DATE DUE

JUN 2 7 2010	
AUG 2 3 2010	
NOV 0 8 2017	

CROSSING THE BORDER

CROSSING THE BORDER

Research from the Mexican Migration Project

Jorge Durand and Douglas S. Massey
Editors

Russell Sage Foundation ❖ New York

The Russell Sage Foundation

The Russell Sage Foundation, one of the oldest of America's general purpose foundations, was established in 1907 by Mrs. Margaret Olivia Sage for "the improvement of social and living conditions in the United States." The Foundation seeks to fulfill this mandate by fostering the development and dissemination of knowledge about the country's political, social, and economic problems. While the Foundation endeavors to assure the accuracy and objectivity of each book it publishes, the conclusions and interpretations in Russell Sage Foundation publications are those of the authors and not of the Foundation, its Trustees, or its staff. Publication by Russell Sage, therefore, does not imply Foundation endorsement.

Library of Congress Cataloging-in-Publication Data
Crossing the border : research from the Mexican Migration Project / Jorge
   Durand, Douglas S. Massey, editors.
      p. cm.
   Includes bibliographical references and index.
   ISBN 0-87154-288-9
      1. Mexican Americans—Research—Congresses. 2. Immigrants—United
States—Research—Congresses. 3. Mexican Americans—Social conditions—Congresses. 4.
Immigrants—United States—Social conditions—Congresses. 5. Alien labor,
Mexican—United States—Research—Congresses. 6. Mexico—Emigration and
immigration—Research—Congresses. 7. United States—Emigration and
immigration—Research—Congresses. I. Durand, Jorge. II. Massey, Douglas S. III.
Mexican Migration Project.

E184.M5B43 2004
305.868′72073—dc22

2004042837

Text design by Genna Patacsil.

RUSSELL SAGE FOUNDATION
112 East 64th Street, New York, New York 10021
10 9 8 7 6 5 4 3 2 1

CONTENTS

Contributors

Jorge Durand is professor in the Department for the Study of Social Movements at the University of Guadalajara and codirector of the Mexican Migration Project.

Douglas S. Massey is professor of sociology and public affairs in the Office of Population Research at Princeton University and codirector of the Mexican Migration Project.

Patricia Arias is full professor at the University of Guadalajara.

María Aysa is a doctoral candidate in demography at the University of Pennsylvania.

Marcela Cerrutti is director of the Centro de Estudios de Población in Buenos Aires.

Enrique Martínez Curiel is associate professor of sociology at the University of Guadalajara, Campus Universitario Valles.

Katharine M. Donato is associate professor of sociology at Rice University and associate professor in behavioral sciences at the University of Texas School of Public Health.

Nadia Y. Flores is a doctoral candidate in sociology at the University of Pennsylvania.

Elizabeth Fussell is assistant professor of sociology at Tulane University.

Rubén Hernández-León is assistant professor of sociology at the University of California, Los Angeles.

William A. Kandel is sociologist at the Economic Research Service of the U.S. Department of Agriculture.

MARGARITA MOONEY is a doctoral candidate in the Department of Sociology at Princeton University.

PIA M. ORRENIUS is senior economist in the Research Department of the Federal Reserve Bank of Dallas.

EMILIO A. PARRADO is assistant professor of sociology at Duke University.

EVELYN PATTERSON is a graduate student in demography at the University of Pennsylvania.

BELINDA I. REYES is assistant professor in the School of Social Science, Humanities, and Arts at the University of California at Merced.

FERNANDO RIOSMENA is a doctoral candidate in demography at the University of Pennsylvania.

ESTELA RIVERO-FUENTES is a consultant for the Gender and Development Group at the World Bank.

Preface

THE CHAPTERS in this volume continue a long tradition of empirical research based on Mexican Migration Project data. They were first presented as papers at a binational conference held in Puerto Vallarta, Mexico, on March 15 and 16, 2002. The conference was held in conjunction with the Programa de Estudios del Cambio Económico y Sustentabilidad del Agro Mexicano, which is codirected by J. Edward Taylor of the University of California at Davis and Antonio Yuñez of the Colegio de México. Its purpose was to promote a cross-fertilization of ideas and research between scholars who were actively engaged in data collection and research on the issue of Mexico-U.S. migration.

In the present book, we have selected papers from that conference that were based on data gathered by the Mexican Migration Project. Although all chapters were written from a common data source, they address a variety of topics: family, gender, regional differences, and policy.

CHAPTER 1

WHAT WE LEARNED FROM THE MEXICAN MIGRATION PROJECT

Jorge Durand and Douglas S. Massey

A SALIENT characteristic of the current debate on U.S. immigration policy is the high ratio of hot air to data. With respect to Mexico-U.S. migration, in particular, political entrepreneurs, ideologues of all stripes, special interests, and many a rank opportunist employ the border as a stage on which to project their hopes, fears, and fantasies about the nation (Andreas 2000; Chavez 2001). With the border as a dramatic prop, immigrants become symbols in a battle of images. For some they symbolize the American Dream; for others, the loss of control in a global economy. Some see them as desperate people fleeing abject poverty and destitution in the third world, and still others as spirited entrepreneurs seeking opportunity and freedom in the United States. Whereas one special interest may portray immigrants as undeserving consumers of public services and an unwanted burden on U.S. taxpayers, another will argue that they are productive workers who are essential to the nation's prosperity.

However presented, narratives about immigrants and their effects are likely to be constructed with few facts and little empirical research. One of the reasons that various parties to the immigration debate can get away with repeated exaggerations and sometimes outright confabulations is the absence of objective data to gainsay any assertion they might make, however wild. In the absence of valid, reliable, and relevant data, one can make almost any claim about the causes, characteristics, and consequences of immigration, find anecdotal evidence of seeming verisimilitude to support it, and then proceed as if the claim were true without fear of falsification.

As is well known to demographers, however, migration data are among the weakest and least reliable statistics routinely collected and published by the federal government, and they were among the last to receive systematic methodological attention in the profession. Unlike events such as birth and death, which are clearly defined and biologically expressed, a "move" is socially constructed and has no obvious biological referent. All demographic events involve crossing a line of one sort or another. For births, the line is tangible, in that it separates the womb from the realm of those who live and breathe. For deaths, the line is equally real, separating a living being in this world from a soul in the great hereafter. Before birth there is no breathing; aging is accompanied by successive breaths and heartbeats; and at death breathing and heartbeats cease. The lines are fairly clear and not amenable to manipulation for political purposes.

When it comes to migration, however, the event—the move—requires the crossing of an intangible line that exists mainly on a map and is often invisible in space. Where, by whom, and for what purpose that line is placed matter a great deal in determining who gets counted as a migrant. In the final analysis, drawing a line and specifying under what circumstances crossing it is meaningful are arbitrary exercises and are therefore subject to a host of purposeful manipulations. As a result, migration statistics in general and immigration statistics in particular are inherently more polit-ical than data on fertility or mortality. Although trends in fertility and mor-tality may have political implications, only with respect to migration is the definition of the event itself subject to serious political manipulation.

Because a geographic move is a social rather than a biological construct, those who study human mobility scientifically have their work cut out for them. Scientists seeking to generate data, construct theories, and test hypotheses about international migration face especially difficult obstacles. Demographers lack good information on legal immigrants to the United States and are especially bereft when in comes to counting those who enter without authorization and reside in the country illegally. All the data sources normally employed by social scientists to study demographic events—the decennial census, intercensal surveys, registration systems, and specialized surveys—are compromised when it comes to studying immigration, usually fatally so (see Massey and Capoferro, forthcoming).

To overcome the serious deficiencies associated with standard data sources and to generate solid, reliable information on Mexico-U.S. migra-tion, we developed a data-gathering method known as the ethnosurvey (described in detail in chapter 16). The method was first used in a pilot project conducted in 1982 and 1983; but since 1987 ethnosurveys have been carried out annually in Mexico under the aegis of the Mexican

Migration Project (MMP). The MMP selects communities in different regions, of varying size, and of diverse patterns of social and economic organization. Respondents are selected using simple random sampling methods, and the data gathered include complete histories of migration, work, and border crossing for all household heads and spouses; basic information on the first and most recent U.S. trips of all household members with migratory experience; and detailed information about experiences on the most recent international trip made by the household head.

In the course of the Mexican survey, we quickly learn where in the United States migrants from a particular community go. Once fieldwork in Mexico ends, we send interviewers to those destinations to compile a proportionate sample of settled out-migrants originating in that community and administer to them the same survey instrument that was applied in Mexico, yielding a comparable set of data on long-term U.S. residents or settlers. Investigators for the MMP have developed a set of sampling weights using the principles of multiplicity sampling to combine the Mexican and U.S. samples into a pooled binational data set that accurately represents the aggregate population of transnational communities created over the years through recurrent processes of migration, settlement, and return (Massey and Parrado 1994).

Chapter 16 presents a detailed description of the content and organization of the MMP database. Since its inception, the MMP has surveyed eighty-one binational communities, yielding reliable data on nearly eighteen thousand current and former U.S. migrants, some 60 percent of whom were undocumented at the time of the survey. The data set contains life histories of around fifty-five hundred migrant households, yielding nearly 260,000 person-years of information on immigration stretching back to the 1920s.

The MMP database offers the largest, most comprehensive, and most reliable source of statistical data on documented and undocumented Mexican immigrants currently available. It has been employed by many investigators in numerous studies that have produced sound scientific research about Mexico-U.S. migration, yielding dozens of publications in peer-reviewed journals of anthropology, demography, sociology, economics, and science generally. A collection of such studies forms the core of this volume, which we believe yield several important lessons about Mexico-U.S. migration.

METHODOLOGICAL LESSONS

Perhaps the first and most fundamental lesson of the Mexican Migration Project is that it is indeed possible to generate accurate and reliable data on immigration, even when much of the movement is transitory, circular, and clandestine and thus outside the purview of normal statistical systems. Moreover, the MMP data have been generated at relatively modest cost, with annual budgets beginning at less than $100,000 in 1982 and rising to a current $225,000 as the project has grown in size and scope. Although by no means trivial, these budgets are small by the standards of survey research, especially considering the size of the sample, the quality of data, and the marginal status of the target population. We offer the MMP as a model for other scholars studying movements between other origins and destinations.

The success of the MMP has been achieved by demarcating specific communities of manageable size and then studying them intensively, using an approach that blends ethnographic and survey methods. The vagaries inherent in migratory decision making are minimized by asking respondents to report behavior rather than intentions or motivations. The project deliberately avoids trying to define who is or is not a migrant and eschews the creation of migrant typologies. We simply ask whether each household member has ever left his or her community of origin to work or to look for work. We then gather basic information about the first and last such trips made both inside and outside of the country. For household heads and spouses, we compile a labor history that lists every activity undertaken for remuneration or support lasting a month or more, noting what that activity was, where it took place, and, if in the United States, whether the respondent held documents that permitted him or her to work legally. We leave it to the data user to decide whether a visit to work in a neighboring Mexican community constitutes a "move" or whether a visit to the United States for one, three, or six months constitutes a "trip."

Despite their reliability and validity relative to other potential sources of information on Mexican migration, however, the MMP data are not perfect. The most serious problem is their limited generalizability. Strictly speaking, the MMP data are representative only of the combined population of eighty-one nonrandomly selected Mexican communities. Though the diversity of community traits has steadily expanded, the data are not representative of Mexico or Mexican immigrants in general. Nonetheless, systematic comparisons between the MMP and nationally representative surveys have generally found a close correspondence between migrant characteristics in the two sources (Massey and Capoferro, forthcoming; Massey and Zenteno 2000; Zenteno and Massey 1999). Data users seeking to represent conditions within Mexico or among Mexican immigrants generally, however, should proceed with caution.

On the U.S. side of the border, the sample of settled out-migrants interviewed in destination areas is representative neither of settled Mexican immigrants nor of settlers from specific sending communities. Samples gathered in the United States are compiled using snowball sampling (also known as the chain-referral method), a serviceable technique imposed by practical constraints but one that ultimately yields data of unknowable representativeness. Although MMP investigators have conducted experiments testing whether representative sampling methods can be applied to select U.S. respondents, their efforts have proved unsuccessful in terms of cost, time, and practicality. Thus, although the MMP's U.S. interviews provide a snapshot of the characteristics of long-term settlers based on a relatively large number of cases, our data cannot be assumed to be representative and certainly cannot be used to estimate the size of the undocumented Mexican population of the United States.

Although MMP data by themselves cannot produce valid estimates of aggregate quantities such as the total number of undocumented migrants in the United States, the volume of undocumented entries in a given year, or the quantity of "migradollars" transmitted to Mexico, they have proved to be extremely useful for characterizing and understanding the social and economic processes that underlie and ultimately produce these aggregate counts (see Massey and Zenteno 1999). Data from the MMP can be used to find the value of many important parameters that determine aggregate trends, and they have been used to calculate otherwise unknowable quantities such as the likelihood of undocumented departure from Mexico, the probability of apprehension at the border, the likelihood of return migration, the odds of remigration, the probability of remitting, and the average size of remittances. Such parameter estimates can be combined with published statistics to generate defensible estimates of larger quantities, such as the annual volume of undocumented migration (Massey and Singer 1995), the annual flow of migradollars back to Mexico (Massey and Parrado 1994), the aggregate effect of remittances on the Mexican economy (Durand, Massey, and Parrado 1996), and the likely size of the future immigrant population (Massey and Zenteno 1999).

In sum, the MMP data, like all other data, have their strengths and weaknesses and appropriate and inappropriate uses. The point is not that other approaches to data collection should be abandoned in favor of the ethnosurvey or that the MMP should be used to the exclusion of information from the Bureau of the Census or the Immigration and Naturalization Service but that the data compiled by the MMP using ethnosurvey methods provide an important and often crucial complement to standard statistical sources, enabling a clearer interpretation of trends and the more effective use of published statistics.

MIGRANTS AND THEIR FAMILIES

A common perception in the United States is that Mexican immigrants are fleeing dire, impoverished circumstances at home and that once across the border they will naturally seek to stay permanently to enjoy the obvious benefits of living in the United States. It logically follows, of course, that if the United States does not vigorously defend its border, a huge fraction of the Mexican population will end up living north of the boundary—hence the imagery of a border under siege, subject to a silent invasion by a flood of immigrants, yielding names for enforcement operations such as blockade, gatekeeper, and hold-the-line (Andreas 2000).

This common perception, however, is fundamentally incorrect. Mexican immigrants are generally not poor and desperate—they would survive without migration to the United States. For the most part, households turn to migration quite rationally and use it instrumentally as an adaptive strategy to compensate for missing and failed markets in Mexico, conditions that are common in a country undergoing transition to a developed, market society. In reality, Mexico is not a poor country. With a per capita gross domestic product in excess of $9,000, it is one of the richest countries in the developing world, and international migration is a consequence of its dynamic growth and development, not its poverty. This figure is nearly three times the average of $3,200 for developing nations as a whole (United Nations 2002).

Because they are migrating to overcome specific market failures at home, the overwhelming majority of Mexican migrants plan to return, seeking to work in the United States for short periods to generate an alternative source of household income (thus overcoming failures in insurance markets) or to accumulate savings for a specific purpose (thus overcoming failures in capital and credit markets). Left to their own devices, most Mexican immigrants would work in the United States only sporadically and for limited periods of time. According to estimates by Douglas Massey and Audrey Singer (1995), for example, between 1965 and 1985 (when the border was relatively open) 85 percent of undocumented entries were offset by departures, yielding a relatively modest net increment to the U.S. population.

A concrete indication that migrants are motivated to return is the leaving behind of families. Historically, undocumented migration from Mexico has been led by young males who leave wives and children behind, arranging for the entry of dependents only once their own migration has become chronic or the duration of their stays abroad too long. In their analysis of long-term trends, however, Marcela Cerrutti and Douglas S. Massey (chapter 2 of this volume) find that the demographic composition of Mexican immigrants is changing, characterized by the rising participation of women, a growing number of nonworking dependents, a shift out of agriculture, and a redirection of flows to new destination states. These changes have been accompanied by a declining probability of return migration among undocumented men and a falling probability of apprehension at the border.

Margarita Mooney (chapter 3 of this volume) finds that the kind of social ties that migrants have north of the border influence the nature and form of the investments they make in Mexico. Those who travel alone and live with kin or friends in the United States tend to make short trips and return with savings, which they invest in housing or production. They appear to be moving to overcome limitations in Mexico's lending markets. In the absence of viable mortgage markets, Mexicans move to self-finance the construction or acquisition of a home; and in the absence of an effective banking system, they move to accumulate capital for business formation.

In contrast, migrants who join social clubs in the United States (such as a hometown association or soccer club) make longer trips, often with other family members, and send money home through monthly remittances rather than accumulated savings. Through U.S.-based social clubs they join with other migrants to make investments in community infrastructure, to maintain and improve homes, and to run businesses in order to claim status and continued membership in their communities of origin.

Perhaps the single most important motivation for Mexican migration to the United States is the need to self-finance home acquisition because of poorly functioning and inaccessible mortgage markets in Mexico. In his analysis of home ownership and quality (chapter 4 of this volume), Emilio Parrado finds that migration to the United States markedly increases the likelihood of home ownership and greatly increases the quality of housing. In general, the greater a household's prior U.S. experience, the higher the odds it will own its home, the greater the number of rooms and appliances in the dwelling, and the more likely the dwelling will be to have a tile or wood floor. U.S. migration lowers a family's reliance on inheritance as a means of home acquisition, and by providing collateral it increases access to bank loans. U.S. migration is thus responsible for much of the growth in the size and quality of Mexico's housing stock.

Given the obvious material benefits associated with migration to the United States, it is hardly surprising that it has a pronounced influence on marriage markets within migrant-sending communities. As Joshua Reichert

(1982) noted long ago, men and women who have unhindered access to the U.S. labor market make unusually attractive marriage partners, yielding what Enrique Martínez (in chapter 5) calls "the green card as a matrimonial strategy." As he shows, one who is able to marry a U.S. citizen or resident alien is guaranteed not only a higher standard of living but also access to legal status through the family reunification provisions of U.S. immigration law. In the community Martínez studied, this reality has produced new mercenary attitudes toward marriage, characterized by a willingness to marry U.S. citizens and legal residents in the absence of love as a means of gaining access to a U.S. visa, a practice associated with rather high subsequent rates of marital dissolution.

WOMEN AND MIGRATION

Although most undocumented Mexican migrants are men, women are always intimately involved in the process of international migration, either as wives and daughters who remain behind or, increasingly, as migrants themselves. Mexico has a rather patriarchal culture, and migration to the United States has created pressures for change that have played an important role in transforming Mexican gender relations. The departure of a male household head for work in the United States immediately increases a wife's authority and autonomy, leaving her in control of daily decisions regarding family discipline, production, and spending.

When the husband returns from the United States, authority relations often do not return to the status quo ante. Women grow accustomed to their autonomy, and their children to their authority, making it difficult for men to reassert their former dominance in family relations when they return. Moreover, as María Aysa and Douglas Massey show (in chapter 7), the departure of men under appropriate circumstances also increases female autonomy by promoting the wife's labor force participation. They find that in settings in which the control of family is weaker and job opportunities more abundant (that is, in urban areas), a wife is likely to enter the labor force following her husband's migration.

Although males are typically the first to migrate from a Mexican household, the more trips a man takes and the longer he remains north of the border, the more likely he is to be joined by his wife and children (Massey et al. 1987). As U.S. authorities progressively militarized the border over the 1990s, men adapted to the higher costs and risks of border crossing by staying longer, and increasingly they have arranged for the entry of their wives and children (see Massey, Durand, and Malone 2002). Katharine Donato and Evelyn Patterson (in chapter 6) undertake the first systematic analysis of undocumented border crossing by Mexican women. They find that compared with men, women are much less likely to cross by themselves and are more likely to retain the services of a paid crossing guide, thus lowering their risk of apprehension. Because most women are first-time migrants, and because once in the United States they tend to stay, the typical female border crosser has substantially less migratory experience than her male counterpart.

REGIONAL AND SECTORAL DIFFERENCES

The traditional heartland for migration to the United States is western Mexico, notably the states of Guanajuato, Jalisco, Michoacán, San Luis Potosí, and Zacatecas, along with smaller and less populous western states such as Aguascalientes, Colima, and Nayarit. As far back as data exist, at least half of all migrants to the United States have come from one of these states (Durand, Massey, and Zenteno 2001). Accordingly, the Mexican Migration Project began by securing samples of communities in this region. Over the years, however, MMP investigators have endeavored to survey communities in other sending regions in the south and north of the country.

Most Americans probably assume that a majority of Mexican immigrants originate in border states—after all, they are closest to the United States. Historically, however, only a small fraction have come from frontier states such as Baja California, Sonora, Chihuahua, Coahuíla, Tamaulipas, or Nuevo León. Before World War II, this region was sparsely populated, and although it grew tremendously after 1945, border communities continue to be relatively marginal participants in the international migratory stream.

In her analysis of migration from the border metropolis of Tijuana, Elizabeth Fussell (chapter 8) argues that cross-border economic integration provides potential migrants with attractive alternatives in Mexico, yielding relatively low rates of migration to the United States. Whereas 15 percent of respondents interviewed in Tijuana had been to the United States, the figure was 24 percent in communities of Mexico's rural interior. Moreover, when people did migrate from Tijuana, they were likely to have documents. Whereas nearly 60 percent of first U.S. trips made by Tijuana residents were legal, fewer than a third of those made from the rural interior were. The odds of documented migration were greater in Tijuana because of the prevalence of cross-border family and business ties, which open up a variety of avenues to legal documents.

Patricia Arias (chapter 9) points out that new patterns of migration are evolving even in traditional migrant-sending regions. Although emigration from the state of Guanajuato has historically been rural in origin, with migrants leaving to self-finance home construction, acquire consumer goods, purchase land, or fund agricultural production, during the 1980s and 1990s Guanajuato underwent a process of rural industrialization, with numerous locally financed factories springing up in former agrarian towns and agriculture itself being transformed into capital-intensive commercial activity. In the course of this transformation, the dynamics of migration shifted as migrants increasingly came from industrializing towns and small cities. Rather than migrating to finance home acquisition or agricultural production, the new immigrants used U.S. labor as a buffer to cover family expenses during periods of local unemployment and as a source of investment capital for business formation.

Nadia Flores, Rubén Hernández-León, and Douglas Massey (chapter 10) note that social and economic trends in Mexico have resulted in a growing number of U.S. migrants originating in urban rather than rural areas. Owing to the greater size, density, and heterogeneity of cities, the authors argue, the logic of migration from cities is very different from that of migration from rural areas. They show that household formation is associated with U.S. migration from rural but not urban areas. Whereas newly formed urban couples simply enter the local market for rental housing to establish an independent residence, in rural communities rental housing markets do not exist, and recently married husbands become migrants to self-finance the construction of a home and free themselves from their parental households. In addition, whereas the migratory behavior of urban dwellers is responsive to fluctuations in interest rates, that of rural dwellers is not. Formal credit is so lacking in the rural sector that interest rates are irrelevant. Finally, the effects of migrant networks are much stronger in rural than in urban areas because rural social networks are stronger and more dense, yielding social capital of greater value and more potential for the cumulative causation of migration.

The hypothesis of cumulative causation posits that the departure of people and the repatriation of earnings change local social and economic structures in ways that promote additional migration. Estela Rivero-Fuentes (chapter 11) extends the analysis of cumulative causation to incorporate internal as well as international migration. She finds that migration within Mexico and to the United States have similar determinants at the community level, with movement occurring largely in response to structural economic changes. Rivero-Fuentes discerns little evidence that the growth of international migration comes at the expense of internal migration. Indeed, she finds that both types of migration are perpetuated through similar mechanisms of cumulative causation linked to the accumulation of social capital. Having a tie to a U.S. migrant and living in a community with many such migrants raises the odds that a person will leave for the United States but does not affect the odds of migrating within Mexico. Similarly, having a tie to an internal migrant and living in a community with many such migrants raises the odds of migration within Mexico but does not affect the odds of going to the United States.

LESSONS FOR POLICY MAKERS

According to William Kandel (chapter 12), the consolidation of the food-processing industry over the past two decades has brought about a radical transformation of rural areas of the United States. Whereas Mexican farm laborers for decades have gone to fields in Texas and California, during the 1990s farming regions throughout the United States began to receive large numbers of Mexican immigrants. Mexicans constitute upwards of 85 percent of all agricultural laborers in the United States and form the backbone of the workforce engaged in the production of tobacco (North Carolina), onions (Georgia), mushrooms (Pennsylvania), cherries (Michigan), poultry (Arkansas, Delaware), meat (Iowa, Nebraska), and seafood (Maryland).

Kandel uses MMP data to construct a social, economic, and demographic portrait of Mexican migrant farmworkers. He shows that relative to skilled and unskilled manual workers, those employed in U.S. agriculture tend to make more trips of shorter duration, working fewer months per year but more hours per week and generally experiencing the lowest wages and harshest working conditions. Compared with migrant workers in other sectors, those in agriculture had very low rates of occupational mobility. Overall, the picture Kandel paints is one of an impoverished, exploited farm workforce skirting the borders of indentured servitude.

A principal reason for the dire circumstances facing farm labor in the United States is the series of repressive immigration and border policies imposed by U.S. authorities since 1986. For the first time in U.S. history, the 1986 Immigration Reform and Control Act criminalized the hiring of undocumented workers, causing employers in agriculture and other industries to shift to labor subcontracting and thereby substantially reducing the amount of money going to workers (Massey, Durand, and Malone 2002). Between 1985 and 2000, moreover, the Mexico-U.S. border was militarized in unprecedented ways, with spending on border enforcement rising by a factor of six, the number of Border Patrol officers doubling, and the hours spent patrolling the border tripling. At present, the Border Patrol is the largest arms-bearing branch of the U.S. government outside of the military itself, with a budget in excess of $1.3 billion a year.

This massive deployment of enforcement resources has produced a variety of unintended negative consequences. Rather than deterring Mexicans from coming to the United States, the militarization of the border has lowered the likelihood of their returning home. In his life-table analysis of return migration, Fernando Riosmena (chapter 13) estimates that before 1992, the probability of returning from a first undocumented trip to the United States generally ranged between .60 and .70, but following the launching of successive border operations in 1993 the likelihood of return plummeted and by 1996 stood at around .45. The drop in the odds of return migration was particularly acute among nonagricultural workers.

This finding is confirmed by Belinda Reyes (chapter 15), using an entirely different methodology. She shows that the sharply falling probabilities of return have substantially increased the length of trips and greatly increased the rate of Mexican population growth in the United States. Thus the border crackdown has turned a temporary strategy adopted to overcome Mexican market limitations into the permanent resettlement of workers and their families, thereby significantly increasing the rate of Mexican population growth within the United States.

U.S. border policies have had other consequences as well. According to Pia Orrenius (chapter 14), the concentration of enforcement resources in specific sectors has prompted undocumented Mexicans to avoid formerly popular crossing sites in California in favor of new locations in Texas and Arizona. Within states, there has also been a shift away from crossing in urban areas such as Tijuana and Juárez toward new crossing points in remote and unpopulated sites located in the mountains and deserts of California and the lower Rio Grande Valley of Texas.

TOWARD THE FUTURE

The chapters of this volume suggest that the 1990s were a decade of radical change in Mexico-U.S. migration and a period in which U.S. policy responses were increasingly misplaced and inadequate. The attempt to make the border impervious with respect to the movement of Mexican labor while opening it with respect to movements of goods, capital, information, commodities, and services has proved worse than a failure; it has achieved counterproductive outcomes in virtually every instance. It has transformed Mexican immigration from a circular movement of workers affecting three states into a national population of settled dependents scattered throughout the country. It has lowered the rate of apprehension on the border but driven up the rate of death and injury during border crossing. It has not deterred Mexican immigrants from coming to the United

States, but it has kept them from going home. It has dramatically accelerated the rate of Mexican population growth in the United States while exacerbating the social and economic marginalization of the population.

These negative consequences follow from the attempt to impose restrictive immigration policies on a wealthy, developing country that is otherwise integrating rapidly with the United States. Restrictive policies rest on the misapprehension that Mexicans are desperately poor and seek to enter the United States to live permanently. But migrants do not come from the poorest regions of the country; they come from communities that are dynamic and rapidly developing, and those who migrate generally seek temporary work to overcome specific market failures at home. Left to their own devices, the vast majority would return to participate in Mexico's growth as an economy and society.

We believe that more enlightened policies could follow from a more accurate understanding of the causes of international migration and a better appreciation of the motivations of migrants. In previous work (Durand and Massey 2001; Massey, Durand, and Malone 2002) we have offered specific recommendations for a more effective and humane immigration policy in North America. The contributors to this volume describe the data and present the kinds of empirical research that have guided our thinking in making these policy recommendations. We trust that the studies collected here will provide others with a more informed window on the complex and changing phenomenon of Mexico-U.S. migration.

REFERENCES

Andreas, Peter. 2000. *Border Games: Policing the U.S.-Mexico Divide.* Ithaca, N.Y.: Cornell University Press.

Chavez, Leo R. 2001. *Covering Immigration: Popular Images and the Politics of the Nation.* Berkeley: University of California Press.

Durand, Jorge, and Douglas S. Massey. 2001. "Borderline Sanity." *American Prospect* 12(7, September 15): 28–31.

Durand, Jorge, Douglas S. Massey, and Emilio A. Parrado. 1996. "Migradollars and Development: A Reconsideration of the Mexican Case." *International Migration Review* 30: 423–44.

Durand, Jorge, Douglas S. Massey, and René M. Zenteno. 2001. "Mexican Immigration to the United States: Continuities and Changes." *Latin American Research Review* 36: 107–27.

Massey, Douglas S., Rafael Alarcón, Jorge Durand, and Humberto González. 1987. *Return to Aztlán: The Social Process of International Migration from Western Mexico.* Berkeley: University of California Press.

Massey, Douglas S., and Chiara Capoferro. Forthcoming. "Measuring Undocumented Migration." *International Migration Review.*

Massey, Douglas S., Jorge Durand, and Nolan J. Malone. 2002. *Beyond Smoke and Mirrors: Mexican Immigration in an Age of Economic Integration.* New York: Russell Sage Foundation.

Massey, Douglas S., and Emilio A. Parrado. 1994. "Migradollars: The Remittances and Savings of Mexican Migrants to the United States." *Population Research and Policy Review* 13: 3–30.

Massey, Douglas S., and Audrey Singer. 1995. "New Estimates of Undocumented Mexican Migration and the Probability of Apprehension." *Demography* 32: 203–13.

Massey, Douglas S., and René Zenteno. 1999. "The Dynamics of Mass Migration." *Proceedings of the National Academy of Sciences* 96(8): 5328–35.

————. 2000. "A Validation of the Ethnosurvey: The Case of Mexico-U.S. Migration." *International Migration Review* 34: 766–93.

Reichert, Joshua S. 1982. "A Town Divided: Economic Stratification and Social Relations in a Mexican Migrant Community." *Social Problems* 29: 411–23.

United Nations. 2002. *Population, Environment, and Development 2001.* New York: United Nations.

Zenteno, René, and Douglas S. Massey. 1999. "Especifidad versus representatividad: Enfoques metodológicos para el estudio de la migración internacional." *Estudios Demográficos y Urbanos* 40: 75–116.

PART I

❖

MIGRATION AND THE FAMILY

Chapter 2

Trends in Mexican Migration to the United States, 1965 to 1995

Marcela Cerrutti and Douglas S. Massey

THE MODERN era of Mexico-U.S. migration began with the end of the Bracero Program in 1964. Although this program was enacted in 1942 as a temporary measure to relieve wartime labor shortages, at the behest of agricultural growers in California and Texas it was successively reauthorized and expanded in the years after 1945. The size of the program was dramatically increased in the late 1950s after a paramilitary crackdown on undocumented migration (Operation Wetback) led to labor disruptions that angered agricultural interests and led to bureaucratic backpedaling (Calavita 1992). Before Operation Wetback, no more than two hundred thousand visas were issued in any year, but from 1955 through 1959 the number exceeded four hundred thousand.

As the United States moved into the civil rights era of the 1960s, the Bracero Program increasingly came to be seen as an exploitative labor relations system that undermined the well-being of Mexican Americans, discouraged the unionization of farmworkers, and subordinated laborers on the basis of ethnicity. U.S. officials began to reduce the number of Bracero recruitments in the early 1960s, and in 1964, the year Congress passed its landmark Civil Rights Act, a coalition of labor unions, civil rights groups, and religious organizations finally succeeded in having the program killed.

In the three decades from 1965 to 1995, U.S. policy toward Mexico underwent profound changes, and the Mexican political economy was radically transformed. To date, however, policy makers and social scientists have lacked a basic description of how patterns of Mexican immigration have fared over this important period. Undocumented migration, in particular, has defied attempts at reliable statistical representation (see the Binational Migration Study [1998a, 1998b, 1998c] for a comprehensive review of what is known).

MILESTONES IN MEXICO–U.S. MIGRATION
The Hart-Celler Act

One of the most important changes in the history of U.S. immigration policy occurred just after the demise of the Bracero Program. In 1965 new amendments to the Immigration and Nationality Act were passed and signed into law by President Lyndon Johnson. Often called after its sponsors, Senator Philip Hart of Michigan and Representative Emanuel Celler of New York, the Hart-Celler Act scrapped the discriminatory national-origins quota system established in the 1920s and replaced it with new limits that seemed more defensible in an era of expanding civil rights. Under the old quota system, Africans and Asians were essentially prohibited from immigrating, and strict limits were established on the entry of eastern and southern Europeans.

The Hart-Celler Act abolished this discriminatory system and replaced it with a new formula under which each country in Europe, Africa, Asia, and the Pacific qualified for up to 20,000 visas per year, which were allocated according to a preference system that gave priority to relatives of U.S. citizens and resident aliens as well as to persons with skills or abilities needed in the United States. These regions (labeled the "Eastern Hemisphere") were limited to an annual total of 170,000 visas per year. The Hart-Celler Act did not apply fixed quotas to individual countries in North America, South America, or the Caribbean, however (the "Western Hemisphere"), though it did cap entries from the entire region at 120,000 per year (yielding a worldwide ceiling of 290,000). In both regions, spouses and children of U.S. citizens were not subject to quantitative restriction and entered outside of these numerical limitations. Although the original preference system contained a category for refugees (later abandoned), most of those who came to the United States after 1965 as refugees or asylum seekers (for example, Cubans, Nicaraguans, Russians, Vietnamese, and Cambodians) were admitted outside of the quotas for political or humanitarian reasons.

The fact may not be widely appreciated, but before 1965 countries in the Western Hemisphere were not subject to any quantitative restrictions on immigration. The old national-origins quotas were silent about immigration from Latin American and the Caribbean, and before the Hart-Celler

Act, Mexicans could enter the United States in any number as long as they met certain qualitative criteria (having to do with health, fitness, and political affiliation). Thus the 1965 amendments involved the first quantitative restrictions ever imposed on immigration from the Western Hemisphere and in no way can be said to have caused the increase in immigration from Latin America. On the contrary, immigration from Mexico and other Latin American countries grew after 1965 *in spite of* the act's restrictive provisions.

After 1968, successive amendments to the Immigration and Nationality Act further tightened restrictions on the entry of Mexicans. In 1976 Congress placed the Western Hemisphere under the 20,000 per country quota system, an action that immediately reduced the inflow of Mexicans by 25 percent. In 1978 the separate hemispheric caps were abolished in favor of a single worldwide ceiling of 290,000, which was further reduced to 270,000 in 1980, when the preference category for refugees was deleted. Under the Hart-Celler Act and its successor amendments, therefore, legal immigration from Mexico has become progressively more difficult.

The Immigration Reform and Control Act

With the termination of the Bracero Program in 1964 and the progressive tightening of legal immigration from Mexico after 1968, undocumented migration began to grow. From a mere 87,000 arrests in 1964 the annual number of aliens apprehended and expelled from the United States rose to a peak of 1.8 million in 1986. Over the same period, the United States experienced considerable economic distress, with high rates of unemployment, recurrent bouts of inflation, stagnating wages, and rising inequality— precisely the combination of characteristics that studies have shown make immigration a salient political issue with the public (Massey 1999; Meyers 1995; Timmer and Williamson 1998). In this context, Congress felt obliged to act, and in late 1986 it passed the Immigration Reform and Control Act (IRCA).

Reflecting the delicate balance of interests needed to secure the bill's passage, IRCA contained four separate provisions: new resources were allocated to the Border Patrol for enforcement along the Mexico-U.S. border; sanctions were enacted to remove the lure of U.S. jobs by penalizing employers who knowingly hired unauthorized workers; long-term undocumented residents of the United States were offered an amnesty to wipe the slate clean (and thus secure the acquiescence of Latino and civil rights groups); and undocumented agricultural workers were offered their own legalization program (thereby securing support from agricultural growers in Texas and California).

The Immigration Reform and Control Act proved to be the first salvo in a long battle over the Mexico-U.S. border. Under the act, the Immigration and Naturalization Service (INS) received a 50 percent budget increase to hire additional Border Patrol officers, and a $35 million contingency fund was established to cover "immigration emergencies" (Bean, Vernez, and Keely 1989; Goodis 1986). Passage of IRCA was followed by a series of highly publicized crackdowns, first in El Paso (Operation Hold-the-Line) and later in San Diego (Operation Gatekeeper). In subsequent years, Congress continued to augment the INS budget for immigration enforcement, resulting in a new militarization of the border (Dunn 1996).

Although IRCA was enacted as a general change in U.S. immigration law and did not single out any particular country for attention, there is little doubt that its primary purpose was to curb undocumented migration from Mexico. Accordingly, migrants from this country have borne the brunt of the law's far-reaching effects: Mexicans constitute 70 percent of those granted amnesty, 80 percent of those legalized as farmworkers, and 95 percent of those apprehended by the U.S. Border Patrol since 1986 (Smith, Kramer, and Singer, 1996; U.S. Immigration and Naturalization Service 1995).

THE 1990 IMMIGRATION ACT

Although since 1980 the number of immigrant visas has theoretically been capped at 270,000, the volume of legal immigration has never actually been this low. Indeed, the smallest immigrant cohort admitted after 1980 was 544,000 (in 1984), and by 1990 annual volume was running at 660,000 per year (not counting the millions of former undocumented migrants legalized under IRCA). Year after year, immigration has exceeded the theoretical cap by an increasingly wide margin because over time earlier waves of immigrants gained access to U.S. citizenship and then sponsored the entry of immediate family members, who could enter outside of the numerical quotas.

In 1990 Congress attempted to control this situation by phasing in a "flexible" cap of 675,000 immigrants per year, consisting of 480,000 family-sponsored migrants, 140,000 employment-based migrants, and 55,000 "diversity" migrants (people from countries underrepresented in current flows who are selected randomly by an annual lottery). Under the 1990 Immigration Act, immediate relatives of U.S. citizens continued to enter without numerical restriction, but they were charged against the next year's total of 480,000 family-sponsored immigrants, thereby reducing the number of positions available to more distant relations. Through this mechanism, Congress sought to apply a brake to the explosive growth in family migration. The cap, however, was designed to be "flexible," in that no more than 226,000 visas could be subtracted from the family category in any single year. As a result, legal immigration has continued to exceed the theoretical cap and in the first half of the 1990s averaged around a million per year.

The Mexican Economic Crisis

For most of the period from 1965 to 1982, the Mexican economy expanded rapidly, and with the exception of a brief downturn in 1975 and 1976 it regularly achieved growth rates in excess of 6 percent per year. This high rate of economic growth derived from a development model applied widely in developing countries after World War II and known as Import Substitution Industrialization. Its fundamental aim was to create and sustain internal markets to serve as springboards for economic growth. In keeping with this philosophy, Mexico's political leaders undertook large-scale spending and investment to generate income and eliminate bottlenecks in production while simultaneously erecting barriers to the entry of foreign goods and services, thereby creating a captive internal market that national producers—both public and private—could use to initiate and sustain industrialization (Hansen 1971).

Although the limits of this model were reached by the early 1970s, yielding a stagnation of economic growth by mid-decade, after 1976 Mexico was granted a reprieve from structural economic reforms because of two fortuitous developments: the rapid inflation in oil prices following the Arab Oil Boycott of 1973 and the sudden discovery of massive new petroleum deposits off the Mexican coast in 1976. With potential access to vast amounts of a valuable and eminently marketable commodity, international loans poured into Mexico not only to finance the development of the petroleum industry but also to support a dramatic increase in social spending and a huge expansion of public employment (Centeno 1994).

In Mexico the period from 1976 to 1982 is generally known as the "Oil Boom" (el boom petrolero). The years of reprieve came to an abrupt halt, however, when the Arab-led oil cartel disintegrated and world petroleum supplies rose, causing the price of oil to drop precipitously and initiating a financial crisis in the summer of 1982 that forced a devaluation of the peso and unleashed successive rounds of hyperinflation that persisted through the 1980s, which came to be called the "lost decade" (la década perdida). From 1980 to 1989, Mexican gross domestic product (GDP) per capita fell by 9 percent, the real urban minimum wage fell by 47 percent, and the percentage of households earning less than twice the minimum wage (an index of poverty) increased by 28 percent (Sheahan 1991).

The Neoliberal Revolution and North American Free Trade Agreement

Spurred on by the World Bank and the International Monetary Fund, and encouraged by the U.S. Treasury, in the late 1980s Mexico embarked on an ambitious program of economic restructuring designed to cure the economic ills responsible for its ongoing crisis. Abandoning its long-standing commitment to Import Substitution Industrialization, Mexico embraced the philosophy of neoliberalism and opened itself to full participation in the global market economy. Beginning in 1986, in quick succession the Mexican government joined the General Agreement on Tariffs and Trade (GATT), lowered tariffs, eliminated restrictions on foreign business ownership, reduced barriers to capital mobility, privatized state enterprises, downsized the state bureaucracy, and phased out subsidies to producers and consumers. In rural areas, it eventually privatized the ownership of communal lands and offered new incentives to private agricultural producers.

Although these changes began under President Miguel de la Madrid Hurtado (1982 to 1988), they accelerated markedly during the presidency of Carlos Salinas de Gortari (1988 to 1994). Having set Mexico decisively on the road toward a free market, Salinas sought a means of institutionalizing his economic program and making it permanent (Durand, Massey, and Parrado 1999). By creating a direct U.S. financial and political interest in Mexico's free market reforms, the North American Free Trade Agreement (NAFTA) ensured that no successor president could undo what Salinas had accomplished, and this was NAFTA's primary political purpose (Massey 1998). Because President Salinas had implemented most of the elements of the new political economy long before the treaty was ratified, however, NAFTA's effects were felt long before it actually took effect.

TRENDS IN MEXICO-U.S. MIGRATION

After 1986, the U.S. implemented increasingly restrictive policies toward Mexican immigration, including the criminalization of hiring undocumented workers by U.S. employers and a massive increase in personnel and funding for the U.S. border patrol. The pursuit of restrictive policies in the context of ongoing economic integration between Mexico and the United States under NAFTA have been counterproductive. The likelihood of undocumented migration has not been affected, and the probability of apprehension at the border declined as migrants shifted from fortified segments of the border to more remote and less-patrolled sectors. Meanwhile, the probability of return migration has fallen, yielding an increase in the number of long-term undocumented residents.

The principal obstacle to the accurate measurement of trends in Mexico-U.S. migration has been the lack of good data. Although they may not be perfect, the best data for our purposes are those of the Mexican Migration Project, described in chapter 16.

Leaving for the United States

The most fundamental fact about migration from Mexico is its annual rate or volume. Although we cannot measure the total number of migrants using MMP data (for this, see Bean et al. 1998; Van Hook and Bean 1998; Woodrow-Lafield 1998), we can estimate the annual probability of leaving Mexico for the United States. Figure 2.1 presents trends in the annual probability of taking a first trip to the United States among Mexican men and women from 1966 through 1995. These probabilities were computed from retrospective life-history data by including in the denominator all persons who had never been to the United States and were at least fifteen years old during the year in question, and in the numerator a count of the number of people who left on a first trip to the United States during that year. Probabilities are estimated separately for those with and without documents; to smooth out irregularities stemming from sampling error, we present three-year moving averages. Readers should also remember that these figures are computed across all communities in the MMP database and that trends may be quite different from place to place (see Donato 1998).

The top panel shows the annual probability of leaving Mexico on a first undocumented trip. For men, this probability rises sharply and steadily through the late 1960s and into the 1970s, going from roughly .006 per year in 1966 to about .021 per year in 1979. The years 1980 to 1982 coincide with Mexico's oil boom, and during this brief period of high prosperity the likelihood of migration fell sharply, reaching about .013 in 1982. But the initiation of the economic crisis in late 1982 brought a quick revival of undocumented migration, which fluctuated around .020 per year during the years 1985 to 1988 before peaking at .0218 in 1989. In the early 1990s the probability of initial undocumented migration fell once again, reflecting the buildup of enforcement resources along the border, but by 1995 the decline had ceased and the probability of out-migration had nudged back up to .0175 per year.

Among women, the likelihood of becoming an undocumented migrant parallels the trend for men but at a much lower level and with swings of much smaller amplitude. The annual probability rises steadily from near

FIGURE 2.1   Three-Year Moving Average of Probability of Taking a
First Trip to the United States, 1965 to 1995

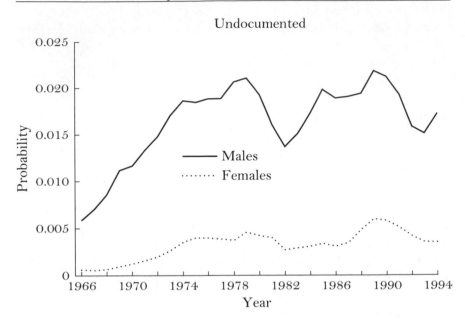

Undocumented

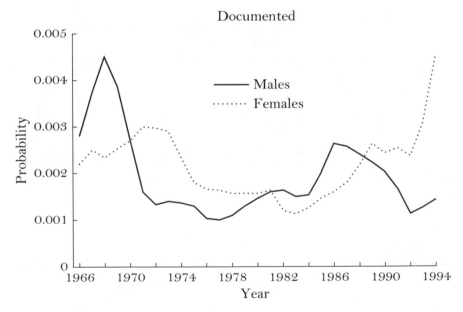

Documented

Source: Data from Mexican Migration Project.

zero in 1966 to peak at .005 in 1979 before declining and then reaching a new peak in 1990. Although the basic time trend is the same, most of the variation for women is in the range .0025 to .006, whereas for men it is in the range of .0125 to .0225. In other words, as Jorge Bustamante and colleagues (1998), Marcela Cerrutti and Douglas Massey (2001), and Katharine Donato (1998) have also found, the odds of becoming an undocumented migrant appear to be far greater for men than for women.

The bottom panel of figure 2.1 shows trends in the likelihood of becoming a documented migrant. The only way for someone to leave on a first trip as a documented migrant is to be sponsored by a relative or employer in the United States. During the brief time between the end of the Bracero Program and the implementation of the new hemispheric quotas (roughly 1965 to 1970), U.S. employers rushed to sponsor the legal immigration of former braceros and their family members under the relatively lax provisions in effect before the Hart-Celler Act took effect (see Reichert and Massey [1979, 1980] for a community case study). In figure 2.1 this phenomenon is observed as a sharp spike in the probability of male documented migration in 1968, followed by a less extreme and flatter peak in the likelihood of female migration a few years later (1970 to 1973). The initial wave of male migration consisted of the sons and brothers of former braceros who were able to garner employer sponsorship through their family connections, and the subsequent wave of female migration was composed of their wives and daughters.

The next peak in documented migration for males came in the wake of IRCA and lasted from 1985 through 1992. Although IRCA's legalization programs theoretically applied only to persons with prior experience in the United States, either as long-term residents or as agricultural workers, subsequent studies have revealed that both programs for both categories involved considerable fraud. The agricultural worker program, in particular, seems to have been so loosely administered and so nebulous in its criteria for qualification that it induced some Mexicans to cross the border specifically in hopes of being legalized. According to Philip Martin, Edward Taylor, and Phil Hardiman (1988), the number of applicants for legalization as farmworkers in California was three times the size of the state's entire agricultural workforce during the reference period. In other words, IRCA seems to have pulled into the migrant workforce many Mexicans who would not otherwise have left for the United States.

In subsequent years, IRCA's legalization encouraged additional migration by family members who were unable to legalize directly under the original act (Massey and Espinosa 1997), accounting for the rapid upswing in the odds of documented migration by females between 1990 and 1995.

These were the spouses and daughters of men who had been legalized in the late 1980s and early 1990s and now qualified for legalization themselves, either as immediate family members of resident aliens (the second preference category) or under special temporary quotas established for relatives of persons legalized under IRCA.

Making Additional Trips

Having migrated to the United States, Mexicans are subject to the risk of remigration. Although the MMP compiled information on the timing of first trips for all members of the sample, it gathered data on subsequent trips only for household heads. Unfortunately, as household heads are overwhelmingly male, we can analyze the process of repeat migration only for men. Figure 2.2 shows the probability of taking a second U.S. trip with and without documents, given that one trip has already occurred. From the retrospective life histories, in each year we determined the number of men aged fifteen and older who had made one prior U.S. trip and were presently in Mexico, which became our denominator. The numerator is simply a count of the number of persons who left for a second U.S. trip in each year. As before, we compute three-year moving averages to smooth out year-to-year sampling variation.

The probability of taking a second undocumented trip closely follows the trend for first trips, rising steadily from 1966 to 1980, then falling to 1983, rising again to peak in 1985 and 1986, and then falling through 1991 before rising once again. Although the trend over time is the same, however, the likelihood of taking a second trip without documents is much higher than the likelihood of taking a first trip undocumented. As others have noted, once a trip has occurred, the odds of future trips rise substantially and, in fact, increase with each trip taken (see Donato 1998; Massey 1986; Massey and Espinosa 1997; Massey et al. 1987). Whereas the annual probability of taking a first trip without documents never exceeds .023, since the mid-1970s the likelihood of taking a second trip without documents has fluctuated between .020 and .030. Thus whereas the likelihood of initial out-migration peaked at about .021 in 1979, the probability of repeat migration reached .031 in that year. Having taken one trip as an undocumented migrant, in other words, increases the odds of a second undocumented trip by around 50 percent.

The bottom panel of figure 2.2 also shows the trend in the likelihood of taking a second U.S. trip with documents. As before, the denominator includes men aged fifteen and older who had made one prior U.S. trip and were in Mexico during the year in question, and the numerator counts the number of persons who left for a second U.S. trip with documents in the

FIGURE 2.2   Three-Year Moving Average Probability of a Second
                  Trip to the United States, 1965 to 1995

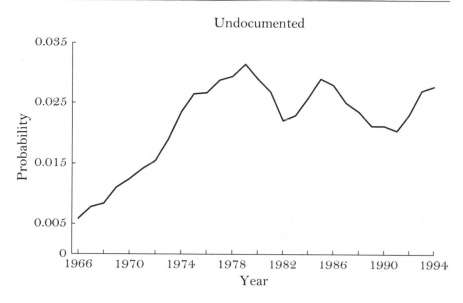

Undocumented

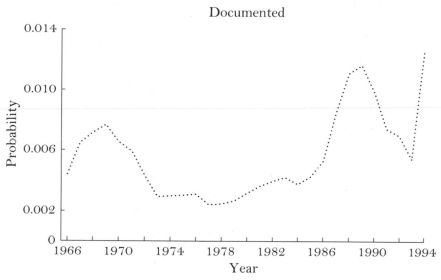

Documented

Source: Data from Mexican Migration Project.

same year. To be at risk of leaving on a second trip with documents, one need not have been documented on the first trip, and in fact most men were not.

The two major peaks in the probability of taking a second trip with documents (1968 and 1989) correspond to the two major waves of legalization. The first is the post-Bracero boom, when employers sponsored the immigration of their former temporary workers to retain unhindered access to their labor. The second is the even larger wave of legalization that occurred under IRCA. The sharp jump in the probability of taking a second trip with documents from 1993 to 1994 may be real, or it may simply be an artifact of the relatively small number of cases for that year.

CHANGES IN THE PROCESS OF BORDER CROSSING

So far, evidence suggests that trends in the likelihood of initial and repeat migration have followed a course shaped—although not entirely determined—by U.S. policies. Not surprisingly, trends in the probability of legal migration have been most strongly affected by U.S. actions, with rather pronounced increases in the likelihood of documented migration during two periods: the final implementation of the Hart-Celler Act (roughly from 1965 to 1970), and the period following the passage of IRCA, when the United States sponsored a mass program of amnesty and farmworker legalization (1987 to 1992). As border enforcement has steadily increased, moreover, the likelihood of return migration by both documented and undocumented men has trended downward, reflecting the increasing cost and difficulty of border crossing faced by migrants and their undocumented dependents. Among women, the receipt of legal documents appears to facilitate movement back and forth.

The probability of illegal migration appears to be connected more strongly to changes in the Mexican political economy than to shifts in U.S. policy, rising during the era of Import Substitution Industrialization from 1965 to 1980, falling during the peak of Mexico's oil boom (1980 to 1982), and rising again during its ensuing economic crisis (1983 to 1991). Given the dramatic increase in resources for border enforcement, the launching of major police actions along the border, and the various anti-immigrant measures enacted since 1986, the disconnection between migration probabilities and enforcement actions might seem strange, and for this reason we examine the process of undocumented border crossing.

Use and Cost of Coyotes

One important action that migrants can take to avoid apprehension is to hire the services of a paid border-crossing guide, known colloquially as a

FIGURE 2.3   Three-Year Moving Average Percentage of
Undocumented Migrants Using a Coyote on
First Trip to the United States, 1965 to 1995

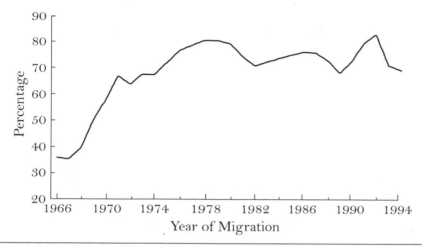

Source: Data from Mexican Migration Project.

coyote (see Conover 1987). Figure 2.3 shows the thirty-year trend in the use of coyotes by undocumented migrants on their first trip to the United States. On a first U.S. trip, migrants have no personal knowledge or experience of border crossing, and paid guides have been shown to play an important role in lowering the odds of apprehension and facilitating entry (López Castro 1998; Singer and Massey 1998).

In the immediate post-Bracero period, most undocumented migrants did not make use of a paid guide on their first trip across the border. In 1966 just a little over one-third of all first-time undocumented migrants reported using a coyote. Over the ensuing years, however, coyotes increasingly came to dominate the process of border crossing, and by 1978 they had become the norm, 80 percent of migrants reporting that they had used a coyote on their first U.S. trip. Since then the rate of coyote usage has fluctuated between 70 and 80 percent, with peaks around the time of IRCA's passage and in 1992 but no consistent trend over time. In the mid-1990s, as in the past, coyotes remain a structural feature of the border-crossing industry, and most first-time migrants avail themselves of the services they provide. Those who do not use coyotes generally cross with unpaid guides who are family or friends; very few migrants report a solo attempt on their first border crossing (Singer and Massey 1998).

FIGURE 2.4   Three-Year Moving Average of Coyote Fees for
Undocumented Migrants on First Trip to the
United States, 1966 to 1994

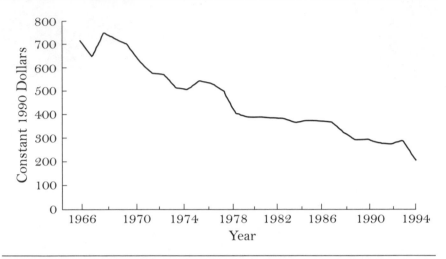

Source: Data from Mexican Migration Project.

Another important indicator of migrants' access to coyotes is the cost of such services. Figure 2.4 plots the average cost reported for retaining the services of a coyote from 1966 to 1995, in constant 1990 dollars. We do not attempt to control for the specific services provided, so the quality and extent of the smuggling services add noise to the picture. Nonetheless, the real cost of hiring a paid border guide seems to have fallen steadily over time, and by 1994 it reached a thirty-year low. In the immediate post-Bracero period, the cost of hiring a coyote stood at around $700, but by 1994 it had declined to about $200 in real terms.

Thus the massive increase in the U.S. enforcement efforts along the border has done little to increase a crucial cost of surreptitious border crossing. Demand for coyotes appears to have reached a relatively high level by 1978, when the vast majority of new border crossers were using them, and since then increases in the supply of coyotes have apparently exceeded demand, yielding a lower cost in real terms. This interpretation makes sense because the number of people who are qualified to become coyotes (those with prior border-crossing experience themselves) has grown steadily over time and reached large numbers by the early 1990s. According to Julie Phillips and Massey (2000), 16 percent of Mexicans of working age have made at least one trip to the United States. As the pool of people from whom coyotes are selected has increased over time, their supply has been sufficient to offset any increases in demand created by U.S. border policies.

The Probability of Apprehension

The most important indicator of the border's permeability is the probability of apprehension; figure 2.5 shows the trend in this indicator, computed for male household heads on their first and second trips. The denominator includes all attempted border crossings in a given year, and the numerator counts those attempts on which an apprehension was reported. As other studies have already shown (Massey and Singer 1995; Singer and Massey 1998), the probability of getting caught while attempting an undocumented entry has generally trended downward since 1970, and by the early 1990s was at historical lows. Whereas the odds of capture were about one in five through 1980, since then apprehension probabilities have steadily fallen, reaching levels below 10 percent by the early 1990s.

FIGURE 2.5   Three-Year Moving Average Probability of Apprehension on First and Second Undocumented Trips to the United States, Male Household Heads, 1966 to 1994

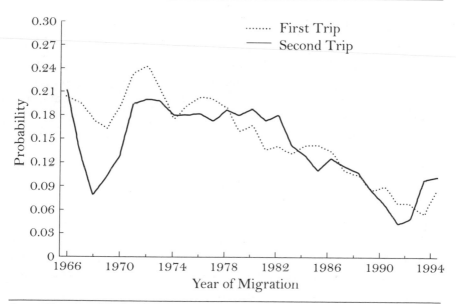

Source: Data from Mexican Migration Project.

It thus appears that U.S. border enforcement policies have had only a limited effect on the likelihood of undocumented migration or the odds of apprehension at the border. Changes in U.S. immigration policies appear to have played a more important role in influencing trends and patterns of legal migration, largely through their effect on the number of immigrant visas accessible to Mexicans in any given year. When the number was relatively large (before the implementation of Hart-Celler and during the IRCA legalization), we observe a sharp increase in the odds of documented migration by men, which is then followed by a lagged upswing in the odds of documented migration by women.

THE CHANGING SELECTIVITY OF MIGRATION

Although U.S. policies appear to have had a limited effect on patterns and processes of undocumented migration, they may nonetheless influence the traits and characteristics of the people who choose to migrate. The following examination of basic demographic and socioeconomic characteristics of undocumented and documented migrants with and without prior U.S. experience illustrates the trends in the selectivity of migration over time.

First-Time Migrants

Table 2.1 presents the demographic characteristics of cohorts of Mexican migrants leaving on their first U.S. trip during successive five-year intervals from 1965 to 1995. We present results for all first-time migrants to the United States and for documented and undocumented migrants separately. Unlike other studies (for example, Bustamante et al. 1998), which examine characteristics for large stocks of migrants enumerated in cross-sectional censuses or surveys, we focus on the characteristics of migrants at the point of initial departure.

Among all migrants, we see few consistent trends. There are two periods (1970 to 1974 and 1990 to 1995) during which emigrant cohorts are rather heavily female (37 to 40 percent of all migrants, compared with 29 to 33 percent at other times). The average age of first-time migrants varies narrowly between nineteen and twenty-two years, dipping somewhat during the late 1970s and early 1980s. The proportion going to California was 72 to 73 percent during three periods (1965 to 1969, 1975 to 1979, and 1985 to 1989) and lower at other times. In general, the greatest systematic variation is in the proportion of each cohort that was undocumented, which starts at 51 percent in 1965 to 1969, rises steadily to 71 percent in 1975 to 1979, and then falls back to under 69 percent in 1990 to 1995.

TABLE 2.1   Demographic Characteristics of Cohorts Leaving Mexico
on Their First Trip to the United States, 1965 to 1995

Characteristics	1965 to 1969	1970 to 1974	1975 to 1979	1980 to 1984	1985 to 1989	1990 to 1995
All migrants						
Percentage female	28.9	39.8	31.3	32.3	30.9	37.1
Mean age	20.4	20.3	19.1	18.8	20.1	21.5
Percentage undocumented	50.8	64.5	71.4	64.5	69.8	68.5
Percentage in California	72.9	67.2	71.8	69.0	73.1	66.1
Percentage in nontraditional states[a]	7.0	7.8	10.1	10.6	12.6	11.7
N	443	907	1,354	1,308	1,544	1,049
Undocumented migrants						
Percentage female	11.1	15.8	21.2	22.8	23.3	27.8
Mean age	22.4	23.6	23.3	24.0	22.9	23.4
Percentage in California	60.9	62.6	69.8	66.4	73.0	66.3
Percentage in nontraditional states[a]	11.1	8.4	10.2	10.6	12.2	12.3
N	225	584	959	842	1,075	716
Documented migrants						
Percentage female	47.3	58.1	57.0	49.7	48.6	57.3
Mean age	18.4	14.2	8.7	9.3	13.6	17.4
Percentage in California	85.3	75.7	77.5	74.1	73.6	65.7
Percentage in nontraditional states[a]	2.3	6.8	9.6	10.6	13.1	10.3
N	218	322	384	486	465	330

Source: Data from Mexican Migration Project.
[a] Traditional states are the four border states plus Illinois.

Given the shifting legal composition of the cohorts, it is probably wise to focus on the selectivity of documented and undocumented migrants separately. In general, the trends are clearer once the cohorts are broken down by legal status. The demographic data on successive cohorts of undocumented migrants display a clear and consistent trend toward feminization. Whereas from 1965 to 1969 only 11 percent of first-time undocumented migrants were women, by 1990 to 1995 the figure had risen to 28 percent, with monotonic increments across the cohorts in the in-between years. Although mean age is relatively stable throughout the period, at around twenty-two to twenty-four years, we see a growing concentration of migration to California from 1965 to 1989, followed by a sharp drop in the early 1990s. The proportion of migrants going to nontraditional receiving states generally increased over time and by the early 1990s stood at 12 percent.

Legal immigration has likewise shifted away from California in recent years, with the proportion of documented migrants going to that state dropping from 85 percent in 1965 to 1969 to 66 percent in 1990 to 1995; but cohorts of documented migrants were substantially feminized only during two eras: after the end of the Bracero Program and following the IRCA amnesty. Waves of legalization during these periods generally involved the initial documentation of male workers, who were either sponsored by their employers (in the post-Bracero period) or legalized under IRCA (after 1985). Having obtained their papers, however, these men then sponsored the legal immigration of their wives and dependents, producing sharp increases in the percentage of women among first-time documented migrants from 1970 to 1974, 1975 to 1979, and 1990 to 1995.

Table 2.2 continues the analysis of changing selectivity by showing trends in the basic socioeconomic characteristics of migrants. The percentage of new Mexican migrants going into agriculture has steadily dropped, while the share employed in services has increased. Education (among those aged fifteen or older) has generally increased, as has the percentage of migrants who did not work on their first trip (although the latter trend is hardly smooth). To interpret trends more accurately, we once again turn to consider undocumented and documented migrants separately.

In general, documented migrants have more schooling than their undocumented counterparts, although the trend across cohorts is toward rising education for both groups. However, both levels and trends in non–labor force participation differ by legal status. Documented migrants are far more likely to report that they did not work on their first trip to the United States, reflecting the fact that first-time legal immigrants are quite likely to be dependents (wives and children) sponsored by migrant men who have already legalized. Among documented cohorts, the proportion of those

TABLE 2.2   Socioeconomic Characteristics of Migrant Cohorts Leaving Mexico on Their First Trip to the United States, 1965 to 1995

Characteristics	1965 to 1969	1970 to 1974	1975 to 1979	1980 to 1984	1985 to 1989	1990 to 1995
All migrants						
Mean schooling (years)	6.4	5.8	5.8	6.1	7.5	7.5
Percentage nonworking	26.9	25.3	30.8	35.6	30.7	39.2
Percentage in agriculture	44.7	44.2	42.0	39.3	30.9	21.3
Percentage in services	13.6	14.4	18.8	19.1	21.7	29.7
N	443	907	1,354	1,308	1,544	1,049
Undocumented migrants						
Mean schooling (years)	5.2	4.4	5.1	5.7	7.1	7.2
Percentage nonworking	10.7	7.2	12.6	12.1	14.3	22.8
Percentage in agriculture	48.2	47.5	42.5	39.7	30.8	22.7
Percentage in services	13.6	14.4	18.8	19.1	21.7	29.7
N	225	584	959	842	1,075	716
Documented migrants						
Mean schooling (years)	7.7	8.6	8.8	8.2	9.0	8.1
Percentage nonworking	43.6	58.1	75.8	78.4	68.8	74.9
Percentage in agriculture	38.8	31.0	38.8	37.1	31.9	8.1
Percentage in services	17.4	21.4	21.2	19.1	26.8	38.7
N	218	322	384	486	465	330

Source: Data from Mexican Migration Project.

who did not work on their first U.S. trip rises from 44 percent in 1965 to 1969 to 78 percent in 1980 to 1984, dips to 69 percent from 1985 to 1989, and then recovers to 75 percent in 1990 to 1995. In contrast, the share of those not working is much lower among undocumented migrants, although after 1970 it tends to rise steadily, from 7 percent in 1970 to 1974 to 23 percent in 1990 to 1995.

The concentration of workers in agriculture is also much greater among undocumented than documented migrants, and it displays a more consistent trend over time. The share of undocumented first-time migrants employed in agriculture was 48 percent from 1965 to 1969, but over succeeding cohorts it fell steadily to reach 23 percent from 1990 to 1995. In contrast, the percentage of documented migrants in agriculture fluctuated between 31 and 39 percent across cohorts between 1965 and 1989 before plummeting to just 8 percent in 1990 to 1995, the period immediately following the IRCA legalizations.

These trends suggest the changing nature of selection in the flow of Mexico-U.S. migrants. New undocumented migrants are steadily becoming more female, and the percentage who are not working has also increased, although nonworkers still account for less than a quarter of all new entrants. The age of entering undocumented migrants has not changed much over time, averaging twenty-two to twenty-four across all cohorts; but new undocumented migrants display a steady and rather pronounced shift away from agriculture and toward services. In general, these trends are steady and stable and are not linked in any obvious way to changes in U.S. immigration policies.

The characteristics of documented first-time migrants are apparently more strongly shaped by shifts in U.S. policy. Specific changes in U.S. immigration policies during the late 1960s (the end of the Bracero Program and the implementation of the Hart-Celler Act) and the late 1980s (IRCA's amnesty programs) led to associated waves of legalization, mostly of men. In the immediate aftermath of these waves, documented migration became substantially feminized and skewed toward non–labor force participation. Among the documented, there has also been a steady movement away from California and a steady increase in the percentage of migrants working in services.

Experienced Migrants

Although it is important to understand trends in the selectivity and characteristics of new migrants, most of those crossing the border in any given year are not new but experienced migrants, having made one or more prior trips. Thus it is also important to understand how migrants are selected into a pattern of recurrent border crossing. Table 2.3 does so by presenting demographic characteristics for cohorts of experienced Mexican migrants (those with at least two trips) on their most recent U.S. trip.

In general, these cohorts, with a mean age of thirty-three to thirty-six, are older than those of new migrants, and they are much less likely to be women (under 20 percent). Moreover, the recent shift away from California toward nontraditional states is more pronounced among experienced migrants, a pattern that is true for both documented and undocumented migrants. Over the thirty-year period studied, the share of experienced migrants who were undocumented first falls, then rises to a peak from 1975 to 1979, and then falls to a very low level (38 percent) in 1990 to 1995. In general, females are unlikely to migrate recurrently without documentation, although there has been an increase over time. In no case, however, has an undocumented cohort been less than 87 percent male.

Interestingly, the number of prior trips by experienced undocumented migrants has generally fallen over time, going from 4.6 between 1964 to 1970 to just 2.8 from 1990 to 1995. This is precisely the trend one would expect if tightened border enforcement were inducing migrants to stop moving recurrently and to instead settle north of the border. Indeed, among documented migrants, for whom border crossing is no problem, the number of prior trips has been steadily increasing and the percentage of women is considerably higher, ranging from 22 to 37 percent (with a peak from 1975 to 1979).

Table 2.4 presents the socioeconomic characteristics of successive cohorts of experienced migrants. Mean schooling levels have steadily risen over time for both documented and undocumented migrants, but the differential in education between these two groups is not as large as for first-time migrants. Recurrent migrants are overwhelmingly labor force participants. Among documented migrants the percentage not working fluctuates between 13 and 28 percent with no clear time trend, while among the undocumented it varies from 2 to 11 percent and generally increases over time. The degree of concentration in agriculture moves in opposite directions across successive cohorts of recurrent documented and undocumented migrants. Among the latter, there is a steady shift away from agricultural employment. Whereas three-quarters of recurrent undocumented migrants were farmworkers from 1965 to 1969, by 1990 to 1995 the percentage had fallen to just 29 percent.

Among documented cohorts, in contrast, concentration in agriculture generally increases, especially after 1985. By 1990 to 1995, 44 percent of recurrently migrating legal migrants were working in agriculture. This

TABLE 2.3   Demographic Characteristics of Recurrent Migrant Cohorts Leaving Mexico on Their Most Recent Trip to the United States, 1965 to 1995

Characteristics	1965 to 1969	1970 to 1974	1975 to 1979	1980 to 1984	1985 to 1989	1990 to 1995
All migrants						
Percentage female	9.1	13.7	17.8	1.8	19.4	18.4
Mean age	35.5	36.4	34.8	35.6	33.2	35.7
Percentage undocumented	62.6	56.0	72.3	67.5	45.6	37.7
Percentage in California	66.3	68.7	67.2	71.2	70.6	54.5
Percentage in nontraditional states[a]	11.1	7.6	10.2	11.2	15.3	19.2
Mean number of prior trips	4.1	4.5	3.5	3.9	4.8	5.7
N	99	211	329	498	1,010	1,213
Undocumented migrants						
Percentage female	0.0	5.1	10.1	8.6	12.5	12.1
Mean age	36.4	36.5	34.9	34.5	32.2	32.1
Percentage in California	57.4	59.0	64.7	70.5	73.4	52.7
Percentage in nontraditional states[a]	3.5	5.3	8.4	10.8	13.8	20.3
Mean number of prior trips	4.6	3.9	3.1	3.1	3.0	2.8
N	62	117	238	335	462	462
Documented migrants						
Percentage female	24.3	25.0	37.4	33.3	25.0	22.0
Mean age	34.0	36.3	34.7	37.6	34.1	37.9
Percentage in California	81.1	81.5	74.7	72.2	67.1	55.7
Percentage in nontraditional states[a]	13.0	10.2	13.8	12.5	19.8	15.6
Mean number of prior trips	3.2	5.2	4.7	5.6	6.4	7.5
N	37	92	88	161	544	749

Source: Data from Mexican Migration Project.
[a] Traditional states are the four border states plus Illinois.

TABLE 2.4   Socioeconomic Characteristics of Experienced Migrant Cohorts Leaving Mexico on Their Most Recent Trip to the United States, 1965 to 1995

Characteristics	1965 to 1969	1970 to 1974	1975 to 1979	1980 to 1984	1985 to 1989	1990 to 1995
All migrants						
Mean schooling (years)	3.8	3.9	4.3	4.6	5.8	6.1
Percentage nonworking	8.1	9.0	7.5	11.6	10.4	3.6
Percentage in agriculture	56.2	41.8	42.6	42.6	37.3	38.3
Percentage in services	11.2	15.9	16.5	16.8	18.3	18.3
N	99	211	329	498	1,010	1,213
Undocumented migrants						
Mean schooling (years)	2.9	3.2	3.6	3.8	5.1	6.3
Percentage nonworking	1.6	4.3	2.9	3.6	7.8	11.2
Percentage in agriculture	74.6	49.6	45.2	47.3	32.3	29.4
Percentage in services	8.5	15.3	18.3	12.9	21.2	21.5
N	62	117	238	335	462	462
Documented migrants						
Mean schooling (years)	5.3	4.9	6.3	6.2	6.3	6.0
Percentage nonworking	18.9	15.2	19.8	27.8	12.7	20.7
Percentage in agriculture	20.0	29.0	34.3	30.2	41.7	44.4
Percentage in services	16.7	17.1	10.0	26.7	15.8	16.1
N	37	92	88	161	544	749

Source: Data from Mexican Migration Project.

new concentration of recurrent legal migrants in farmwork probably stems from the employer sanctions enacted by IRCA in late 1986, which made it illegal for employers to hire undocumented workers. In response to the criminalization of the hiring of undocumented workers, agricultural growers shifted to a new practice: labor subcontracting (Durand 1997; Martin 1996; Martin and Taylor 1991; Taylor 1996; Taylor, Martin, and Fix 1997; Taylor and Thilmany 1993). Under subcontracting arrangements, a legal immigrant (usually a recurrent migrant) contractually agrees to provide an employer with a specific number of workers for a certain period of time to undertake a defined task at a fixed rate of pay per worker. Neither the subcontractor nor the workers themselves are technically employees of the firm or person entering the contract, so the employer avoids IRCA's burdensome paperwork requirements and escapes liability under the law. In return for providing this buffer, the subcontractor retains a portion of the workers' wages as payment, thus lowering their effective rate of pay (Phillips and Massey 1999).

CONCLUSION

Our research suggests that U.S. border enforcement policies have had relatively small effects on the likelihood of undocumented migration between Mexico and the United States. To the extent that we observe any effects at all, they tend to be perverse. By the time the border crackdown began in 1987, the use of paid border-crossing guides was already widespread among undocumented migrants, and a coyote industry had become institutionalized in border cities. As the pool of people with the knowledge and ability to become coyotes (former migrants) grew steadily larger, their supply generally kept pace and even exceeded demand. Among the migrants themselves, stocks of migration-related human and social capital steadily accumulated to reach very high levels (see Phillips and Massey 2000).

As a result, border enforcement has failed to affect the odds of apprehension (which have, in fact, fallen sharply since the early 1970s), the real cost of border crossing. As the demand for border-crossing guides increased over time, so did the supply of coyotes, yielding falling fees; and as enforcement resources increased they also became more concentrated geographically, leading migrants to shift their crossing preferences away from San Diego toward other locations on the two-thousand-mile border. Under these circumstances, it is not surprising that U.S. immigration policies have had a minimal effect on the probability of taking a first or second trip without documents. To the extent that these probabilities have varied over time, they seem to have been in response to shifts in the Mexican political economy rather than to changes in U.S. immigration policy.

We estimate that the probability of taking a first undocumented trip in 1995 was .018 for men and .003 for women and that in the same year the probability that a man would make a second trip was .029 (we were unable to estimate the corresponding probability for women). Among a cohort of men going through life subject to this risk of taking a first trip to the United States, 15 percent would have done so after ten years, and after going back to Mexico another 25 percent of the returnees would have remigrated within another ten years.

We uncovered little evidence that U.S. policy has strongly affected the characteristics of undocumented migrants either. They appear, rather, to be evolving steadily according to their own rhythm (see Massey, Goldring, and Durand 1994; Massey et al. 1998). The percentage of women has steadily increased among both first-time and recurrent migrants (especially the former), non–labor force participation has gone up, average schooling levels have increased, and the percentage employed in agriculture has fallen.

Changes in U.S. policy have had far greater effects on the likelihood and selectivity of documented migration. During two historical epochs, Mexicans enjoyed unusual access to U.S. visas for permanent residence. After the demise of the Bracero Program, U.S. growers energetically worked to sponsor the legal immigration of their Mexican workers under the liberal provisions of U.S. immigration law that prevailed until the Hart-Celler Act took full effect in 1968, resulting in a notable increase in the likelihood of legal migration, predominantly of men, from 1965 to 1969. Similarly, the two legalization programs authorized by IRCA provided legal papers to some 2.3 million Mexicans, again predominantly men, yielding another sharp increase in the probability of legal migration from 1985 to 1989. These two waves of legalization were followed by legalization "echoes" in subsequent periods, as the newly legalized men sponsored the legal entry of their spouses and children, producing elevated probabilities of documented migration by women from 1970 to 1974 and from 1990 to 1995, with accompanying shifts in the composition of migrant cohorts toward feminization and non–labor force participation.

Among all cohorts of first-time migrants, both documented and undocumented, there has been a shift away from agricultural employment toward services and a movement away from California toward nontraditional destinations, as well as steadily rising levels of educational achievement. These patterns also characterize cohorts of recurrent migrants (those with prior U.S. experience), except that recurrent legal migrants are showing a greater concentration in agriculture, probably reflecting their new role acting as labor subcontractors in the wake of IRCA's employer sanctions.

REFERENCES

Bean, Frank D., Rodolfo Corona, Rodolfo Tuirán, and Karen A. Woodrow-Lafield. 1998. "The Quantification of Migration between Mexico and the United States." In *Binational Study of Migration Between Mexico and the United States*, vol. 1, *Thematic Chapters*. Washington: U.S. Commission on Immigration Reform.

Bean, Frank D., George Vernez, and Charles B. Keely. 1989. *Opening and Closing the Doors: Evaluating Immigration Reform and Control*. Washington, D.C.: Urban Institute.

Binational Migration Study. 1998a. *Binational Study of Migration Between Mexico and the United States*, vol. 1, *Thematic Chapters*. Washington: U.S. Commission on Immigration Reform.

———. 1998b. *Binational Study of Migration Between Mexico and the United States*, vol. 2, *Research Reports and Background Materials*. Washington: U.S. Commission on Immigration Reform.

———. 1998c. *Binational Study of Migration Between Mexico and the United States*, vol. 3, *Research Reports and Background Materials*. Washington: U.S. Commission on Immigration Reform.

Bustamante, Jorge A., Guillermina Jasso, J. Edward Taylor, Gustavo López Castro, and Katharine Donato. 1998. *Binational Study of Migration Between Mexico and the United States*, vol. 1, *Thematic Chapters*. Washington: U.S. Commission on Immigration Reform.

Calavita, Kitty. 1992. *Inside the State: The Bracero Program, Immigration, and the I.N.S.* New York: Routledge.

Centeno, Miguel Angel. 1994. *Democracy within Reason: Technocratic Revolution in Mexico*. University Park: Pennsylvania State University Press.

Cerrutti, Marcela, and Douglas S. Massey. 2001. "On the Auspices of Female Migration from Mexico to the United States." *Demography* 38: 187–200.

Conover, Ted. 1987. *Coyotes: A Journey Through the Secret World of America's Illegal Aliens*. New York: Random House.

Donato, Katharine. 1998. "Mexican Migration Project Data." In *Binational Study of Migration Between Mexico and the United States*, vol. 3, *Research Reports and Background Materials*. Washington: U.S. Commission on Immigration Reform.

Dunn, Timothy J. 1996. *The Militarization of the U.S.-Mexico Border, 1978–1992: Low-Intensity Conflict Doctrine Comes Home*. Austin: University of Texas, Center for Mexican American Studies.

Durand, Jorge. 1997. "De enganchadores a contratistas: La difusión de un nuevo sistema de contratación de mano de obra Mexicana." Paper presented to the Congress Latin American Studies Association. Guadalajara (April 17–19, 1997).

Durand, Jorge, Douglas S. Massey, and Emilio A. Parrado. 1999. "The New Era of Mexican Migration to the United States." *Journal of American History* 86: 518–36.

Goodis, Tracy Ann. 1986. "A Layman's Guide to the 1986 U.S. Immigration Reform." Discussion Paper on the Impacts of Immigration in California. Washington, D.C.: Urban Institute.

Hansen, Roger D. 1971. *The Politics of Mexican Development.* Baltimore, Md.: Johns Hopkins University Press.

López Castro, Gustavo. 1998. "Coyotes and Alien Smuggling." In *Binational Study of Migration Between Mexico and the United States*, vol. 2, *Research Reports and Background Materials.* Washington: U.S. Commission on Immigration Reform.

Martin, Philip L. 1996. *Promises to Keep: Collective Bargaining in California Agriculture.* Ames: Iowa State University Press.

Martin, Philip L., and J. Edward Taylor. 1991. "Immigration Reform and Farm Labor Contracting in California." In *The Paper Curtain: Employer Sanctions' Implementation, Impact, and Reform*, edited by Michael Fix. Washington, D.C.: Urban Institute.

Martin, Philip L., J. Edward Taylor, and Phil Hardiman. 1988. "California Farmworkers and the SAW Legalization Program." *California Agriculture* 42: 4–6.

Massey, Douglas S. 1986. "The Settlement Process Among Mexican Migrants to the United States." *American Sociological Review* 51: 670–85.

———. 1998. "March of Folly: U.S. Immigration Policy After NAFTA." *American Prospect* 37: 22–33.

———. 1999. "International Migration at the Dawn of the Twenty-First Century: The Role of the State." *Population and Development Review* 25: 303–23.

Massey, Douglas S., Rafael Alarcón, Jorge Durand, and Humberto González. 1987. *Return to Aztlán: The Social Process of International Migration from Western Mexico.* Berkeley: University of California Press.

Massey, Douglas S., Joaquín Arango, Graeme Hugo, Ali Kouaouci, Adela Pellegrino, and J. Edward Taylor. 1998. *Worlds in Motion: Understanding International Migration at the End of the Millennium.* Oxford: Oxford University Press.

Massey, Douglas S., and Kristin E. Espinosa. 1997. "What's Driving Mexico-U.S. Migration? A Theoretical, Empirical, and Policy Analysis." *American Journal of Sociology* 102: 939–99.

Massey, Douglas S., Luin P. Goldring, and Jorge Durand. 1994. "Continuities in Transnational Migration: An Analysis of Nineteen Mexican Communities." *American Journal of Sociology* 99: 1492–1533.

Massey, Douglas S., and Audrey Singer. 1995. "New Estimates of Undocumented Mexican Migration and the Probability of Apprehension." *Demography* 32: 203–13.

Meyers, Eytan. 1995. "The Political Economy of International Migration Policy: A Comparative and Quantitative Study." Ph.D. diss., University of Chicago.

Phillips, Julie A., and Douglas S. Massey. 1999. "The New Labor Market: Immigrants and Wages After IRCA." *Demography* 36: 233–46.

———. 2000. "Engines of Immigration: Stocks of Human and Social Capital in Mexico." *Social Science Quarterly* 81: 33–48.

Reichert, Joshua S., and Douglas S. Massey. 1979. "Patterns of Migration from a Central Mexican Town to the United States: A Comparison of Legal and Illegal Migrants." *International Migration Review* 13: 599–623.

———. 1980. "History and Trends in U.S.-Bound Migration from a Mexican Town." *International Migration Review* 14: 475–491.

Sheahan, John. 1991. *Conflict and Change in Mexican Economic Strategy: Implications for Mexico and Latin America.* La Jolla: University of California at San Diego, Center for U.S.-Mexican Studies.

Singer, Audrey, and Douglas S. Massey. 1998. "The Social Process of Undocumented Border Crossing Among Mexican Migrants." *International Migration Review* 32: 561–92.

Smith, Shirley J., Roger G. Kramer, and Audrey Singer. 1996. *Characteristics and Labor Market Behavior of the Legalized Population: Five Years Following Legalization.* Washington: U.S. Government Printing Office.

Taylor, J. Edward. 1996. "IRCA's Effects in California Agriculture." In *Immigration Reform and U.S. Agriculture,* edited by Philip L. Martin, Wallace Huffman, Robert Emerson, and J. Edward Taylor. Oakland: California Division of Agriculture and Natural Resources.

Taylor, J. Edward, Philip L. Martin, and Michael Fix. 1997. *Poverty amid Prosperity: Immigration and the Changing Face of Rural California.* Washington, D.C.: Urban Institute.

Taylor, J. Edward., and Dawn Thilmany. 1993. "Worker Turnover, Farm Labor Contractors, and IRCA's Impact on the California Farm Labor Market." *American Journal of Agricultural Economics* 75: 350–60.

Timmer, Ashley S., and Jeffrey G. Williamson. 1998. "Immigration Policy Prior to the 1930s: Labor Markets, Policy Interactions, and Globalization Backlash." *Population and Development Review* 24: 739–72.

U.S. Department of Justice. Immigration and Naturalization Service. 1995. *1994 Statistical Yearbook of the Immigration and Naturalization Service.* Washington: U.S. Government Printing Office.

Van Hook, Jennifer, and Frank D. Bean. 1998. "Estimating Unauthorized Migration to the United States: Issues and Results." In *Binational Study of Migration Between Mexico and the United States,* vol. 2, *Research Reports and Background Materials.* Washington: U.S. Commission on Immigration Reform.

Woodrow-Lafield, Karen A. 1998. "Estimating Authorized Immigration." In *Binational Study of Migration Between Mexico and the United States,* vol. 2, *Research Reports and Background Materials.* Washington: U.S. Commission on Immigration Reform.

CHAPTER 3

MIGRANTS' SOCIAL CAPITAL AND INVESTING REMITTANCES IN MEXICO

Margarita Mooney

STUDYING WHAT conditions lead migrants to invest their remittances is of great practical importance, given the enormous sums of money migrants send to their countries of origin, estimated at $75 billion worldwide in 1995 (Taylor et al. 1996). In 1999 migrants sent $6.8 billion in remittances to Mexico alone. This sum exceeds the value of all Mexican agricultural exports, almost equals the country's income from tourism, is more than two-thirds the value of oil exports, and represents more than half the foreign direct investment in Mexico (Multilateral Investment Fund 2001). How migrants and their families spend this money has practical implications for the local and national economy.

Alejandro Portes (1995) theorizes that social relations influence economic action both by defining the goals that actors pursue and by providing them the means to achieve their goals. This idea can be applied to migration and remittances in several ways. First, social networks facilitate the transfer of goods and information between Mexico and the United States, becoming social capital. Second, migrants invest their remittances to establish a solid basis for claiming membership in their communities of origin. Third, different kinds of social ties affect the way migrants spend monthly remittances compared with savings brought back at the end of a migration trip.

NETWORKS, COMMUNITIES, AND REMITTANCES

Numerous studies have shown that networks reduce the cost and risk of migration (Massey et al. 1987; Portes 1995). Migrant networks also increase the likelihood that remittances will be invested in the community of origin. Networks reduce monitoring and transaction costs of sending remittances (Roberts and Morris 2003). In addition, migrants who wish to make an investment in their hometown can use social networks first to transfer the money and then to obtain information on how that investment is progressing.

Several studies have found that social and family networks among migrants are an important predictor of investment of remittances in a business (Lopez and Seligson 1991; Massey et al. 1987). Rubén Hernández-León (1997) finds that migrants who participate in networks with other migrants have greater information about investment opportunities centered precisely on the needs of migrants and their families. Portes and Luis Guarnizo (1991) also find that interethnic networks facilitate immigrant entrepreneurship in both places of settlement and origin. In a study of four Mexican communities, Douglas Massey and Lawrence Basem (1992) find that social ties increased migrants' likelihood of investing remittances and savings.

Migrants who are embedded in social networks of other migrants in the United States maintain their hometown as the source of their identity, and their remittances are used to signify continuing membership in the community of origin (Connell and Conway 2000; Goldring 1998; Levitt 1997; Massey et al. 1987; Roberts and Morris 2003). One way migrants maintain ties to other migrants is by living with family members or other townspeople (paisanos) while abroad, which reinforces norms about sending remittances. In addition, migrants who wish to invest in their hometowns draw on relations of kinship and friendship to supplement their own funds in making those investments. In other cases, migrants form voluntary associations with other migrants, such as hometown associations or social clubs. These clubs reinforce migrants' identification with their place of origin and provide them with an opportunity to exchange information about what is happening at home, encouraging them to channel money to their hometowns (Massey et al. 1987).

The central research question addressed in this chapter is how migrant networks influence the way migrants spend remittances. Some studies have found that migrants use remittances for conspicuous consumption, buying items such as televisions, cars, and parabolic television antennas (Cornelius 1991). Migrants often spend savings on social activities during their visits home, including religious Christmas festivals and celebration of the day of the community's patron saint (Cornelius 1991; Durand et al. 1996; Massey et al. 1987). This type of consumption has led some researchers to speak of a migrant syndrome (Reichert 1982) whereby returned migrants raise consumption norms in their places of origin, leading other community members to emulate those consumption patterns by migrating themselves.

Other migrants make short trips and live with family members or townspeople to save money to invest in a business or farm they already own (Durand et al. 1996; Massey and Basem 1992; Massey et al. 1993). Migrants who retain ties to their hometowns may use their foreign earnings to buy or repair a home, signifying a solid base of membership in their community of origin even if they continue to make migration trips (Goldring 1998; Grasmuck and Pessar 1991; Massey et al. 1987).

Under certain conditions, migrants use their remittances both to make a status claim and to make an investment. Migrant networks promote investment in a home or productive activity both because such investments constitute a more visible and durable status claim than consumption and because they are a way to improve a migrant family's economic condition.

To explain what conditions limit or facilitate investing remittances, previous studies have looked to family conditions, trip characteristics, access to productive resources before departure, and community and macroeconomic conditions. I hypothesize that, after controlling for these factors, those migrants with social ties to other migrants in the United States are more likely to invest their remittances and savings in their places of origin.

PREVIOUSLY TESTED THEORIES OF MIGRATION

According to the new economics of labor migration, households use migration as a strategy for diversifying their labor resources to overcome the risks and constraints to production. For example, families lacking money for a productive activity may send a migrant abroad to obtain capital for investment. This proposition is supported by Massey and Basem (1992) and Jorge Durand and colleagues (1996), who find that migrants are more likely to invest remittances if they own a business, land, or a home before migrating.

The current stage in a migrant family's life cycle obviously influences its consumption needs and its ability to invest. Married migrants, particularly those with young children, have greater needs for family sustenance than unmarried migrants or those with few or older children. Migrants from these families are thus more likely to dedicate remittances and savings to current consumption than to productive investment (Massey and Basem 1992).

According to the new economics of labor migration, the circumstances of a particular trip also affect the likelihood of investing remittances and savings. Migrants whose immediate families are in Mexico have greater consumption needs, while those who migrate with their families have more opportunities to save money for investment. Extended trips also allow migrants more time to accumulate money to send home. Many migrants who "settle" in the United States also build a house in their place of origin as part of an eventual plan to return (Goldring 1998; Grasmuck and Pessar 1991; Massey et al. 1987). The amount of money sent home also affects the way in which it is spent (Durand et al. 1996).

Similarly, some forms of human capital appear to predict remittance behavior. Migrants with higher levels of education are less likely to send remittances to their places of origin, though when they do remit, the amounts are greater (Funkhouser 1995; Itzigsohn 1995; Menjivar et al. 1998). Durand and colleagues (1996) also find that migrants with greater education are more likely to spend remittances and savings on both production and housing, and individuals with more work experience tend to have more opportunities for investment. Other kinds of human capital, such as occupational skill and proficiency in English, affect a migrant's economic success in the United States, but they do not appear to be significant predictors of remitting behavior (Durand et al. 1996).

When deciding how to spend remittances and savings, migrants must consider local economic conditions. Often, the same factors that lead to out-migration, such as a small and poorly educated workforce, limited transportation, poor communications, and restricted local markets, simultaneously discourage investment (Lindstrom 1996; Taylor et al. 1996). However, studies have found that in Mexican communities undergoing economic growth, U.S. earnings constitute an important source of funding for business enterprises (Lindstrom 1996; Massey et al. 1987).

Broader macroeconomic conditions also affect local business prospects and condition investment decisions. On the one hand, rising inflation translates into higher consumer prices, declining purchasing power, and increasing consumption costs (Cornelius 1991; Durand et al. 1996), hitting small-scale producers particularly hard (Taylor et al. 1996). On the other hand, inflation in Mexico creates investment opportunities for those with U.S. dollars, as it reduces the cost of capital goods and productive resources in dollar-denominated terms. For someone with liquid dollars, a sudden devaluation of Mexican currency may create a window of opportunity to acquire productive equipment at bargain prices.

METHODS

The Mexican Migration Project gathered data from household heads who had migrated to the United States at least once, who were asked detailed questions about their most recent trip (see chapter 16). For my analysis I used data gathered from 4,082 household heads living in the fifty-two communities surveyed through 1997 and focused on answers to questions about whether they had sent home monthly remittances or returned home with savings. Among those who reported savings or remittances, respondents were asked to select the top-five end uses for these funds from thirteen options listed in the survey. These data were supplemented with longitudinal data compiled for the migrant's community and the Mexican political economy.

While previous studies have generally constructed a single model to predict who remits, how much is remitted, and how remittances are spent, my theory focuses exclusively on what factors make certain migrants more likely than others to invest their remittances and savings. I consider variables that I take to influence how migrants spend remittances and savings, and my sample includes only those migrants who reported positive remittances or savings on their last U.S. trip, yielding subsamples of 1,750 migrants with remittances and 1,496 with savings. I dropped observations that were missing values on independent variables or were outliers, yielding final samples of 1,284 remitters and 968 savers. Although some studies (Durand et al. 1996; Massey and Basem 1992) combine monthly remittances and savings brought back at the end of a trip into a single dependent variable, my aim here is to determine how social networks influence the way savings and remittances are used, so I created two separate dependent variables.

Specifically, I created separate, mutually exclusive categories for spending on housing, production, and consumption and then used a multinomial logit regression to relate these dependent variables to a set of independent variables (described later in this chapter). The baseline category was always spending on consumption. Although migrants were asked to list the top-five ways they used their savings and remittances, they were not asked how much was spent on each end use. To classify each migrant into one of three mutually exclusive spending categories, I used the top-reported end use.

Following Durand and colleagues (1996), I reduced the thirteen reported end uses to three categories as follows: the consumption category comprises reported spending on consumer goods, recreation, family maintenance, and debts; housing includes money dedicated to the purchase, construction, or repair of a home; and production includes money spent to purchase farmland, livestock, or tools, to help finance a business enterprise, or to acquire a motor vehicle. Although it is impossible to know whether vehicles were used as items of consumption (for pleasure and recreation) or production (launching a taxi or hauling service), the results of my analysis were robust whether vehicles were counted as consumption or production, so I included them in production, as acquisition of a car for business purposes is quite common in migrant-sending regions (Massey et al. 1987).

Exponentiation of the odds of a multinomial regression produces a relative risk ratio, which represents the odds that an observation falls into the comparison category versus the baseline category. Thus my models predict the relative risk that migrants spent remittances or savings on housing and production rather than consumption. A ratio of 1.0 indicates a risk equal to that of the baseline or comparison category. A ratio greater than 1.0 represents an increased likelihood of falling into the comparison category, and a ratio less than 1.0 represents the converse—a decreased likelihood of falling into the comparison category versus the baseline. I also correct for community clustering in my models because regressions that assume a simple random sample tend to underestimate standard errors, thereby inflating significance levels.

I use Durand and colleagues (1996) as a reference to create a nested model (model 1) predicting how migrants spend their remittances and savings. I include only variables from their model that are theorized to affect how migrants spend remittances or savings, not those that affect which migrants are more likely to remit or how much they send. In model 2, I add variables that measure social networks to test the hypothesis that migrants who have social ties with other migrants in their place of settlement are more likely to invest remittances and savings at home.

All independent variables are defined as of the year of the most recent U.S. trip or, in the case of property owned, as of the year before the last trip. Table 3.1 presents operational definitions for the theoretical and control variables employed in the analysis. To measure social ties in the United States, my leading theoretical variable, I chose what I considered to be the best indicators of regular social contact with other migrants at places of destination: whether the respondent belonged to a U.S. social club, lived with relatives, or lived with paisanos on the last U.S. trip. Although Massey and colleagues (1987) translate the word "paisano" to mean a person from the same origin community, a looser translation would be a person from the same country (in this case, any Mexican), but this nuance in meaning does not significantly affect my interpretation of results.

Means and standard deviations for all variables are presented in table 3.2. Whereas the numbers presented in this table were computed using sample weights to represent the collective population of all communities sampled, the multinomial regression analyses were unweighted (see Durand et al.

TABLE 3.1   Independent Variables Included in Model Predicting Migrant Remittances and Savings

Independent Variable	Definition
Social networks	
Lived with relatives	1 if lived with relatives on last U.S. trip, 0 otherwise
Lived with townspeople	1 if lived with townspeople on last U.S. trip, 0 otherwise
Belonged to social club	1 if member of U.S. social club on last trip, 0 otherwise
Household resources	
Owns farmland	1 if household owned farmland before last U.S. trip, 0 otherwise
Owns business	1 if household owned business before last U.S. trip, 0 otherwise
Owns home	1 if household owned home before last U.S. trip, 0 otherwise
Family life cycle	
Married	1 if married at time of last U.S. trip, 0 otherwise
Number of minors	Number of minor children in household at time of last U.S. trip
Trip characteristics	
Previous U.S. experience	Months of U.S. experience before last trip
Total number of trips	Number of prior trips to the United States
Wages earned	Final wage earned on last U.S. trip
Settled in United States	1 if migrant surveyed in U.S. out-migrant community, 0 otherwise
Duration of trip	Length in years of last U.S. trip
Spouse on trip	1 if spouse present on last U.S. trip, 0 otherwise
Children on trip	1 if son or daughter present on last U.S. trip, 0 otherwise
Total amount of remittances or savings	Amount of monthly remittances or savings brought back at the end of last migration trip, measured in dollars (thousands)
Human capital	
Work experience	Migrant's age at last U.S. trip minus education minus six
Education	Years of schooling completed at time of last U.S. trip

(*Table continues on p. 52.*)

TABLE 3.1   Independent Variables Included in Model Predicting
Migrant Remittances and Savings (*Continued*)

Independent Variable	Definition
Community characteristics	
Percentage twice minimum wage	Percentage of workers earning more than twice the minimum wage in migrant's community of origin at time of last migration trip
Percentage females in manufacturing	Percentage of female workers employed in manufacturing in migrant's community of origin at time of last migration trip
Percentage males in agriculture	Percentage of male workers employed in agriculture in migrant's community of origin at time of last migration trip
Macroeconomic context	
Mexican inflation rate	Percentage change in interest rate during year of last U.S. trip

Source: Data from Mexican Migration Project.

1996 for a description of the sample weights). As can be seen in table 3.2, around 7 percent of migrants who sent remittances and 2 percent of migrants who sent savings belonged to a social club. To see whether people who belong to social clubs differ from the rest of the sample, I computed a t-test on the difference in the means for various characteristics of migrants who belonged to social clubs compared with those who did not. I found that migrants who were in social clubs had significantly more U.S. experience and total trips than those who were not. However, social club membership was not clustered at the community level.

To gauge a household's access to productive resources, I included dummy variables indicating whether the migrant's household owned farmland, a business, or a house or lot before the head of household's most recent migration trip. In some cases, a migrant bought a home or land or started a business during the same year as his last migration trip. As it is impossible to determine whether he made the trip before or after the purchase, for these observations I coded this variable as missing. In the analysis of remittances, about 10 percent of the households owned farmland, 15 percent owned a business, and 39 percent owned a home before going to the United States. In the analysis of savings, the respective figures were 11, 12, and 51 percent.

TABLE 3.2   Means and Standard Deviations of Variables Used in Analysis of Remittances and Savings (Percentage)

| | Analysis of Remittances | | Analysis of Savings | |
Variable	Mean	Standard Deviation	Mean	Standard Deviation
Social networks				
Lived with relatives	0.627	0.484	0.579	0.494
Lived with townspeople	0.662	0.473	0.713	0.453
Belonged to social club	0.066	0.248	0.019	0.135
Household resources				
Owns farmland	0.101	0.301	0.113	0.317
Owns business	0.145	0.352	0.116	0.320
Owns home	0.388	0.487	0.511	0.500
Family life cycle				
Married	0.806	0.396	0.850	0.358
Number of minors	2.471	2.245	2.748	2.251
Trip characteristics				
Previous U.S. experience	88.983	87.252	57.968	71.000
Total number of trips	4.697	4.897	4.938	5.560
Wages earned	5.861	4.296	4.869	3.938
Settled in United States	0.331	0.471	0.025	0.157
Duration of trip	2.678	4.363	1.223	2.464
Spouse on trip	0.282	0.450	0.090	0.287
Children on trip	0.315	0.465	0.132	0.338
Total remittances (in thousands)	5.472	8.812		
Total savings (in thousands)			1.005	1.183
Human capital				
Work experience	22.298	12.994	24.128	13.101
Education	5.774	4.219	5.172	3.967
Community characteristics				
Percentage twice minimum wage	29.029	10.723	27.409	10.785
Percentage females in manufacturing	15.898	10.438	16.243	10.840
Percentage males in agriculture	46.300	17.000	46.800	18.000
Macroeconomic context				
Mexican inflation rate	31.949	22.676	31.665	23.315

Source: Data from Mexican Migration Project.

I measured family life cycle in two ways: marital status and the number of children in the household under the age of eighteen. Migrants in a religious, civil, or common-law marriage at the time of their most recent migration trip were coded as being married. The vast majority of the respondents (81 percent in the remittance analysis, 85 percent in the savings analysis) were married at the time of their last U.S. trip. The number of minors in the household was a continuous variable that averaged 2.5 in the remittance model and 2.7 in that for savings.

The amount of prior U.S. experience was measured in months. Whereas in the remittance analysis the average migrant had 89 months (7.4 years) of accumulated experience, in the savings analysis the figure was only 58 months (4.8 years). This experience was accumulated over 4.7 trips in the former case and 4.9 trips in the latter. Wages earned in the United States ranged from an average $5.86 per hour for remitters to $4.87 for savers. The duration of the migrant's last trip was measured in years, yielding respective averages of 2.7 and 1.2 years. Migrants interviewed in the United States were coded as being settled abroad. According to this definition, a third of remitters were settled migrants, compared with just 2.5 percent of savers. Dummy variables were used to indicate whether a migrant's spouse and children accompanied him on his most recent trip. Whereas 28 percent of the migrants who remitted had spouses present and 32 percent had children present, among those who saved the respective figures were only 9 and 13 percent. The means of the total amount of remittances and savings are not comparable because the length of time over which the money was earned is different for each observation.

In general, these differences between the two samples suggest that migrants who send remittances are more likely than those who return with savings to be settled in the United States, to make longer migration trips, and to be accompanied by immediate family members. In general, those who bring home savings are staying in the United States only temporarily, make shorter trips, and more often migrate alone. This contrast suggests that sending remittances and returning with savings represent two related, but slightly different, strategies for migrating to obtain money for an investment.

I measured years of education as a continuous variable (yielding respective averages of 5.8 and 5.2 years), and I calculated migrants' work experience as their age minus their years of schooling minus six (to represent the years before they would have entered school). On average, respondents had around twenty-two to twenty-four years of labor market experience. Local economic conditions were measured using the characteristics and earnings of the workforce. More developed areas in Mexico typically have a high percentage of women in manufacturing, while areas with low numbers of working women are usually rural, subsistence economies (Durand et al. 1996; Lindstrom 1996). In both analyses, roughly 16 percent of women were employed in manufacturing. The percentage of the economically active population earning twice the minimum wage indicates the potential purchasing power of community residents, which in turn affects the viability of investments. This figure was 29 percent in the analysis of remittances and 27 percent in the analysis of savings. Finally, the percentage of men working in agriculture indicates the extent of the rural basis of the economy, and rural economies generally offer fewer opportunities for investment. The typical respondent came from a community in which nearly half of all men (46 to 47 percent) worked in agriculture.

I did not include measures of access to land used in Durand and colleagues (1996) because they are only available for the time of the survey and not for the year corresponding to the migrant's most recent trip. Nonetheless, I did incorporate one indicator of the condition of the Mexican economy at the time of the migrant's last trip. Reflecting the instability of recent years, the average migrant left during a year in which inflation ran at an annual rate of 32 percent, but the standard deviation of around 23 indicates wide fluctuations over time.

USE OF SAVINGS AND REMITTANCES

Table 3.3 presents odds ratios corresponding to multinomial logit models estimated to predict whether migrants channeled their savings into housing or production rather than consumption (the reference category). Model 1 includes the controls for household resources, family life cycle, trip characteristics, human capital, community characteristics, and the macroeconomic context; model 2 adds the three social network indicators. The addition of these explanatory variables significantly increases explanatory power (p < .001 for a chi squared of difference) and indicates that social connections are indeed important in determining the spending behavior of Mexican migrants to the United States.

The coefficients for social networks generally support my hypothesis that social ties in the United States increase a migrant's likelihood of investing earnings in housing and production rather than spending them on current consumption. For example, migrants who lived with relatives on their most recent trip to the United States were 1.4 times more likely to channel their savings into housing than into consumption and 1.8 times more likely to allocate savings to production than to consumption. Similarly, migrants who lived with townspeople while in the United States were 2.2 times more likely to invest their savings in production than to spend them on consumption.

TABLE 3.3   Multinomial Logit Regression Predicting Top-End
Use of Savings

	Invested in Housing		Invested in Production	
Variable	Model 1 Risk Ratio	Model 2 Risk Ratio	Model 1 Risk Ratio	Model 2 Risk Ratio
Social networks				
Lived with relatives	—	1.353*	—	1.825*
Lived with townspeople	—	1.406	—	2.179*
Belonged to social club	—	1.279	—	1.056
Household resources				
Owns farmland	0.951	0.942	3.725***	3.633***
Owns business	1.032	1.020	1.956	1.904*
Owns home	2.895***	2.982***	0.271	0.871
Family life cycle				
Married	0.767	0.730	0.511*	0.446**
Number of minors	1.000	0.999	1.051	1.051
Trip characteristics				
Months of U.S. experience	0.999	0.999	1.001	1.002
Total number of U.S. trips	0.994	0.992	0.999	0.994
Wages on last U.S. trip	1.029	1.030	1.014	1.017
Settled in United States	2.768*	2.980*	1.225	1.477
Trip duration	0.976	0.977	0.987	0.985
Spouse on trip	1.880	1.935	0.899	0.945
Kids on trip	0.682	0.661	1.633	1.527
Total savings	1.519***	1.524***	1.468***	1.503***
Human capital				
Work experience	0.992	0.996	0.997	1.005
Education	0.953	0.956	0.970	0.978
Community characteristics				
Percentage twice minimum wage	0.995	0.994	0.979	0.977

(continued)

TABLE 3.3   Multinomial Logit Regression Predicting Top-End
Use of Savings (*Continued*)

| | Invested in Housing | | Invested in Production | |
Variable	Model 1 Risk Ratio	Model 2 Risk Ratio	Model 1 Risk Ratio	Model 2 Risk Ratio
Percentage females in manufacturing	0.999	0.999	0.991	0.993
Percentage males in agriculture	0.944	0.873	0.156	0.124
Macroeconomic context				
Mexican inflation rate	1.006*	1.006*	0.998	0.998
N		865		865
Pseudo R-squared		0.085		0.096
Log likelihood		-747.062***		-737.831***

Source: Data from Mexican Migration Project.
*p < .05   **p < .01   ***p < .001

Table 3.4 repeats the foregoing analysis focusing on remittances rather than savings. As before, addition of the social network variables significantly increases explanatory power (p < .05). According to the estimates of model 2, migrants who belonged to a social club while in the United States were 3.1 times more likely to spend remittances on housing than on consumption, and they were 4.5 more likely to channel them into production (p = .06). Taken together, these variables demonstrate that social ties to other migrants increase a migrant's relative propensity to invest remittances and savings.

In addition to corroborating my own hypotheses about social networks, the estimates in tables 3.3 and 3.4 support several propositions derived from the new economics of labor migration. For example, migrants who owned productive resources before leaving for the United States were more likely to invest. Migrants who owned a home before departing were 3.0 times more likely to invest savings in housing and 2.9 times more likely to channel remittances toward this end. Similarly, owning a business increased the odds of productively investing savings by a factor of 1.9, and ownership of farmland raised the odds by a factor of 3.6. In other words,

TABLE 3.4   Multinomial Logit Regression Predicting Top-End Use of Remittances

| | Invested in Housing | | Invested in Production | |
Variable	Model 1 Risk Ratio	Model 2 Risk Ratio	Model 1 Risk Ratio	Model 2 Risk Ratio
Social networks				
Lived with relatives	—	0.943	—	1.675
Lived with townspeople	—	0.980	—	1.105
Belonged to social club	—	3.124*	—	4.464+
Household resources				
Owns farmland	0.999	1.014	1.927	1.975
Owns business	0.900	0.915	1.086	1.040
Owns home	2.879***	2.933***	1.195	1.261
Family life cycle				
Married	0.722	0.751	0.211***	0.202***
Number of minors	0.978	0.974	0.997	0.993
Trip characteristics				
Months of U.S. experience	0.998	0.998	0.998	0.997
Total number of U.S. trips	1.018	1.015	1.024	1.010
Wages on last U.S. trip	1.050**	1.050*	0.868**	0.867**
Settled in United States	1.760	1.758	2.592*	2.294+
Trip duration	0.760**	0.744***	0.585***	0.573**
Spouse on trip	0.711	0.645	1.144	1.022
Children on trip	2.143**	2.224**	2.713*	2.663*
Total remittances	1.068***	1.072***	1.090***	1.101***
Human capital				
Work experience	0.972*	0.970*	0.993	0.998
Education	0.970	0.966	1.159	1.165
Community characteristics				
Percentage twice minimum wage	1.020	1.021	1.033	1.033

(continued)

TABLE 3.4   Multinomial Logit Regression Predicting Top-End Use of Remittances (*Continued*)

	Invested in Housing		Invested in Production	
Variable	Model 1 Risk Ratio	Model 2 Risk Ratio	Model 1 Risk Ratio	Model 2 Risk Ratio
Percentage females in manufacturing	1.003	1.003	1.020*	1.025*
Percentage males in agriculture	1.951	1.994	7.230	7.095
Macroeconomic context				
Mexican inflation rate	1.008	1.008	1.005	1.004
N		1,112		1,112
Pseudo R-squared		0.110		0.100
Log likelihood		-460.233***		-455.220***

Source: Data from Mexican Migration Project.
†p < .1   *p < .05   **p < .01   ***p < .001

when migrants have a tangible target in which to invest their earnings in the United States, they are very likely to do so.

Life cycle and trip characteristics also affect how migrants spend remittances and savings. Married migrants have a lower propensity to spend remittances and savings on production relative to consumption. Contrary to my expectations, however, each additional year of trip duration decreased the likelihood of spending remittances on housing or production, though this effect does not appear in the savings equation. Migrants settled in the United States were also 3.0 times more likely to spend savings on housing and 2.3 times more likely to spend remittances on production (though the latter effect is significant only at p = .08). Finally, an increase in the amount of remittances and savings raised the risk that migrants spend them on production and housing rather than consumption, indicating that greater sums of money are more likely to be invested.

Human capital variables had relatively small effects in the models. The only significant relationship was work experience: each year of experience lowered the odds of investing remittances by 0.3. Similarly, macroeconomic conditions were significant only in the savings equation, where a percentage point increase in the Mexican inflation rate raised the odds of investing in housing by 0.6. Hyperinflation decreases the dollar-denominated cost of real property in Mexico, apparently causing migrants to invest their U.S. savings in housing.

CONCLUSION

The three indicators of migrants' social ties while living in the United States—whether they lived with family, whether they lived with other townspeople, and whether they belonged to a social club while in the United States—appear to influence the way migrants chose to allocate their remittances and savings. These ties suggest that a stronger identification with place of origin tends to enforce social norms to repatriate U.S. earnings.

However, different kinds of social ties were found to have different effects on the use of remittances versus savings. Belonging to a social club in the United States increased the likelihood of investing remittances in both housing and production, compared with consumption; but had no effect on the allocation of savings. Living with relatives or townspeople had no effect on the allocation of remittances but worked to channel savings toward production and housing. Such differences highlight the fact that migrant networks do not function equally under all circumstances.

In general, I found that migrants who bring savings home tend to make trips of relatively short duration and to migrate alone. They live with friends and kin in order to save money to invest in a productive activity or a dwelling at home. In contrast, migrants who send remittances tend to make longer trips and are more likely to be settled in the United States. They appear to join migrant social clubs to secure a reliable avenue for channeling resources back to the home community and to monitor their investments indirectly by means of information transmitted through social networks. Migrants who spend long periods of time away from their hometowns seem to join social clubs with other migrants and invest their remittances in a home or a business to create a stable basis for claiming continuing membership and status in their hometown.

Previous studies have claimed that competition for social status among migrants led them to spend their remittances and savings on conspicuous consumption. I offer an alternative explanation. While most remittances and savings may indeed be channeled into consumption, my data indicate that migrants possessing adequate economic resources and appropriate family circumstances seek to demonstrate the economic gain they have achieved through migration by investing their remittances and savings. In other words, migrants with prior access to productive resources and low family consumption needs can be expected to spend more of their

remittances and savings on durable and visible assets, such as a home, land, or an economically productive activity.

Such assets offer a greater claim on social status than does spending on short-term consumption, such as recreation. In addition, investing remittances in their hometowns gives migrants a basis for claiming continued membership in their community of origin. Finally, migrants use social ties to get information and to monitor their investments, thereby transforming those ties into social capital. Both of these explanations support my argument that researchers should view migrants' savings and remittances as a socially organized practice that has a collective meaning within migrant communities. Future studies should explore the mechanisms through which social ties promote investment.

An earlier version of this chapter appeared in *Social Forces* (Mooney 2003).

REFERENCES

Connell, John, and Dennis Conway. 2000. "Migration and Remittances in Island Microstates: A Comparative Perspective on the South Pacific and the Caribbean." *International Journal of Urban and Regional Research* 24(1): 52–78.

Cornelius, Wayne. 1991. "Labor Migration to the United States: Development Outcomes and Alternatives in Mexican Sending Communities." In *Regional and Sectoral Development in Mexico as Alternatives to Migration*, edited by Sergio Díaz-Briquets and Sidney Weintraub. Boulder, Colo.: Westview Press.

Durand, Jorge, William Kandel, Emilio A. Parrado, and Douglas S. Massey. 1996. "International Migration and Development in Mexican Communities." *Demography* 33(2): 249–64.

Funkhouser, Edward. 1995. "Remittances from International Migration: A Comparison of El Salvador and Nicaragua." *Review of Economics and Statistics* 77(1): 137–46.

Goldring, Luin. 1998. "The Power of Status in Transnational Social Fields." In *Transnationalism From Below*, edited by Michael Peter Smith and Luis Eduardo Guarnizo. New Brunswick, N.J.: Transaction Publishers.

Grasmuck, Sherri, and Patricia R. Pessar. 1991. *Between Two Islands: Dominican International Migration*. Berkeley: University of California Press.

Hernández-León, Rubén. 1997. "El circuito migratorio Monterrey-Houston." *Ciudades* 33(July–September): 26–33.

Itzigsohn, José. 1995. "Migrant Remittances, Labor Markets, and Household Strategies: A Comparative Analysis of Low-Income Household Strategies in the Caribbean Basin." *Social Forces* 74(2): 633–55.

Levitt, Peggy. 1997. "Transnationalizing Community Development: The Case of Migration Between Boston and the Dominican Republic." *Nonprofit and Voluntary Sector Quarterly* 26(4): 509–26.

Lindstrom, David P. 1996. "Economic Opportunity in the United States and Return Migration from the United States." *Demography* 33: 357–74.

Lopez, Jose Roberto, and Mitchell Seligson. 1991. "Small Business Development in El Salvador: The Impact of Remittances." In *Migration, Remittances, and Small Business Development: Mexico and Caribbean Basin Countries*, edited by Sergio Díaz-Briquets and Sidney Weintraub. Boulder, Colo.: Westview.

Massey, Douglas S., Rafael Alarcón, Jorge Durand, and Humberto González. 1987. *Return to Aztlán: The Social Process of International Migration from Western Mexico*. Berkeley: University of California Press.

Massey, Douglas S., Joaquín Arango, Graeme Hugo, Ali Kouaouci, Adela Pellegrino, and J. Edward Taylor. 1993. "Theories of International Migration: A Review and Appraisal." *Population and Development Review* 19(3): 431–66.

Massey, Douglas S., and Lawrence C. Basem. 1992. "Determinants of Savings, Remittances, and Spending Patterns among U.S. Migrants in Four Mexican Communities." *Sociological Inquiry* 62(2): 185–207.

Menjívar, Cecilia, Julie Davanzo, Lisa Greenwell, and R. Buruaga Valdez. 1998. "Remittance Behavior among Salvadoran and Filipino Immigrants in Los Angeles." *International Migration Review* 32(1): 99–128.

Mooney, Margarita. 2003. "Migrants' Social Ties in the U.S. and Investment in Mexico." *Social Forces* 81(4, June): 1147–70.

Multilateral Investment Fund. 2001. *Remittances to Latin America and the Caribbean: Comparative Statistics*. Washington, D.C.: Inter-American Development Bank.

Portes, Alejandro. 1995. *The Economic Sociology of Immigration: Essays on Networks, Ethnicity, and Entrepreneurship*. New York: Russell Sage Foundation.

Portes, Alejandro, and Luis E. Guarnizo. 1991. "Tropical Capitalists: U.S.-Bound Immigration and Small-Enterprise Development in the Dominican Republic." In *Migration, Remittances, and Small Business Development*, edited by Sergio Díaz-Briquets and Sidney Weintraub. Boulder, Colo.: Westview Press.

Reichert, Joshua S. 1982. "A Town Divided: Economic Stratification and Social Relations in a Mexican Migrant Community." *Social Problems* 29(4): 413–23.

Roberts, Kenneth, and Michael Morris. 2003. "Fortune, Risk, and Remittances: An Application of Option Theory to Village-Based Migration Networks." *International Migration Review* 37(4): pp. 1252–81.

Taylor, J. Edward, Joaquín Arango, Graeme Hugo, Ali Kouaouci, Douglas S. Massey, and Adela Pellegrino. 1996. "International Migration and National Development." *Population Index* 62: 181–212.

CHAPTER 4

U.S. MIGRATION, HOME OWNERSHIP, AND HOUSING QUALITY

Emilio A. Parrado

OWNING A HOME is highly valued for its connection to personal development, family formation, and economic independence. In Mexico, unfortunately, high interest rates and a lack of access to credit have prevented
home acquisition by families of modest means (Centro de Información para
el Desarrollo 1991). The economic effects of these constraints are long
lasting, as owning a home is the primary means by which families build
long-term assets, protect against economic instability, and accumulate
financial worth. Through its effect on inheritance and family support,
home ownership also influences the intergenerational transmission of
wealth. The acquisition of a home thus represents a crucial life-course
transition, potentially breaking the cycle of poverty and inequality that
now traps so many low-income families.

Little is known about the economic strategies that households employ
to cope with financial constraints in Mexico. Given the significance of
home ownership for both personal development and social mobility, one
might expect a wide range of adaptive strategies to be employed in an
effort to overcome the lack of access to capital markets and persistent
wage inequality in Mexico (Fletcher 1999). One such strategy is "la tanda,"
a popular form of collective saving and financing widely used in urban
Mexico (Arias 1997); but a more popular strategy, especially in rural areas,
is international migration.

Remittances and savings repatriated by Mexicans working in the United
States constitute a major source of income for migrant-sending communities and households, often more than doubling locally earned incomes

(Lozano Ascencio 1993; Massey and Parrado 1994). Temporary labor in the United States provides an important means of overcoming capital market constraints for low-income and middle-income households. For those with scarce resources who cannot afford the large expenditures involved in purchasing a home, sending out a household member for temporary labor in the United States offers an alternative path to capital accumulation. The extent to which remittances and savings are diverted to housing thus has direct implications for assessing the role of international migration on wealth accumulation and economic development in Mexico. Accordingly, this chapter concentrates on understanding the contribution of U.S. migration to two dimensions of housing investment in Mexico: ownership and quality.

Previous studies have found positive effects of international migration from Mexico on development outcomes, such as business formation (Durand et al. 1996; Portes and Guarnizo 1991) and land acquisition (Massey et al. 1987). However, most of these studies fail to account for the possibility that migration and investment decisions might be jointly determined. Failure to control for endogeneity and simultaneity of these decisions might overestimate the positive effect of migration on development in Mexico.

This chapter presents an alternative model of housing investment that treats migration and housing decisions as endogenous and jointly estimates the transition into U.S. trips and home acquisition while controlling for potential bias in parameter estimates stemming from unobserved heterogeneity. Even after controlling for endogeneity, migration facilitates home acquisition in Mexico; U.S. remittances and savings lower reliance on inheritance and family in the purchase of housing; and U.S. migration improves housing quality. Overall, the study reported here supports the view of international migration as a strategy to overcome market constraints in Mexico, as predicted by the new economics of labor migration, and challenges the view that migration perpetuates the dependency of developing countries.

HOME OWNERSHIP, MIGRATION, AND DEVELOPMENT

Although it is often overlooked in demographic and sociological studies of development, access to housing is a central feature of economic progress in nations such as Mexico. According to a report from the Centro de Información para el Desarrollo (1991), three main problems limit home ownership in Mexico. First are the financial constraints that families face in trying to obtain credits and loans. As in other Latin American countries, capital markets in Mexico are underdeveloped or absent; one consequence is an almost total lack of access to credit or access only at very high interest rates, which significantly deters housing investments. These effects are particularly strong among lower-income families, which typically lack the collateral to obtain credit and the income stream necessary to finance a loan.

Second, economic constraints over and above those associated with limited capital markets restrict possibilities for capital accumulation. Low wages, widespread unemployment and underemployment, informal economic relations, and the persistence of a subsistence economy in many rural areas virtually eliminate the possibility of savings accumulation among the lower classes. In addition, high levels of inequality with respect to wealth and income perpetuate the cycle of poverty. Given the lack of access to well-paid employment, Mexican households are highly dependent on inheritance and family support to achieve home ownership, and inequalities are thereby reinforced and perpetuated across generations.

The third obstacle to more widespread home ownership in Mexico is judicial. Legal regulations and bureaucratic requirements increase housing prices and discourage the construction of rental housing. Restrictions on access to land, high real estate taxes, and statutory protection for renters have also limited housing investments. In many ways, legal regulations simply end up protecting those who already own their homes and do little to increase the supply of housing.

International migration has potentially important effects on the first two dimensions of the housing problem in Mexico. The remittances and savings returned by Mexican migrants to the United States provide individuals and families with the necessary capital and income to buy a house, thereby reducing their dependence on inheritance in acquiring homes. Not surprisingly, therefore, Mexican migration to the United States has become a common and massive phenomenon. According to Julie Phillips and Douglas Massey (2000), 40 percent of household heads in western Mexico have been to the United States, and in many communities the figure exceeds 70 percent. For the nation as a whole, it is estimated that one-quarter of all households have at least one member working in the United States at any given moment (Castañeda 1996).

High levels of migration are likely to continue, making Mexican migration to the United States the largest sustained international population movement in the world (Durand, Massey, and Parrado 1999). A report by Mexico's Consejo Nacional de Población (CONAPO 2000) estimates that four hundred thousand persons would migrate each year to the United States, even if Mexican economic growth averaged 5 percent per year, and the number would increase to five hundred thousand if growth averaged only 1.5 percent a year. Needless to say, the economic performance of Mexico since the implementation of neoliberal policies has been uneven and has continued to fuel migration to the United States. In the year 2001, for example, the gross domestic product of Mexico declined by 0.4 percent, and it grew by only 1.2 percent in 2002 (World Bank 2003).

A large component of Mexico's migratory flow consists of circular and recurrent migration. According to Massey and Audrey Singer (1995), 85 percent of Mexican entries to the United States between 1965 and 1985 were offset by departures. The Consejo Nacional de Población (2000) reports that close to 70 percent of migrants crossing the border have been to the United States before, and the vast majority expect to return to Mexico after a short stay, more than 30 percent intending to return within six months. However, there are recent indications that Mexico-U.S. migration is becoming more permanent (Massey, Durand, and Malone 2002). For example, from 1994 to 1997 the proportion intending to stay in the United States "as long as possible" increased from 36 percent to 40 percent (CONAPO 2000).

The time orientation and dynamic nature of Mexico's migrant flow have significant effects on the economic conditions in sending communities (Roberts 1995). Migrant remittances and savings have become a significant source of foreign capital in Mexico. According to estimates from the Bank of Mexico, in 1998 the country received close to $6 billion in remittances. This figure was more than double the revenues from agricultural exports, equal to the amount received from tourism, and equivalent to 60 percent of direct foreign investment. The effect of remittances on economic conditions is probably even more important at the household and community levels. According to Consejo Nacional de Población (CONAPO 2000) estimates, in 1996 1.1 million Mexican households received income transfers from the United States, representing almost half of their total income. Effects were especially pronounced in rural areas and small communities, where remittances often constitute the main source of cash income.

Despite the economic significance of migrant savings and remittances, there has been considerable debate about their effects on economic development in Mexico (Russell 1986). On the positive side, researchers have identified several important contributions: small business formation, poverty reduction, and aggregate indirect effects on consumption and investment (Durand et al. 1996; Taylor et al. 1996). On the negative side, others (Cuestas 2002; Paus 1995; Reichert 1981) have noted the dependence of families and communities on income generated abroad, which, they argue, ultimately perpetuates the cycle of poverty and migration. Part of the controversy, however, stems from different underlying notions of economic development and divergent expectations about the ability of migrants to promote economic growth. In general, it has been easier to identify positive effects of remittances and savings on individual and family dimensions of well-being than on aggregate dimensions of economic growth and development. But as one migrant put it in an interview, "Why expect from migrants what the Mexican government cannot achieve?"

This chapter employs a limited definition of economic development focused on household living standards. In contrast to other international transfers—such as foreign aid, direct foreign investment, and sales of commodities such as oil—migrant remittances and savings constitute a direct transfer to Mexican households that enables a higher level of consumption while improving liquidity to enable larger investments such as land acquisition, agricultural production, business formation, and, most relevant for this analysis, housing.

However, methodological problems and data limitations have complicated prior attempts to establish a clear causal connection between migration and housing investment. The application of a life-course perspective to the analysis of migration has led scholars to recognize that migration is not a single event but a process that evolves over time and is closely connected to other life-course transitions, such as marriage and childbearing (Massey et al. 1987; Parrado 2004). One of the most important features of the Mexican Migration Project data is their ability to connect different life-course transitions, such as migration and home ownership, with one another in a statistically reliable fashion, thus solving many data problems.

However, the interconnectedness of life-course events also presents important methodological challenges (Ahituv and Tienda 2004). A particular problem is that life-course transitions tend to occur over a short time span. In the course of a few years, usually during late adolescence and early adulthood, people can migrate for the first time, marry, begin families, and buy a first house. The short time span between decisions suggests that they are interconnected and not necessarily independent of one another. On the contrary, they are likely to be determined simultaneously. In general, previous studies of the effect of migration on development have failed to account for the potential endogeneity of migration and investment decisions. If migrants are not randomly selected, unobserved characteristics such as psychological predispositions, friendship networks, and the desire for personal growth may determine not only the purchase of a home but also the decision to migrate. Under these circumstances, studies that do not control for endogeneity will overestimate the positive effect of migration on simultaneously determined outcomes (Smith and Thomas 1997; Stark 1988).

Consider, for instance, the case of a Mexican man interested in purchasing or building a home. He chats with other people and discusses different ways of obtaining capital to acquire a home. He is certainly more likely to talk to home owners than to people who do not already have a house. He evaluates different alternatives, such as obtaining a loan, borrowing from family members, or saving money over time. At this point, his personal connections make him aware of the possibility of migrating to the United States to accumulate capital. In this case, an empirical connection between migration and home ownership may not identify the relevant social influence. If the man had been made aware of an alternative strategy, such as migrating to Mexico City or obtaining a second job, then the end result of purchasing a home might have remained unchanged but it would have no association with U.S. migration. If unobserved influences are not accounted for, conclusions about the positive effect of U.S. migration on investments in Mexico are likely to be exaggerated.

METHODS

For my analysis I use detailed retrospective data on home purchase and housing quality available from the life-history files of the Mexican Migration Project as well as information about the sources of capital for home investment (see chapter 16). Such information is generally absent in standard migration or employment surveys. In combination with other retrospective life-history data on marriage, childbearing, and migration, the Mexican Migration Project data permit me to follow men as they age and to relate indicators of housing wealth, including home ownership and quality, to their various life-course transitions.

For the purpose of this analysis, I limit the sample to the sixty-six communities that were surveyed after 1987 and have complete samples in both Mexico and the United States. To reduce the potential bias arising from the close connection between home ownership and household formation in Mexico, I also restrict the analysis to households headed by males aged thirty to seventy at the time of the survey. While this decision limits the number of households in my sample, it provides a more accurate representation of the population in these communities, since close to 90 percent of Mexican men marry by the age of thirty. Applying these selection criteria yields a total of 7,620 male household heads for the final sample.

The analysis is undertaken in two parts. The first focuses on the relationship between a household head's U.S. migration experience and home ownership. The second considers the connection between migration experience and various dimensions of housing quality and financing, including the type of flooring, the number of rooms, the number of appliances, and how the property was acquired. The two sets of analyses require different estimation strategies. The study of home ownership uses event-history analysis to follow individuals over time and estimate the likelihood of acquiring a house given certain time-varying individual and household characteristics. The models of housing quality and financing, in contrast, use cross-sectional regression to measure the effect of selected independent variables on the characteristics and acquisition strategies of dwellings.

As discussed earlier, although the life-history data provided by the Mexican Migration Project record the timing of different life events, they also raise issues of unobserved heterogeneity and endogeneity surrounding migration and housing decisions. Several statistical procedures are available to control for the effect of unobserved characteristics affecting both predictors and outcomes, including fixed effects, random effects, and instrumental variables. Here I follow a sequential and dynamic choice framework that considers first the likelihood of migrating to the United States before purchasing a home and then the subsequent likelihood of purchasing a home. By estimating these behaviors jointly I seek to control for person-specific unobserved heterogeneity that might influence both decisions and thus bias estimates of the effect of U.S. migration on development in Mexico (Heckman and Walker 1992; Trussell and Richards 1985).

I specify the likelihood of buying house h at time t as follows:

$$h_h(t \mid Z,M,\theta) = \exp[\alpha_{0h} + \alpha_{1h}(\text{time}) + \alpha_{2h}(\text{time})^2 + Z(t)\beta_h + M(t)\gamma_h + c_h\theta],$$

where Z is a vector of independent variables corresponding to different individual- and household-level predictors; M includes the endogenous variables that measure whether a person is in the United States during the year before buying a house and accumulated months of U.S. experience; and θ is a person-specific unobserved variable assumed to have a log-normal distribution. The model assumes quadratic duration dependence, and the coefficients α, β, γ, and c are parameters to be estimated.

Table 4.1 lists the variables included in the analysis, together with their time-varying specifications. The predictors include birth cohort (to capture changes in propensity toward home ownership over time), human capital (years of education and occupational status), family status (whether marriage was formed in that year, whether currently in a union, and number of minor children), and migratory experience (whether in United States during prior year and accumulated months of U.S. experience). The model also controls for particular housing conditions prevalent in rural communities.

In addition to the equation predicting home ownership, I also estimate the likelihood of first migration before first house purchase among Mexican

TABLE 4.1   Variables Included in the Independent and Joint Event-History Models of Home Ownership and First Migration

Variable	Specification	Home Ownership	First Trip Before Ownership
Baseline hazard	Quadratic duration dependence	X	X
Birth cohort	Set of dummy variables corresponding to birth period (reference: born after 1961)	X	X
Before 1931			
1931 to 1940			
1941 to 1950			
1951 to 1960			
Human capital characteristics			
Years of education[a]	Accumulated years of education	X	X
Occupational characteristics[a]	Set of dummy variables indicating occupational type in any given year. (reference: agricultural worker)	X	X
Not working			
Skilled nonmanual			
Unskilled nonmanual			
Skilled manual			
Unskilled manual			

Family status			
Year of marriage[a]	1 if marriage year, 0 otherwise	X	X
Currently in union[a]	1 if yes, 0 otherwise	X	X
Number of minor children[a]	Number of children in household under the age of eighteen	X	X
Migration experience			
In the United States during previous year[a]	1 if yes, 0 otherwise	X	
Months of U.S. experience[a]	Accumulated months of U.S. experience	X	
Rural community	1 if community population less than 2,500, 0 otherwise	X	
Migrant networks[a]			
Father U.S. migrant[a]	1 if yes, 0 otherwise		X
Mother U.S. migrant[a]	1 if yes, 0 otherwise		X
Percentage ever migrating in community[a]	Proportion of adult males in community with U.S. migration experience		X
Log normal heterogeneity	Heterogeneity control	X	X

Source: Data from Mexican Migration Project.

[a] Time-varying variable.

men. The model accounts for the joint nature of these decisions by estimating a common unobserved factor, assumed to have a log-normal distribution, that is allowed to have different effects in the migration and home ownership equations. Instrumental variables are used to specify the migration equation, predicting the hazard of migrating m at time t as follows:

$$h_m(t \mid K,\theta) = \exp[\alpha_{0m} + \alpha_{1m}(\text{time}) + \alpha_{2m}(\text{time})^2 + K(t)\beta_m + c_m\theta],$$

where K includes the same three measures of migrant networks and individual- and household-level predictors as the home ownership model: whether the respondent's father ever migrated to the United States, whether the respondent's mother was a U.S. migrant, and the percentage of people in his community who have migrated to the United States at a given point in time (see table 4.1).

The covariance structure of the unobserved component is of the form

$$\text{Cov}(c_h\theta, c_m\theta) = c_h c_m \text{Var}(\theta) \, m,$$

so that the products of the factor loadings ($c_h c_m$) determine the direction of the association between unobserved effects across equations (Ahituv and Tienda 2004). The models were estimated using the continuous time model (CTM) of Kei-Mu Yi, James Walker, and Bo Honoré (1986). I use cross-sectional multinomial logit models to estimate the effect of different variables on the likelihood of living in a house with different kinds of flooring and the likelihood of acquiring a house using different kinds of financing. I employ ordinary least squares (OLS) regression models to predict the number of rooms and appliances in the house.

MIGRATION AND HOME OWNERSHIP

Table 4.2 reports descriptive statistics. As can be seen, a majority of Mexican migrants to the United States remitted money home (63 percent) and returned with savings (55 percent). The average amount remitted on the last trip was nearly $300 a month, and repatriated savings averaged just short of $1,600 dollars. How savings and remittances are used is a prima facie indicator of the relative importance of migration for home acquisition. As many studies have found, family maintenance is the main destination for both remittances and savings. However, 15 percent of household heads reported having used remittances for housing expenditures, and 25 percent said they had used savings for this purpose; spending on housing ranks second in the use of migrant remittances.

TABLE 4.2   Migration, Remittances, and Savings in Relation to
Home Ownership Among Mexican Men

Characteristic	Remittances	Savings Returned
Remittances and savings returned to Mexico during last trip to the United States		
Percentage of migrants remitting or returning with savings	62.8	55.3
Average amount remitted during last trip	282.0 per month	1,591.0
Standard deviation	(365.4)	(4,762.1)
Reported use of remittances or savings returned to Mexico (percentage of migrants)		
Family maintenance (including food, education, health, and recreation expenditures)	88.0	64.8
Housing (including purchasing and fixing a house)	15.3	24.6
Purchase of consumer goods (including vehicles)	8.3	13.5
Purchase of inputs of production (including tools, livestock, and other inputs)	1.8	6.0
Business formation	1.6	4.4
Debt repayment	8.1	7.6
Savings	2.5	11.8
Other	9.9	10.7

Source: Data from Mexican Migration Project.

My analysis yielded interesting connections between home ownership and international migration (not shown). Seventy-two percent of men in the sample owned a house, 43 percent migrated before purchasing their house, and almost 20 percent said they financed home acquisition with money earned in the United States. Results also show that among men who migrated and bought a house, there is less than a five-year difference between age at home purchase (29.3 years) and age at return from the first trip to the United States (24.5 years), suggesting a close connection between these transitions.

Table 4.3 presents results from a multivariate analysis estimating both independent and joint models to assess the extent to which endogeneity

TABLE 4.3   Independent and Joint Event-History Models of Home Ownership and First Migration

| | Home Ownership | | Joint Models | | | |
| | | | First Trip Before Home Ownership | | Home Ownership | |
Characteristic						
Constant	−4.452**	(0.104)	−4.016**	(0.112)	−4.933**	(0.089)
Baseline hazard						
Time	0.104**	(0.007)	0.187***	(0.011)	0.097***	(0.006)
Time squared	−0.003**	(0.000)	−0.012***	(0.001)	−0.003***	(0.000)
Birth cohort (reference is after 1961)						
Before 1931	−0.792**	(0.077)	−0.406**	(0.101)	−0.660**	(0.065)
1931 to 1940	−0.599**	(0.069)	−0.531***	(0.090)	−0.516***	(0.059)
1941 to 1950	−0.238**	(0.061)	−0.894***	(0.089)	−0.243***	(0.054)
1951 to 1960	−0.034*	(0.058)	−0.408***	(0.079)	−0.054*	(0.051)
Human capital characteristics						
Years of education	0.005	(0.005)	0.030**	(0.007)	0.003	(0.004)
Occupational characteristics (reference is agricultural worker)						
Not working	−0.349**	(0.102)	−1.712**	(0.131)	−0.335**	(0.098)
Skilled nonmanual	0.203**	(0.074)	−3.293**	(0.245)	0.203**	(0.064)
Unskilled nonmanual	−0.056	(0.054)	−1.993***	(0.114)	−0.021	(0.049)
Skilled manual	0.028	(0.044)	−1.086***	(0.070)	0.006	(0.038)
Unskilled manual	−0.060	(0.043)	0.338**	(0.045)	−0.039	(0.039)

	(1)		(2)		(3)	
Family status						
Year of marriage	2.291**	(0.055)	−0.018	(0.088)	2.268**	(0.057)
Currently in union	1.103**	(0.049)	−0.271**	(0.065)	1.140**	(0.052)
Number of minor children	−0.009	(0.008)	−0.036**	(0.018)	−0.011	(0.008)
Migration experience						
In the United States during previous year	0.349**	(0.046)	—		0.424**	(0.044)
Months of U.S. experience	0.002**	(0.001)	—		0.003**	(0.001)
Rural community	0.209**	(0.031)	—		0.232**	(0.037)
Migrant networks						
Father U.S. migrant	—		0.846***	(0.063)	—	
Mother U.S. migrant	—		1.079***	(0.136)	—	
Percentage ever migrating in community	—		3.607***	(0.141)	—	
Log normal heterogeneity						
c	−0.025	(0.030)	−0.913**	(0.100)	−0.527**	(0.082)
Chi squared			7,786.4		4,414.4	
df			38		19	
N			7,620		7,620	

Source: Data from Mexican Migration Project.
Note: Standard deviations in parentheses.
*p < .1   **p < .05

affects parameters. Results from the independent model of home ownership reveal that the likelihood of acquiring a home at a given age increases consistently across cohorts, suggesting a significant improvement in the chances for home ownership over time in Mexico. The transition into home ownership, however, is a function not of the educational characteristics of Mexican men but rather of their occupational position. More than education, occupational skill is an income-generating asset, and as a result it more directly connects with housing investment. Estimates show that relative to agricultural workers, unemployed men are less likely to buy a house and those in skilled nonmanual occupations are more likely to do so.

Family characteristics are key determinants of home ownership. The likelihood of buying a home rises considerably during the year of marriage and continues to remain high while a respondent is in a union. The number of minors in the household does not affect the propensity for home acquisition. These results highlight the close connection between home ownership, marriage, and home acquisition and suggest the extent to which home buying is part of the broader process of household formation in Mexico. Results also show that the transition to home ownership is more likely in small rural communities than in large urban areas, most likely because of lower housing prices and the possibility of subdividing or sharing land in rural contexts.

Estimates of the effect of migration on home acquisition generally confirm theoretical expectations. Both the immediate effect of having been in the United States in the previous year and the long-term effect of migration experience significantly accelerate the transition to home ownership. Having been in the United States during the prior year raises the likelihood of acquiring a home 1.5 times ($\exp[0.424] = 1.52$), and every additional year of U.S. experience increases the likelihood of home ownership by another 4 percent ($\exp[12*0.003] = 1.04$). The positive effect of having been in the United States during the previous year is particularly interesting as it suggests that migration and home acquisition are not conflicting events. Contrary to other life-course processes such as marriage, which requires the migrant to be in his home community in order to participate in the marriage market (Parrado 2004), housing purchases can be made while the migrant is still abroad.

In-depth interviews I conducted with migrants in the United States support this interpretation. In many cases, migrants pay for the purchase of a house with remittances they regularly send back to Mexico. In other cases, they finance the construction of a house with remittances and the periodic repatriation of savings. These interviews suggest that the dependence of home construction on flows of foreign capital is so strong that when migrants lose their U.S. jobs, they often are forced to stop construction in Mexico. In the absence of migration, there appears to be a dearth of alternative sources of credit in Mexico that allow migrants to continue investing in housing.

The last two columns of table 4.3 report results from the joint models of migration and housing behavior. According to these estimates, the likelihood of migrating to the United States has increased tremendously among men born after 1965, reflecting market failures in Mexico after economic restructuring and the implementation of neoliberal policies (Parrado 2002). Although migrants are positively selected with respect to education, it is those in agricultural and unskilled employment who are most likely to migrate to the United States. Family status variables support the conclusion that migration is particularly prevalent among single men. Finally, migrant networks are significant triggers of taking a first trip to the United States. Having a father or mother with migratory experience and the prevalence of migration in the home community both increase the odds of migration by reducing the costs and risks of international movement.

The main objective of estimating the model of first U.S. migration, however, was to estimate the likelihood of home ownership while accounting for unobservable characteristics that might affect both decisions. The last column of table 4.3 reports estimates from a joint model of home ownership that treats migration as endogenous. Results confirm the findings from the independent model and suggest that migration still increases the likelihood of home ownership once unobserved heterogeneity is taken into account. However, the size of migration's apparent effect on home ownership diminishes considerably. According to my estimates, the effect of having been in the United States during the previous year is reduced by 20 percent once unobserved heterogeneity is controlled. Moreover, the positive effect of U.S. experience on home ownership is 30 percent smaller in the joint than in the independent model. These results are further confirmed by the direction of heterogeneity's effect: those who are less likely to migrate are also less likely to buy a house.

Together, the accumulated empirical evidence suggests that previous studies linking migration and investment decisions that do not control for the simultaneity of these transitions indeed overestimate the positive effect of migration to the United States on development in Mexico. Nonetheless, even after appropriate controls are introduced, international migration still has a significant positive net effect on home ownership, above and beyond that resulting from the common selectivity of migrants and home owners. In other words, without the resource of migration, the rate of home ownership observed in the Mexican Migration Project sample would have been significantly lower.

MIGRATION, FINANCIAL STRATEGIES, AND HOUSING QUALITY

The next set of analyses addresses the association between U.S. migration, the financial strategies adopted for home acquisition, and housing quality. A simple description of the data suggests that a positive effect of migration on housing quality can be expected. As table 4.4 shows, houses whose acquisition was financed with U.S. savings are more likely to have tile or wooden floors (as opposed to dirt). They also tend to be larger, with four or five rooms instead of 1 to 3, and to have more appliances, compared with houses not financed with U.S. savings. In addition, U.S. savings

TABLE 4.4   Differences in Housing Quality, by Source of Financing (Percentage)

	Financed with U.S. Savings	Not Financed with U.S. Savings
Type of floor		
Dirt	3.5	11.6
Cement	35.9	50.9
Tile	49.2	37.0
Wood	11.4	0.5
Number of rooms		
One to three	21.4	39.5
Four to five	42.2	36.9
Six to seven	25.2	16.7
Eight or more	11.2	6.9
Number of appliances in household		
Zero to three	21.1	36.1
Four to five	34.1	30.5
Six to seven	44.8	33.4
Form of acquisition		
Savings	76.8	61.3
Loan from bank	3.9	1.1
Loan from family or friends	3.2	3.7
Inheritance	16.1	34.0

Source: Data from Mexican Migration Project.

appear to reduce the reliance on inheritance as a strategy for home ownership in Mexico. Thirty-four percent of houses not financed with U.S. savings were inherited, compared with just 16 percent of those financed with U.S. savings.

Table 4.5 models these characteristics to assess whether the association between migration and housing quality remains once we control for associated socioeconomic factors. Results confirm that Mexican men with higher accumulated U.S. experience are less likely to reside in houses with dirt floors and more likely to reside in houses with tile or wood floors (the reference category is houses with cement floors). In addition, as months of accumulated experience increase, the average number of rooms in the house also rises, net of other family and personal variables including household size. The same pattern is found with respect to the number of appliances: as the number of previous months of U.S. experience increase, so too, on average, does the number of appliances available in the household. The multinomial model that predicts the strategy of financing indicates that migration reduces the dependency on family of origin to achieve home ownership in Mexico. At the same time, it increases the likelihood of financing a home purchase with a bank loan.

DISCUSSION

Taken together, these results suggest that migrating to the United States not only facilitates home acquisition but also significantly improves living standards in Mexico. In addition to short-term improvements in housing quality, the long-term effects are also important. Migration reduces the reliance of families on inheritance as a strategy for home acquisition and counteracts the negative effects of family poverty on the likelihood of ownership. Not only are current living standards affected by international migration, but also the intergenerational transmission of inequality can be reduced through a series of temporary trips to the United States.

There has been considerable discussion about the effect of international migration on economic development in Mexico. The remittances and savings of Mexican migrants to the United States have generally been recognized as a central contribution to the economy of families with modest resources. However, that most foreign-earned income is spent on consumption and family maintenance has led researchers to argue that international migration has not necessarily been conducive to long-term economic improvements. Our analysis contradicts this view and provides support for an alternative perspective that more positively connects migration to economic development in Mexico.

TABLE 4.5   Models Predicting Different Dimensions of Housing Quality

	Multinomial Logit Predicting Floor Type[a]			OLS Predicting Number of Rooms	OLS Predicting Number of Appliances	Multinomial Logit Predicting Form of Acquisition[b]		
	Dirt	Tile	Wood			Bank	Family or Friends	Inheritance
Age	−0.015**	0.012**	−0.041**	0.045**	0.032**	0.003	0.024*	−0.050**
	(0.005)	(0.003)	(0.013)	(0.003)	(0.002)	(0.030)	(0.016)	(0.009)
Human capital characteristics								
Years of education	−0.122**	0.098**	0.122**	0.146**	0.163**	0.013	−0.019	0.026
	(0.019)	(0.009)	(0.031)	(0.007)	(0.007)	(0.064)	(0.048)	(0.018)
Occupational characteristics[c]								
Skilled nonmanual	−0.697**	0.094	0.807*	0.231*	0.203**	0.646	−0.785	−0.534**
	(0.318)	(0.139)	(0.508)	(0.119)	(0.104)	(1.014)	(0.832)	(0.281)
Unskilled nonmanual	−0.921**	0.254**	0.708*	0.651*	0.759**	−0.295	−1.048*	−0.626**
	(0.198)	(0.095)	(0.421)	(0.082)	(0.071)	(0.959)	(0.663)	(0.230)
Skilled manual	−1.001**	0.036	1.283**	0.279*	0.425**	−0.190	−0.218	−0.427**
	(0.157)	(0.087)	(0.329)	(0.073)	(0.064)	(0.914)	(0.457)	(0.195)
Unskilled manual	−0.151	−0.045	0.973**	0.042*	0.294**	0.659	−0.364	−0.870**
	(0.139)	(0.096)	(0.319)	(0.079)	(0.069)	(0.679)	(0.459)	(0.200)

Household characteristics

In union	−0.290	−0.118	−0.583	0.288	0.852**	−0.431	−0.300	−0.031
	(0.248)	(0.159)	(0.477)	(0.133)	(0.116)	(0.797)	(0.558)	(0.216)
Number of members	0.043*	−0.008	−0.195**	0.069**	−0.029**			
	(0.023)	(0.015)	(0.064)	(0.013)	(0.011)			
Number of workers	−0.078*	−0.026	0.362**	0.060**	0.058**			
	(0.043)	(0.027)	(0.095)	(0.023)	(0.020)			
Months of U.S. experience	−0.014**	0.006***	0.019**	0.006**	0.006**	0.010**	−0.009	−0.005*
	(0.002)	(0.001)	(0.001)	(0.000)	(0.000)	(0.003)	(0.008)	(0.003)
Rural	0.642**	−0.696***	−1.039**	−0.092*	−0.651**	−0.462	−0.310	0.169
	(0.102)	(0.076)	(0.291)	(0.060)	(0.052)	(0.639)	(0.393)	(0.154)
Constant	0.001	−1.120***	−2.996***	0.374	1.026***	−3.982**	−2.896**	1.044***
	(0.414)	(0.263)	(0.879)	(0.219)	(0.190)	(1.392)	(0.851)	(0.354)
Chi squared / R squared	1,407.64			0.17	0.27	116.09		
df	33			11	11	27		
N	5,388			5,396	5,401	1,128		

Source: Data from Mexican Migration Project.

Note: Standard deviations in parentheses.

[a] Reference category is cement floor.

[b] Reference category is acquisition through savings.

[c] Reference category is agricultural worker.

*p < .1   **p < .05

One potential caveat about previous studies connecting migration and investment behavior in Mexico is that they may have overstated the positive effect of remittances and savings on development. These decisions are closely connected and tend to be mutually dependent. Unmeasured individual factors can affect both migration and investment behaviors, and failure to account for the joint nature of these decisions might produce biased results. Accordingly, our analysis accounts for the simultaneous nature of these decisions by formulating a joint model of migration and housing investments to account for the potential endogeneity between trips to the United States and home purchases.

However, the results presented here indicate that even after controlling for unobserved heterogeneity, migration experience directly contributes to home ownership. Although the largest share of foreign-earned income is spent on consumption, the second-largest form of expenditure is housing, and acquiring housing is arguably the most salient constraint that low-income and middle-income families face in their attempts to achieve a higher standard of living in Mexico. Given the poor state of financial markets and the general lack of access to credit, a temporary trip to the United States appears to offer a successful economic strategy for families that lack the possibility of inheriting.

The long-term effects of migration on home investment cannot be overlooked. Housing is a central dimension of capital accumulation, and home ownership is the main form of savings among many low-income families. Moreover, to the extent that housing investments directly affect the intergenerational transmission of wealth, the capacity to save and divert a large part of migrants' remittances and savings toward housing represents a direct contribution to families' attempts to break the cycle of poverty and inequality in Mexico.

At the same time, these results corroborate the finding that failure to account for the endogeneity of migration and housing overstates the positive effect of remittances and savings on capital investments. After modeling these two processes jointly, the effects of migration on home purchase are reduced 20 to 30 percent. This implies that some migrants would have acquired a house even in the absence of migration. Nevertheless, for the majority of migrants, having the alternative of a temporary trip to the United States represents a central economic strategy to overcome the lack of financial markets in Mexico.

The main policy implication to be drawn from this study is that migrants by themselves have been very successful at fostering long-term capital investments—in this case, housing. The increase in the number of Mexican migrants to the United States and in the volume of remittances and savings sent back to Mexico has attracted the attention of public officials and international financial institutions (Lowell and de la Garza 2000). The prevailing assumption is that remittances and savings can be more efficiently channeled to promote long-term growth.

At the same time, however, a cautionary note is necessary. My results show that the unregulated market for remittances and savings has been very efficient in directly affecting the living standards and housing conditions of low- and middle-income Mexican households. Attempts to regulate such flow might not necessarily improve the current allocation of funds. Lack of accountability on the part of financial officers, misguided investment decisions, depletion of funds, and bureaucratic inefficiencies have plagued the Latin American experience with financial institutions. The remittances and savings of international migrants is a clear example of foreign-earned income directly reaching those families most in need of financial assistance. Certainly, community organizations and government support can be an important stimulus to channel these funds toward investments in infrastructure and community development. However, strong community and personal involvement is necessary to guarantee the appropriate use of remittances and protect the individual savings of Mexican migrants.

REFERENCES

Ahituv, Avner, and Marta Tienda. 2004. "Employment, Motherhood, and School Continuation Decisions of Young White, Black, and Hispanic Women." *Journal of Labor Economics* 22(1): 115–56.

Arias, Patricia. 1997. "La 'tanda' en tiempos de globalización." *Ciudades* 9(35): 41–46.

Castañeda, Jorge G. 1996. "Mexico's Circle of Misery." *Foreign Affairs* 75(4): 92–105.

Centro de Información para el Desarrollo. 1991. *Vivienda y estabilidad política: Reconcebir las políticas sociales.* Mexico City: Centro de Investigación y Desarrollo.

Consejo Nacional de Población (CONAPO). 2000. *Migración México–Estados Unidos: Presente y futuro.* Mexico City: Consejo Nacional de Población.

Cuestas, Jose. 2002. "Export-Led Growth and the Distribution of Incomes in Honduras." Unpublished paper. United Nations Development Program, Honduras.

Durand, Jorge, William Kandel, Emilio A. Parrado, and Douglas S. Massey. 1996. "International Migration and Development in Mexican Communities." *Demography* 33(2): 249–64.

Durand, Jorge, Douglas S. Massey, and Emilio A. Parrado. 1999. "The New Era of Mexican Migration to the United States." *Journal of American History* 86(2): 518–36.

Fletcher, Peri. 1999. *La casa de mis sueños: Dreams of Home in a Transnational Community.* Boulder, Colo.: Westview.

Heckman, James, and James R. Walker. 1992. "Understanding Third Births in Sweden." In *Demographic Applications of Event History Analysis,* edited by James Trussell, Richard Hankinson, and Judith Tilton. Oxford: Clarendon Press.

Lowell, Lindsay B., and Rodolfo O. de la Garza. 2000. *The Developmental Role of Remittances in U.S. Latino Communities and in Latin American Countries: A Final Project Report.* San Antonio, Tex.: Tomás Rivera Policy Institute and the Inter-American Dialogue.

Lozano Ascencio, Fernando. 1993. *Bringing It Back Home: Remittances to Mexico from Migrant Workers in the United States.* La Jolla: University of California at San Diego, Center for U.S.-Mexican Studies.

Massey, Douglas S., Rafael Alarcón, Jorge Durand, and Humberto González. 1987. *Return to Aztlán: The Social Process of International Migration from Western Mexico.* Berkeley: University of California Press.

Massey, Douglas S., Jorge Durand, and Nolan J. Malone. 2002. *Beyond Smoke and Mirrors: Mexican Immigration in an Era of Free Trade.* New York: Russell Sage Foundation.

Massey, Douglas S., and Emilio A. Parrado. 1994. "Migradollars: The Remittances and Savings of Mexican Migrants to the United States." *Population Research and Policy Review* 13(2): 3–30.

Massey, Douglas S., and Audrey Singer. 1995. "New Estimates of Undocumented Mexican Migration and the Probability of Apprehension." *Demography* 32(2): 203–13.

Parrado, Emilio A. 2002. "Globalization and Labor Market Mobility Over the Life-Course of Men: The Case of Mexico." Working paper. Bamberg, Germany: Globalife Project.

———. 2004. "International Migration and Men's Marriage in Western Mexico." *Journal of Comparative Family Studies* 35(1): 51–72.

Paus, Eva. 1995. "Exports, Economic Growth and the Consolidation of Peace in El Salvador." *World Development* 23(12): 2173–93.

Phillips, Julie A., and Douglas S. Massey. 2000. "Engines of Immigration: Stocks of Human and Social Capital in Mexico." *Social Science Quarterly* 81(1): 33–48.

Portes, Alejandro, and Luis Guarnizo. 1991. *La inmigración en los Estados Unidos y el desarrollo de la pequeña empresa en la República Dominicana.* Santo Domingo, Dominican Republic: Facultad Latino-Americana de Ciéncias Sociales.

Reichert, Joshua S. 1981. "The Migrant Syndrome: Seasonal U.S. Wage Labor and Rural Development in Central Mexico." *Human Organization* 40: 56–66.

Roberts, Bryan. 1995. "Socially Expected Durations and the Economic Adjustment of Immigrants." In *The Economic Sociology of Immigration,* edited by Alejandro Portes. New York: Russell Sage Foundation.

Russell, Sharon Stanton. 1986. "Remittances from International Migration: A Review in Perspective." *World Development* 14(6): 677–96.

Smith, James P., and Duncan Thomas. 1997. "On the Road: Marriage and Mobility in Malaysia." *Journal of Human Resources* 33(4): 805–32.

Stark, Oded. 1988. "On Marriage and Migration." *European Journal of Population* 4: 23–37.

Taylor, J. Edward, Joaquín Arango, Graeme Hugo, Ali Kouaouci, Douglas S. Massey, and Adela Pellegrino. 1996. "International Migration and National Development." *Population Index* 62(2): 181–212.

Trussell, James, and Toni Richards. 1985. "Correcting for Unmeasured Heterogeneity in Hazard Models Using the Heckman-Singer Procedure." *Sociological Methodology* 15: 242–76.

World Bank. 2003. *World Development Indicators.* Washington, D.C.: The World Bank.

Yi, Kei-Mu, James Walker, and Bo Honoré. 1986. *CTM: A User's Guide.* Unpublished manuscript. National Opinion Research Center and the University of Chicago.

CHAPTER 5

THE GREEN CARD AS A MATRIMONIAL STRATEGY: SELF-INTEREST IN THE CHOICE OF MARITAL PARTNERS

Enrique Martínez Curiel

ACCORDING TO Pierre Bourdieu (1980, 250), "Marriage strategies always attempt . . . to ensure a 'good marriage' and not just a marriage; that is, to maximize the economic and symbolic benefits associated with the establishment of a new relationship." In this chapter I argue that undocumented migrants from the city of Ameca, Jalisco, go to the United States to establish marital relationships with U.S. citizens as part of a well-defined matrimonial strategy based on self-interest and that the pursuit of this deliberate social strategy has become more common in recent years. This strategy is a fundamental part of individual life projects. The concept of a life project is here defined as "an open, personal project that creates new demands and new anxieties" (Giddens 1998, 18) in which our "interpersonal existence is completely transfigured by involving ourselves in everyday social experiments, to which we are subjected by wider social changes" (Giddens 1998, 19). Many Mexican migrants pursue a strategy of union formation with U.S. citizens and permanent legal residents to achieve individual social mobility.

Most undocumented migrants who are able to legalize by marrying a U.S. citizen continue thereafter to live with their spouse as a married couple. This chapter considers the manifold motives that push migrants to formalize unions with U.S. citizens, motives that in many cases have resulted in marriages that last longer than either spouse originally planned or expected. For a number of reasons, some migrants opt for common-law arrangements (living together in free union) instead of legal or religious matrimony.

WHY MARRY A U.S. CITIZEN?

Any Mexican who migrates to the United States without documents faces the possibility of remaining there for a prolonged period of time. Indeed, the question of settlement versus return has become increasingly salient in the years since the 1986 Immigration Reform and Control Act authorized two massive legalization programs, one for farmworkers and the other for long-term U.S. residents. Since then, the Mexico-U.S. border has been militarized, and the costs and risks of undocumented border crossing have increased, causing millions of migrants to avoid crossing the border by prolonging trips and remaining longer in "el Norte" (Massey, Durand, and Malone 2002). At the same time, however, the procedures for legalizing have become more complicated, and the processes for regularizing relatives more drawn out.

At this point, one of the few fast and sure ways to legalize one's migratory status is by marrying a U.S. citizen. For migrants from Ameca, going to work regularly in the United States has long constituted a popular strategy for socioeconomic mobility, enabling households to finance the construction of a home, improve family consumption, invest in education, and finance new productive enterprises. Until the 1990s, the circulation of Mexicans back and forth in irregular status was relatively easy, and marriage to a U.S. citizen was not a significant part of the conscious calculus of undocumented migrants. With the tightening of border controls, however, marriage to a U.S. citizen has become increasingly salient as a part of the migrant life project, for by choosing to marry a U.S. citizen migrants can legalize, remain indefinitely in the United States, and cross the border as they please. Marriage to a U.S. citizen opens up wider avenues of economic mobility and more possibilities for increasing material well-being in personal and family lives. In this sense, contracting a mixed marriage has become fundamental to achieving success as a migrant.

Moreover, as undocumented migrants remain north of the border for longer periods, they are increasingly likely to select U.S. citizens as marriage partners because distance minimizes family pressures to choose someone from the local home community. As a result, the decision to enter into a mixed marriage has increasingly become a personal rather than a family decision. In many cases, a male migrant will simply tell his parents that he is going to get married so that he can legalize and then return home for visits without the complications of clandestine border crossing. For many parents, the possibility of seeing a son more often mitigates their desire for him to marry within the community. In some cases, migrants do not bother to inform their parents they have married someone from the United States until they actually arrive and introduce their parents to a new grandchild. Still others—a small minority—inform their elders of a relationship only after it has ended.

Consider the case of Timoteo, who emigrated to the United States in 1973 to make a better life for himself; the situation in his village was not going well, and he felt that things would be better north of the border. With the assistance of an older brother he migrated to Lake Tahoe, where he found work in the hospitality industry. Although the job was steady, he was still undocumented and could be deported at any unlucky moment. To increase the security of his existence in the United States, Timoteo says,

> in 1974 I married an [American] woman, and seven months later I emigrated. When I got my papers arranged I said good-bye. My idea was to see how she worked out as a wife, but soon I began to see that she wasn't worthwhile, that all she wanted to do was go to restaurants and casinos. She didn't want to work; she didn't do anything to get money; she just enjoyed herself, and that bothered me. So I began to think about leaving her, because she even used to go to parties with her sisters and tell me that that was how life was in the United States; but it was all a lie, and that's why what happened to her happened to her.

Timoteo ended up leaving his wife, but only after he had achieved his objective of obtaining legal residence papers. Once he had documentation and could cross the border freely, and after his divorce, Timoteo returned to Mexico. "In 1980 I got married again," Timoteo says, "to a girl from the rancho Lagunillas in the same municipality; she's six years younger than me, and we have two children. . . . Both of them were born here [in the U.S.]." Timoteo believes he did well to marry a woman from the United States, despite the ephemeral nature of their relationship. Because he was able to arrange his citizenship papers, his wife and parents are now also U.S. residents who can enter and leave the country freely, which gives the family greater security and wider possibilities in "the land of opportunity."

Another case of intermarriage to a U.S. citizen is that of Miguel, a worker from Ameca's sugar mill. By the late 1960s, the mill faced an uncertain future, and in 1969, like many other insecure workers, he decided to migrate to the United States to "try his luck" for a few months before the next sugarcane harvest. He went to Chicago but had been there only a short time when he began to think about staying longer. Because the economic future at home was so uncertain, he was not concerned about leaving his job as a seasonal worker in the sugar mill to remain in the United States. There was one thing that worried him, however, and kept him from settling down more definitively to accumulate savings that he might eventually invest in a business: his lack of documentation. Because his undocumented status constrained his ability to rise economically, he decided to "arrange my papers any way I could, so I could be more at ease and not have problems with [migration officials] or looking for work; and to do it, all I had to do was marry a gringa or something like that." One day after leaving work, Miguel met a Puerto Rican woman on the subway: "She always caught the subway two blocks after the station where I got on when I left the factory. We started to talk and get to know each other. That was how we got together and then lived together for a while. But after that, she introduced me to a friend of hers, also Puerto Rican, and I got involved with her, and one day she found us together." After his infidelity, the first Puerto Rican woman refused to marry him, and the legalization process came to an abrupt halt. As Miguel puts it, "We were going to get married so that I could apply for residence, but after that everything just went up in smoke."

Miguel's good luck continued, however, because the second woman was also "something like" a gringa. She had U.S. citizenship and so "could help me get my documents, as long as I decided to stay with her." Miguel was honest about his intentions: he told her, "I'm just looking to get my papers, and that's it; if that's what you want from me, then I accept." But they remained together for several years and had two children. In the second year after their marriage, Miguel made his application for permanent residence from Toronto, Canada, because a notary public had told him it was better to start the procedure from outside the United States. Eight months later, Miguel received his answer. He had finally obtained what he had so longed for: the document that would allow him greater stability in his life in the United States. Six years later, however, Miguel got divorced. In Miguel's view, "I had gotten what I wanted, and things weren't going very well between us, so the best thing to do was get divorced." He then went to live in Lake Tahoe, where he remarried, this time with a woman from Ameca.

THE GREEN CARD AS A MATRIMONIAL STRATEGY

Whatever their emotions may be, a salient reason for an undocumented man to take an American wife is the possibility of legalizing his migrant status. For many new migrants who have no legal migrants in their immediate family, marrying a U.S. citizen represents the only quick and viable way to obtain a residence card—the so-called green card. At present, the identity card that accredits migrants as U.S. residents is no longer green. As a security measure adopted by the Immigration and Naturalization Service, the green card has been replaced with a pink laser-readable card, but the moniker "green card" has stuck, though some migrants now call it a "laser card." Whatever its color, a visa for permanent residence in the United States confers legal status and facilitates employment security and mobility. It represents a fundamental step toward realizing a more fulfilling life project of work in the United States. After five years, moreover, card holders are eligible to apply for U.S. citizenship, opening up new possibilities for sponsoring the legal entry of close relatives.

Obtaining the green card, then, is of singular importance in the lives of migrants, and marriage to a U.S. citizen is one of the most feasible ways available to a man of modest origins. A strategy of "marriage mobility" becomes especially likely considering the constraints placed on the "marriage market" for migrants, who lose regular contact with women in their home communities. Given the increasing difficulty, risk, and expense of crossing the border without authorization, the only viable place for migrants to look for a spouse is in the U.S. communities in which they live and work. Therefore, their status as undocumented workers makes migrants, especially those arriving in the repressive 1990s, relatively more prone to exogamy than their documented counterparts. As illustrated in the chart shown in figure 5.1, 62 percent of migrants from Ameca who entered into a mixed marriage were undocumented, which suggests that undocumented migrants enter mixed marriages far more often than do their legalized counterparts.

To explore in greater detail the relationship between choice of spouse and premarital documentation, figure 5.2 shows the distribution of nationalities among spouses of intermarried migrants from Ameca. Clearly, migrants most often turn to citizens of the United States, who make up almost three-quarters (74 percent) of all exogamous spouses. More revealing, however, is the fact that of those migrants who chose to establish a relationship with a U.S. citizen, 77 percent were undocumented workers at the time of their marriage, while only 23 percent had already obtained papers (not shown). Of the 115 mixed couples from Ameca, 85 were formed with U.S. citizens, and among these, only three were common-law relationships. Almost all migrants forming a union with an American partner have thus sought to formalize the relationship.

The case of Mario illustrates how matrimony may be used as a migratory strategy to obtain the green card. Mario left for the United States in mid-1996 at the tender age of sixteen because of his involvement in drug trafficking and his drug consumption at home. To shield him from the law—and to save him from the ill effects of drugs—his family sent him to live under the guiding hand of an elder brother in Los Angeles.

Mario had no difficulty crossing the border, but it was hard for him to adapt to the demands of his brother, who imposed a rigid, disciplined

FIGURE 5.1   Migratory Status at Time of Marriage Among
Migrants from Ameca

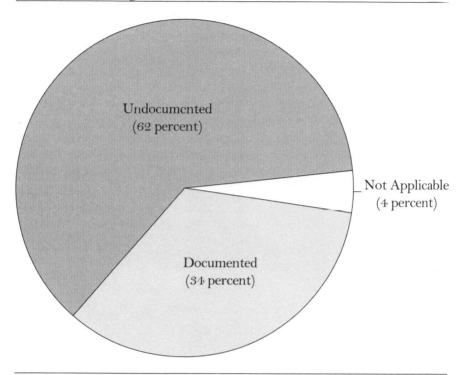

Source: Data from Mexican Migration Project.

lifestyle upon him to prevent him from going back to drugs. His brother found Mario a job in the same junkyard where he worked, so that he could keep a close eye on him and take him to and from work every day. That way, he knew exactly what time his brother started work and what time he got off at the end of the day, leaving Mario no opportunity to get into trouble.

Although Mario had originally left Mexico only to seek refuge from his drug problems, over time he began to see the opportunities for a better life in the United States. He was not bothered by the hard work or the long hours he had to spend at the junkyard; but the same could not be said of his brother's extreme rigidity, something he had never known with his parents in Ameca. In December 1997 he met a young woman in the neighborhood in which he lived. Her name was Wendy, and she had been born in California, though her parents were from Mexico. She was five years older than Mario, but they went out for several months and enjoyed their courtship.

FIGURE 5.2   National Origin of Spouse of Migrants from Ameca in
Mixed Marriages

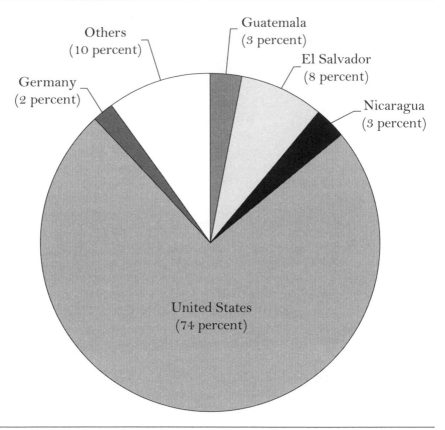

Source: Data from Mexican Migration Project.

Mario's brother did not accept this American girlfriend: she was independent, and her manners and values were quite different from those of women from Ameca. He himself had already promised to marry a Mexican woman, although he was living far from home. He preferred to continue living without documents rather than marry an American woman, even one of Mexican origin. Though his only realistic chance for legalization was to marry an American, he chose as his wife a woman from Ameca, who was herself undocumented.

Almost a year after they met, Mario and Wendy decided to get married in a civil ceremony in Reno, Nevada, without his brother in attendance, as the latter had clearly let it be known that he opposed the union. Mario decided to marry Wendy "because I found the person who understood me and supported me, where my own family didn't. I married her though I wasn't really sufficiently in love with her like one ideally would be."

Both he and Wendy suspected that this relationship would not be as lasting as they might have wished. It was clear that Mario had decided to get married to get out from under his brother's yoke and, above all, to legalize his migratory status. Wendy knew that once Mario had obtained his papers he might leave her, but she rationalized this risk by saying, "I want[ed] to give him the chance to have more opportunities, and one of them is for him to get his green card. Mario only knows Ameca and Bellflower [in California], so by living with me he could see more places and widen his horizons. It doesn't matter if he leaves me some day, that's up to him."

Similar "marriages of convenience" often occurred in England during the seventeenth and eighteenth centuries. In a novel published in 1749, the aristocratic protagonist states, "I married for a fortune, she for a title. Once we had both obtained what we wanted, the sooner we separated the better" (cited in Stone 1990, 153). Though such marriages also occurred historically in Mexico (Seed 1988), intermarriages among migrants from Ameca are distinct in several ways. First, they are arranged exclusively by the couple without taking the views of parents or family members into account. Second, both spouses are well aware of the practical self-interest underlying the marriage. In contrast, traditional marriages in Mexico are typically made by the couple's families as part of an explicit attempt to improve *the family's* economic position (Leonard 1992; Seed 1988; Stone 1990).

Modern society opens up many possibilities in terms of marital strategies that migrants may pursue when selecting a spouse. Contemporary couples consider the range of possibilities and a variety of objectives and interests when deciding to form mixed marriages. As a result, most migrants from Ameca decide to marry American women in full knowledge that they are using matrimony as a tactic to fulfill life plans, allowing them to live under more favorable circumstances than would be possible without documentation. Far from being an event in each individual's private life, outmarriage to an American has profound social and legal consequences, conditioning the migrant's prospects for assimilation and integration into the United States. When explaining their decision to marry a U.S. citizen, migrants frequently express a desire to remain in the United States for a long time and to accelerate their social integration (Collet 1993).

MIXED MARRIAGES FROM A LEGAL PERSPECTIVE

In the context of the many controls and sanctions that surround clandestine immigration, marriage to an American citizen offers one of the few, and often the only, means of achieving a stable legal status. For this reason, undocumented migrants with U.S. citizen partners generally opt for matrimony rather than a common-law union because the latter offers no legal advantages. In the neighborhoods of Ameca surveyed by the Mexican Migration Project in 1992, 45 percent of all migrants were undocumented on their most recent U.S. trip (Martínez 1997). It is no coincidence that among unions formed between these migrants and American women, the vast majority were legalized through matrimony. Sixty-eight percent of all those in a mixed union were legally married at the time of the survey; if those who were widowed, separated, or divorced are added, a total of 91 percent of all mixed unions were formalized as legal marriages.

Unions with American citizens are especially likely to end in marriage compared with unions with other nationalities. Table 5.1 shows the distribution of couples in mixed marriages by nationality and current marital status. Whereas 74 percent of currently married migrants have an American partner, only 10 percent of cohabiting migrants do so. Among those migrants who are widowed, separated, or divorced, 100 percent of the spouses are from the United States. Fewer than 13 percent of Amecan migrants were in legally established unions with Guatemalans, Salvadorans, and Nicaraguans. Despite sharing a common language, spouses from these nations cannot help migrants to obtain a green card unless they themselves have already achieved legal residence or citizenship.

Although most intermarriages among Amecans involve men marrying American women, female Amecans also go to the United States and marry men who are U.S. citizens. Teresa migrated without papers in 1971 at the age of twenty. With the help of an aunt, she took up residence in Los Angeles. After seven years in undocumented status, she met Ignacio, a

TABLE 5.1   Current Marital Status of Migrants from Ameca in Mixed Marriages, by Nationality of Spouse (Percentage)

Spouse's Nationality	Married	Divorced	Cohabiting	Separated	Widowed	Total
United States	74.3	100.0	10.0	100.0	100.0	75.0
El Salvador	7.7	0.0	30.0	0.0	0.0	7.8
Guatemala	3.8	0.0	10.0	0.0	0.0	3.5
Nicaragua	1.3	0.0	30.0	0.0	0.0	3.5
Other	12.8	0.0	20.0	0.0	0.0	10.4
N	78	17	10	5	5	115

Source: Data from Mexican Migration Project.

Chicano eight years her elder, in the factory where she was employed. They were introduced by a friend of hers, and after a brief courtship they decided to marry. A few months later, they tried to travel to Mexico to visit Teresa's parents, but because of her undocumented status the trip had to be postponed. Her husband then suggested they attempt to legalize her status, saying, "Let's arrange it as soon as we can so that you can come and go as you please."

The process of legalizing Teresa's situation took around a year, and the couple had no particular problem with the procedure, as she was legally married to an American citizen. Teresa did have to make seven visits to the offices of the Immigration and Naturalization Service to complete interviews that were part of the legalization process. Immigration officials also visited Ignacio and Teresa's home several times to confirm that they were, in fact, living together and that theirs was not a "ghost marriage" (which Ameca townspeople call a "fixed" marriage). They asked permission to enter the house, where they opened closets to make sure they held both men's and women's clothes, as a way of proving that Ignacio and Teresa were living together as man and wife. Thus Teresa did have to submit to a series of intrusive procedures before obtaining her legal residence. After all this her marriage lasted just a short time, and Teresa actually received her green card after being divorced.

Amecans who married more recently find that the legalization process now takes much longer than it did during the 1980s. The process used to be completed in less than twelve months, but presently it can take as long as three years to obtain the new "laser card." During this time, of course, the marital relation must be sustained according to the laws of the civil registry. The process has become more time-consuming because of the large number of applications from migrants who are seeking to legalize and the growing number of already legalized Mexicans who are applying for U.S. citizenship, which has slowed the immigration bureaucracy considerably (see Massey, Durand, and Malone 2002).

MIXED MARRIAGES AS MARRIAGES OF CONVENIENCE?

A union between an undocumented migrant and an American citizen is always under suspicion of being one of convenience, for it carries a huge benefit for the undocumented migrant. Under such circumstances, an objective observer might naturally conclude that the true purpose of the marital relationship was legalization rather than loving union and that the marriage is based on material self-interest rather than affection. However, though mixed marriage may well be convenient for an undocumented migrant, emotions inevitably enter the picture and influence both the choice of partner and the duration of the relationship beyond their instrumental value in obtaining residence papers.

Although marital histories compiled in Ameca suggest that many exogamous unions are indeed "marriages of convenience," other data indicate that most of them persist many years after the convenience has passed. If mixed marriages were arranged solely on the basis of convenience, then we would expect them to be short-lived and ephemeral, but this is apparently not the case. As figure 5.3 shows, 68 percent of all mixed marriages contracted by migrants from Ameca were still intact at the time of the survey, compared with 15 percent that ended in divorce and 4 percent in separation.

FIGURE 5.3   Marital Status of Migrants from Ameca in
            Mixed Marriages

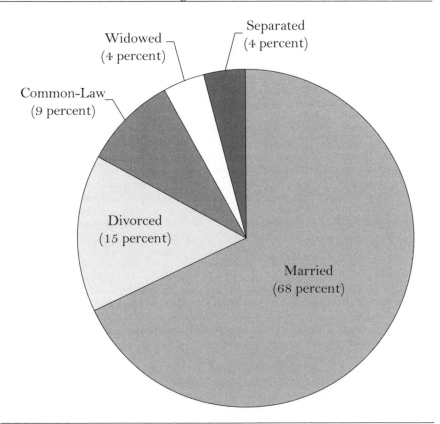

Source: Data from Mexican Migration Project.

If the number of those widowed is included, nearly three-quarters of the unions (72 percent) proved to be durable.

Carrying the analysis further, I selected the unions most likely to be marriages of convenience: those contracted while the migrant from Ameca was in undocumented status. I then examined the current marital status of the migrants by gender. The results are displayed in table 5.2. Among both men and women, "married" is the most frequent category, accounting for 70 percent of the unions involving male migrants and 57 percent of those involving females. Although these figures may suggest that women are more likely to enter into marriages of convenience, the gender differential is entirely the result of women's higher likelihood of widowhood. When the 14 percent who were widowed are added, the share of all marriages between undocumented women and U.S. citizens lasting until the death of the husband or the survey date rises to 71 percent. With the addition of the 2 percent of male migrants who were widowers, the total share of unions of undocumented males and women with U.S. citizenship lasting until death or survey is nearly identical, at 72 percent. Only about a quarter appear to terminate in separation or divorce.

The arrival of children typically convinces even shaky couples to continue their relationship well after the "convenience" has ended. As figure 5.4 illustrates, of the forty-seven unions between undocumented migrants and U.S. citizens that were still intact at the time of the survey, forty-four (94 percent) had children. In contrast, among fifteen comparable unions that ended in divorce, only a third had children.

Thus the arrival of children appears to be closely related to the stability of marriage, an effect that is independent of other factors such as culture and religion (Martínez 1996). Children cement marital relationships

TABLE 5.2   Current Status of Mixed Marriages Contracted by Undocumented Migrants from Ameca, by Gender (Percentage)

Current Status	Male	Female	Total
Married	70.0	57.1	66.2
Divorced	20.0	14.3	18.3
Cohabiting	2.0	9.5	4.2
Separated	6.0	4.8	5.6
Widowed	2.0	14.3	5.6
N	50	21	71

Source: Data from Mexican Migration Project.

FIGURE 5.4   Status of Mixed Marriages Between Undocumented
Migrants from Ameca and U.S. Citizens, With and
Without Children, 1992

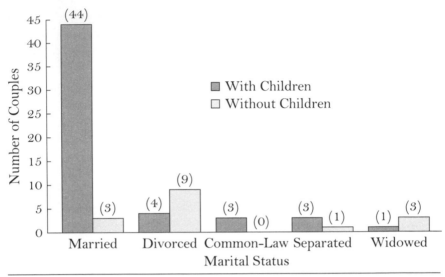

Source: Data from Mexican Migration Project.

and cause the couple to make joint plans that lead to greater stability and permanence. However, the presence of children is just one of three factors that enhance marital stability. The others are a sound financial condition and adequate communication between spouses. The saying in Ameca, "Love comes later," captures the fact that people who enter a marriage of convenience often fall in love after living together as a couple for a period of time and thus decide to continue the relationship longer than originally planned.

MIXED MARRIAGES: CONVENIENT FOR WHOM?

The stability of mixed marriage is also affected by the actions of the exogamous spouse. It is unreasonable to think that in all mixed marriages convenience is entirely a matter for Mexicans. The exogamous spouse may also benefit from the union. Indeed, many U.S. citizens and resident aliens view marrying a Mexican immigrant as part of their life project. In a kind of role reversal, for example, a previously legalized migrant from Ameca may serve as the documented spouse for a "foreign" undocumented mate, the most common partner being someone from Central America. In marriages of this type, cultural similarities are an important factor, raising expectations for a compatible life. In anthropology and sociology, an affinity of interests is called "homogamy" (see Kalmijn 1998), and in the case of marriage between Mexicans and Central Americans, of course, a common interest is the construction of a new life in the United States.

One must also consider what is viewed as convenient from the viewpoint of Anglo-Americans who marry undocumented migrants from Ameca. Here the notion of convenience is bound up in the U.S. stereotype of Mexican families as united and cohesive and likely to contribute to a happy and contented communal life. Michael Parfit reports, in *National Geographic* magazine, that "the family [in Mexico] is very important, it is the vital force that characterizes the Mexican." "The family is seen as an example of the vital difference between the United States and Mexico," he notes, and "is the base and nucleus of the society" (Parfit 1996c, 30; 1996b, 54; 1996a, 76). One way that Americans can aspire to this kind of idealized family life, escaping an American life that lacks commitment and love, is through marriage to a Mexican immigrant.

Consider the case of Sebastián, who was born in Ameca and at the age of eighteen entered the school of aviation in Mexico's military service. He had been studying there for three years when he deserted over disciplinary issues. He then looked for work in Guadalajara for a few months but with little success because his military training opened few doors of employment. He therefore decided to migrate to the United States, where three of his siblings were already living—one brother in Chicago, another in Lake Tahoe, and a sister in Los Angeles. Of these three potential U.S. destinations, Sebastián chose Lake Tahoe. When he arrived there in June 1974, he was not thinking about a long-term stay. He always supposed he would return to Ameca to marry and settle down. Indeed, the idea of staying permanently in the United States did not really take shape until 1992, when he began to take steps to purchase a house in that casino city.

In the fall of 1974, Sebastián got a job as a houseman at a recently opened hotel. The following year, a young American woman named Patricia Ellis began to work there also. As she was a chambermaid, they had frequent contact. They had similar levels of education, including some professional studies, so there was a certain affinity between them, and they began to develop a friendship, despite differences in culture and language. After a while, their friendship turned into flirtation, and their working hours together allowed them not only to get to know each other better but also to begin a courtship. According to Sebastián, "What really got my attention about Patricia was her liberal way of thinking." Patricia, on the other hand, was attracted precisely by the opposite: Sebastián's more conservative ways. These differences eventually brought them closer together, and they became a couple.

Two and a half years after they first met, Patricia accepted Sebastián's invitation to visit his hometown, though they were not living together at the time. Sebastián's parents were somewhat taken aback by the presence of the young lady in their home, but they never took a position with respect to their son's relationship with her. Sebastián's mother just said, "If you love her, then go ahead!" Patricia had to cut short her visit and return to the United States earlier than planned. Sebastián stayed on for a few more weeks, because he had not seen his parents in three years.

When he returned to the United States, Patricia met him at the airport in San Diego and drove him back to Lake Tahoe. "[He] didn't have any-where to stay," she relates, "so he stayed with me, and then he just stayed and stayed. . . . It's been twenty years now, and he's still there. It all happened without thinking, no plans for the future. We never plan."

For the first few years, this couple lived in a common-law relationship. "It was all passion," they now say. As time went by, however, they decided to get married, and in 1981 Patricia became pregnant. Sebastián sees the child as "a beautiful thing, a gift from God, a blessing; it strengthened our relationship." After a year of marriage, Sebastián decided to legalize his status. The procedure took six months, but by then he knew that his relationship with Patricia was going to last a long time and that his legal residence in the country would help them establish a secure relationship and work situation. He also became concerned about the financial stability of the family. The couple's purchase of a house in Lake Tahoe consolidated Sebastián's life project and cemented his permanence in the United States.

The couple has maintained a certain familial closeness with Sebastián's relatives in other parts of the United States, especially by getting together on holidays. At Thanksgiving, for example, the two sides of the family normally visit Sebastián's sister, who still lives in Los Angeles and, like her brother, is married to an American. On these occasions, Patricia cooks the traditional turkey, while her sister-in-law prepares a Mexican-style birria (a typical Mexican dish for festive occasions, made with goat and a special sauce), thereby mixing the culinary preferences of these two mixed families.

The years of their marriage have been pleasant and harmonious for Sebastián and Patricia, together with their two children, primarily because they have formed a united family, more like a typical Mexican family, just as Patricia had hoped. As she says, "I grew up without a mother [because] she died when I was just three, and my father was always out working. I was always alone, [so] for me it was a dream to have a family like this."

She "had that hope" and, thanks to Sebastián, has been able to form a more "Mexican" family. I have encountered many cases similar to this one, in which an American woman seeks to marry a man of Mexican origin in hopes of forming a happy couple and a united extended family.

Another case study bears on the motivations of spouses who marry migrants from Ameca. Jorge was an Amecan who married a Guatemalan woman named Loyda, whom he met in Lake Tahoe. Before he left for the United States, Jorge studied law for one year at the University of Guadalajara. He then decided to go north, to "see what it was like," and planned to work only for a few months. Early in 1988 he arrived in Salinas, California, where he stayed with an uncle for a month and a half before relocating to Lake Tahoe and getting a job at a hotel and casino.

Given the timing of his arrival in the United States, Jorge was able to apply for legal residence under the Special Agricultural Workers program. He simply purchased an agricultural work card from one of many labor contractors who worked the black market in false documents. By then Jorge was twenty-one years old, but he had never had a girlfriend, even in Ameca. His natural timidity and a certain unattractiveness had not brought him much luck as far as women were concerned. In the United States, however, his potential marriage market widened, and he soon found a woman who, as he puts it, "returned his attentions."

Loyda herself was not particularly attractive or enchanting. Their mutual plainness created a certain balance, however, and they soon found themselves attracted to each other. Loyda had left Guatemala in 1989, a year after the period for legalizing under the Immigration Reform and Control Act had closed. She had come to the United States because

> there was no sense in living there [in Guatemala]. There was no interest, my family was very disunited, everybody was going their own way. I was raised by my aunt and uncle, and then my sister said, "Why don't you come over here with me? At least that way the two of us would be together." I came as an undocumented migrant. . . . [I] arrived first in Los Angeles, and after that I came to Lake Tahoe, where my sister was [living]. After a year here I applied for political asylum, and each year I renewed my work permit.

The couple met at the hotel where they both had jobs, Jorge as a houseman and Loyda as a chambermaid. As they worked in the same area they had many chances for contact, but little came of their meetings at first. As Loyda recalls, "We always chatted, but we never imagined that I would come to like him or that he would come to like me." According to Jorge,

"Everything began with a hug when we were just playing around. We were working, she was over by the cart they use for their work, and I went up to her and picked her up, but without saying anything, and all I managed to do that time was make her cry; that's all." In her own words, Loyda "cried out of shame, out of embarrassment. . . . It didn't bother me, maybe I even liked it, that was where our relationship started. After that he invited me for an ice cream."

Their courtship lasted three years. Loyda was wary: "My sister just told me to be careful if I was going to go out with him, not because he was a Mexican or anything, because she's married to a [guy] from Puebla; but because we didn't know him very well." It may well be that her sister's experience influenced Loyda's decision to marry Jorge, but also her marriage market was narrow as she had little contact with people from her native country—only with Mexicans and Americans.

They got married in April 1995, but it was a civil marriage because they had different religions, she belonging to an evangelical church and he being a Catholic. Though they only formalized their marriage before the state, she decided to wear a white dress because, as Jorge says, "that was how she wanted to leave her house, even though she wasn't going to the church. . . . It was her 'dream.' " Jorge purchased the wedding dress in Guadalajara, on a visit to thank the Virgin of Talpa for a divine favor he had received, after his mother had fallen ill. Jorge and Loyda had agreed that they would get married once he had fulfilled this obligation.

Their years together have brought Loyda to change some of her ideas: "Before, I didn't go to parties, I didn't dance, I didn't use earrings, but now I do. Now I don't even go to my church, he convinced me to do all these things." In fact, she is "now convinced that we should get married in the Catholic church, but in Ameca, because I've got my papers now, and I can come and go from the United States with no problems; he wants us to get married there with his family and then go to visit my family in Guatemala."

Loyda's parents did not find out that she and Jorge had gotten married until she could work up the courage to tell them she had married a Mexican. But her father said only, "As long as he's a good man, it doesn't matter if he's from another country or if he has a different religion." At the beginning of their relationship, Loyda "felt scared and believed that things weren't going to work out well or that after a little while they'd have arguments, not because we're from different places but because we have different religions; but everything has worked out well." Jorge did not believe that their religious differences would be an obstacle to a harmonious, lasting relationship, because "we have always respected what the other one believes, that's why we haven't had problems."

A few months after they got married, Jorge decided to apply for American citizenship in order to legalize his wife more quickly. If he attempted to legalize Loyda as a permanent resident alien, the procedure would be more complicated and could take years because the entry of spouses of permanent residents is numerically restricted. In addition, "as an American citizen there would be more benefits for me and my family." For this reason, Loyda was able to get legal residence quickly, just one year after Jorge became an American citizen.

The final case study also shows a combination of self-interest and emotional attraction in the selection of a spouse. This case involves Martín and Irma, both of whom were migrants living in the United States when they met. Martín is from Ameca and emigrated to the United States for the first time in 1980, when he was just eighteen years old. He was enrolled at the time at the Teacher's College in Ciudad Guzmán, located in southern Jalisco, and he planned to migrate for a few months during summer vacation. He lived with a sister in Stockton, California, and worked in the nearby agricultural fields.

Over the next five years he continued to work in Stockton for two months every summer as an agricultural fieldworker to earn money to pay for his studies. After graduating from Teacher's College, he taught for a couple of years, first in the state of Guerrero and later in Jalisco, but he continued to go to the United States periodically during summer vacations to spend time with his family, most of whom were living in California. He also wanted to get enough money together to buy an automobile and take it back to Mexico. Throughout this period, he entered the United States as an undocumented worker, though his father was living in Los Angeles and some of his brothers and sisters were working in Lake Tahoe. When the Immigration Reform and Control Act took effect in 1986, offering legalization to undocumented farmworkers, Martín decided not to return to Mexico but instead to establish himself in Lake Tahoe, where his brothers and sisters were living.

Irma is from Guatemala. She left her country at the end of 1988, when she was just seventeen. She crossed Mexico with a tourist visa and entered the United States as an undocumented migrant, as so many thousands of Central Americans have done. The first place she settled was Los Angeles, but she later moved on to Lake Tahoe, where she was reunited with her sister, who had come to the United States several years earlier.

Through the early 1990s, Martín and Irma did not know each other, but chance eventually brought them together. Both were attending an English class for adult migrants. Although they were in different groups, one day they had a joint session in which a policeman was scheduled to give them a driver's education class. On that occasion, they only looked at each other without exchanging words, but a few days later Martín ran into Irma again in a busy supermarket. Irma was with a friend who knew Martín, and they were introduced. During this brief encounter they spoke few words, but they exchanged telephone numbers. After that, they called each other to set up more formal dates, with the intention of establishing a relationship.

Irma reports that she was lonely and wanted to find a companion, and in Martín she felt she had found just what she was looking for. Martín, who was by then twenty-eight, also felt the need to establish a relationship. Their courtship lasted a short time, and soon they decided to move in together, just for a few months. However, one of Irma's brothers, who also lived in Lake Tahoe, "didn't want his sister going around with a Mexican because of the bad reputation they have. He prohibited me from even turning around to look at a Mexican, he didn't like them because he said they were drunkards, gamblers, and really 'machos.' " Irma paid little heed to her brother, because she wanted a companion with whom she could have a more active sexual relationship without the kinds of prohibitions that her brother was trying to impose on her. Her sister was already married to a Mexican, so she could see that everything her brother was telling her was untrue.

According to Irma, "The idea was to live together before getting married in a civil ceremony, to see if it would work out. If it worked out then we would get married, and if not, we'd just split up. For us, this was good, to live like that, because love began to grow bit by bit, so it was good that way." Martín adds, "We lived together in order to share expenses. Here it isn't like Mexico, here you're on your own, you have to pay your rent, pay your bills. Over in Mexico you depend on your parents. . . . That's why it's better to [live] where you can share the costs; and what better way than with a woman!" Both Martín and Irma agree that "after a while together love began to grow between us; at first we lived together out of economic necessity, later for sex, and finally for love."

Within a year of meeting, Irma and Martín had decided to live together before formalizing their relationship by getting married. Martín never consulted his parents about marrying a Guatemalan woman—not until after they were married and had their first son, some four years later. It was not strange for Martín's parents to see one of their children marrying a foreigner: three of their other children had formed mixed marriages, and two of his father's brothers also had foreign wives. Irma's parents said only, "If you love each other, then go ahead and get married!" By 1994 Irma was applying for legal residence, thanks to Martín, who had previously achieved legal status through the Immigration Reform and Control Act. After four years, however, she still had not received permission to reside legally in the United States, and as my fieldwork ended she was still waiting.

COUPLES WHO PREFER JUST "LIVING TOGETHER"

It is possible, of course, that the decision to establish a common-law union in a mixed relationship follows a different logic from the decision to marry. First, it is clear that "some couples who live together do so out of a principled rejection of the institution of marriage itself" (Collet 1993, 16). Second, other couples see living together as "an acceptable alternative to a civil or religious marriage" (Collet 1993, 16). Finally, living together "often constitutes a step on the road to legal marriage" (Robichaux 1997, 107).

Although only 10 couples in my sample of 115 mixed relationships were living in common-law situations, representing just 9 percent of the total, cohabitation occupies third place in the ranking of the most common marital events in the Mexican Migration Project sample, following marriage and divorce. According to official vital statistics for Ameca, however, common-law union ranks second, preceding divorce (Instituto Nacional de Estadística, Geografía, e Informática 2001a), and the same finding holds at the national level (Robichaux 1997). Another recent study indicates that in the year 2000, 71 percent of adult Mexicans were married, while another 16 percent were in common-law relationships; cases of divorce, separation and widowhood together made up the remaining 13 percent (Instituto Nacional de Estadística, Geografía, e Informática 2001b).

Table 5.3 presents the nationality, legal status, number of children, and the year and order of the union for the ten cohabiting mixed couples in my sample of mixed unions. Most of the relationships were with Central Americans, especially Salvadorans and Nicaraguans (three cases each). The sample also includes one spouse from Guatemala, one from the United States, one from Germany, and one from the Philippines. That all but one of the exogamous partners are from countries other than the United States suggests an absence of practical incentive to marry among mixed couples. Although in most historical periods participants in common-law marriages tend to be drawn from the same social group, often from marginal minorities (see Martínez-Alier 1989; Seed 1988; Flandrin 1979; and Robichaux 1997), in this case half of the ten partners are themselves documented, as are seven of the ten migrants from Ameca. Thus there is little practical incentive to marry.

Among common-law unions in which both members have legal status, the majority decided not to have children. This leads us to believe that their

TABLE 5.3   Characteristics of Mixed Common–Law Unions Among Migrants from Ameca

Union	Spouse's National Origin	Spouse's Status	Respondent's Status	Number of Children	Year of Union	Previously Married?
1	United States	Citizen	Legal	0	1995	No
2	Germany	Illegal	Illegal	2	1982	No
3	Philippines	Legal	Legal	0	1993	Yes
4	Guatemala	Legal	Legal	2	1993	Yes
5	El Salvador	Illegal	Illegal	1	1993	No
6	El Salvador	Legal	Legal	0	1996	Yes
7	El Salvador	Legal	Legal	0	1992	Yes
8	Nicaragua	Illegal	Illegal	1	1993	No
9	Nicaragua	Illegal	Legal	1	1998	Yes
10	Nicaragua	Legal	Legal	1	1998	No

Source: Data from Mexican Migration Project.

common-law relationship is part of an alternative lifestyle or represents a rejection of the institution of marriage, as there is nothing that might compel them to stay together if things do not work out as planned. This, of course, would be quite different if there were children or an agreement to legalize the undocumented member. In addition, of the four relationships in which the documented foreign spouse of a documented migrant was previously married, three have no children, probably because the common-law arrangement allows them greater comfort in their relationship or perhaps because after a short time these couples may be added to the small but significant group of unstable mixed couples.

Translated from the Spanish by Paul C. Kersey.

REFERENCES

Bourdieu, Pierre. 1980. *Le sens pratique*. Paris: Les Editions de Minuit.

Collet, Beate. 1993. "Couples mixtes en France, Couples binationaux en Allemagne." *Hommes & Migrations* 1167: 15–19.

Flandrin, Jean-Louis. 1979. *Families in Former Times: Kinship, Household, and Sexuality*. Cambridge: Cambridge University Press.

Giddens, Anthony. 1998. *La transformación de la intimidad*. Madrid, Spain: Ediciones Cátedra.

Instituto Nacional de Estadística, Geografía, e Informática. 2001a. *Estadísticas vitales, Cuaderno Número 3, Jalisco*. Aguascalientes, Mexico: Instituto Nacional de Estadística, Geografía, e Informática.

———. 2001b. *Mujeres y hombres en México*. Aguascalientes, Mexico: Instituto Nacional de Estadística, Geografía, e Informática.

Kalmijn, Matthijs. 1998. "Intermarriage and Homogamy: Causes, Patterns, Trends." *Annual Review of Sociology* 24: 395–421.

Leonard, Karen Isaksen. 1992. *Making Ethnic Choices: California's Punjabi Mexican Americans*. Philadelphia, Pa.: Temple University Press.

Martínez Curiel, Enrique. 1996. "Matrimonios mixtos y migración internacional: Exogamia en el caso de Ameca, Jalisco." Paper presented to the Coloquio Internacional: Las Relaciones México–Estados Unidos desde la Perspectiva Regional. San Luis Potosí, Mexico (August 26–28, 1996).

———. 1997. "En el Norte y en el pueblo hay zafra para el obrero: La migración laboral a Estados Unidos: Un estudio de caso en Ameca, Jalisco." Unpublished paper. Universidad de Guadalajara, Mexico.

Martínez-Alier, Verena. 1989. *Marriage, Class and Color in Nineteenth-Century Cuba: A Study of Racial Attitudes and Sexual Values in a Slave Society*. Ann Arbor: University of Michigan Press.

Massey, Douglas S., Jorge Durand, and Nolan J. Malone. 2002. *Beyond Smoke and Mirrors: Mexican Immigration in an Age of Economic Integration.* New York: Russell Sage Foundation.

Parfit, Michael. 1996a. "Heartland and the Pacific: Eternal Mexico." In "Emerging Mexico," special issue, *National Geographic* 190(2): 70–93.

———. 1996b. "Mexico City Pushing the Limits." In "Emerging Mexico," special issue, *National Geographic* 190(2): 24–43.

———. 1996c. "Monterrey Confronting the Future." In "Emerging Mexico," special issue, *National Geographic* 190(2): 52–61.

Robichaux, David. 1997. "Las uniones consensuales y la nupcialidad en Tlaxcala rural y México: Un ensayo de interpretación cultural." *Ispiral, Estudios sobre Estado y Sociedad* 4(10): 101–42.

Seed, Patricia. 1988. *Amar, honrar y obedecer en el México colonial: Conflictos en torno la elección matrimonial, 1574–1821.* Mexico City: Editorial Alianza.

Stone, Lawrence. 1990. *Familia, sexo y matrimonio en Inglaterra, 1500–1800.* Mexico City: Fondo de Cultura Economica.

PART II

❖

MIGRATION AND GENDER

CHAPTER 6

WOMEN AND MEN ON THE MOVE: UNDOCUMENTED BORDER CROSSING

Katharine M. Donato and Evelyn Patterson

MEXICO IS well known as a nation that has long sustained high levels of out-migration to the United States. Mexican men, in particular, have migrated for more than a hundred years, especially from traditional sending areas in the western central part of the country (Durand 1998). During the past two decades, women have become migrants in increasing numbers (Donato 1993). Douglas Massey, Jorge Durand, and Nolan Malone (2002) describe the "feminization of migration" as one of the unintended consequences of heightened border enforcement in the late twentieth century and one of the hallmarks of the "new era" of Mexican migration (Durand, Massey, and Parrado 1999, 133).

Despite the recent attention focused on border enforcement and immigration policy, not much is known about women's clandestine border crossing. We know little about how women make their way across the now well-guarded Mexico-U.S. frontier, women's chances of being arrested by the Border Patrol, and variance in the odds of arrest by mode of border crossing. To date, the only evidence that speaks to these issues is qualitative, and it suggests important sex differences in patterns and processes of border crossing.

CURRENT KNOWLEDGE ABOUT BORDER CROSSING

A variety of studies of undocumented border crossing have been undertaken during the past decade. Whether quantitative or ethnographic, these studies have greatly improved our knowledge of clandestine entry. During the late 1980s and early 1990s, the process of border crossing constituted a "game of cat and mouse" (Kossoudji 1992, 160), in which U.S. Border Patrol agents arrested migrants attempting to enter surreptitiously and deported them "voluntarily" back to Mexico, whereupon the migrants simply tried to enter again—and usually succeeded (Chavez 1992; Durand 1994; Graham 1996; Heyman 1995).

The origins of this "game" lie in the organizational interests of the Immigration and Naturalization Service (INS) (Andreas 2000; Heyman 1995). As a bureaucratic agency the INS faces contradictory demands, with agricultural growers, business interests, and immigrant advocates lined up on one side seeking to hire more immigrant workers (either explicitly or implicitly) and labor unions, nativists, and the unskilled lined up on the other side to oppose any expansion of immigration. Both sets of players are potentially powerful, and their conflicting demands create a difficult political landscape for the INS.

Temporary worker programs put in place from 1942 to 1964 finessed the contradiction and served both sets of interests (Calavita 1992). As Audrey Singer and Douglas Massey (1998, 563) point out, however, when the program finally ended, "political heat" generated by contradictions once again emerged to reignite immigration as a divisive political issue. In response, the INS developed a new strategy: it sought to win widespread public support by directing its enforcement efforts to visible entry points, at the same time participating in popular causes such as the so-called war on drugs (Andreas 2000; Dunn 1996; Hagan and Baker 1993). Congress also responded by passing the Immigration Reform and Control Act (IRCA) in 1986 and the Illegal Immigration Reform and Immigrant Responsibility Act in 1996. Designed to curb undocumented migration, the legislation imposed new costs and penalties against migrants repeatedly apprehended for unauthorized entry.

Despite its get-tough provisions, undocumented migration nonetheless persisted. Few migrants apprehended more than once faced criminal charges under the 1996 immigration reform legislation because Project IDENT, which sought to fingerprint apprehended migrants before deportation, has never been able to produce reliable results and also because the INS has lacked the resources to track and fingerprint all those it apprehends (Spener 2003). As a result, the game of cat and mouse has continued, though with deadlier consequences to migrants and at much higher cost to U.S. taxpayers (Massey, Durand, and Malone 2002; Eschbach et al. 1999).

As is known from participant observer studies, oral histories, letters, votive paintings, and published testimonials, migrants can generally count on substantial social support when seeking to cross the border (Chavez 1992; Conover 1987; Davis 1990; Durand 1996; Durand and Massey 1995; Halsell 1978; Hellman 1994; Siems 1992; Spener 2003; Waumbaugh 1984).

The border can be a frightening place for first-time migrants; friends and relatives with migratory experience help overcome these fears by providing useful information and serving as crossing guides. Personal experience also matters: the probability of apprehension while crossing generally falls as the number of prior trips increases, and over time most migrants substitute their own knowledge of border crossing for the help of others (Singer and Massey 1998).

Quantitative studies of border crossing have yielded several important findings. First, among undocumented migrants the average probability of apprehension per attempt was about .32 during the late 1970s and early 1980s (Crane et al. 1990; Espenshade 1990; Massey and Singer 1995, 204). Second, between 1974 and 1979, the use of a border smuggler, or "coyote," increased the odds of a successful crossing but also increased the duration of U.S. trips, as migrants had to work in the United States longer to pay coyotes' fees (Kossoudji 1992). Third, trip durations were shorter from communities in which migration was more prevalent, as access to social capital reduced the costs of crossing and cut the time needed to pay off coyotes (Kossoudji 1992). Fourth, as the number of arrests on prior crossings increased, so did the odds of capture on any subsequent crossing, a pattern that Singer and Massey (1998) take to indicate socialization into the norms of border crossing. Fifth, the number of border crossing attempts was generally equal to the number of apprehensions plus one—meaning that everyone ultimately gets in (Donato, Durand, and Massey 1992; Espenshade 1990). Finally, macro-level policies did have an effect on the number of apprehensions and the likelihood of arrest (Espenshade and Acevedo 1995; Singer and Massey 1998).

Based on these and other findings, Singer and Massey (1998) have developed a theoretical model of border crossing, viewing it as a social process determined by the quantity and quality of human and social capital at a potential migrant's disposal and contingent on the strength and nature of U.S. enforcement efforts. In undertaking our analysis of female border crossing, we base our equations and estimates on their model.

BORDER CROSSING AS A GENDERED EXPERIENCE

Although prior studies offer insights into the process of undocumented border crossing, they share one key shortcoming: all focus only on the experience of men. A variety of studies, however, suggest that patterns and processes of border crossing for men and women may be quite different. Several studies have described how migrant decision making is constrained by patriarchal norms and gender-linked power differences (Cerrutti and Massey 2001; Goldring 1996; Hondagneu-Sotelo 1994; Pedraza 1991). As a result, substantially fewer Mexican women than men undertake undocumented migration (Donato 1993; Donato and Carter 1999; Kanaiaupuni 2000).

For much of the twentieth century, the preference of Mexican families to send out males as migrant workers matched the structure of U.S. labor demand—especially that for farmworkers—and led to a disproportionate representation of men in the pool of migrant workers, both undocumented and those with legal but temporary labor permits (Donato 1994; Grindle 1988; Massey et al. 1987; Stephen 1992). The U.S. Congress itself encouraged male migration through its support of the Bracero Program, which from 1942 to 1964 imported some 4.5 million men for short-term agricultural labor (Calavita 1992). Congress also promoted male entry through the 1986 Immigration Reform and Control Act, which legalized former undocumented migrants, the vast majority of whom were men (Donato 1994; Hagan 1998; Kanaiaupuni 2000).

During the 1990s, Congress steadily increased funds for border enforcement; undocumented migrants responded to the consequent increases in the costs and risks of clandestine entry by minimizing crossings and prolonging their stays in the United States. As trip durations lengthened, undocumented migrants arranged for the entry of their wives and children, yielding a sharp drop in the probability of return migration and a sudden increase in the size of the undocumented population. At the same time, after 1990 newly legalized Mexican men began to sponsor the legal entry of their dependents in record numbers. As a result, migratory flows—both legal and illegal—have been substantially feminized (Massey, Durand, and Malone 2002).

When women migrate, Mexican families attempt to safeguard traditional gender roles by controlling their trips and seeking extra protection in the process of border crossing. Mexican women are much less likely than men to migrate independently, and their moves are strongly linked to relatives already living north of the border (Cerrutti and Massey 2001; Donato 1993; Lindstrom 1991). However, because women generally follow their husbands and sons in migration, when they do travel they have access to more financial and social resources, which they draw upon to ensure a safer and more secure crossing.

Many women and their families choose not to be smuggled surreptitiously across the border but to enter openly with some kind of legal or legal-appearing document. The use of fraudulent documents carries serious risks of arrest and incarceration—not simply deportation—and is avoided by many families. A common strategy is for women to obtain and carry valid documents but to use them inappropriately. A woman may "borrow" a green card or other visa from a look-alike sister and cross with it, counting on the inspecting officer (who is processing dozens of entries an hour) not to notice or care that the person in the picture looks slightly different. Another strategy is for a woman to go to a U.S. consulate and try to convince a consular officer to grant a tourist visa to allow her to visit relatives north of the border. Although most such requests are rejected, some women nonetheless get "lucky" and obtain a valid tourist visa, which they use to cross into the United States and then overstay the period of authorized entry.

In frontier cities, an increasingly common approach for women is to obtain a legal border-crossing card. According to David Spener (2003), Operation Blockade (launched in 1993) substantially increased the use of border-crossing cards by Mexican women. These documents, given to border residents, allow the holder to enter the United States for short trips of shopping or recreation. Until recently, these cards had no expiration date and were obtained simply by documenting border residence and steady employment at a well-paid job. Thus another pathway for female entry is for women to migrate to the border, get work in a maquiladora (assembly plant), and use this employment to get a border-crossing card, which is then used to cross legally into the United States to work illegally (Quintanilla and Copeland 1996). Rather than stopping undocumented migration, the buildup of enforcement resources seems to have done little more than blur the lines between legal and illegal migration.

In this chapter we do not focus on open crossings. Our goal is to understand gender differences in the process of clandestine border crossing, about which the literature suggests several hypotheses. First, with respect to mode of crossing, we expect women to be more likely than men to use a guide, either paid (a coyote) or unpaid (a friend or relative). Moreover, given the border buildup and the desire of Mexican families to ensure the safety of female migrants, we expect this tendency to increase over time. Second, partly because of their more frequent use of crossing guides, we expect that the probability of apprehension on a first U.S. trip will be lower for women than for men. Finally, given the growing intensity of border enforcement, we expect that women who made their first trip after 1986 will be different from those who migrated before that date. Specifically, later migrants should evince a higher risk of arrest because they are less likely to have prior U.S. experience and may be moving more for reasons of family reunification than autonomous employment.

DATA AND METHODS

Our analysis combines data from the Mexican Migration Project (see chapter 16) with information from the Health and Migration Survey (see www.mexmah.com). From the Mexican Migration Project we employ data from seventy-one communities surveyed through 1997, which are located mainly in states that have traditionally sent large numbers of migrants to the United States. Despite the relatively large size of this data set, information on border crossing was available only from the life histories of household heads, of whom just 241 were women. Among these female heads, moreover, only 78 had been to the United States.

To supplement the small number of migrant women from the Mexican Migration Project, we added data gathered from an additional 187 female household heads and spouses interviewed in 1996 in the Health and Migration Project. This binational project, directed by Katharine Donato at Rice University and Shawn Kanaiaupuni at the Kamehameha Schools, Kamehameha, seeks to collect and analyze longitudinal data on the health consequences of Mexico-U.S. migration through surveys of eleven communities in the state of San Luis Potosí. As with the communities in the Mexican Migration Project, these communities were selected to reflect a range of climatic conditions, population compositions, and levels of economic development. In the United States, two urban barrios were sampled, one in the Houston metropolitan area and another in the metropolitan region of San Diego, which field interviews indicate were the two primary destinations for migrants from the eleven communities.

In each household, we conducted interviews with the señora of the household, who was either the wife of a male head or in some cases the head herself. We defined the two U.S. neighborhoods (using census tract and block information from the 1990 census) that contained high concentrations of Mexican immigrants. Because these data were already dated by the time of the survey, investigators spent several days walking through the neighborhoods to refine the boundaries, a process that was especially important in Houston, which has no zoning laws. As a result of this exercise, the neighborhoods were redefined to exclude groups of one or two blocks that contained large commercial establishments, typically located at the edges of neighborhoods. Once the boundaries had been established, investigators compiled a list of all homes in the neighborhood and randomly chose from this list.

One strength of these data is that the two U.S. neighborhoods offer very different demographic profiles. The San Diego neighborhood contains a relatively young population, with many children, few home owners, and numerous recently arrived immigrants. The Houston neighborhood is more established and the residents generally older, with fewer recent arrivals but more home owners and two-parent families. To the extent that other destination areas share these characteristics, our data are representative of migrants settled in the United States.

For female household heads and spouses in the combined sample, we developed a set of data weights that were the inverse of the sampling fraction. In both Mexico and the United States, sampling fractions were computed as the number of households in the sample divided by the number of eligible households on the sampling frame. These weights reflect the relative contribution of households to the representative sample of all binational communities combined. The Mexican samples represent conditions in Mexican origin communities at the time of the survey, whereas the U.S. samples depict conditions in U.S. destinations. When pooled and weighted, they offer a portrait of a diverse set of binational communities.

This analysis is based on border-crossing histories compiled for household heads in the Mexican Migration Project and for heads and spouses in the Health and Migration Project. For each undocumented trip, respondents gave the year of the crossing and the number of times they were apprehended by the Border Patrol. These data were arranged into an event-history file that links mode of crossing and likelihood of apprehension in year $t + 1$ with individual and household characteristics defined in year t (t being the year of the undocumented trip). Following Singer and Massey (1998), three modes of border crossing were identified: alone (the reference category), with family or friends, and with a paid smuggler. A migrant who reported having crossed with a smuggler was coded into that category, even if friends or relatives were also along for the trip. Singer and Massey argue that a coyote, if employed, always serves as the primary crossing guide.

The independent variables included in our analysis are sex, age, prior U.S. trip experience, place of origin, and period. Age is a measure of general human capital and is taken to indicate increasing maturity, judgment, and wisdom. As human capital increases, we expect migrants to be more likely to use a guide for border crossing. We also expect that increasing human capital and the use of a guide will, in turn, lower the odds of apprehension.

On later trips, migration-specific human capital is measured using the number of prior U.S. trips as a proxy. We expect that as this kind of human capital increases (that is, as experience and knowledge of border crossing rises with each trip), the odds of crossing with a guide (either coyote or friend or relative) will decline and the mode of crossing should have a smaller effect on the likelihood of being apprehended. As Singer and Massey (1998) have shown, over time people substitute their own migration-specific capital for the use of paid smugglers and social capital. Finally, we control for region and period of entry with sets of dummy variables.

SEX DIFFERENCES IN BORDER CROSSING

In table 6.1 we present means by gender for all variables in our analysis. On both first and later trips, neither men nor women were likely to cross the border alone: only 4 percent of women and 6 percent of men entered by themselves on their first U.S. trip. On later trips, the respective percentages rose somewhat but reached only 9 percent among the former and 13 percent among the latter. Both men and women were likely to cross in the company of others, but females were much more likely to rely on the services of a paid guide. Whereas 39 percent of women crossed with a coyote on their first trip and 27 percent did so on subsequent trips, the respective percentages for men were only 13 and 10 percent. Men were relatively more likely to cross with friends or other family members: 81 percent on first trips and 77 percent on later trips, compared with 57 and 64 percent, respectively, among women.

Consistent with our hypotheses and with their heavier reliance on professional border crossing services, women's probabilities of apprehension were much lower than those of men. Whereas the likelihood of apprehension for females was 12 percent on the first trip and 14 percent on later trips, the probability was 29 percent for men, irrespective of trip order. The figure for males is very close to the figure of 32 to 33 percent found in prior studies (Espenshade 1990; Massey and Singer 1995, 204).

With respect to our indicator of general human capital, women are, on average, older than men on both the first and subsequent trips: twenty-nine years old on their first trip and thirty-nine years old on later trips, compared with average ages of twenty-seven and thirty-three, respectively, for men. In addition, the age gap between women and men appears to grow as one progresses from first to later trips (from two years to six years). Pronounced gender differences in the number of trips are also evident: as of their most recent U.S. trip, men reported having taken slightly more than four prior trips, compared with just two for women.

Community distributions reveal substantial variability in the geographic origins of migrants by sex (owing mainly to the combination of data from the Mexican Migration Project and the Health and Migration Project). Among women, for example, 55 percent were interviewed in Houston or San Diego, another 8 percent each from Michoacán and Guanajuato

TABLE 6.1   Means of Variables Used in Analysis of Undocumented Border Crossing

Variable	All Trips Male	All Trips Female	First Trip Male	First Trip Female	Later Trips Male	Later Trips Female
Final outcome: apprehension	0.29	0.13	0.29	0.12	0.29	0.14
Mode of crossing						
Alone	0.11	0.05	0.06	0.04	0.13	0.09
Family or friends	0.78	0.59	0.81	0.57	0.77	0.64
Coyote	0.11	0.36	0.13	0.39	0.10	0.27
Age						
Average (years)	31.2	31.3	27.0	28.8	32.9	38.9
0 to 24	0.31	0.37	0.53	0.45	0.22	0.15
25 to 34	0.36	0.30	0.27	0.30	0.40	0.32
35 to 44	0.21	0.17	0.13	0.14	0.24	0.26
45 and older	0.12	0.15	0.08	0.11	0.13	0.27
Migration-specific human capital						
Prior U.S. trips	3.00	0.52	—	—	4.20	2.10
Prior apprehensions	0.45	0.10	0.67	0.10	0.35	0.09
Interview state						
Jalisco	0.15	0.04	0.12	0.05	0.15	0.04
Michoacán	0.11	0.08	0.10	0.03	0.12	0.21
Guanajuato	0.15	0.08	0.15	0.05	0.15	0.15
Nayarit	0.03	0.07	0.05	0.05	0.03	0.12
Zacatecas	0.21	0.04	0.11	0.03	0.25	0.05
Guerrero	0.03	0.04	0.03	0.03	0.03	0.07
San Luis Potosí	0.14	0.04	0.13	0.05	0.14	0.04
Colima	0.03	0.02	0.04	0.02	0.03	0.00
Oaxaca	0.03	0.00	0.06	0.00	0.02	0.00
Sinaloa	0.01	0.02	0.02	0.01	0.01	0.03
Puebla	0.02	0.01	0.05	0.01	0.01	0.00
Baja California	0.02	0.01	0.03	0.01	0.01	0.00
Aguascalientes	0.05	0.01	0.06	0.01	0.05	0.00
Houston or San Diego	0.03	0.55	0.07	0.64	0.01	0.29
Period						
1980 to 1986	0.60	0.37	0.57	0.37	0.62	0.40
1987 to 1992	0.31	0.47	0.34	0.48	0.29	0.45
1993 to 1997	0.09	0.15	0.09	0.15	0.09	0.15
N	4,967	291	1,483	218	3,484	73
Percentage from Health and Migration Survey	2.9	55.3	7.0	64.2	1.2	28.8

Source: Data from Mexican Migration Project and Health and Migration Project.

samples, and 7 percent from surveys in Nayarit. Among men, 15 percent were surveyed in Jalisco, 15 percent in Guanajuato, and 21 percent in Zacatecas. Together, Houston and San Diego accounted for just 3 percent of the male interviews.

DETERMINANTS OF MODE OF CROSSING

The descriptive results presented so far confirm our leading hypotheses: women are more likely than men to make use of paid crossing services; they experience lower odds of apprehension; and their background characteristics are different from those of men, being older and having had less experience in the United States. Our analytic strategy is to examine actual border-crossing behavior to see whether, ceteris paribus, the social process differs for men and women and whether female border-crossing behavior is different now from what it was in the past. To consider these issues fully, ideally we would seek to estimate separate models for men and women. But even with our merging of the Mexican Migration Project and Health and Migration Project data sets, the number of women is too small to sustain reliable multivariate analyses.

We therefore combined men and women and included a dummy variable to represent gender in the equation. To test for differences in female behavior over time, in a separate regression we interacted the female dummy variable with dummies for period. Table 6.2 presents coefficients for two multinomial logit models estimated to predict the mode of border crossing. The first model (on the left-hand side) includes no interactions between gender and period, whereas the second model (right-hand side) includes terms to capture this contingency. Like Singer and Massey (1998), we pooled the data for initial and subsequent trips because separate models (not shown) did not reveal significant differences in the determinants of mode of crossing by trip order.

In the additive model, female undocumented migrants were more likely than their male counterparts to cross with family or friends but just as likely to cross with coyotes. Irrespective of gender, respondents were more likely to cross with others (either coyotes or friends or family) if they were under the age of forty-five, left after 1992, or were interviewed in the states of Nayarit or Zacatecas. Compared with migrants from Jalisco (the reference category), those from Baja California were less likely to cross either with family or friends or with a coyote. Migrants interviewed in Guanajuato, San Luis Potosí, and in the United States (Houston or San Diego) were notably less likely to have crossed the border using a coyote,

TABLE 6.2   Multinomial Logit Models Predicting Mode of Undocumented Border Crossing

	Additive Model						Interactive Model					
	With Family or Friends		With Coyote				With Family or Friends		With Coyote			
Variable	B	Standard Error	B	Standard Error			B	Standard Error	B	Standard Error		
Sex												
Male	—	—	—	—			—	—	—	—		
Female	0.726*	0.423	0.532	0.447			0.155	0.514	−0.086	0.545		
Age												
0 to 24	—	—	—	—			—	—	—	—		
25 to 34	0.059	0.249	−0.127	0.215			0.069	0.249	−0.119	0.215		
35 to 44	0.173	0.293	−0.321	0.233			0.191	0.292	−0.307	0.232		
45 and older	−0.960**	0.308	−0.981**	0.236			−0.946**	0.309	−0.974**	0.238		
Period												
1980 to 1986	—	—	—	—			—	—	—	—		
1987 to 1992	0.220	0.208	0.039	0.169			0.158	0.219	−0.079	0.171		
1993 to 1997	0.793**	0.379	0.545*	0.325			0.553	0.447	0.534	0.336		
Interview state												
Jalisco	—	—	—	—			—	—	—	—		
Michoacán	−0.045	0.395	0.248	0.284			−0.038	0.395	0.262	0.286		
Guanajuato	0.195	0.281	−1.350**	0.195			0.194	0.281	−1.340**	0.195		
Nayarit	1.460**	0.561	0.963**	0.455			1.470**	0.552	0.980***	0.444		
Zacatecas	0.731**	0.292	0.519**	0.208			0.728***	0.293	0.515**	0.208		

(Table continues on p. 122.)

TABLE 6.2   Multinomial Logit Models Predicting Mode of Undocumented Border Crossing (Continued)

| | Additive Model | | | | Interactive Model | | | |
| | With Family or Friends | | With Coyote | | With Family or Friends | | With Coyote | |
Variable	B	Standard Error	B	Standard Error	B	Standard Error	B	Standard Error
Guerrero	0.341	0.826	1.400**	0.637	0.375	0.825	1.410**	0.636
San Luis Potosí	0.226	0.425	−0.844**	0.360	0.243	0.425	−0.849**	0.362
Colima	−1.460**	0.594	−0.518	0.382	−1.440**	0.588	−0.508	0.372
Oaxaca	−0.178	0.610	−0.085	0.383	−0.116	0.610	−0.064	0.383
Sinaloa	1.170*	0.701	−0.072	0.623	1.250*	0.688	−0.048	0.612
Puebla	−0.284	0.603	−0.348	0.475	−0.213	0.603	−0.334	0.475
Baja California	−1.660**	0.497	−2.360**	0.393	−1.610**	0.491	−2.360**	0.396
Aguascalientes	1.480	0.940	1.550**	0.489	1.520*	0.950	1.560**	0.489
Houston or San Diego	0.514	0.362	−1.960**	0.318	0.483	0.355	−2.020**	0.309
Migration-specific human capital: prior U.S. trips	−0.967**	0.239	−0.895**	0.214	−0.992**	0.244	−0.917**	0.220
Interactions								
Female* 1987 to 1992	—	—	—	—	1.170	0.752	1.550*	0.758
Female* 1993 to 1997	—	—	—	—	1.180	1.140	0.508	1.120
Intercept	0.543	0.340	3.160**	0.268	0.586*	0.348	2.210**	0.277
Log likelihood	−2,971.29**				−2,961.56***			
N	4,685				4,685			

Source: Data from Mexican Migration Project and Health and Migration Project.
Note: B = unstandardized coefficients.
*p < .1   **p < .05

whereas those from Guerrero and Aguascalientes were significantly more likely to do so. As in earlier studies, the number of prior trips is negatively related to the odds of crossing with others. With more trips and therefore greater knowledge about the border and how to cross it, migrants grow more likely to cross by themselves.

Coefficients in the interactive model provide a further indication that gender matters in border crossing. The inclusion of the interaction term reduces the main effect of gender to insignificance, and the coefficient for the interaction between being female and leaving between 1987 and 1992 is now positive and significant in predicting the use of a coyote. Thus the descriptive result that females are more likely than males to use coyotes appears to reflect a heightened propensity on the part of women to rely on paid smuggling services during the period immediately following the implementation of the 1986 Immigration Reform and Control Act.

GENDER AND THE LIKELIHOOD OF APPREHENSION

Following Singer and Massey's (1998) analysis of the social process of undocumented border crossing, we move on to consider what determines the odds of apprehension by the U.S. Border Patrol, including the mode of crossing. Table 6.3 presents the results of simple logit regressions estimated to predict the likelihood of apprehension during a given attempt at crossing, where the outcome is coded 1 if an apprehension is observed and 0 otherwise. The left-hand columns show additive and interactive models predicting the odds of apprehension on first trips to the United States. The controls for place of interview generally show that odds of apprehension were generally lower in places other than Jalisco, and notably for those surveyed in Guerrero, Colima, Baja California, and Houston or San Diego.

Unlike those in the descriptive results presented in table 6.1, however, the coefficients here indicate no gender differences in the odds of apprehension, implying that the lower chances observed earlier stemmed from the greater proclivity of females to cross with others, particularly coyotes. As can be seen, both crossing with others and crossing with coyotes sharply reduce the odds of apprehension, meaning that if women are more likely to cross with others than by themselves, they will be apprehended less often, other things being equal. The addition of gender-period interactions does not change the main effects much, but it does indicate a heightened risk of female apprehension after 1992, when the border enforcement buildup truly began. During

TABLE 6.3   Multinomial Logit Model Predicting Mode of Undocumented Border Crossing, First Trip and Later Trips

| | First Trip | | | | Later Trips | | | |
| | Additive Model | | Interactive Model | | Additive Model | | Interactive Model | |
Variable	B	Standard Error	B	Standard Error	B	Standard Error	B	Standard Error
Sex								
Male	—	—	—	—	—	—	—	—
Female	0.139	0.076	−0.055	0.097	−1.550**	0.126	−1.680**	0.183
Age								
0 to 24	—	—	—	—	—	—	—	—
25 to 34	−0.071	0.052	−0.078	0.053	−0.373**	0.042	−0.372**	0.042
35 to 44	0.036	0.071	0.061	0.072	−0.358**	0.042	−0.357**	0.042
45 and older	−0.415**	0.098	−0.399**	0.098	−0.382**	0.061	−0.383**	0.061
Period								
1980 to 1986	—	—	—	—	—	—	—	—
1987 to 1992	−0.568**	0.050	−0.590**	0.053	−0.228**	0.038	−0.233**	0.038
1993 to 1997	−0.449**	0.091	−0.696**	0.107	−0.471**	0.076	−0.480**	0.077
Mode of crossing								
Alone	—	—	—	—	—	—	—	—
With family or friends	−0.619**	0.100	−0.625**	0.100	−0.009	0.067	−0.013	0.068
With coyote	−0.459**	0.087	−0.449**	0.087	0.132**	0.053	0.131**	0.053

Interview state	B	SE	B	SE	B	SE	B	SE
Jalisco	—	—	—	—	—	—	—	—
Michoacán	−0.068	0.087	−0.073	0.087	−0.347**	0.057	−0.346**	0.058
Guanajuato	−0.236**	0.090	−0.234**	0.090	0.196**	0.061	0.197**	0.061
Nayarit	−0.264**	0.087	−0.265**	0.087	−0.651**	0.071	−0.650**	0.071
Zacatecas	−0.217**	0.105	−0.222**	0.105	−0.770**	0.068	−0.771**	0.068
Guerrero	−0.844**	0.131	−0.837**	0.132	−0.158*	0.113	−0.158*	0.113
San Luis Potosí	−0.585**	0.100	−0.570**	0.100	−0.305**	0.074	−0.304**	0.074
Colima	−1.200**	0.127	−1.180**	0.127	−1.960**	0.172	−1.960**	0.172
Oaxaca	0.212	0.150	0.242*	0.106	−0.604**	0.220	−0.600**	0.220
Sinaloa	0.104	0.200	0.140	0.201	1.810**	0.241	1.820**	0.242
Puebla	−0.094	0.151	−0.052	0.151	0.150	0.209	0.155	0.209
Baja California	−1.640**	0.170	−1.600**	0.171	0.157	0.159	0.157	0.159
Aguascalientes	0.178	0.113	0.137	0.113	0.190**	0.091	0.193**	0.091
Houston or San Diego	−1.590**	0.017	−1.610**	0.109	−0.429**	0.092	−0.427**	0.090
Interactions								
Female* 1987 to 1992	—	—	0.214	0.155	—	—	0.239	0.265
Female* 1993 to 1997	—	—	1.060**	0.203	—	—	0.344	0.400
Intercept	−0.067	0.111	−0.058	0.111	−0.461**	0.072	−0.459**	0.072
Log likelihood	−6,941.96**		−6,228.82**		−11,044.11**		−11,043.52	
N	1,630		1,630		3,029		3,029	

Source: Data from Mexican Migration Project and Health and Migration Project.

Note: B = unstandardized coefficients.

*p < .1   **p < .05

this period, men's and women's odds of apprehension were considerably different. By combining the main and interactive effects we can see the contrast. For women leaving after 1992, the relative odds of being apprehended are indicated by the sum of the coefficients for gender, period, and their interaction: $-.055 + -.696 + 1.060 = .309$, compared with a coefficient for men of $-.696$.

The models estimated for later trips (shown in right-hand columns of table 6.3) show that experienced women generally face much lower odds of apprehension than experienced men and that there is no significant interaction with period of departure. Whether they crossed from 1987 to 1992 or from 1993 to 1997, women's chances of being arrested were significantly lower on later trips. The results also suggest that age plays an important role in determining the odds of apprehension among experienced migrants. As the sample ages, the chances of being arrested drop considerably. Also important in this respect were period of entry and crossing with a coyote. Compared with those entering before 1987, experienced migrants entering from 1987 to 1997 evinced a declining likelihood of apprehension, but other things being equal, using a smuggler increased the likelihood of being arrested. Once again there is considerable variability in place effects. For example, compared with Jalisco, the probability of arrest was significantly lower among those surveyed in Michoacán, Nayarit, Oaxaca, and especially Colima but higher for those interviewed in Guanajuato, Aguascalientes, particularly in Sinaloa.

CONCLUSION

Although prior qualitative work suggests the process of clandestine entry might differ between men and women, the quantitative studies done to date have focused exclusively on males. Drawing upon new data available from the Health and Migration Project and combining it with information from the Mexican Migration Project, we created a sample of female migrants sufficient to sustain an analysis of undocumented border crossing. Even after pooling the two data sets, however, multivariate analyses could only be carried out on men and women together, with gender indicated as a dummy variable.

Nonetheless, descriptive results reveal patterns consistent with hypotheses derived from the qualitative research literature. First, women are much less likely to cross by themselves compared with men, and when they cross in the company of other people women are much more likely than men to use the services of a paid guide, or coyote. Second, the odds of female migration are generally lower than those of men on both first and subsequent trips. Third, when women migrate without documents they do so at older ages, and on any given trip to the United States they have less accumulated migratory experience than men.

Multivariate analyses confirm that, other things being equal, women are more likely than men to cross with others rather than alone, and the interactive model suggests that the female tendency to rely on coyotes was characteristic of the period immediately following implementation of the Immigration Reform and Control Act, from 1987 through 1992. Results also suggest that men and women display a common underlying tendency to migrate alone as they get older and to substitute personal knowledge of border crossing for the use of guides as migratory experience increases. The latter tendencies are only suggestive, however, as limited degrees of freedom did not permit the estimation of separate models for men and women.

Multivariate analyses also show that on their initial U.S. trips, the likelihood of apprehension did not differ for men and women, once mode of crossing was controlled. Crossing with others sharply lowered the odds of apprehension. Thus women's more frequent use of family, friends, or coyotes as guides appears to explain their lower risk of arrest during crossing, at least on first trips. However, the odds of apprehension seem to have risen differentially for women after the border began to be militarized in 1993.

On later trips, women experienced a systematically lower risk of apprehension no matter what the period or mode of crossing. We also observe a relatively strong effect of age in reducing the odds of apprehension among experienced U.S. migrants. The meaning of the latter findings cannot be fully understood given the limitations of our data. Nonetheless, our admittedly preliminary evidence suggests that there are important differences between men and women in the process of undocumented border crossing and that the size and nature of these differences may have changed over time. If the peculiarities of female border crossing are ever to be characterized with any precision, investigators will have to make a greater effort to gather border-crossing histories from female migrants. To date, efforts have focused almost exclusively on men; but until women are incorporated into data sets as fully as men, there will not be enough cases for the sort of multivariate analyses that have proved so useful in understanding and characterizing the process of male undocumented migration.

References

Andreas, Peter. 2000. *Border Games: Policing the U.S.-Mexico Divide*. Ithaca, N.Y.: Cornell University Press.

Calavita, Kitty. 1992. *Inside the State: The Bracero Program, Immigration, and the I.N.S.* New York: Routledge.

Cerrutti, Marcela, and Douglas S. Massey. 2001. "On the Auspices of Female Migration from Mexico to the United States." *Demography* 38(2): 187–200.

Chavez, Leo R. 1992. *Shadowed Lives: Undocumented Immigration in American Society.* New York: Harcourt Brace Jovanovich.

Conover, Ted. 1987. *Coyotes: A Journey Through the Secret World of America's Illegal Aliens.* New York: Random House.

Crane, Keith, Beth J. Asch, Joanna Zorn Heilbrunn, and Danielle C. Cullinane. 1990. *The Effect of Employer Sanctions on the Flow of Undocumented Immigrants to the United States.* Santa Monica, Calif.: RAND Corporation.

Davis, Marilyn P. 1990. *Mexican Voices/American Dreams: An Oral History of Mexican Immigration to the United States.* New York: Holt & Company.

Donato, Katharine M. 1993. "Current Trends and Patterns of Female Migration: Evidence from Mexico." *International Migration Review* 27(4): 748–71.

———. 1994. "U.S. Policy and Mexican Migration to the United States, 1942–92." *Social Science Quarterly* 75(4): 705–29.

Donato, Katharine M., and Rebecca S. Carter. 1999. "U.S. Policy on Illegal Immigration: A Thirty Year Retrospective." In *Illegal Immigration in America: A Reference Handbook*, edited by David W. Haines and Karen E. Rosenblum. Westport, Conn.: Greenwood Press.

Donato, Katharine M., Jorge Durand, and Douglas S. Massey. 1992. "Stemming the Tide? Assessing the Deterrent Effects of the Immigration Reform and Control Act." *Demography* 29: 139–57.

Dunn, Timothy J. 1996. *The Militarization of the U.S.-Mexico Border, 1978–1992: Low-Intensity Conflict Doctrine Comes Home.* Austin: University of Texas, Center for Mexican American Studies.

Durand, Jorge. 1994. *Más allá de la línea: Patrones migratorios entre México y Estados Unidos.* Mexico City: Consejo Nacional de la Cultura y las Artes.

———. 1996. *El Norte es como el mar: Entrevistas a trabajadores migrantes en Estados Unidos.* Guadalajara, Mexico: University of Guadalajara.

———. 1998. "¿Nuevas regiones migratorias?" In *Población, desarrollo y globalización*, edited by René M. Zenteno, vol. 2, *V reunión de Investigación Sociodemográfica en México.* Mexico City: Sociedad Mexicana de Demografía and El Colegio de la Frontera Norte.

Durand, Jorge, and Douglas S. Massey. 1995. *Miracles on the Border: Retablo Paintings of Mexican Migrants to the United States.* Tucson: University of Arizona Press.

Durand, Jorge, Douglas S. Massey, and Emilio A. Parrado. 1999. "The New Era of Mexican Migration to the United States." *Journal of American History* 86: 518–36.

Eschbach, Karl, Jacqueline M. Hagan, Nestor P. Rodríguez, Rubén Hernández-León, Stanley Bailey. 1999. "Death at the Border." *International Migration Review* 33(2): 430–40.

Espenshade, Thomas J. 1990. "Undocumented Migration to the United States: Evidence from a Repeated Trials Model." In *Undocumented Migration to the United*

States: IRCA and the Experience of the 1980s, edited by Frank D. Bean, Barry Edmonston, and Jeffrey S. Passel. Washington, D.C.: Urban Institute.

Espenshade, Thomas J., and Dolores Acevedo. 1995. "Migrant Cohort Size, Enforcement Effort, and the Apprehension of Undocumented Aliens." *Population Research and Policy Review* 14: 145–72.

Goldring, Luin. 1996. "Gendered Memory: Constructions of Rurality among Mexican Transnational Migrants." In *Creating the Countryside: The Politics of Rural and Environmental Discourse*, edited by E. Melanie DuPuis and Peter Vandergeest. Philadelphia, Pa.: Temple University Press.

Graham, Wade. 1996. "Masters of the Game: How the U.S. Protects the Traffic in Cheap Mexican Labor." *Harper's*, July 1996, 35–50.

Grindle, Merilee. 1988. *Searching for Rural Development*. Ithaca, N.Y.: Cornell Press.

Hagan, Jacqueline M. 1998. "Social Networks, Gender and Immigrant Settlement: Resource and Constraint." *American Sociological Review* 63(1): 55–67.

Hagan, Jacqueline M., and Susan Gonzalez Baker. 1993. "Implementing the U.S. Legalization Program: The Influence of Immigrant Communities and Local Agencies on Immigration Policy Reform." *International Migration Review* 27: 513–37.

Halsell, Grace. 1978. *The Illegals*. New York: Stein and Day.

Hellman, Judith. 1994. *Mexican Lives*. New York: The New Press.

Heyman, Josiah M. 1995. "Putting Power in the Anthropology of Bureaucracy: The Immigration and Naturalization Service at the Mexico–United States Border." *Current Anthropology* 36: 261–87.

Hondagneu-Sotelo, Pierrette. 1994. *Gendered Transitions: Mexican Experiences of Immigration*. Berkeley: University of California Press.

Kanaiaupuni, Shawn M. 2000. "Reframing the Migration Question: An Analysis of Men, Women and Gender in Mexico." *Social Forces* 78(4): 1311–48.

Kossoudji, Sherrie A. 1992. "Playing Cat and Mouse at the U.S.-Mexican Border." *Demography* 29(2): 159–80.

Lindstrom, David. 1991. "The Differential Role of Family Networks in Individual Migration Decisions." Paper presented to the Population Association of America annual meeting, Washington, D.C., March 21–23.

Massey, Douglas S., Rafael Alarcón, Jorge Durand, and Humberto González. 1987. *Return to Aztlán: The Social Process of International Migration from Western Mexico*. Berkeley: University of California Press.

Massey, Douglas S., Jorge Durand, and Nolan J. Malone. 2002. *Beyond Smoke and Mirrors: Mexican Immigration in an Era of Free Trade*. New York: Russell Sage Foundation.

Massey, Douglas S., and Audrey Singer. 1995. "New Estimates of Undocumented Mexicans: Migration and the Probability of Apprehension." *Demography* 32: 203–13.

Pedraza, Silvia. 1991. "Women and Migration: The Social Consequences of Gender." *Annual Review of Sociology* 17: 303–25.

Quintanilla, Michael, and Peter Copeland. 1996. "Mexican Maids: El Paso's Worst-Kept Secret." In *U.S. Borderlands: Historical and Contemporary Perspectives,* edited by Oscar J. Martinez. Wilmington, Del.: Scholarly Resource Books.

Siems, Larry. 1992. *Between the Lines: Letters Between Undocumented Mexican and Central American Immigrants and Their Families and Friends.* Hopewell, N.J.: Ecco Press.

Singer, Audrey, and Douglas S. Massey. 1998. "The Social Process of Undocumented Border Crossing Among Mexican Migrants." *International Migration Review* 32: 561–92.

Spener, David. 2003. "Controlling the Border in El Paso del Norte: Operation Blockade or Operation Charade?" In *Ethnography at the Border,* edited by Pablo Vila. Minneapolis: University of Minnesota Press.

Stephen, Lynn. 1992. *Zapotec Women.* Austin: University of Texas Press.

Waumbaugh, Joseph. 1984. *Lines and Shadows.* New York: Morrow.

CHAPTER 7

WIVES LEFT BEHIND: THE LABOR MARKET BEHAVIOR OF WOMEN IN MIGRANT COMMUNITIES

María Aysa and Douglas S. Massey

MIGRATION FROM developing to developed countries has been widely studied over the past two decades. Much of this research has focused on the causes and consequences of Latin American migration to the United States. Although studies have described the process by which migrants and their partners integrate within U.S. labor markets (see Cerrutti and Massey 2001; Dinerman 1978; Gurak and Kritz 1996; Ortiz 1996), studies of the labor market behavior of family members left behind, particularly women, remains limited (Fernández 1997; Massey et al. 1987; Pessar 1982).

Whatever the effects of male migration, women's labor force participation is obviously influenced by the social context in which women live. In the case of women left behind, an important context is the social construction of gender. Mexico is a patriarchal culture characterized by a high degree of female subordination within the household combined with low rates of marital dissolution and family instability (Goldring 1996; Hondagneu-Sotelo 1992, 1994). Cohabitation, separation, and divorce are rare, though their frequency has been growing in recent years (Fernández, Avil, and Garcia 1999).

Female labor force behavior is also dependent on the immediate economic context—the array of opportunities available locally for paid employment—which we proxy by community size. In small towns and villages, most jobs are in agriculture and are frequently unpaid, yielding few opportunities for work outside the household. In Latin America women are employed infrequently in both peasant and capital-intensive agriculture (Ward 1985),

131

yielding few opportunities for income generation in rural areas. Large metropolitan areas, in contrast, contain robust manufacturing and service sectors that create dynamic labor markets that offer many opportunities for female employment.

We hypothesize that the economic pressure caused by the departure of a husband pushes women into the paid workforce. With the militarization of the border during the 1990s, especially, undertaking a trip to the United States became quite costly. According to Douglas Massey, Jorge Durand, and Nolan Malone (2002), the average cost of a coyote (a border smuggler) went from $189 in 1990 to $482 in 1998. As a result of these rising costs, men frequently must go into debt to pay the up-front costs of undocumented migration; even if they do not have to borrow, it still takes time and money to move, acquire housing, and find a job. As a result, wives and children left behind face a growing period of time without regular financial support from an absent husband. It may be several months before a male migrant finds himself in a position to remit money back to his family on a regular basis, creating a short-term cash-flow crisis that creates strong incentives—and, at times, the necessity—for wives to find paid employment as a means of bolstering family income, at least temporarily.

We generally expect these incentives to be expressed in terms of higher rates of female employment. But we hypothesize that the effect will be observed more in urban than in rural areas. The labor market in small communities is necessarily limited in size, offering few opportunities for paid labor outside the household; and Mexico's patriarchal culture is generally much stronger in small towns than in large cities, yielding strong, community-enforced expectations that remittances will be sent and discouraging the entry of wives into the public sphere of work. Patriarchal constraints on women tend to be much weaker in large Mexican cities, where female employment opportunities are relatively abundant and female labor force participation is commonplace.

HUSBANDS' MIGRATION AND WIVES' BEHAVIOR

Previous studies examining the effect of husbands' international migration on the economic and social roles of their wives are inconclusive. Evidence suggests that wives respond in different ways to the absence of their husbands. Charles Wood (1981) claims that household behavior should be conceptualized as a series of sustenance strategies undertaken to maintain a dynamic balance between consumption needs, labor power, and the alternatives for generating monetary and nonmonetary resources. International migration constitutes one kind of strategy (Massey et al. 1998) in which costs of absent migrant members are met through the income-generating activities of those left behind until remittances are received from abroad (Meillassoux 1981).

Massey and colleagues (1987) have found that in the course of recurrent male migration to the United States, Mexican wives assumed total responsibility for the care and education of the children and occasionally for their support, as well. In her analysis of a rural migrant-sending community in northern Mexico, Leticia Fernández (1997) finds that, controlling for a wife's age and the length of her husband's absence, educated wives were more likely to undertake income-generating activities than those without schooling. For all women, each additional month the husband was absent from the household lowered the odds of a wife's employment. Fernandez notes, however, that wives of migrating husbands were expected to take charge of feeding the family even if remittances were not immediately forthcoming, though local income-generating activities for women were few and offered low pay.

Rosa Espinoza and María Cebada (1999) have examined the behavior of wives left behind in three towns of Guanajuato, a state with a relatively high prevalence of emigration. Their interviews reveal that women who received insufficient remittance income were able to look for income-generating activities in nearby urban areas, which contained an abundance of maquiladoras and packing plants, as well as opportunities for domestic service. They generally preferred the former to the latter. During the past decade many urban and semiurban communities have been explicitly organized to produce goods and services relying on female labor.

Feminist theory suggests that decisions concerning labor supply and consumption at the household level are conditioned by the relative bargaining power of husbands and wives, which is constrained by cultural norms (Manser and Brown 1980; Rao and Greene 1996). According to Sherri Grasmuck and Patricia Pessar (1991), the internal hierarchies of power within Latin American households are based largely on income generation and gender. Under these circumstances, a wife can engage in income-generating activities to raise her position only when permitted to do so by local cultural conventions. Gendered power relations are frequently enforced by the extended family, which is committed to household well-being but also to the respectability of all its members. In the absence of the husband, an extended family may be obliged to protect and support the wife, but she, in turn, is obliged to respect traditional gender roles and customs regarding work outside the home. In Mexico, women can and do influence family decisions, but their bargaining power varies by age, household position, and rural versus urban location (Ortiz 1996).

Ethnographic studies have documented the mechanics of gendered power relations in both Mexico and the Dominican Republic. In a study of a rural Dominican community, Eugenia Georges (1990) finds that women in formal marriages were more constrained in their decision making than women in consensual unions. In many instances, a married woman was expected to move in with her parents or in-laws upon the departure of her husband for work in the United States. A husband who sent remittances remained in his normative role as breadwinner, thus preserving his decision-making authority within the household.

In her analysis of a rural community in Mexico, Macrina de Alarcón (1983) has found a similar pattern in which young wives moved in with their mothers-in-law, who received remittances directly from their migrant sons, once again preserving male power. Family power relations in Mexico continue to be dominated by males (Oliveira 1998). Although women are gradually becoming more autonomous in Mexican society, in the working classes and rural areas male dominance is still strong, though it varies with age, education, and occupation (Benería and Roldán 1987; Oliveira 1998).

To analyze the effects of a husband's migration on a wife's labor market participation in the areas of origin, it is necessary to take account of a woman's life-cycle stage. In her conceptualization of the family life cycle, Linda Waite (1980) argues that systematic changes in family circumstances over time bring about shifts in the behavior of different family members. Although age is a factor, the most important changes are those involving marriage, childbearing, and children leaving home. She identifies a first stage that starts at marriage and ends with the birth of the first child. The second stage begins with the birth of the first child and ends with the birth of the last child; and the third stage begins when all the children have been born and ends just before they begin to leave the household. Women in the later part of the second stage and in the third stage are generally more responsive to family financial circumstances and to labor market opportunities than married women without children or those who expect to have more children.

Another issue to be considered in analyzing the effect of a male head's absence on wives' labor market behavior is the frequency, level, and certainty of remittances. Massey and colleagues (1987) analyze household budgets in four Mexican communities, comparing households with different configurations of internal and international migrants. They find that for households with members working in the United States, monthly remittances were the principal economic resource. Mariano Sana (2001) points out that the strong cohesion of Mexican families generates a relatively high degree of certainty that remittances will be sent. If remittances are received with certainty and in adequate amounts, then the wives left behind do not need to work and can dedicate their time to taking care of the children and the household. Whatever the effect of remittances, to accurately assess the labor market participation of wives it is necessary to control for the socioeconomic status of the household. Katharine Donato (1993) argues that land ownership generally binds women to the community and that business ownership reduces the likelihood that women work outside the home, if only because women are often the ones managing the household business.

Although the aforementioned studies offer valuable insights into the labor market behavior of women with migrant husbands, they do not explicitly model the cultural and economic context in which women live. We remedy this situation by specifying a model of wives' labor force participation and estimating it separately for rural and urban areas. We hypothesize that, contingent on life-cycle stage, human capital, family dependency, and economic resources, a married woman is more likely to participate in the paid workforce when her husband is away working in the United States than when he is at home in the community. However, we expect that such an increase in labor force participation will be expressed in urban but not rural areas, because of both the looser patriarchal constraints and the wider array of employment opportunities in the former.

Our model of female labor force participation may be specified in terms of a simple prediction equation:

$$LFP = f(HMS, DEM, HC, HER), \tag{1}$$

where LFP refers to a married woman's labor force participation, HMS is the husband's migration status, DEM stands for the woman's demographic condition (life-cycle stage), HC is her human capital, and HER refers to the set of household economic resources at her disposal. We propose to estimate this equation separately in rural and urban areas and expect to find that migration increases female labor force participation in the latter but not the former.

DATA

Data come from the Mexican Migration Project. Table 7.1 shows means and standard deviations for the variables used to operationalize the various constructs included in equation (1). Two sets of measures are shown: one computed cross-sectionally for all married women aged fifteen to sixty-four at the time of the survey and another computed longitudinally for all

TABLE 7.1   Means and Standard Deviations for Variables Used in
             Analysis of Married Women's Labor Force Participation

	Married Women		Person-Years of Married Women	
Variable	Mean	Standard Deviation	Mean	Standard Deviation
Outcome: in labor force	0.182	0.386	0.191	0.342
Husband's status				
Migrant in Mexico	0.094	0.291	0.053	0.224
Migrant in United States	0.038	0.197	0.065	0.247
Demographic background				
Age	39.714	11.740	31.783	12.509
Number of children under the age of eighteen	2.560	2.063	2.550	2.245
First union	0.924	0.266	—	—
Urban residence	0.482	0.500	0.516	0.500
Human capital: education	5.335	4.022	5.103	3.968
Economic resources				
Monthly remittances (hundreds of dollars)	2.083	2.706	—	—
Home owned	0.686	0.464	0.571	0.495
Business owned	0.311	0.463	0.141	0.348
Land owned	0.199	0.399	0.166	0.372
Real estate owned	0.100	0.300	—	—
N	8,732		57,267	

Source: Data from Mexican Migration Project.
Note: The sample is married women aged fifteen to sixty-four at time of survey.

person-years lived by married women aged fifteen to sixty-four. We rely on data from communities surveyed after 1996, when spouses' labor histories were added to the Mexican Migrant Project questionnaire.

At the time of the survey, around 18 percent of working-age women were employed or looking for work, whereas in the average person-year that figure is around 19 percent. The absence of husbands through migration was not a frequent occurrence. At the time of the survey, 9 percent of husbands were absent elsewhere in Mexico, and 4 percent had gone to the United States. In the average person-year, however, 5 percent of women had a husband away somewhere in Mexico, and nearly 7 percent had a husband working in the United States. In terms of the woman's demographic situation at the time of the survey, the average working-age woman was almost forty years old with 2.6 children. Around half (48 percent) were living in an urban community (more than twenty-five thousand inhabitants), and 92 percent were in their first union. Information on the order of the union is not available in the life-history data, but the percentage is probably as high as or higher than that in the cross-section. In the average person-year observed, wives were around thirty-two years of age and had 2.6 children, and 52 percent lived in an urban setting.

Human capital is measured by educational attainment, which at the time of the survey stood at 5.4 years of schooling in the cross-section and 5.1 in the average person-year. Considering economic characteristics of the household, at the time of the survey 69 percent of wives lived in an owned home, 31 percent of their families owned a business, 20 percent owned land, and 10 percent owned some other kind of real estate. Of those receiving remittances, the average amount received was $208 per month. In the typical person-year, 57 percent of the women lived in an owned home, 14 percent had a family business, and 17 percent owned land. Unfortunately, data on remittances and information on other real estate holdings are not available from the life histories.

LABOR MARKET BEHAVIOR OF MIGRANTS' WIVES

Table 7.2 presents the results of a logistic regression equation predicting wives' labor force participation at the time of the survey, estimated separately for women living in urban and rural areas. As expected, the absence of a husband has no detectable effect on the labor market behavior of wives in rural areas. For them, participation is positively predicted by education and family business ownership, and it has a curvilinear relationship to age, at first rising and then falling with age (the typical age profile for employment). The number of minor children has no apparent effect in rural areas.

TABLE 7.2   Logistic Regression of Married Women's Female Labor Force Participation at Time of Survey on Selected Independent Variables

Independent Variable	Urban Communities		Rural Communities	
	B	Standard Error	B	Standard Error
Husband's status				
At home	—	—	—	—
Migrant in Mexico	−0.081	0.133	0.155	0.156
Migrant in United States	0.399[+]	0.242	0.029	0.224
Demographic background				
Age	0.257***	0.032	0.184***	0.031
Age squared	−0.003***	0.0004	−0.002***	0.0004
Children under the age of eighteen	−0.132**	0.030	−0.004	0.024
First union	0.255	0.171	0.120	0.170
Human capital: education	0.199***	0.011	0.186***	0.013
Economic resources				
Monthly remittances (hundreds of dollars)	−0.001	0.028	−0.044*	0.022
Home owned	−0.040	0.096	0.078	0.104
Business owned	0.905***	0.089	1.270***	0.088
Land owned	−0.130	0.176	0.005	0.096
Real estate owned	0.508***	0.128	0.178	0.134
Intercept	7.617***	0.617	7.066***	0.609
Likelihood ratio	677.549***		609.409***	
Wald chi squared	531.836***		517.029***	
N	4,214		4,158	

Source: Data from Mexican Migration Project.
Note: The sample is married women aged fifteen to sixty-four at time of survey.
B = coefficient estimate for each variable.
[+]$p < .1$ *$p < .05$ **$p < .01$ ***$p < .001$

The only other significant effect is remittances from the United States: the greater the remittances, the lower the likelihood that a wife will be productively engaged in work. With every hundred dollars received, the odds of working go down by around 4 percent (determined by taking the exponent of the regression coefficient). In rural areas, it is not the absence of the husband in the United States but the amount of money he is remitting home on a monthly basis that affects a woman's odds of working.

In urban communities, however, remittances have no effect on the likelihood of a wife's participation in the labor force. For urban wives, it is the absence of the husband in the United States that raises the odds of working, though the effect is significant only at the 10 percent level. (The effect is significant at 5 percent, however, when a one-tailed test is used.) Thus, irrespective of the amount of remittance sent home each month by a husband working in the United States, his mere absence increases the odds of employment outside the household. As with rural women, the effect of age is curvilinear, and the influence of education is positive, although both effects are slightly larger in the rural equations. However, unlike its effect in rural areas, the presence of minor children has a strong negative influence on the likelihood of female labor force participation in urban areas. Most likely, women in villages and towns have access to more relatives and trusted friends, and in any event are likely to work near to their children, compared with the situation in cities, where most neighbors are unknown, family members are absent or scattered, and places of work tend to be distantly separated from places of employment. As in rural areas, ownership of a family business increases the odds of female employment, as does ownership of real estate apart from the family home and agricultural land.

Table 7.3 continues the analysis by using dynamic methods of event-history analysis (Allison 1995, 1998) on the person-year data available from the life histories compiled from household heads and spouses. Women are followed year-by-year from the age of fifteen until either the age of sixty-five or the survey date (whichever comes first), and logistic regression is used to predict whether a wife is in the labor force in a particular year based on the migratory status of her husband and observed values of demographic, human capital, and economic control variables. As can be seen, as in the cross-sectional analysis there is no evidence that her husband's migration to the United States has any effect on the likelihood that a wife works; but in this analysis we do find a significant negative effect of internal migration from rural communities. Those wives living in rural areas with husbands working elsewhere in Mexico appear to be significantly less likely to enter the labor force than those with nonmigrant husbands. Similarly, in both urban and rural areas the effect of having minor children is strongly

TABLE 7.3   Event-History Analysis of Married Women's Labor Force Participation Across Person-Years

Independent Variable	Urban Communities		Rural Communities	
	B	Standard Error	B	Standard Error
Husband's status				
At Home	—	—	—	—
Migrant in Mexico	−0.018	0.062	−0.303**	0.126
Migrant in United States	0.099+	0.054	0.099	0.069
Demographic background				
Age	0.016+	0.008	0.018*	0.009
Age squared	−0.0006***	0.0001	−0.004**	0.0001
Children under the age of eighteen	−0.109***	0.010	−0.079***	0.004
Human capital: education	0.111***	0.004	0.107***	0.004
Economic resources				
Home owned	0.134***	0.034	−0.108**	0.037
Business owned	0.813***	0.041	0.816***	0.040
Land owned	0.395***	0.060	0.147***	0.039
Intercept	−1.939***	0.120	−2.117***	0.126
Likelihood ratio	2088.942***		1589.197***	
Wald chi squared	1,859.877***		1,547.987***	
N	29,561		27,706	

Source: Data from Mexican Migration Project.
Note: The sample is married women aged fifteen to sixty-four at time of survey.
B = coefficient estimate for each variable.
+$p < .1$ *$p < .05$ **$p < .01$ ***$p < .001$

negative when considered longitudinally. As before, business ownership and rising education increase the odds of female labor force participation, whereas the effect of age is curvilinear.

Although home ownership has no apparent influence in the cross-section, it exerts a significant negative influence on female employment in rural areas when viewed dynamically across the life course. Many migrants from rural communities go to the United States to raise capital for the construction or purchase of a home, and wives, by working as well, may shorten the time that a husband needs to stay away. If this important asset is already owned by the family, the husband must be migrating for other reasons to which the work contributions of the wife are less relevant. Nonetheless, ownership of real estate other than the home increases the odds of female employment in rural areas, perhaps by supplying a venue for commercial operations.

As before, having a husband away in the United States has a modest positive effect in elevating the odds of a wife's labor force participation in urban areas. The effect is marginally significant ($p < .10$) using a two-tailed test but stronger when a one-tailed test is employed ($p < .05$). In cities, the loss of a husband's financial and moral contributions to the family through international migration is more likely to push women into the workforce. As in the cross-sectional analysis, the effect of age is curvilinear, and the influences of education, business ownership, and land holding are positive; but so now is home ownership (whose effect was insignificant in the cross-sectional regression). It must be recalled, however, that owing to data limitations we are unable to control for the size of the remittance flow in any year.

CONCLUSION

In this chapter we have considered the consequences of male migration for women by comparing the labor force participation of wives with husbands who do and do not migrate. We hypothesized that, owing to the unique costs and risks of border crossing and the likely longer duration of trips to the United States, wives of international migrants would be "pushed" into the labor force out of economic necessity but that this effect was likely to be observed only in urban settings, where patriarchal constraints are weaker and opportunities for outside employment more abundant. Because of the lower costs, shorter trip durations, and more frequent visits from husbands working elsewhere in Mexico, we expected that the wives of internal migrants would not experience the same push toward employment in either urban or rural settings.

In general, estimates were consistent with expectations. There is no empirical evidence that internal migration by husbands in any way increases the propensity of wives to enter the labor force, either in the cross-section or across time. We did find that the migration of a husband to the United States increased the odds of a wife's labor force participation, but only in urban areas; and even in cities the effect was not particularly strong ($p < .10$, using a two-tailed test). We thus conclude that international migration has only a modest effect on the likelihood that women in urban areas will work. Apart from the migratory behavior of the husband, female labor force participation is more strongly determined by the variables one would expect: age, the presence of minor children, education, and asset ownership.

Finally, cross-sectional analyses suggest that her husband's migration influences a woman's labor force behavior in urban areas primarily through the size of the remittance flow. As the quantity of monthly remittances increases, the odds that a wife works outside the home steadily decline, by about 4 percent for each additional hundred dollars received.

To the extent that migration takes male breadwinners temporarily out of the family and pushes wives into the workforce, the resulting earnings of wives can be expected to increase their power and bargaining position in the family. Although using the crude data at our disposal we cannot measure this effect, we also suspect that the absence of the husband through international migration enhances the autonomy of women in other ways, by making them the sole authority in child rearing and daily household decision making, a shift in status that might also differ from rural to urban settings. Developing quantitative data to test this possibility should be a high priority for researchers interested in the interplay between migration and gender in developing-country settings such as Mexico.

REFERENCES

Alarcón, Macrina de. 1983. *La función social de las esposas de los migrantes: el caso de Chavinda, Michoacán*. Michoacán, Mex.: El Colegio de Michoacán.

Allison, Paul D. 1995. *Survival Analysis Using the SAS System: A Practical Guide*. Cary, N.C.: SAS Institute.

———. 1998. "Logit and Loglinear Analysis Using the SAS System." Unpublished manuscript. University of Pennsylvania, Population Studies Center.

Benería, Lourdes, and Martha Roldán. 1987. *The Crossroads of Class and Gender: Industrial Homework, Subcontracting, and Household Dynamics in Mexico City*. Chicago: University of Chicago Press.

Cerrutti, Marcela, and Douglas S. Massey. 2001. "On the Auspices of Female Migration from Mexico to the United States." *Demography* 38: 187–200.

Dinerman, Ina R. 1978. "Patterns of Adaptation Among Households of U.S.-Bound Migrants from Michoacán, Mexico." *International Migration Review* 12: 485–501.

Donato, Katharine M. 1993. "Current Trends and Patterns of Female Migration: Evidence from Mexico." *International Migration Review* 27: 748–71.

Espinoza, Rosa Aurora, and Maria del Carmen P. Cebada Contreras. 1999. "Mujeres sedentarias, hombres nomadas: Notas sobre la migración rural en Guanajuato." *Cuadernos del CICSUG*. Manuscript no. 20. Guadalajara: Universidad de Guanajuato, Centro de Investigaciones Sociales.

Fernández, Leticia. 1997. "Paternal Migration, Maternal Autonomy and Child Health in Mexico." Ph.D. diss., University of Pennsylvania.

Fernández, Patricia, Diana Avil, and Juan Enrique Garcia. 1999. "La Nupcialidad en México, patrones de continuidad y cambio en el ultimo cuarto de siglo." In *La Situación Demográfica de México 1999*, edited by Consejo Nacional de Población. Mexico City, Mex.: Consejo Nacional de Población.

Georges, Eugenia. 1990. *The Making of a Transnational Community: Migration, Development and Cultural Change in the Dominican Republic.* New York: Columbia University Press.

Goldring, Luin. 1996. "Gendered Memory: Constructions of Rurality among Mexican Transnational Migrants." In *Creating the Countryside: The Politics of Rural and Environmental Discourse*, edited by E. Melanie DuPuis and Peter Vandergeest. Philadelphia, Pa.: Temple University Press.

Grasmuck, Sherri, and Patricia R. Pessar 1991. *Between Two Islands: Dominican International Migration.* Berkeley: University of California Press.

Gurak, Douglas T., and Mary M. Kritz. 1996. "Social Context, Household Composition and Employment Among Migrant and Nonmigrant Dominican Women." *International Migration Review* 30: 399–422.

Hondagneu-Sotelo, Pierrette. 1992. "Overcoming Patriarchal Constraints: The Reconstruction of Gender Relations Among Mexican Immigrant Women and Men." *Gender and Society* 6: 393–415.

————. 1994. *Gendered Transitions: Mexican Experiences of Immigration.* Berkeley: University of California Press.

Manser, Marilyn, and Murray Brown. 1980. "Marriage and Household Decision-Making: A Bargaining Analysis." *International Economic Review* 21: 31–44.

Massey, Douglas S., Rafael Alarcón, Jorge Durand, and Humberto González. 1987. *Return to Aztlán: The Social Process of International Migration from Western Mexico.* Berkeley: University of California Press.

Massey, Douglas S., Joaquín Arango, Graeme Hugo, Ali Kouaouci, Adela Pellegrino, and J. Edward Taylor. 1998. *Worlds in Motion: Understanding International Migration at the End of the Millennium.* Oxford: Oxford University Press.

Massey, Douglas S., Jorge Durand, and Nolan Malone. 2002. *Beyond Smoke and Mirrors: Mexican Immigration in an Era of Free Trade.* New York: Russell Sage Foundation.

Meillassoux, Claude. 1981. *Maidens, Meals, and Money: Capitalism and the Domestic Community.* Cambridge: Cambridge University Press.

Oliveira, Orlandina. 1998. "Familia y relaciones de género en México." In *Familias y relaciones de género en transformación: Cambios trascendentales en America Latina y el Caríbe*, edited by Beatriz Schmukler. Mexico City: Population Council and EDAMEX.

Ortiz, Vilma. 1996. "Migration and Marriage among Puerto Rican Women." *International Migration Review* 30: 460–84.

Pessar, Patricia R. 1982. "The Role of Households in International Migration and the Case of U.S.-Bound Migration from the Dominican Republic." *International Migration Review* 16: 342–64.

Rao, Vijayendra, and Margaret E. Greene. 1996. "Marital Instability, Spousal Bargaining and Their Implications for Fertility in Brazil: An Interdisciplinary Analysis." Working paper. University of Chicago, Population Research Center.

Sana, Mariano. 2001. "Family Structure, Market Development and Remittances." Working paper. University of Pennsylvania, Population Studies Center.

Waite, Linda J. 1980. "Working Wives and the Family Life Cycle." *American Journal of Sociology* 86: 272–94.

Ward, Kathryn B. 1985. "Women and Urbanization in the World-System." In *Urbanization in the World-Economy*, edited by Michael Timberlake. Orlando, Fla.: Academic Press.

Wood, Charles H. 1981. "Structural Changes and Household Strategies: A Conceptual Framework for the Study of Rural Migration." *Human Organization* 40: 338–44.

PART III

❖

REGIONAL VARIATIONS

CHAPTER 8

TIJUANA'S PLACE IN THE MEXICAN MIGRATION STREAM: DESTINATION FOR INTERNAL MIGRANTS OR STEPPING STONE TO THE UNITED STATES?

Elizabeth Fussell

OVER THE PAST century the Mexico-U.S. border region, and Tijuana in particular, has had stronger economic and social ties to the United States than to central Mexico (Lorey 1999). A look at Tijuana's population history helps explain why. Tijuana's population growth during the twentieth century came mainly from internal migration within Mexico and return migration from the United States (Bustamante 1990; Zenteno 1995). In the early part of this century Tijuana was a small town, cut off from the rest of Mexico and accessible primarily by way of San Diego, California. The Mexican population living there was mainly employed in tourist services related to the casinos and race-tracks frequented by California's growing population and owned primarily by U.S. citizens.

The first surge in Tijuana's population occurred in the 1930s, when, in an effort to increase employment in California during the depression, U.S. government officials rounded up thousands of persons of Mexican origin and "returned" them to Tijuana—though many of those deported had never lived in Mexico. Around the same time, Mexico's president, Lázaro Cárdenas, encouraged the voluntary return of Mexicans living in the United States in order to populate the northern border and prevent U.S. economic interests from appropriating valuable Mexican

147

territory (Bustamante 1990). Ironically, therefore, Tijuana's population growth began with migrants from the United States.

Between the 1940s and the mid-1960s, Tijuana's growth was associated with the increasing demand for agricultural labor in California and the southwestern United States, owing initially to U.S. war mobilization and then to the expansion of the Bracero Program, a temporary worker program that admitted Mexican agricultural laborers into the United States on short-term employment visas. Braceros were almost all males, and most were recruited from rural communities in the central states of western Mexico. Often they brought families with them to Tijuana to establish a home base closer to the United States. In addition, internal migrants were attracted by the good prospects for work in cross-border commerce and tourism.

Population growth along the border slowed temporarily after the termination of the Bracero Program in 1965. However, export-oriented manufacturing began to grow in the early 1970s and helped maintain the economic vitality of Tijuana, which continues to attract some of Mexico's largest internal population flows (INEGI 1999). Indeed, the restructuring of industry and the creation of new export-processing zones has shifted development away from primary metropolitan centers and toward secondary urban areas, such as Tijuana, thereby creating more urban-to-urban migration flows toward the north. As a result, the origins and characteristics of international and border migrants are increasingly similar (Fussell and Massey 2004; Lozano Ascencio, Roberts, and Bean 1999). Both streams flow between urban labor markets and include workers seeking stable urban employment rather than the seasonal agricultural work typical of earlier migrants.

Although prior research has examined movement to and through the border, it has shed little light on movement from the border into the United States. California's border region has been conceptualized as a single urban system (Rubin-Kurtzman, Ham-Chande, Van Arsdol 1996) with frequent cross-border movements facilitated by a host of formal and informal institutions. Mexican border residents, for example, are allowed to hold "local passports" that allow them to travel within twenty-five miles of the border and to stay for up to seventy-two hours to visit relatives and friends or shop in U.S. stores (U.S. Department of Justice 1999). Although these border-crossing cards do not allow Mexicans to work, some inevitably do, though they risk losing the card if they cross too frequently and attract the attention of border inspectors. Border crossings by pedestrians and automobile passengers through Tijuana's checkpoints numbered more than 47 million in 1997 (U.S. Department of Transportation 2002, n.p.). Most crossers went into San Diego to shop, work, or pay social visits (Cox 1994).

Undocumented migration has historically been intense through the San Diego–Tijuana corridor. During 1993 nearly 45 percent of all undocumented migrants were apprehended in this sector (though this figure declined to 24 percent in 1997, after the implementation of Operation Hold-the-Line in September of 1993—see U.S. General Accounting Office 1997). In the other direction, many California residents travel to Baja California for social visits, shopping, or tourism (without needing documentation), thus contributing to the range of social and economic ties binding the two sides of the border together. Such individual-level movements are complemented by the growth of trade since 1965, when the Border Industrialization Program was first established, and especially since 1994, when the North American Free Trade Agreement took effect.

Long-standing social and economic ties within the border region distinguish international migration from Tijuana from that originating in the interior. I hypothesize that as a result of long-standing cross-border connections, Tijuana's residents are, in general, less likely than other Mexicans to migrate to the United States but more likely to travel with documents when they do migrate. In contrast to interior settings, Tijuana does not lack for employment or consumption opportunities. Indeed, residents have ample access to U.S. dollars by working in Tijuana's service, commercial, and tourist sectors. In addition, government employment surveys indicate that nearly 8 percent of Tijuana's labor force actually works in the United States, commuting daily to jobs across the border (Alegría 2000). In sum, high levels of cross-border trade, the free flow of dollars into the local economy, the existence of numerous cross-border linkages, and the unique opportunity for daily commuting to U.S. jobs all act to diminish the likelihood of undocumented migration and, to a lesser extent, documented migration from Tijuana to the United States.

DATA AND METHODS

The research reported here is based on data from a household survey conducted in Tijuana in conjunction with the Mexican Migration Project (see chapter 16). Using data on first and most recent trips to the United States, I select household members aged fifteen and older and examine means and percentage distributions to compare migrants originating in different kinds of communities with respect to frequency of migration, duration of trip, place of destination, and type of documentation. I then refine the sample to focus on household heads, who offer detailed data on employment characteristics during their most recent U.S. trip. Comparisons across communities demonstrate that more migration-related resources are available to Tijuana's migrants than to those from the interior and suggest that the city's binational economy constitutes a single labor market for border residents.

In the second part of the analysis, I undertake an event-history analysis predicting whether household heads make a documented or undocumented U.S. trip in a given year. The dependent variable has three categories: making an undocumented trip, making a documented trip, or not migrating at all. A U.S. trip is defined as change in the usual place of residence and excludes short trips for shopping, family visits, and daily commuting for work. I focus only on male household heads, since female heads evince distinct patterns of migration (Cerrutti and Massey 2001). Independent variables are time-varying indicators of demographic characteristics, occupation, human capital, and social capital. The event history selects person-years lived in the United States after 1964 and follows each person from the age of fifteen onward, noting annual changes in independent and dependent variables. For the analysis of first trips, I include all person-years up to the date of the survey or first migration and exclude others; for the analysis of most-recent trips, I include all person-years lived between the first trip and the date of the survey or the last trip, whichever came first. By taking into account change in a household head's characteristics and his probabilities of making a trip to the United States, the event-history method accounts for bias owing to right-hand censoring (that is, the failure to observe respondents after the time of the survey).

MIGRANTS FROM TIJUANA AND THE INTERIOR

Although Tijuana has historically been the primary passageway for Mexican migrants to the United States, the percentage of Tijuana's residents who have been in the United States is surprisingly low. Table 8.1 presents information on migrants originating in Tijuana, in urban areas of Mexico's interior (those with more than one hundred thousand in population), and in rural areas of the interior (those with fewer than one hundred thousand persons). As indicated at the bottom of the table, only 15 percent of Tijuana's residents have ever migrated to the United States, a percentage closer to the level observed in interior urban areas (10 percent) than that in rural areas (24 percent). Furthermore, U.S. migrants from

TABLE 8.1   Comparison of Migrants from Tijuana and Urban and Rural Interior Communities

Variable	Tijuana	Urban Interior	Rural Interior
Total migratory experience			
Number of U.S. trips	1.3	1.8	2.9
Months of U.S. experience	136.3	91.2	82.8
Destination on first U.S. trip (percentage)			
California	93.8	63.1	66.2
Other border state	2.1	10.9	13.8
Northwestern state	0.0	1.7	3.5
Midwestern state	1.4	1.5	5.9
Southern (nonborder) state	0.2	1.2	1.5
Northeastern state	0.6	5.8	1.3
Other	0.2	0.9	0.3
Missing	1.7	14.9	7.6
Documentation on first U.S. trip (percentage)			
Legal resident	22.9	11.1	10.1
Tourist visa or crossing card	33.1	10.2	5.6
U.S. citizen	0.8	16.2	9.0
No or false documents	40.9	57.8	69.3
Other	2.4	4.7	6.0
Number of migrants	632	1,370	15,484
Percentage of sample ever migrated	14.6	10.0	23.7

Source: Data from Mexican Migration Project.

Tijuana have made fewer trips than others (1.3 versus 1.8 in the urban interior and 2.9 in the rural interior); when they do migrate, they spend more time abroad than their counterparts from rural and urban interior communities (136 months versus 91 and 83 months, respectively). Their greater accumulation of U.S. experience may reflect a tendency to work in urban labor markets that offer full-year employment, compared with migrants from the interior, who are more likely to engage in seasonal agricultural employment.

California is the preferred destination for Mexicans from all sending regions; but it is almost the only destination for those from Tijuana. As shown in the second panel of table 8.1, 94 percent of Tijuana's migrants go to California on their first trip, compared with 63 percent from urban interior communities and 66 percent from rural interior communities, respectively. Figures for last trips (not shown) are similar. Although some recurrent migrants do relocate their families to Tijuana to form a base there (see Zabin and Hughes 1995), this does not appear to happen often enough to substantially raise the percentage of migrants emanating from Tijuana, nor does it increase the average number of trips. These findings support my contention that there is a distinct migration dynamic in Tijuana, one that is facilitated by proximity to the United States and the range of cross-border ties that it allows.

One way of measuring these ties is by the frequency of formal, legal arrangements for movement across the border. As previously discussed, border residents have access to local crossing cards that allow them to enter the United States for short periods within a restricted geographic area. In addition, cross-border relationships that have developed over time within families have allowed many people in Tijuana to become legal resident aliens in the United States. Both of these facts are reflected in the kinds of documents used by border and nonborder residents on their first U.S. trip, as shown toward the bottom of table 8.1.

Whereas nearly a quarter of Tijuana migrants made their first U.S. trip as legal resident aliens, only a tenth of migrants from urban and rural interior communities do so. Another third of Tijuana's migrants made their first trip with a tourist visa or border-crossing card, in contrast to 10 and 6 percent, respectively, of migrants from urban and rural interior communities. Thus greater access to legal documents along the border appears to diminish the likelihood of first-time border crossing without authorization (only 41 percent of first trips from Tijuana, compared with 58 and 69 percent, respectively, from urban and rural interior areas).

With their greater array of cross-border ties, and greater access to legalization, migrants from border communities enjoy wider opportunities for U.S. employment. They can choose from the full range of jobs, not just those designated for "illegals," for which employers do not ask for documentation or accept false papers. Table 8.2 presents selected characteristics of the last U.S. job held by migrants from Tijuana, urban interior areas, and rural interior areas. As can be seen, the search strategies used by migrants from Tijuana are different from those used by migrants from the interior. Compared with the latter, the former more often look for employment on their own (47 versus 29 percent in the urban interior and 24 percent in the rural interior) and are less likely to rely on recommendations from relatives.

TABLE 8.2   Characteristics of Employment of Male Household
Heads on Most Recent Trip to the United States
(Percentage Except as Indicated)

Variable	Tijuana	Urban Interior	Rural Interior
How job was found			
Search by oneself	46.5	29.4	24.4
Recommended by relative	19.7	26.5	27.0
Recommended by friend	25.0	20.6	27.0
Recommended by paisano	0.4	0.0	2.5
Recommended by coyote	0.0	0.0	0.3
Contracted	4.8	2.9	9.5
Missing	3.5	20.6	9.1
U.S. occupation: undocumented migrants			
Professional, managerial, technical	0.0	9.5	0.3
Manufacturing	39.1	47.6	38.8
Transportation	2.3	0.0	0.3
Service employee	18.4	33.3	27.5
Agricultural worker	34.5	9.5	27.6
Not in labor force	4.6	0.0	3.9
Missing	1.1	0.0	1.6
U.S. occupation: documented migrants			
Professional, managerial, technical	0.7	0.0	0.0
Manufacturing	30.5	46.2	10.9
Transportation	2.8	7.7	0.0
Service employee	27.7	38.5	9.1
Agricultural worker	19.9	0.0	69.1
Not in labor force	10.6	7.7	9.7
Missing	7.8	0.0	1.2
Hourly wage (U.S. dollars)			
Undocumented migrants	8.38	5.72	6.28
Documented migrants	9.60	4.68	5.84
Mean	8.99	5.20	6.06
Number of migrants			
Undocumented	87	21	742
Documented	141	13	165
Total	228	34	907

Source: Data from Mexican Migration Project.
Note: To make these characteristics, which are period sensitive, comparable, I used only communities that were surveyed between 1996 and 1998. As a result, the sample sizes are smaller for urban and rural interior communities than for Tijuana.

The binational nature of the border economy is evident as well in the similar distributions of occupations for undocumented and documented migrants. Although undocumented migrants from Tijuana are more often agricultural workers than are their counterparts who carry documentation (35 versus 20 percent), this is a result of the concentration of undocumented agricultural migrants who use Tijuana as a home base. Documentation status of migrants from urban interior communities makes relatively little difference; most are concentrated in manufacturing and service sector occupations. The effect of legal status in shaping placement in the U.S. labor market is strongest among migrants from rural interior communities. Nearly 70 percent of rural migrants who hold legal documentation are employed in agriculture. This is an outcome of the Special Agricultural Workers provision of the Immigration Reform and Control Act of 1986, which gave documentation to vast numbers of migrants who could show that they had worked previously in agricultural occupations in the United States. In contrast, undocumented rural migrants are more evenly distributed across manufacturing, service, and agricultural occupations. Whereas the legalization of agricultural workers has created a specific labor market concentration of migrants from rural interior communities, for Tijuana's migrants the prevalence of cross-border ties that provide legal status has allowed most to settle into a variety of occupations.

The advantageous position of border migrants is further suggested by the U.S. earnings they report. Whereas being a legal migrant increases wages among border residents, it appears to confer a disadvantage on those from interior communities. The mean hourly wage earned by migrants from Tijuana was about $3.00 to $4.00 higher than that earned by interior migrants, regardless of documentation or rural or urban location. Undocumented migrants from Tijuana earned an average of $8.38 per hour compared with $6.00 for those from the interior. Moreover, whereas documented migrants from the border earned an average of $9.60 per hour, those from the urban interior earned just $4.68 and those from the rural interior just $5.84.

PREDICTING INITIAL MIGRATION

The advantages conferred on border residents are the outcome of a reiterative process by which migration-related social and human capital are accumulated (Fussell and Massey 2004; Massey and Zenteno 1999). For this reason, it is instructive to look at the life histories of migrants and nonmigrants alike and to measure which factors lead some to initiate migration and others to stay put. Table 8.3 presents means and standard deviations for variables used to predict initial migration to the United States, distinguished by the type of community (see Fussell 2004 and Fussell and Massey 2004 for related analyses). The means represent average characteristics across person-years of study. These data suggest that household heads are fairly similar across different types of communities. The typical household head migrating from Tijuana was a few years younger, had fewer children, and was slightly less likely to be married. However, all respondents report similar levels of labor force experience: around thirteen or fourteen years. Not surprisingly, respondents from Tijuana reported having had considerably more schooling (7.4 years) than those in urban interior communities (6.5 years) or those in rural interior communities (4.4 years).

There are important differences across communities with respect to the degree of prior migratory experience within families. The parents of male heads in both Tijuana and urban interior communities were less likely to have had migratory experience than those in rural interior communities (10 and 12 percent, respectively, versus 18 percent), which is to be expected given the long history of U.S. migration from the latter. However, roughly a quarter of all male household heads in border communities and a third of those in rural interior communities had a sibling who had migrated, whereas only 16 percent of urban interior male household heads had a sibling with prior U.S. experience. Border and interior communities appear to have lower levels of family-based, migration-related social capital, as they have only recently entered into the migration stream.

Having prior migratory experience within Mexico may predict migration to the United States simply because someone who has moved once is more likely to move again. To control for this, I include separate measures of internal migration to Baja California and elsewhere in Mexico (these moves had to have been of at least twelve months' duration to be counted). In this way I sought to differentiate the propensity to move anywhere from a person's strategic move to a crossing point on the Mexico-U.S. border. As table 8.3 shows, residents of Tijuana are quite likely to be internal migrants: more than half of male household heads in Tijuana were themselves migrants to Baja California, and a slightly larger proportion moved from somewhere else in Mexico. This profile is quite different from that prevailing in interior urban or rural communities, where only 1 percent of migrating residents had ever moved to Baja California and 36 to 38 percent migrated within Mexico.

TABLE 8.3   Means and Standard Deviations Used in Event–History Analysis of Migration of Male Household
Heads to the United States

	Tijuana		Urban Interior		Rural Interior	
Variable	Mean	Standard Deviation	Mean	Standard Deviation	Mean	Standard Deviation
Dependent variable						
Took undocumented trip	0.008	0.09	0.006	0.007	0.013	0.113
Took documented trip	0.002	0.05	0.001	0.003	.0009	.030
Demographic background						
Age	35.2	13.9	36.9	13.9	37.6	14.8
Number of minors	1.6	1.8	2.3	2.3	2.5	2.5
Percentage ever married	0.70	0.46	0.77	0.42	0.76	0.44
Human capital						
Years of education	7.4	4.3	6.5	4.7	4.4	4.2
Months of labor force experience	168.0	109.8	155.0	98.3	156.2	99.6
Family-based social capital						
Parent migrant	0.10	0.30	0.12	0.33	0.18	0.38
Sibling migrant	0.25	0.43	0.16	0.37	0.33	0.47

Migration-based human capital					
Internal migrant in Mexico	0.58	0.49	0.38	0.47	0.36	0.48
Internal migrant to Baja California	0.52	0.50	0.01	0.10	0.01	0.12
Number of U.S. trips	0.56	1.06	0.59	2.14	2.36	4.84
Occupation in prior year					
Agriculture	0.04	0.19	0.08	0.27	0.47	0.50
Manufacturing	0.36	0.48	0.43	0.50	0.26	0.44
Services	0.40	0.49	0.27	0.45	0.15	0.36
Transportation	0.09	0.28	0.08	0.27	0.04	0.18
Professional, managerial	0.07	0.26	0.09	0.28	0.05	0.23
Not in labor force	0.04	0.20	0.05	0.23	0.03	0.17
Period (percentage)					
1965 to 1969	0.08	0.26	0.12	0.32	0.12	0.33
1970 to 1974	0.09	0.29	0.14	0.35	0.15	0.36
1975 to 1979	0.12	0.32	0.17	0.38	0.17	0.38
1980 to 1984	0.16	0.36	0.19	0.39	0.19	0.39
1985 to 1989	0.18	0.39	0.20	0.40	0.20	0.40
1990 to 1998	0.39	0.48	0.18	0.38	0.17	0.38
Number of person-years	12,272		37,590		183,115	

Source: Data from Mexican Migration Project.

To measure a person's accumulated U.S. migratory experience, I include the number of prior U.S. trips. It is readily apparent that residents of small interior communities have much higher levels of accumulated U.S. experience than those in other locations. In areas of the rural interior, subjects made an average of 2.4 trips to the United States, compared with just 0.6 trips in either border or interior cities.

I include sector of employment during the prior year to measure employment opportunities within the home labor market. In the absence of information on annual wages, sector of employment is the best time-varying indicator of class position just before the migration decision. As expected, respondents from small interior communities were employed in agriculture in nearly half of all person-years under observation, and a quarter were employed in manufacturing. In contrast, respondents in Tijuana and urban interior communities spent 70 to 76 percent of their person-years working in manufacturing and services, as one would expect in an urban economy. Tijuana displays a slightly greater concentration in the service sector, owing to the strength of commerce and recreational services on the border. This fact may be surprising given the growth of Tijuana's maquiladora sector, but it is important to remember that maquiladoras tend to hire more women than men. Finally, I include dummy variables to control for period effects, dividing years from 1965 to 1989 into five-year intervals, and a final category covering 1990 to 1998.

Before I turn to the results of the event-history analysis, recall that my central argument is that cross-border social and economic ties shape the logic of migration from Tijuana. Specifically, I hypothesize that (1) residents of Tijuana are less likely to migrate than are those from rural interior areas; (2) family-based social ties to migrants are most powerful in predicting migration from rural interior communities (despite significant effects across all communities); and (3) employment in more economically vibrant sectors negatively predicts migration in all kinds of communities but especially in Tijuana.

Table 8.4 presents coefficients and standard errors for a multinomial logistic regression equation estimated across person-years to predict whether a respondent took a documented or undocumented trip to the United States (the reference category is no migration). Consistent with the history of migration from Mexico to the United States, the odds of undocumented migration from Tijuana and urban areas in the interior of Mexico are significantly lower than from rural interior areas. Other things equal, the odds that a Tijuana resident undertakes a first trip to the United States are 67 percent lower than those of residents of rural interior communities (determined by taking $[e^{\beta} - 1]*100$, where β is the

TABLE 8.4   Multinomial Logit Coefficients Predicting a First Trip to the United States With and Without Documents

Independent Variables	Undocumented Migration		Documented Migration	
	Logged Odds	Standard Error	Logged Odds	Standard Error
Current residence				
Rural interior	—	—	—	—
Urban interior	−0.96**	0.07	−0.63**	0.21
Tijuana	−1.10**	0.11	1.51**	0.19
Demographic background				
Age	0.04**	0.01	−0.07*	0.03
Age squared	−0.002**	0.0002	0.001*	0.0004
Number of minors	−0.004	0.01	−0.01	0.05
Ever married	−0.12*	0.06	−0.08	0.17
Human capital				
Years of education	−0.07**	0.01	0.08**	0.01
Labor force experience	−0.002**	0.001	−0.004*	0.001
Family-based social capital				
Parent migrant	0.66**	0.05	1.19**	0.14
Sibling migrant	1.28**	0.04	1.03**	0.13
Migration-based human capital				
Internal migrant in Mexico	0.07*	0.04	−0.14	0.15
Internal migrant to Baja California	0.41**	0.09	−0.41	0.25
Occupation in prior year				
Agriculture	—	—	—	—
Manufacturing	0.62**	0.05	0.70**	0.16
Services	0.59**	0.06	0.45**	0.18
Professional, managerial	−1.49**	0.23	−0.68	0.53
Not in labor force	0.57*	0.14	1.81**	0.23
Period				
1965 to 1969	—	—	—	—
1970 to 1974	0.83**	0.09	−0.69**	0.21
1975 to 1979	1.12**	0.09	−0.99**	0.22
1980 to 1984	0.97**	0.09	−0.92**	0.22
1985 to 1989	1.30**	0.09	−0.57	0.22
1990 to 1996	1.12**	0.11	−0.98**	0.26
Intercept	−4.68**	0.23	−5.81**	0.48
Likelihood ratio			25360.17**	
N			168,624	

Source: Data from Mexican Migration Project.
*p < .05   **p < .01

regression coefficient shown in table 8.4). Similarly, the odds of taking a first undocumented trip for urban interior residents are 62 percent less than those for residents of rural interior communities.

Such differences between urban and rural areas are easily explained by the fact that Mexico-U.S. migration has historically been driven by a strong U.S. demand for agricultural workers. Tijuana was a major passageway for these laborers, and its residents might easily have been drawn into the migration stream; therefore the lower odds of migration from Tijuana are less easily explained than those prevailing in urban interior communities. To examine how the determinants of migration differ between Tijuana and the interior communities, I reestimated the model after including interactions between place of residence and measures of social capital, internal migration experience, and occupation and period controls and compared the results with those of the baseline model shown in table 8.4. The results are displayed in table 8.5.

Earlier I mentioned two possible reasons for the lower likelihood of undocumented migration from Tijuana (and interior urban areas) relative to rural interior communities: fewer kin ties to migrants and more attractive economic opportunities locally. I test these hypotheses by interacting measures of family-based social capital, internal migration experience, and occupation in the previous year with place of residence. Once these interactions are included, the indicators for Tijuana and urban interior areas fall below statistical significance, which suggests that cross-locality differences in the quantity of social capital, internal migration experience, and the distribution of occupations account for the lower likelihood of undocumented migration from the border.

The use of family-based migration-related social capital is well known as a means for entering the migration stream, whether from urban or rural communities. There are important differences, however, between communities in access to this type of social capital (see table 8.3). As table 8.5 shows, family-based migration-related social capital and place of residence interact in expected ways. In rural interior communities, having a relative with migrant experience greatly increases the chances of making a first undocumented trip. Specifically, having a parent with U.S. experience raises the odds of making a first U.S. trip by 86 percent whereas having a migrant sibling increases the odds by 252 percent. In Tijuana, having a migrant parent or migrant sibling has no significantly greater effect on the likelihood of making a first undocumented trip to the United States than in rural areas. In urban interior communities, however, having a migrant parent increases the likelihood of making a first undocumented trip by an additional 77 percent. In other words, family-based social capital is

TABLE 8.5   Multinomial Logit Coefficients Predicting First Documented and Undocumented Migration, with Interactions

Independent Variables	Undocumented Migration		Documented Migration	
	Logged Odds	Standard Error	Logged Odds	Standard Error
Current residence				
Rural interior	—	—	—	—
Urban interior	−0.71**	0.16	−0.60	0.49
Tijuana	−0.63*	0.29	1.37**	0.37
Demographic background				
Age	0.04*	0.02	−0.07*	0.03
Age squared	−0.001**	0.0002	0.00	0.00
Number of minors	−0.005	0.01	−0.01	0.05
Ever married	−0.12*	0.06	−0.06	0.19
Human capital				
Years of education	−0.07**	0.01	0.08**	0.02
Labor force experience	−0.002**	0.0005	−0.001	0.001
Family-based social capital				
Parent migrant	0.62**	0.05	1.13**	0.17
Sibling migrant	1.26**	0.04	1.14**	0.17
Social capital by place interactions				
Parent migrant × Tijuana	−0.17	0.40	0.56	0.35
Sibling migrant × Tijuana	−0.09	0.26	−0.60	0.35
Parent migrant × urban interior	0.57**	0.17	−0.38	0.50
Sibling migrant × urban interior	0.30	0.16	−0.05	0.49
Migration-based human capital				
Internal migrant in Mexico	0.06	0.05	−0.17	0.15
Internal migrant to Baja California	0.51**	0.10	−0.85	0.72
Migration-based human capital by place interactions				
Internal migrant to Baja California × Tijuana	−0.76**	0.27	0.53	0.77
Internal migrant to Baja California × Urban	0.17	0.31	2.01	1.03

(*Table continues on p. 162.*)

TABLE 8.5   Multinomial Logit Coefficients Predicting First Documented and Undocumented Migration, with Interactions (*Continued*)

Independent Variables	Undocumented Migration		Documented Migration	
	Logged Odds	Standard Error	Logged Odds	Standard Error
Occupation in prior year				
Agricultural	—	—	—	—
Manufacturing	0.64**	0.05	0.52**	0.18
Services	0.70**	0.06	0.50*	0.22
Professional, managerial	−1.57**	0.26	−1.48	1.01
Not in labor force	0.54**	0.15	2.04**	0.25
Occupation by place interactions				
Manufacturing × Tijuana	0.14	0.33	0.55	0.42
Services × Tijuana	−0.72	0.38	−0.05	0.47
Professional, managerial × Tijuana	0.66	0.81	1.42	1.28
Not in labor force × Tijuana	0.95	0.67	−1.75	1.10
Manufacturing × interior urban	−0.53**	0.18	0.34	0.56
Services × interior urban	−1.01**	0.23	−0.04	0.63
Professional, managerial × interior urban	−0.24	0.65	−1.45	1.49
Not in labor force × interior urban	−0.26	0.42	−1.04	0.22
Period				
1965 to 1969	—	—	—	—
1970 to 1974	0.83**	0.09	−0.71**	0.24
1975 to 1979	1.12**	0.09	−1.02**	0.25
1980 to 1984	0.96**	0.09	−0.94**	0.25
1985 to 1989	1.29**	0.09	−0.59**	0.24
1990 to 1996	1.11**	0.10	−0.98**	0.26
Intercept	−4.68**	0.23	−5.75**	0.48
Likelihood ratio			25497.58**	
N			168,624	

Source: Data from Mexican Migration Project.
*p < .05   **p < .01

no more influential in Tijuana than it is in smaller interior communities, though it still has a positive overall effect on the odds of undocumented migration.

Mexican men also enter the migrant stream to the United States through internal migration to the border. Those migrants who earlier migrated to Baja California are 67 percent more likely than those who never moved to Baja California to undertake a first undocumented trip to the United States. Since most of these internal migrants were surveyed in Tijuana, this finding suggests that migrating to the border and settling there is a common strategy for gaining entry to the United States. Thus for those who lack authorization to enter the United States, relocating to the border is a strategy for acquiring access to migration-related social capital through friends and acquaintances as well as through employers on both sides of the border.

Labor market opportunities also differentiate potential U.S. migrants from nonmigrants. Those with skills that are in demand locally are more likely to stay than to leave in search of U.S. employment. Among those in rural areas, the effects of occupation clearly show that male heads in professional or managerial occupations were less likely than agricultural workers to migrate to the United States. In contrast, those who were not in the labor force or who worked in manufacturing or services were more likely than agricultural workers to make a first undocumented trip. These patterns were similar in Tijuana, even though its occupational distribution is less agriculturally based. In interior urban communities, however, those who worked in manufacturing and services were no more likely than agricultural workers to make a first U.S. trip. Thus the composition of the local labor market in the origin community, and the respondent's position within it, influences the likelihood of a making a first undocumented trip.

Conversely, Tijuana's male household heads had a greater likelihood of making a first documented U.S. trip than those from interior urban and rural communities. Subjects from Tijuana were nearly three times more likely to make a first documented trip than were those from the rural or urban interior, indicating the much greater access of Tijuana's residents to legal avenues of border crossing and U.S. employment. In other words, as predicted, although Tijuana's residents were less likely than residents of rural interior communities to migrate, when they did migrate they were more likely to use some kind of legal document.

Although men from Tijuana were more likely to make a first documented trip, however, this does not necessarily mean they were more likely to have "legalized" family networks. If Tijuana residents were more likely to make a first documented trip because of access to legal documents through family sponsorship, then we would expect to see a significant interaction between social capital and place of origin. Instead, as table 8.5 indicates, when they have a relative with migrant experience, residents of Tijuana are no more likely than those from rural interior communities to make a first documented trip, which suggests that the greater likelihood of documented migration from the border stems from other means of accessing legal documentation, such as acquiring the border-crossing cards or the sponsorship of a U.S. employer. Indeed, Tijuana's greater stock of human capital (more education, greater facility with English, and familiarity with Southern Californian culture) probably increases the access of Tijuana residents to both sponsorship and crossing cards.

The demographic profile of undocumented migrants is consistent with that found in earlier investigations (Massey et al. 1987; Massey and Espinosa 1997). Most men made their first undocumented U.S. trip while they were young. The odds of undocumented migration rise to an early peak and then fall as the sample moves into older ages (see the positive effects of age and the negative effects of age squared in tables 8.4 and 8.5). Among men taking their first U.S. trip with documents, however, age was a less significant factor. Having been married or having minor children in the household neither deterred nor promoted U.S. migration, with or without documents. Education, however, lowered the likelihood of undocumented migration but raised the odds of legal migration. The effect of Mexican labor market experience was generally to reduce the odds of going to the United States in both statuses.

PREDICTING LATER TRIPS

How the likelihood of making a later U.S. trip was changed by having made a first trip, and how this varied by place of residence, is considered in table 8.6. Having made a first trip to the United States, a male household head has acquired knowledge about how to cross the border and where to find housing and employment, a form of migration-specific human capital. This effect is captured in the indicator of the number of previous trips made to the United States, where each additional U.S. trip increased the likelihood of making a later undocumented trip by around 15 percent and that of making a later documented trip by 18 percent. Notably, in Tijuana, this effect is amplified: each additional U.S. trip significantly increased the odds of taking an undocumented U.S. trip by an additional 30 percent. These career migrants account for most of the undocumented U.S. trips from Tijuana. Many of these career migrants were internal migrants to the border, for whom

TABLE 8.6   Multinomial Logit Equation Predicting Later Trips for All Migrants, with Interactions

Independent Variables	Undocumented Migration		Documented Migration	
	Logged Odds	Standard Error	Logged Odds	Standard Error
Current residence				
Rural interior	—	—	—	—
Urban interior	0.43**	0.17	−0.40	0.32
Tijuana	−2.11**	0.72	−1.39*	0.64
Demographic background				
Age	0.01	0.01	0.06**	0.01
Age squared	−0.001**	0.0001	−0.001**	0.0001
Number of minors	0.06**	0.01	−0.04**	0.01
Ever married	0.10*	0.05	0.22**	0.07
Human capital				
Years of education	−0.07**	0.01	0.04**	0.01
Months of labor force experience	−0.01**	0.0003	−0.01**	0.001
Family-based social capital				
Parent migrant	−0.10**	0.04	0.54**	0.05
Sibling migrant	0.18*	0.04	0.60**	0.05
Family-based social capital				
Parent migrant × Tijuana	−0.78	0.78	0.23	0.37
Sibling migrant × Tijuana	0.86	0.52	−0.70*	0.36
Parent migrant × interior urban	0.24	0.18	−0.17	0.28
Sibling migrant × interior urban	−0.30	0.17	−0.56*	0.28
Migration-based human capital				
Internal migrant in Baja California	0.76**	0.13	0.39	0.21
Internal migrant to Mexico	0.35**	0.04	−0.15**	0.05
Number of previous U.S. trips	0.14**	0.002	0.17**	0.003
Migration capital by location interactions				
Internal migrant in Baja California × Tijuana	1.22*	0.55	0.14	0.43
Internal migrant to Baja California × interior urban	−0.02	0.55	0.80	0.79

(*Table continues on p. 166.*)

TABLE 8.6   Multinomial Logit Equation Predicting Later Trips for All Migrants, with Interactions (*Continued*)

Independent Variables	Undocumented Migration		Documented Migration	
	Logged Odds	Standard Error	Logged Odds	Standard Error
U.S. trips × Tijuana	0.26**	0.10	0.22**	0.08
U.S. trips × urban interior	0.00	0.01	−0.02*	0.01
Occupation in prior year				
Agriculture	—	—	—	—
Manufacturing	0.07	0.04	−0.57**	0.06
Services	0.07	0.05	−0.56**	0.07
Professional, managerial	−1.68**	0.24	−1.37	0.27
Not in labor force	−0.56**	0.16	−0.43**	0.14
Occupation by place interactions				
Manufacturing × Tijuana	−1.17	0.70	1.11	0.61
Service × Tijuana	−1.56*	0.78	0.97	0.63
Professional, managerial × Tijuana	—	—	—	—
Not in labor force × Tijuana	—	—	0.84	1.20
Manufacturing × interior urban	−0.90**	0.18	0.62	0.33
Service × interior urban	−1.01**	0.23	−0.10	0.43
Professional, managerial × interior urban	−0.49	0.64	1.78**	0.53
Not in labor force × interior urban	−1.09	0.62	−0.50	0.67
Period				
1965 to 1969	—	—	—	—
1970 to 1974	0.74**	0.07	0.42*	0.10
1975 to 1979	1.15**	0.07	0.39**	0.10
1980 to 1984	1.47**	0.07	0.32**	0.10
1985 to 1989	1.82**	0.07	1.65**	0.09
1990 to 1996	1.62**	0.08	2.16**	0.10
Intercept	−3.11**	0.20	−6.32**	0.23
Likelihood ratio	44956.02**			
N	75,420			

Source: Data from Mexican Migration Project.
*p < .05   **p < .01

the odds of making additional U.S. trips were twice those of native-born Tijuanenses.

The effect of migration-based human capital in Tijuana distinguishes career migrants from all others. Overall, however, being a resident of Tijuana strongly reduced the probability of repeat undocumented migration. To some extent, former U.S. migrants may not make repeated trips because they find more attractive employment locally. For example, in all places, male household heads who spent the previous year employed as professionals or managers were less likely to take subsequent undocumented trips to the United States. In Tijuana, working in the service sector had an additional deterrent effect on repeat undocumented migration, as did manufacturing and service sector employment in urban interior communities. Thus opportunities available in the origin community appear to strongly influence the likelihood of making a career of international migration, and Tijuana's labor market and other urban labor markets appear to compete well with economic opportunities in the United States.

There is little that positively predicts later documented U.S. trips. As in the equation predicting later undocumented trips, the number of previous U.S. trips increased the likelihood of taking a later documented trip to the United States by 19 percent. Furthermore, in Tijuana this effect is amplified by an additional 25 percent. Evidently, there were both undocumented and documented career migrants based there. Overall, however, Tijuana's residents were much less likely to make repeat documented U.S. trips than were those in both rural and urban interior areas. Later documented trips to the United States appear best explained by one's place in the labor market, agricultural workers being most likely to make additional documented U.S. trips—a fact well documented in the literature on Mexican migration (Fussell 2004; Massey et al. 1987). Notably, however, those who worked in professional and managerial jobs in the previous year were significantly more likely to make repeated documented U.S. trips, suggesting an incipient stream of urban professional migrants.

DISCUSSION

The integration of Tijuana with San Diego has diminished undocumented migration by providing potential migrants with attractive alternatives in the local labor market. At the same time, however, cross-border integration has increased the odds of documented migration by providing greater access to papers through family ties and, most important, employer sponsors. The binational nature of Tijuana's economy, therefore, fundamentally alters the logic of international migration from that part of Mexico.

The descriptive statistics presented in tables 8.1 and 8.2 support this assertion. Compared with migrants from communities in Mexico's interior, those from Tijuana took longer and less frequent trips to the United States that were more targeted on California and more likely to be made with documentation. Moreover, when migrants from Tijuana arrived in the United States, they more often found jobs on their own rather than through friends or family; and their jobs were more likely to be in services or manufacturing than in agriculture. The most striking difference observed among migrants by place of origin concerns earnings. Migrants from Tijuana, especially those with legal documents, earned substantially more than others. In contrast, the earnings of migrants from urban and rural interior communities generally suffered when they migrated with documents. This paradoxical relationship between legal status and earnings underscores that Tijuana's migrants participate in an aboveground portion of the U.S. labor market, while those from interior communities are generally confined to a segmented, underground economy that offers few returns to legal status.

Multivariate analyses confirm the distinct logic of Tijuana's migration system. While I expected the higher likelihood of documented migration to stem from greater access to legalization in Tijuana, however, I found that access to the United States through family networks was about the same at the border as in the interior. Nor did type of employment in Mexico strongly affect the probability of making a first documented U.S. trip. Simply being a resident of Tijuana increased the probability of making a first documented U.S. trip, apart from these mechanisms. While one might assume that high rates of legal migration stem from the use of border-crossing cards (which residents of interior communities cannot get), in multivariate analyses the dependent variable was constructed so that a person who worked after entering the United States with a local passport or temporary visa would be coded as undocumented. Instead, I suggest it has to do with the greater access that residents of Tijuana have to employers in the United States who can sponsor their work visa.

The greater proportion of first-time migrants from Tijuana who are documented may diminish the probability of first undocumented migration from that city generally; but this represents only a partial explanation. Local socioeconomic characteristics also play an important role. A greater stock of human capital in Tijuana (greater education and more skilled occupations) keeps men out of the undocumented migration stream. Since men in Tijuana have more education and are more likely to be in professional, technical, managerial, or service occupations than those in interior communities, they are self-selected out of the international migration stream. In other words, the composition of the local population plays a strong role in diminishing the probability of the initiation of undocumented migration in Tijuana. The deterrent effect of Tijuana's economy is further indicated by the fact that internal migrants to Tijuana are unlikely to make a first undocumented U.S. trip, most likely because they find Tijuana's economy to be more attractive than migration to the United States.

The depressive effect of residence in Tijuana on U.S. migration persists in the analysis of later trips. The probability of taking either a documented or undocumented trip from Tijuana and urban interior areas is lower than that from rural interior communities. Multivariate results also suggest that while some share of people from each type of community persist in making repeated U.S. trips, it is migrants working in agriculture (mostly from rural communities) who make up the bulk of these repeat migrants. Those migrants from Tijuana who make repeat undocumented and documented U.S. trips are career migrants who have relocated there, making it a home base.

Cross-border economic and social ties thus appear to play an important role in explaining Tijuana's unique migration dynamic. Paradoxically, these ties suppress the tendency to migrate rather than augment it. Linkages between the economies on either side of the border provide greater employment opportunities for residents of Tijuana, who also tend to possess more human capital and thus are more salable within the binational, transborder economy. Despite their proximity to the labor markets of San Diego and Los Angeles, there is no flood of U.S. emigrants from Tijuana. Instead, the transborder economy provides ample opportunities to satisfy and thereby deter many potential migrants.

References

Alegría, Tito. 2000. "Demand and Supply Among Mexican Cross-Border Workers." Paper presented to the Association of Collegiate Financial Planning, Forty-second Annual Conference. Atlanta (November 2–5, 2000).

Bustamante, Jorge A. 1990. *Historia de la colonia Libertad.* Tijuana, Mexico: El Colegio de la Frontera Norte.

Cerrutti, Marcela, and Douglas S. Massey. 2001. "On the Auspices of Female Migration from Mexico to the United States." *Demography* 38: 187–200.

Cox, Millicent. 1994. *Who Crosses the Border: A View of the San Diego/Tijuana Metropolitan Region.* Report of the San Diego Dialogue. University of California at San Diego.

Fussell, Elizabeth. 2004. "Sources of Mexico's Migration Stream: Rural, Urban, and Border Migrants to the United States." *Social Forces* 82: 937–67.

Fussell, Elizabeth, and Douglas S. Massey. 2004. "The Limits to Cumulative Causation: International Migration from Mexican Urban Areas." *Demography* 41: 151–71.

Instituto Nacional de Estadística, Geografía e Informática (INEGI). 1999. *Migración reciente en México, 1985–1990.* Mexico City: INEGI.

Lorey, David E. 1999. *The U.S.-Mexican Border in the Twentieth Century.* Wilmington, Del.: Scholarly Resources.

Lozano Ascencio, Fernando, Bryan Roberts, and Frank Bean. 1999. "The Interconnections of Internal and International Migration: The Case of the United States and Mexico." In *Migration and Transnational Social Spaces,* edited by Ludger Pries. Brookfield, Vt.: Ashgate.

Massey, Douglas S., Rafael Alarcón, Jorge Durand, and Humberto González. 1987. *Return to Aztlán: The Social Process of International Migration from Western Mexico.* Berkeley: University of California Press.

Massey, Douglas, and Kristen E. Espinosa. 1997. "What's Driving Mexico-U.S. Migration? A Theoretical, Empirical and Policy Analysis." *American Journal of Sociology* 102: 939–99.

Massey, Douglas S., and René Zenteno. 1999. "The Dynamics of Mass Migration." *Proceedings of the National Academy of Sciences* 96(8): 5328–35.

Rubin-Kurtzman, Jane R., Roberto Ham-Chande, and Maurice D. Van Arsdol Jr. 1996. "Population in Trans-Border Regions: The Southern California–Baja California Urban System." *International Migration Review* 30: 1020–45.

U.S. Department of Justice. Immigration and Naturalization Service. 1999. "25-Mile Zone—Regulatory History." *Backgrounder,* October 8, 1999. Available at: http://uscis.gov/graphics/publicaffairs/backgrounds/bground.htm.

U.S. Department of Transportation. Bureau of Transportation Statistics. 2002. *U.S.-Mexico Border Crossing Data.* Available at: http://www.bts.gov/itt/cross.

U.S. General Accounting Office. 1997. *Illegal Immigration: Southwest Border Strategy Results Inconclusive; More Evaluation Needed.* GAO/GGD-98-21. Report to the Committee on the Judiciary, U.S. Senate and the Committee on the Judiciary, House of Representatives (December).

Zabin, Carol, and Sallie Hughes. 1995. "Economic Integration and Labor Flows: Stage Migration in Farm Labor Markets in Mexico and the United States." *International Migration Review* 29(2): 395–422.

Zenteno, René. 1995. "Del rancho de la Tía Juana a Tijuana: Una breve historia de desarrollo y población en la Frontera Norte de México." *Estudios Demográficos y Urbanos* 10: 105–32.

CHAPTER 9

OLD PARADIGMS AND NEW SCENARIOS IN A MIGRATORY TRADITION: U.S. MIGRATION FROM GUANAJUATO

Patricia Arias

FIFTEEN YEARS ago, Jorge Durand (1987) noted that migration to the United States was especially widespread in the state of Guanajuato. He reviewed the small number of reliable studies then available to explicate the long-standing and deeply rooted history of migration to "el otro lado" (the other side) from this state. These studies showed that Guanajuato generally had the highest rate of out-migration, surpassing even that prevailing in other west-central states such as Jalisco and Michoacán. High rates of U.S. migration have persisted in Guanajuato through the twentieth century. During the 1920s, for example, migrants from Guanajuato stood out both among those who returned voluntarily and among those who were summarily deported with the onset of the Great Depression in 1929.

According to Manuel Gamio (1930), early U.S. migration was rooted in conditions of agriculture and small landholding that obliged peasants to search for supplemental income or investments for production. This situation did not change much after the implementation of agrarian reform in Mexico in the 1930s; and when the United States resumed labor recruitment in 1942, large numbers of men from Guanajuato quickly signed up to participate in the Bracero Program, which arranged for the temporary importation of migrant farmworkers. Their predominance was aided by the fact that the governors of Michoacán and Jalisco initially prohibited bracero contractors from operating in their states (Martínez 1948).

When the Bracero Program finally shut down in 1964, many Guanajuatenses continued to migrate without documents, a pattern of migration that continued to expand through the early 1980s. During the period of bracero and undocumented migration, international movement was predominantly temporary, characterized by high rates of return and remittance.

Although exhaustive in its day, Durand's review covers a relatively small number of studies and a disparate collection of authors, periods, and topics. Since its publication, many new studies of Guanajuatense migrants have appeared. María Cebada (1993), for example, uses participant observation and qualitative interviews to study emigration from two communities in the municipality of Haunímaro, located in the southeast corner of Guanajuato. Similarly, Laurent Faret (1998) analyzes quantitative data gathered from a sample of households in the large northern municipality of Ocampo, along with a parallel survey of out-migrants located in the United States. Francisco Argüello (1993) studies migration to Canada from two small communities located near the city of Irapuato, and Laura González (1996) examines several small municipalities in the southern part of the state and, more recently, surveys Guanajuatenses settled in the Dallas–Fort Worth area (González n.d.). Victor García has studied the involvement of migrants from Guanajuato in the mushroom harvest of southeastern Pennsylvania. According to him, U.S. migration has become "a way of life in the Mexican countryside" (García 1998, 26).

Despite these recent contributions, studies of migration from Guanajuato are still rather scarce, and most focus on the state's southern and Bajío regions, usually surveying small rural communities where strong ties to the land predominate. Under these circumstances, it is almost impossible *not* to "discover" that migration is somehow associated with conditions in agriculture. Although emigration may be disproportionately rural, however, significant numbers of migrants have always come from cities, and even those from agrarian backgrounds often end up in other vocations when they return to Mexico.

Guillermo Martínez (1948), for example, shows that whereas 15 percent of braceros from Guanajuato worked in agriculture before migrating to the United States, only 2.5 percent did so after their return. Similarly, Mercedes Carreras (1974) has discovered that migrants returning to the small city of Pénjamo, Guanajuato, often brought back automobiles from the United States and set themselves up as taxi drivers; and Durand (1987) finds that migrants returning to San Francisco del Rincón avoided investments in agriculture and preferred instead to put their U.S. earnings into manufacturing and livestock trading (see also Durand 1994).

Even among landowning farmers, moreover, it is not those with the poorest lands who migrate but generally those with the most productive acreage. Kenneth Roberts (1982), for example, has found the highest rates of U.S. migration not among households dependent on rain-fed fields but among those who own irrigated land. Rodolfo Corona (1987) similarly finds that municipalities with the highest rates of U.S.-bound migration tended to be those with the richest agricultural land. Fragmentary evidence thus questions the commonly held view that Mexican migration to the United States is associated with limited agricultural development, segmented production, and few opportunities for farm employment.

Guanajuato, in particular, has always been much more than an agricultural state whose destiny is anchored in the fields. Indeed, over the past several decades, it has been characterized by a rapid process of urbanization, by the emergence of a set of small and medium-sized cities that are economically specialized but functionally interdependent, and by the existence of an entrepreneurial culture that has served to break down the traditional dichotomy between static agrarian communities and dynamic industrial centers. The present diversity of Guanajuato's economic landscape raises fundamental questions about the nature and process of international migration: Does it occur in the same way at all levels and in all places, rural and urban? How has it been transformed by urbanization and other structural economic changes in the state?

GUANAJUATO AND THE MEXICAN MIGRATION PROJECT

According to the sources reviewed by Durand (1998a), Guanajuato was consistently among the three most important migrant-sending states of Mexico. Table 9.1 draws on his review to show the percentage of migrants emanating from Jalisco, Michoacán, and Guanajuato as reported in selected national-level data sets compiled between 1980 and 1994. Based on responses to a question about place of residence five years earlier, Corona's (1987) analysis of the 1980 census finds that of those with prior U.S. experience, around 15 percent were from Guanajuato, 15 percent from Michoacán, and 22 percent from Jalisco. A 1986 survey of recently deported migrants interviewed by the Mexican Department of Labor presents lower percentages for all three states, 8 percent claiming to be from Guanajuato, 11 percent from Michoacán, and 10 percent from Jalisco (see Ranney and Kossoudji 1983).

A 1987 survey of former undocumented migrants who received amnesty under the 1986 Immigration Reform and Control Act (IRCA) finds only around 7 percent of those legalized were born in Guanajuato, compared with 14 percent born in Michoacán and 20 percent born in Jalisco (see Smith, Kramer, and Singer 1996). According to Mexico's National Survey of Population Dynamics, conducted in 1992, 9 percent of those who had

TABLE 9.1   U.S. Migrants from the Three Most Important Mexican Migrant-Sending States, by Data Sources, 1980 to 1994 (Percentage)

Source	Jalisco	Michoacán	Guanajuato
Census of Mexico (1980)	21.6	14.9	14.8
Mexican survey of undocumented workers deported from the United States (1986)	10.0	11.1	7.7
Legalized alien population survey (1987)			
Place of birth	20.0	14.3	6.5
Place of last residence	18.2	11.5	6.5
National Survey of Population Dynamics (1992)	11.7	14.5	8.6
Survey of migrants to the northern border (1994)			
Migrants heading north	7.7	12.1	13.1
Migrants heading south	8.5	11.1	15.2

Source: Data from Durand (1998a).

worked or looked for work in the United States during the prior year were from Guanajuato, 15 percent were from Michoacán, and 12 percent from Jalisco (see Durand, Massey, and Zenteno 2001). Finally, a 1994 survey of migrants crossing or intending to cross the Mexico-U.S. border, fielded by the Colegio de la Frontera Norte, finds that 13 percent were from Guanajuato, 12 percent from Michoacán, and 8 percent from Jalisco.

Thus across a variety of large-scale surveys, Guanajuato always emerges as one of the top-three migrant-sending states in Mexico, though its precise ranking depends on the time and nature of the survey and the particular population of migrants being studied. Over roughly the same period, from 1987 to 1992, the Mexican Migration Project (MMP) undertook representative ethnosurveys of nine communities in Guanajuato; two additional surveys from this state were conducted and added to the MMP database in 1998 (see chapter 16).

The eleven communities surveyed by the MMP are located in five of the six regions into which the state of Guanajuato has been divided by Mexico's Ministry of Social Development: one in the north, one in the northeast, two in the south, two in the southwest, and five in the west-central region, which includes the Bajío (see table 9.2). Two of the communities were classified as metropolitan areas, with more than seventy thousand inhabitants; five were medium-sized cities, with populations ranging from fifteen thousand to seventy thousand; and four were classified as "ranchos" of fewer than three thousand inhabitants. Unfortunately, the surveys of Guanajuato did not include any towns with populations of three thousand to fifteen thousand. Clearly, this lack introduces a bias into the data, though probably not a severe one, as few settlements in Guanajuato were in this size category at the time. According to data from the 2000 census, of forty-six municipalities in Guanajuato, twelve were metropolitan areas, seventeen were medium-sized cities, and five were ranchos, leaving a dozen in the town category. Although another town was added to the MMP database in 2001, its data are not yet available for analysis.

INTERNATIONAL MIGRATION FROM GUANAJUATO

In the 1980s the main migrant-sending municipalities (not distinguishing between national and international migration) generally appeared to be in the northern and southeastern regions of the state (CONAPO 1987). The MMP survey recorded the year in which the first migrant from each community left for the United States. In addition to the size classification, region, and survey date, table 9.2 presents this year for each of the eleven

TABLE 9.2   Communities in Guanajuato Sampled by the Mexican Migration Project, 1987 to 1998

Community Number	Classification	Region	Survey Date	Year of First U.S. Trip
Community 1	Metropolitan area	West central	1987	1920
Community 2	Metropolitan area	West central	1991	1909
Community 3	Medium city	West central	1987	1920
Community 4	Medium city	West central	1988	1929
Community 5	Medium city	South	1992	1915
Community 6	Medium city	South	1992	1920
Community 7	Medium city	North	1990	1920
Community 8	Rancho	West central	1991	1924
Community 9	Rancho	Northeast	1988	1940
Community 10	Rancho	Southwest	1998	1942
Community 11	Rancho	Southwest	1998	1942

Source: Data from Mexican Migration Project.

surveyed Guanajuato communities. These data suggest the existence of a much older international migration emanating from Guanajuato. The earliest recorded U.S. trip occurred in 1909, from community 2, followed by a 1915 trip from community 5. Several communities (1, 3, 4, 6, 7, and 8) began sending migrants to the United States in the 1920s.

Despite these early departures, in three communities (9, 10, and 11), international out-migration began much later, during the early 1940s. What these three communities have in common is that they are all rural villages—ranchos—whose migrants were early participants in the Bracero Program. Located in the northeast and southwest, they are also regionally distinct from communities in the north, south, and central (the Bajío) regions that began sending emigrants earlier. Thus the Bracero Program appears to have had direct effects in Guanajuato: first, it incorporated residents of ranchos into the international migratory flow as never before; second, it extended the traditional migratory spaces that earlier had been concentrated in the Bajío region, where the lines of transportation and communication northward were concentrated.

In most of the communities (with the exception of the two metropolitan areas, one city, and one rancho), international migration is considerably more prevalent than internal movement (see table 9.3). Especially in the rancho communities 8, 10, and 11, the proportion of migrants to the United States identified by the MMP was three to five times the proportion of internal migrants. Migrants from Guanajuato thus appear to "specialize" in international movement to the exclusion of internal trips, a tendency that is particularly marked in rural settings.

Table 9.4 shows the distribution of international migrants from Guanajuato by the period of their first U.S. trip. As can be seen, international out-migration began modestly in the years before 1942 (1.4 percent of all first trips occurred during this period), increased during the bracero period from 1942 to 1964 (around 11.7 percent of all first trips), and then surged markedly during the era of undocumented migration from 1965 to 1986 (59.7 percent) before declining somewhat in recent years (27.2 percent of first trips occurred after 1987).

Although one of the two metropolitan areas (community 2) was an important center for bracero recruitment, and both were directly connected by rail to the United States, the frequency of departure from 1942 to 1964 was no higher, on average, from the metropolitan areas than from other communities; this probably reflects the fact that recruitment was directed toward agricultural, not urban, workers (Durand 1998b). In all communities, the remarkable era of growth was from 1965 to 1986, during which undocumented migration predominated. Anywhere from half to three-

TABLE 9.3   Internal and International Migration from Eleven Guanajuato Communities, 1987 to 1997

Community and Classification	Percentage of All Migration		Sample Size (N = 14,127)
	International	Internal	
Metropolitan area			
Community 1	4.5	5.5	1,574
Community 2	11.8	19.4	1,331
Medium city			
Community 3	18.2	3.2	1,799
Community 4	14.2	9.4	1,580
Community 5	23.0	70.8	1,664
Community 6	23.5	17.9	1,406
Community 7	22.5	18.4	1,482
Rancho			
Community 8	17.2	4.8	883
Community 9	8.7	20.8	1,075
Community 10	31.0	6.2	600
Community 11	30.3	6.1	733

Source: Data from Mexican Migration Project.

quarters of all Guanajuato migrants left for the United States during this time, suggesting a process of out-migration that no internal transition in Mexico could dampen. Whether boom years (1970 to 1974 and 1977 to 1982) or bust (1974 to 1976 and 1982 to 1985), migration continued apace.

For the period that began in 1987 with the implementation of IRCA, data from the MMP must be handled with some caution: because nine of the eleven communities were surveyed between 1987 and 1992, most of the migratory experiences recorded happened before IRCA's provisions took full effect. Nonetheless, some observations can be made. First, although U.S. migration took off from 1965 to 1986, in the twelve years that followed it continued at significant levels, despite the buildup of border enforcement by the United States. The persistence of U.S. migration is most clearly seen in communities 10 and 11, both surveyed in 1998, from which 37 and 47 percent, respectively, of first U.S. trips occurred after the United States began increasing immigration restrictions.

Second, in the two communities surveyed in 1991 (communities 2 and 8), just five years after IRCA's passage, the number of first trips nearly equals those observed over the prior years of the undocumented era, meaning that

TABLE 9.4   International Migration from Eleven Guanajuato
                 Communities, by Period of First U.S. Trip (Percentage)

Community and Classification	Before 1942	1942 to 1964	1965 to 1986	After 1987	Total (N = 2,480)
Metropolitan area					
Community 1	5.6	14.1	71.8	8.8	71
Community 2	1.3	10.2	47.1	41.4	157
Medium city					
Community 3	2.5	12.5	72.5	12.5	327
Community 4	1.3	15.8	69.9	13.8	224
Community 5	1.3	11.5	52.7	34.5	383
Community 6	1.2	12.1	52.9	33.8	331
Community 7	0.6	13.5	72.4	13.5	333
Rancho					
Community 8	2.6	13.2	48.0	36.2	152
Community 9	1.1	4.3	77.7	17.0	94
Community 10	0.5	12.4	50.0	37.1	186
Community 11	0.5	5.9	47.3	46.9	222

Source: Data from Mexican Migration Project.

the rate of out-migration substantially *increased* in both places. There were 74 departures from community 2 and 73 from community 2 from 1965 to 1986, an average departure rate of of 3.5 and 3.4, respectively, per year. After 1986, however, we observe sixty-five departures from community 2 and fifty-five from community 8, yielding respective annual averages of 5.9 and 5.0. At least from this traditional migrant-sending state, IRCA and successive border operations do not seem to have accomplished their goal of stopping undocumented migration.

The escalation of out-migration from community 2 is surprising in that it has experienced substantial growth in recent years. Table 9.5 presents various indicators of demographic growth, sex composition, migration, and economic structure for the eleven communities. As can be seen, community 2 experienced a robust demographic increase of 1.89 percent during the 1990s and housed an economy that was among the most diversified and prosperous in the state, with 24 percent of its labor force employed in manufacturing, 21 percent in commerce, and just 9 percent in agriculture. This community, located in the heart of the Bajío, has excellent agricultural land and the largest number of modern agro-industrial businesses in the entire region. It is also the epicenter of a prosperous and well-known clothes-

TABLE 9.5   Indicators of Internal and International Migration in Eleven Guanajuato Communities

Community and Classification	Year 2000 Population	1990 to 2000 Growth Rate	U.S. Migration Rate	Sex Ratio	Labor Force Participation (Percentage)		
					Agriculture	Manufacturing	Commerce
Metropolitan area							
Community 1	1,020,800	3.04	4.5	95.2	1.6	38.2	20.0
Community 2	319,100	1.89	11.8	92.4	9.1	23.6	20.9
Medium city							
Community 3	65,200	2.25	18.2	94.7	9.4	53.2	13.0
Community 4	18,400	1.07	14.2	90.5	42.8	14.1	11.6
Community 5	22,100	−0.69	23.0	89.8	30.1	18.2	15.2
Community 6	34,000	0.16	23.5	88.3	25.5	14.1	19.2
Community 7	24,900	1.93	22.5	86.7	33.4	12.8	13.3
Rancho							
Community 8	1,200	1.23	17.2	87.3	9.1	23.5	20.9
Community 9	2,200	1.07	8.7	93.1	21.0	12.7	17.0
Community 10	1,200	−0.58	31.0	80.8	38.6	21.0	12.6
Community 11	1,500	0.53	30.3	89.2	38.5	20.9	12.7

Source: Data from Mexican Migration Project.

making industry, and it functions as the commercial and service center for an important agricultural area of the Bajío (Arias and Wilson 1997).

Despite the robust economy and the plethora of local economic opportunities, people nonetheless continue to migrate from community 2 to work in the United States, which suggests two simultaneous flows: in-migration of technical and professional workers, linked to the intensive modernization of local activities, and out-migration of workers, especially males, from the low-income neighborhoods of the city. The example of community 2 shows that no matter how dynamic and economically diversified a community may be—above all, in agriculture—it may offer insufficient opportunities to satisfy the local demand for employment and thus continue to encourage migratory flows, instead of detaining them.

Other communities that display high indexes of international migration include communities 5, 6, and 7, in each of which around 23 percent of the population has been to the United States. These are medium-sized cities located in the southern and northern areas of the state. The two cities in the south (communities 5 and 6) are primarily agricultural communities, which, like community 2, are experiencing intense agrarian change and agro-industrial modernization. In both locations, demographic growth is stagnant, and agriculture continues to be the most important employment sector (at 30 and 25 percent, respectively), thus confirming the hypothesis that agricultural modernization is generally accompanied by substantial out-migration.

The inverse relationship between the level of migration and the sex ratio suggests that such migration is predominantly male. In no community are the numbers of male and female migrants equal (which would be indicated by a sex ratio of 100). Sex ratios range from a low of 80.8 in community 10 (a small rancho) to a high of 95.2 in community 1 (a large metropolitan area), but as the prevalence of U.S. migration rises, the sex ratio generally falls. Employment for women, especially in the form of home-based work in the clothes-making industry, has grown dramatically in many communities in Guanajuato, and such employment seems to be combined and intertwined with male international migration as part of a common household strategy (Arias and Wilson 1997).

Community 7, located in the extensive but depressed northern region, displays a relatively high prevalence of international migration (around 22.5 percent), even though it has continued to grow demographically (1.93 percent from 1990 to 2000). The combination of growth with out-migration and a rather low sex ratio (86.7) suggests that the community is receiving flows of ever poorer immigrants from its rural hinterlands while at the same time expelling people, mainly men, to the United

States. In community 7, agricultural activities are still the main source of employment for local labor (accounting for roughly a third of all jobs), suggesting that arriving immigrants exert even more pressure on an already highly circumscribed, limited, and inflexible labor market, which, in turn, obliges both natives and newcomers to emigrate, the preferred destination being the United States.

Finally, the two ranchos surveyed in 1998 reflect the pattern typical for these kinds of localities. Communities 10 and 11 are both located in the southwest region, an agricultural and livestock-raising area that is geographically quite close to community 2 and is clearly articulated with that city's dynamic economy and its burgeoning regional labor markets. The municipality in which these ranchos are located is still predominantly agricultural in terms of employment (nearly 40 percent of all workers are agrarian), and demographic growth in both communities has been curtailed as people continue to leave, mainly for the United States (both communities display migration prevalence rates in excess of 30 percent). The low sex ratios indicate that this movement continues to be largely male, although female migration has also increased in recent years.

CONCLUSION

To date, the MMP offers the only database for the state of Guanajuato that has examined international migration in a systematic, reliable way from a long-term perspective in different regions and population centers. Research undertaken since 1987 has detected, measured, and mapped patterns of U.S. migration and has helped to deepen our understanding of dynamic migratory processes in a state that constitutes a key source of both past and current migration to the United States.

Although firm conclusions are not easily drawn from these data, nor can the data necessarily be generalized to other migrant-sending regions, the findings are consistent with the basic hypothesis of cumulative causation theory, which holds that once processes of international migration begin, they weave extensive social networks that steadily increase the number of migrants. These networks yield social capital that community members can draw upon to gain access to U.S. jobs as a means of adapting to profound structural changes occurring around them. Thus migratory pressures arise not from the conditions of unemployment, poverty, or intense need but rather from the spread of dynamic economic development to rural areas.

The state of Guanajuato has experienced an unusually intense and diverse process of economic change in both rural and urban settings. Some of these changes have clearly produced increasing hardship, social marginalization, and the exclusion of local actors and local knowledge from broader economic activities. At the same time, however, these changes have thrust Guanajuato and its people into the front line, the vanguard, of globalization and development, especially in the agricultural and manufacturing sectors. Today, the Bajío area of Guanajuato seems to be functioning as a living laboratory of agro-industrial modernization and agrarian change.

In all sectors, international migration, embedded as it is in the historical memory of the people and constantly expressed in everyday life, represents a key resource that households can draw upon as they adapt to change. Migration to "el otro lado" has been, and continues to be, the means by which Guanajuatenses confront and resolve the successive, uncontrollable, and incomprehensible transitions to which their lives and work have been subjected through the workings of the global economy. In this sense, the MMP's data suggest that as long as no better adaptive alternatives exist, people from Guanajuato will continue to leave their communities and swell the long lines of international migrants heading northward.

Translated from the Spanish by Paul C. Kersey.

REFERENCES

Argüello, Francisco J. 1993. "Experiencias migratorias de campesinos de Guanajuato en Canadá." *Regiones* 1: 89–105.

Arias, Patricia, and Fiona Wilson. 1997. *La aguja y el surco: Cambio regional, consumo y relaciones de género en la industria de la ropa en México.* Guadalajara, Mexico: University of Guadalajara, Center for Development Research.

Carreras, Mercedes. 1974. *Los Mexicanos que devolvió la crisis 1929–1932.* Mexico City: Secretaría de Relaciones Exteriores.

Cebada, María Del Carmen. 1993. "La migración hacia Estados Unidos y dos comunidades de origen en el estado de Guanajuato." *Regiones* 1: 73–87.

Consejo Nacional de Población (CONAPO). 1987. *Guanajuato demográfico: Breviario 1985.* Mexico City: Consejo Nacional de Población.

Corona, Rodolfo. 1987. "Estimación de número de indocumentados a nivel estatal y municipal." Unpublished paper. Universidad Nacional de México, Centro de Estudios Sobre Identidad Nacional en Zonas Fronterizas.

Durand, Jorge. 1987. "Guanajuato: Cantera de migrantes." *Encuentro* 4: 49–62.

———. 1994. *Más allá de la línea: Patrones migratorios entre México y Estados Unidos.* Mexico City: Consejo Nacional par la Cultura y las Artes.

———. 1998a. "¿Nuevas regiones migratorias?" In *Población, desarrollo y globalización,* edited by René M. Zenteno. Mexico City: Sociedad Mexicana de Demografía and El Colegio de la Frontera Norte.

———. 1998b. *Política, modelos y patrón migratorios: El trabajo y los trabajadores Mexicanos en Estados Unidos.* San Luis Potosí, Mexico: El Colegio de San Luis.

Durand, Jorge, Douglas S. Massey, and René Zenteno. 2001. "Continuities and Changes in Mexico-U.S. Migration." *Latin American Research Review* 36: 107–27.

Faret, Laurent. 1998. *Les Territoires de la mobilité: Champ migratoire et espaces transnationaux entre le Mexique et les États Unis.* Toulouse, France: Université de Toulouse–Le Mirail.

Gamio, Manuel. 1930. *Mexican Immigration to the United States.* Chicago: University of Chicago Press.

García, Víctor. 1998. "Guanajuatense and Other Mexican Immigrants in the United States: New Communities in Non-Metropolitan and Agricultural Regions." *Regiones* 10: 125–41.

González, Laura. 1996. "La red de migrantes Guanajuatenses." *Cuadernos del centro de investigación en ciencias sociales.* Guanajuato, México: Universidad de Guanajuato.

———. n.d. "The Migration Network: A Case Study of Guanajuatenses in Dallas, Texas." Unpublished paper. Universidad de Guanajuato, Centro de Investigación en Ciencias Sociales.

Martínez, Guillermo. 1948. "Los braceros: Experiencias que deben aprovecharse." *Revista Mexicana de Sociología* 10: 177–95.

Ranney, Susan, and Sherrie Kossoudji. 1983. "Profiles of Temporary Mexican Labor Migrants to the United States." *Population and Development Review* 9(3, September): 475–93.

Roberts, Kenneth D. 1982. "Agrarian Structure and Labor Mobility in Rural Mexico." *Population and Development Review* 8: 299–322.

Smith, Shirley J., Roger G. Kramer, and Audrey Singer. 1996. *Characteristics and Labor Market Behavior of the Legalized Population Five Years Following Legalization.* Washington: U.S. Department of Labor.

CHAPTER 10

SOCIAL CAPITAL AND EMIGRATION FROM RURAL AND URBAN COMMUNITIES

Nadia Y. Flores, Rubén Hernández-León, and Douglas S. Massey

THROUGHOUT ITS long history, Mexican migration to the United States has been predominantly rural in origin. Little attention has been paid to emigrants from urban areas and to differences they might exhibit compared with their rural counterparts. In response to the continued urbanization of Mexico, researchers have come to pay more attention to emigration originating in cities and, more particularly, metropolitan areas (Durand, Massey, and Parrado 1999). Recent studies have documented the changing proportion of urbanites among migrants to the United States (Cornelius 1992; Durand, Massey, and Zenteno 2001; Lozano-Ascencio 2000; Marcelli and Cornelius 2001), the causes of emigration from urban areas (Hernández-León 2001; Roberts and Escobar Latapí 1997), and the social organization of urban-origin emigration (Hernández-León 1997, 1999; Massey et al. 1987; Roberts, Frank, and Lozano-Ascencio 1999).

Despite this new interest in out-migration from urban areas, however, few studies have directly compared patterns and processes with those prevailing in rural settings. We contend that such a comparison is necessary to understand the dynamics of emigration from urban as opposed to rural contexts and to determine the applicability of current theories to migration from each setting. This chapter seeks to undertake these tasks by comparing the characteristics of rural- and urban-origin migrants and by contrasting the determinants of emigration from rural and urban settings.

THEORIZING RURAL AND URBAN SETTINGS

Most theorizing about Mexico–U.S. migration, in seeking to explain how conditions common to agricultural villages yield strong motivations for seasonal wage labor in the United States, implicitly assumes an outflow that is rural in origin. According to the new economics of labor migration, in particular, the absence of reliable markets in the countryside prompts single males from rural communities to emigrate for wage labor as a means of self-financing agricultural production, self-insuring against risks to family well-being, and acquiring capital for housing (Massey et al. 1998). The migrants are assumed to be target earners seeking to make investments at home in anticipation of their eventual return. Owing to their undocumented status, rural migrants display little tendency to settle abroad permanently or seek out nonagricultural occupations (Durand 1998).

According to social capital theory, interpersonal networks arise in the course of recurrent movement for seasonal wage labor abroad. These networks connect sending and receiving areas to create a social infrastructure that channels and sustains future migration by lowering the costs and risks of particular cross-border movements (Massey et al. 1987). The diffusion of migratory behavior through such networks reduces the original selectivity of flow and over time gives rise to a "culture of migration" that functions independently of its original economic causes (Alarcón 1992; Kandel and Massey 2002; Reichert 1981). This sequence of events provides evidence for a larger process of *cumulative causation* (Massey 1990). Causation becomes cumulative when out-migration leads to changes in individual motivations and social structures that function to increase the odds of additional migration (Reichert 1982).

This self-feeding dynamic, wherein migration produces more migration, is rooted in the social structure of peasant communities (Smith 2001) and in characteristic practices such as reciprocity (Foster 1942), solidarity (Flores 2000), and endogamy (Mummert 1999). Economic institutional arrangements such as the ejido (communal farmland) emphasize cooperation and orientation toward the collectivity, whereas reciprocity and endogamy reinforce networks to produce overlapping, multiplex social ties (superimposing kinship, friendship, and paisanaje [common community origins]). Taken together, these institutional arrangements and norms offset, at least in part, tendencies toward social differentiation that stem from the incorporation of rural migrants into national and international markets.

Substantially less is known theoretically about international migration emanating from urban areas. Some scholars have questioned the generalizability of theories developed with rural communities in mind. Though the "dynamics of international migration from large metropolitan areas have not been well studied," they "are sufficiently different from those of smaller towns and cities to warrant separate study" (Massey, Goldring, and Durand 1994, 1503, 1506). The paucity of studies conducted in cities and the fact that prevailing theories of international migration tend to be modeled on rural archetypes leave unanswered questions of whether and how current theoretical knowledge applies to international migrants originating in urban settings.

Theories such as the new economics of labor migration explicitly discuss international migration as a household strategy deployed to overcome failures in labor, financial, and insurance markets that are characteristic of rural Mexico. In urban Mexico, however, there is greater access to unemployment insurance, pensions, low-cost housing programs, and lending through both formal and informal means, potentially reducing the importance of market failures in motivating urban-origin emigration. Although a minority of jobs may be covered by unemployment insurance, a large and dynamic informal sector provides abundant jobs; and though most urban workers do not have bank accounts, they nonetheless have access to a rather diverse web of informal credit and savings institutions.

In Monterrey, Nuevo León, for example, where large corporations and formal employment dominate the labor market, households often borrow money from their employers at little or no interest, and they also request pension advances from their federal social security accounts (Hernández-León 2001). Many companies also offer savings plans wherein contributions made by employees are matched by the firm, yielding a source of personal capital.

In León, Guanajuato, however, where small manufacturing shops and informal labor relations prevail, workers resort to "cajas populares"— savings and loans institutions that follow a cooperative model and charge low interest rates. Individuals also frequently participate in the tanda system to accumulate savings (Flores 2001). "Tandas" are rotating credit associations in which each member receives a one-shot amount made of all the funds accumulated during the savings cycle. The tanda, of which the most common form is that composed of neighbors and work colleagues, represents an informal mechanism to overcome a lack of access to banks and other formal lending institutions (Vélez-Ibáñez 1983a).

The conditions of city life also undermine the mechanisms postulated by social capital theory. In contrast to rural villages, large cities are generally characterized by differentiation, anonymity, and mobility (Wirth 1938). These conditions may not permit the operation of self-feeding processes of network formation and other mechanisms of cumulative causation. A long sociological tradition has noted changes in the forms and sources of social solidarity and cohesion as human societies undergo urbanization (see Durkheim 1984; Simmel 1971). Social solidarity does not disappear in urban settings, but the bases of societal cohesion shift as weaker ties of friendship and acquaintance predominate over the stronger ties of kinship and paisanaje (Fischer 1982).

Strong ties survive and reproduce in urban settings under certain conditions, such as segregation by race, class, or ethnicity (Gans 1962); transplantation from rural areas (Lomnitz 1977); and common adaptations to economic marginalization (Vélez-Ibáñez 1983b). However, recent studies have shown contradictory results regarding the dynamics of networks and cumulative causation in cities. Whereas Douglas Massey (1987) finds that working-class residents of a Guadalajara neighborhood, unable to develop their own networks, relied on rural villages to access social capital, Rubén Hernández-León (2001) finds that residents of a working-class district of Monterrey used neighborhood-level contacts to migrate, find shelter, and obtain jobs in Houston, Texas.

It thus seems that more empirical work is needed to determine whether cumulative causation takes place in cities, albeit in a less forceful way, or whether the processes of network expansion and social capital formation that power the self-feeding dynamics of migration function differently in urban areas. In this analysis, therefore, we specify a statistical model that links the likelihood of taking a first undocumented trip to measures of human, physical, and social capital while controlling for conditions in the binational economy, and we estimate the model separately for rural and urban areas. Of particular interest are the relative strength of human capital, social capital, and economic conditions in determining the odds of emigration from each setting.

DATA AND METHODS

To compare the causes of urban and rural migration from Mexico to the United States, we use data from the Mexican Migration Project (MMP) (see chapter 16). For simplicity, we decided to split the data into rural and urban settings based on population, which is an obviously arbitrary but nonetheless necessary exercise for the comparative analysis we sought to conduct. Mexico's national statistical institute uses an official cutoff of twenty-five hundred inhabitants to distinguish rural from urban areas, but researchers have employed a variety of thresholds ranging from ten thousand (Marcelli and Cornelius 2001) to fifteen thousand (Durand, Massey, and Zenteno 2001) to twenty thousand (Lozano Ascencio 2000) inhabitants.

Since previous studies have all shown that migrants from rural communities are more prone than their urban counterparts to migrate to the United States (Massey et al. 1987), we decided to establish a cutoff number based on the likelihood of undertaking a first trip to the United States as a function of community population size. Using logistic regression, we modeled the odds of migration by household heads as a function of dummy variables representing community size in increments of five hundred people. We found that a threshold of six thousand persons yielded a marked discontinuity in predicting the odds of migration. Below this cutoff, community residents had a high probability of migration; above it, the odds were uniformly lower.

Therefore, we divided the MMP sample into rural and urban segments depending on whether the community was above or below 6,000 inhabitants (rural is less than or equal to 6,000; urban is 6,001 or more). Within each set of communities we selected male heads of household (98 percent of all heads) and used discrete-time event-history methods to predict the odds of undertaking a first undocumented trip to the United States as a function of selected variables. Predictor variables, defined in table 10.1, include indicators of demographic background, human capital, physical capital, social capital, and national economic conditions for each respondent. Data were obtained from life histories, and units of analysis are person-years observed after 1965 for respondents aged fifteen or older. Each respondent was followed from age fifteen until age sixty-five, first migration to the United States, or the survey date, whichever came first. If no undocumented move occurred, the outcome was coded as 0; if the respondent left for the United States in undocumented status, it was coded as 1, and all subsequent person-years were excluded. In this way we predict the annual probability of taking a first undocumented trip to the United States.

All independent variables are measured during the year before the occurrence of the migratory event $(t-1)$. Demographic variables include age (with a squared term to capture nonlinearities), marital status (whether currently married), and number of children in the household under the age of eighteen. Human capital is measured by years of schooling, a dummy variable for occupational status (whether nonagricultural), and the number of prior migratory trips taken within Mexico. Three dummy variables take into account access to physical capital: possession of agricultural land, ownership of a business, and ownership of real estate. Similarly, two dichotomous variables indicate access to social capital: whether a parent had been to the United States and whether any sibling had ever migrated there.

We also include the migration prevalence ratio to measure social capital accessible at the community level. It is defined as the share of community

TABLE 10.1   Definition of Variables Used in Comparative Analysis
of Initial Out-Migration from Rural and Urban
Mexican Communities

Variable	Definition
Outcome: first trip	1 if left for United States without documents in person-year; 0 otherwise
Demographic background	
Age	Age during person-year
Married	1 if in union during person-year; 0 otherwise
Number of minor children	Number of children under the age of eighteen in household during person-year
Human capital	
Education	Years of schooling completed
Nonagricultural skills	1 if worked in nonagrarian job; 0 otherwise
Number of internal trips	Cumulative number of trips within Mexico taken by person-year
Physical capital	
Landowner	1 if owns agricultural land during person-year; 0 otherwise
Business owner	1 if owns business during person-year; 0 otherwise
Real estate owner	1 if owns house or lot during person-year; 0 otherwise
Social capital	
Migrant parent	1 if parent had migrated by person-year; 0 otherwise
Migrant sibling	1 if sibling had migrated by person-year; 0 otherwise
Prevalence ratio	Proportion of persons over the age of fifteen with U.S. experience in person-year
Economic conditions	
U.S.-Mexico wage ratio	Ratio of average wage in United States to average wage in Mexico in person-year
Mexican interest rate	Average real Mexican interest rate during person-year

Source: Data from Mexican Migration Project.

residents aged fifteen or over who had ever been to the United States within a given person-year (see Massey, Goldring, and Durand 1994). Finally, to capture yearly fluctuations in macroeconomic circumstances, we introduce two national-level variables: the ratio of average wages in the United States to average wages in Mexico and Mexico's real interest rate. To discern whether there are significant differences in effects between equations estimated for rural and urban respondents, we conducted Wald chi-squared tests between coefficients (Allison 1999a).

U.S. MIGRANTS FROM RURAL AND URBAN AREAS

Table 10.2 presents average characteristics of U.S. migrants from rural and urban areas of Mexico during the year they made their first undocumented

TABLE 10.2   Characteristics of Migrant Household Heads from Rural and Urban Mexican Communities During the Year of Their First Undocumented Trip to the United States

Variable	Rural	Urban
Demographic background		
Age	25.50	19.97
Married	0.92	0.95
Number of minor children	1.44	1.16
Human capital		
Education	5.30	6.31
Nonagricultural skills	0.32	0.46
Number of internal trips	0.57	0.94
Physical capital		
Landowner	0.13	0.06
Business owner	0.05	0.08
Real estate owner	0.31	0.24
Social capital		
Migrant parent	0.51	0.43
Migrant sibling	0.88	0.87
Prevalence ratio	0.24	0.22
Economic conditions		
U.S.-Mexico wage ratio	7.59	7.48
Mexican interest rate	2.61	3.43

Source: Data from Mexican Migration Project.

trip. As can be seen, urban-origin migrants were significantly younger (by more than five years) than their rural counterparts. Nonetheless, both groups were quite young, with an average age of 25.5 for rural-origin migrants and 20.0 for those from urban areas. The overwhelming majority of migrants from both settings were married at the time they first left for the United States (more than 90 percent), though those from rural areas had slightly more minor children at home (1.4 versus 1.2), as would be expected given higher levels of rural fertility.

In terms of human capital, urban-origin migrants possessed an additional year of schooling (an average of 6.3 years compared with 5.3 for rural-origin migrants). Moreover, whereas nearly half (46 percent) of urban-origin migrants held nonagricultural occupations, only a third (32 percent) of rural-origin migrants did so. As might be expected given the growth of Mexican cities through internal migration, urban-origin migrants had made more domestic trips (an average of 0.9) than those of rural origin (0.6).

In general, migrants from rural and urban areas had similar access to human capital at the time of their first trip. Eighty-eight percent of rural migrants and 87 percent of urban migrants reported having a sibling with U.S. experience; the migration prevalence ratio was .24 in rural communities and .22 in urban areas. The principal difference with respect to human capital concerned parental ties. Whereas more than half (51 percent) of those migrating from rural areas had a parent who had been to the United States, only 43 percent of migrants leaving urban areas did so. Apart from this modest difference, however, those rural and urban dwellers who ended up migrating had similar access to social capital at the time of their departure.

Consistent with the economic structure of rural communities, a greater proportion of rural-origin migrants owned agricultural land (13 percent) than urbanites (6 percent). In contrast, migrants of urban origin were more likely to own businesses (8 percent) than their rural counterparts (5 percent), though the fraction of owners in both cases (farmland and business enterprises) was quite small. Real estate ownership was more common. Nearly a third of rural-origin migrants owned a house or lot, compared with a quarter of those in urban settings. In general, urbanites are more likely to be renters than home owners.

Not surprisingly, the overall U.S.-Mexico wage ratio was essentially the same in both rural and urban settings, at around 7.5. During the year of their departure, however, the real interest rate was significantly higher for migrating urbanites than for respondents leaving rural areas (3.4 versus 2.6). Thus it seems that rural- and urban-origin migrants are selected to have similar marital statuses and comparable access to social capital, but those of rural origin tend to be older, have less education, and are less likely to own businesses, while urbanites are less likely to own homes and farmland and are more likely to leave during periods characterized by higher interest rates.

DETERMINANTS OF EMIGRATION: RURAL VERSUS URBAN

As with the descriptive comparison of rural and urban migrants, the event-history analysis estimated to predict the likelihood of leaving on a first undocumented trip from both settings yields both similarities and differences. Table 10.3 presents coefficients for two discrete-time event-history modes—rural and urban—both estimated with logistic regression procedures using person-years as units of analysis. The coefficients show the relative size, direction, and effects of variables on the likelihood of undocumented migration. By applying the formula $(e^B - 1) \times 100$, these coefficients can be transformed to give the percentage change in the odds of initial out-migration per unit of change in the independent variable (see Allison 1999b).

Among demographic factors, number of children affect the probability of undocumented migration similarly in rural and urban settings. In both cases, the likelihood of out-migration decreases with the addition of each child. Indeed, each minor child added to the household reduces the odds of head's migration by around 15 percent (in this section, all the percentage changes in the odds of out-migration were computed using the formula given in the preceding paragraph). Although marriage acts strongly to affect the relative likelihood of undocumented migration from both rural and urban settings, the direction of the effect is opposite: being in a union increases the odds of migration from rural areas by 70 percent but decreases the odds of emigration from urban areas by 36 percent.

In rural areas, migration appears to be intertwined with the process of family formation, which begins with marriage. Marriage creates strong pressures for the formation of a separate household, which requires a young man to obtain a separate dwelling. In rural areas, homes are generally owned rather than rented, so in practical terms marriage and family formation create an acute need to accumulate capital for the construction or purchase of a home, which in the ranchos and villages of rural Mexico can be achieved only through migration. In contrast, home ownership is not as common in urban areas, and the rental markets are larger and more vibrant. Although marriage may create new demands for housing, these can easily be satisfied without resorting to international migration simply by renting an apartment.

TABLE 10.3   Discrete-Time Event-History Analysis of Undocumented Out-migration from Rural and Urban Areas of Mexico to the United States

Variable	Rural Areas		Urban Areas	
	Beta Coefficient	Standard Error	Beta Coefficient	Standard Error
Demographic background				
Age	−0.070	0.057	0.023	0.048
Age squared	0.004**	0.001	0.002*	0.001
Married	0.530**	0.151	−0.453**	0.159
Number of minor children	−0.165**	0.049	−0.169**	0.039
Human capital				
Education	−0.043**	0.015	−0.021	0.012
Nonagricultural skills	−0.224**	0.096	−0.166*	0.076
Number of internal trips	−0.137**	0.040	−0.061**	0.016
Physical capital				
Landowner	−0.223	0.140	0.186	0.166
Business owner	−0.133	0.201	0.182	0.133
Real estate owner	0.176	0.112	−0.145	0.087
Social capital				
Migrant parent	1.039**	0.098	0.710**	0.078
Migrant sibling	0.333**	0.043	0.244**	0.030
Prevalence ratio	0.652**	0.289	1.010**	0.250
Economic conditions				
U.S.-Mexico wage ratio	0.053**	0.014	0.029**	0.011
Mexican interest rate	0.004	0.003	0.012**	0.003
Intercept	−3.078**	0.688	−3.249**	0.571
Likelihood ratio	857.21**		702.00**	
Chi squared	857.21**		702.00**	
Person-years	28,956		45,096	

Source: Data from Mexican Migration Project.
*p < .05   **p < .01

Prior work has generally shown the likelihood of international migration to be negatively related to human capital. According to Edward Taylor (1986, 1987), skills and education acquired in Mexico are not readily transferable to the U.S. labor market; but they are likely to be rewarded in Mexico's metropolitan economy. Hence rural residents with human capital are more likely to migrate internally than internationally. Whereas a secondary school graduate migrating illegally to the United States is confined to the same low-skilled jobs as an illiterate peasant, by moving to a Mexican city he or she is able to achieve a higher-status, even white-collar job. Thus internal migration constitutes an attractive alternative to international migration for educated rural dwellers. Since urban dwellers are already in the city, however, these disincentives to international movement do not apply to them to the same degree.

Consistent with this reasoning, the coefficients in table 10.3 generally show human capital to be negatively related to the likelihood of illegal out-migration in both rural and urban areas, but the strength of the effects is generally greater in the former. Whereas each year of education reduces the odds of migration by around 4 percent among rural dwellers (significant at $p < .01$), it lowers them by only 2 percent among urban residents. Similarly, each additional domestic trip lowers the odds of undocumented migration to the United States by 13 percent in rural settings but by only 6 percent in urban areas ($p < .01$). Finally, having skills sufficient for a nonagricultural occupation reduces the odds of undocumented migration by 20 percent in rural areas but only by 15 percent in urban settings, though this difference between coefficients is not statistically significant. These results are generally consistent with earlier studies that have shown internal migration to constitute an alternative to international wage labor, especially for rural dwellers (Arizpe 1981, 1985; Massey and Espinosa 1997; Zendejas and Mummert 1998).

Interestingly, none of the physical capital indicators has a statistically significant influence on the likelihood of undocumented migration, either in rural or urban settings. This pattern of results may reflect the fact that a relatively small share of households in either setting owned a business or farmland, although larger shares in both places did possess real estate. In contrast, access to social capital has strong, positive, and consistent effects on the odds of international migration, in keeping with the findings of many earlier studies (Massey and Espinosa 1997; Massey and García España 1987; Massey et al. 1987; Taylor 1987).

Among both rural and urban heads of household, having a parent with prior U.S. experience strongly increases the odds of taking a first migratory trip. However, the effect of this predictor is significantly higher in rural than in urban areas—183 percent compared with 103 percent ($p < .01$). By the same token, having a sibling with previous U.S. experience operates in a positive direction across both community types, but the variable has a much stronger effect on the odds of out-migration from rural areas (40 percent) than from urban settings (28 percent), a difference that is nearly significant statistically ($p < .09$). In sum, having kin connections to U.S. migrants seems to have similar effects on out-migration from rural and urban areas, but the effects are more powerful in the former than in the latter.

Given the greater mistrust and anonymity prevalent in urban areas, we might expect the generalized social capital indexed by the prevalence ratio to have less influence there than in rural areas. If 30 percent of a rural community's adults have been to the United States, the chances are that most of them will be personally known to someone seeking help in migrating abroad; but if 30 percent of those living in a dense urban neighborhood have been abroad, many of these people will be unknown to potential emigrants. Although they are physically close, urban migrants are socially removed from neighborhood residents, even when they live on the same block and especially when they live several blocks away. Moreover, whereas town residents are likely to be interrelated through strong kinship ties, city residents tend to be interconnected through weaker ties of friendship and acquaintance.

Contrary to this line of reasoning, however, we find that the migration prevalence ratio had strong positive effects on out-migration from both rural and urban environments. Indeed, the effect was stronger in urban settings, though the difference between the coefficients was not statistically significant. Whereas each point increase in the prevalence ratio raised the odds of out-migration from urban areas by 1 percent, it raised the odds of undocumented migration from rural areas by just 0.7 percent. We initially thought that this contrast stemmed from the rather low threshold for urbanism—just six thousand inhabitants—but we found that it held even when we increased the cutoff to one hundred thousand persons.

Our finding of a strong positive effect of migration prevalence on out-migration from urban areas contrasts with the reasoning and findings of earlier studies (Massey et al. 1987; Roberts, Frank, and Lozano-Ascencio 1999), which generally cast doubt on the power of cumulative causation to operate within urban environments. In settings where neighbors were more likely to be nonkin than kin, where most nonkin neighbors were unknown or superficially known to residents, and where the sense of paisanaje among neighborhood residents was rather weak, the presence of migrants in the immediate environment was neither found nor expected to yield quantities of social capital sufficient to lock in the self-feeding cycle of social capital formation to create a local "culture of migration."

Our results appear to be more consistent with sociological and anthropological studies that expect and find a recreation and transplantation of solidarity ties from rural to urban settings. As noted earlier in this chapter, Herbert Gans (1962), Larissa Lomnitz (1977), and Carlos Vélez-Ibáñez (1983a) all emphasize the role of social bonds based on class, ethnicity, and common origin in the social organization, survival, and reproduction of urban households. The positive effect of the migration prevalence ratio on undocumented migration from urban areas suggests that at least some of these social bonds may be mobilized to support international migration to the United States (Hernández-León 2001).

Finally, the two national-level economic measures shown appear to have different effects. On the one hand, wage differentials between Mexico and the United States are good predictors of international mobility in general but not of differences between urban and rural settings. Although the positive coefficient is larger for rural than for urban dwellers (.053 versus .029) and each unit increase in the size of the wage ratio correspondingly yields an increase of 5.4 percent in rural areas but only 2.9 percent in urban areas, the differences are not statistically significant. Mexico's real interest rate, on the other hand, has a positive and highly significant effect only in the urban sample. For each point increase in the real interest rate, the odds of undocumented migration rise by 1.2 percent among urbanites, compared with virtually no effect among rural dwellers.

This finding is generally consistent with hypotheses derived from the new economics of labor migration, which sees migration as a response to barriers to capital and credit. Since rural Mexican communities are excluded altogether from capital and credit markets, variations in interest rates are irrelevant to rural dwellers but bear directly on the access urbanites have to capital and credit. Thus when the "peso crisis" of 1994 led to a rapid increase in interest rates, it led also to a sharp increase in out-migration by working- and middle-class people from urban areas (Durand, Massey, and Parrado 1999; Massey and Espinosa 1997).

CONCLUSION

This initial exploration of the causes of undocumented migration from rural and urban Mexican communities, defined according to a cutoff of six thousand inhabitants, yields several important conclusions. First, we find that household formation is associated with international migration in rural but not in urban areas. Whereas urban couples simply enter the rental market to establish an independent residence, rural couples must finance the construction or purchase of a home, leading recently married household heads to migrate northward to accumulate the necessary savings through employment in the United States. In both cases, however, the presence of young children strongly reduces the propensity to migrate.

Second, although human capital acquired in Mexico is negatively associated with the odds of undocumented migration in both rural and urban areas, the effect is generally greater in the former than in the latter. Among rural dwellers, human capital tends to promote internal migration to metropolitan areas as an alternative to international migration, since they are likely to achieve significant returns to Mexican skills and education in urban labor markets. Among urban dwellers, however, internal migration is less of an option because, by definition, they are already present in an urban labor market, and, indeed, many have already migrated from rural areas. Although human capital exerts a negative effect on urban out-migration to the United States, therefore, it is not as powerful as in the countryside.

Third, kin ties to U.S. migrants yield a valuable source of social capital for residents of both rural and urban areas, but the effect in promoting undocumented migration is generally greater in rural settings. In a milieu of community solidarity, kin ties in rural areas tend to be stronger and yield greater quantities of social capital. Consistent with the theory of social capital and cumulative causation, we find that a rising prevalence of migrants within the surrounding community strongly increased the odds of an individual's out-migration. Contrary to some prior reasoning, however, we find no significant differences between rural and urban areas. Across settings, rising prevalence ratios increased the odds of undocumented migration at rates that were statistically indistinguishable.

Finally, we find that both rural and urban dwellers migrated in response to shifts in the size of the binational wage differential, as predicted by neoclassical economics. Moreover, the effect of the wage differential was roughly comparable across settings. In terms of macroeconomic effects, we find that undocumented migration from urban areas was responsive to fluctuations in real interest rates, whereas rural-origin migration was not. We take this to mean that banks and other formal credit institutions are so totally lacking in rural areas that real interest rates are irrelevant to migration decisions, whereas urban dwellers have greater access to a variety of formal and informal sources of capital and credit, so that interest rates do matter.

This research offers only an initial exploration of rural-urban differences in the process of international migration. Other contextual variables need to be added to the models in future work, and perhaps new indicators need to be developed to capture the social and economic realities of cities. Here we have noted the similarities and differences in the determinants of male undocumented migration from rural and urban areas and confirmed resulting differences in migrant characteristics. Theories of international migration have often been developed with rural-origin migrants in mind, and our research suggests that some propositions may not apply so readily to those of urban origin. It is not that current theories should never be applied to urban settings but rather that the application should be done with fore-thought so as to take into account the unique characteristics of urban neighborhoods that follow from their large size, density, and social heterogeneity.

References

Alarcón, Rafael. 1992. "Norteñización: Self-Perpetuating Migration from a Mexican Town." In *U.S.-Mexico Relations: Labor Market Interdependence*, edited by Jorge A. Bustamante, Clark W. Reynolds, and Raúl A. Hinojosa. Stanford, Calif.: Stanford University Press.

Allison, Paul D. 1999a. "Comparing Logit and Probit Coefficients Across Groups." *Sociological Methods and Research* 28: 186–208.

———. 1999b. *Logistic Regression Using the SAS System: Theory and Application.* Cary, N.C.: SAS Publishing.

Arizpe, Lourdes. 1981. "The Rural Exodus in Mexico and Mexican Migration to the United States." *International Migration Review* 15: 626–49.

———. 1985. *Campesinado y migración.* Mexico City: Secretaría de Educación Pública.

Cornelius, Wayne A. 1992. "From Sojourners to Settlers: The Changing Profile of Mexican Immigration to the United States." In *U.S.-Mexico Relations: Labor Market Interdependence*, edited by Jorge Bustamante, Clark Reynolds, and Raúl Hinojosa. Stanford, Calif.: Stanford University Press.

Durand, Jorge. 1998. *Política, Modelo y Patrón Migratorios: El trabajo y los trabajadores mexicanos en Estados Unidos.* San Luis Potosí, Mex.: El Colegio de San Luis.

Durand, Jorge, Douglas S. Massey, and Emilio A. Parrado. 1999. "The New Era of Mexican Migration to the United States." *Journal of American History* 86: 518–36.

Durand, Jorge, Douglas S. Massey, and René Zenteno. 2001. "Mexican Immigration to the United States: Continuities and Changes." *Latin American Research Review* 36(1): 107–26.

Durkheim, Émile. 1984. *The Division of Labor in Society.* New York: Free Press.

Fischer, Claude S. 1982. *To Dwell Among Friends: Personal Networks in Town and City.* Chicago: University of Chicago Press.

Flores, Nadia Y. 2000. "Reciprocity, Solidarity and Altruism in Mexican Migration to the United States: A Case Study." Paper presented to the American Sociological Association annual meetings, "Oppression, Domination, and Liberation: Challenges for the Twenty-first Century." Washington, D.C., August 12–16.

———. 2001. "León, Guanajuato as a Place of Origin for Mexican Migrants to the United States." Working paper. University of Pennsylvania, Population Studies Center.

Foster, George M. 1942. *A Primitive Mexican Economy.* New York: J. J. Augustin.

Gans, Herbert. 1962. *The Urban Villagers.* New York: Free Press.

Hernández-León, Rubén. 1997. "El circuito migratorio Monterrey-Houston." *Ciudades* 35: 26–33.

————. 1999. "¡A la aventura! Jóvenes, pandillas y migración en la conexión Monterrey-Houston." In *Fronteras fragmentadas*, edited by Gail Mummert. Zamora, Mexico: El Colegio de Michoacán.

————. 2001. "Urban Origin Migration from Mexico to the United States: The Case of the Monterrey Metropolitan Area." Ph.D. diss., Department of Sociology, State University of New York at Binghamton.

Kandel, William, and Douglas S. Massey. 2002. "The Culture of Mexican Migration: A Theoretical and Empirical Analysis." *Social Forces* 80: 981–1004.

Lomnitz, Larissa Adler. 1977. *Networks and Marginality: Life in a Mexican Shantytown*. New York: Academic Press.

Lozano-Ascencio, Fernando. 2000. "Migration Strategies in Urban Contexts: Labor Migration from Mexico City to the United States." Paper presented to the Latin American Studies Association, Twenty-third International Congress. Miami, Florida, March 16–18.

Marcelli, Enrico, and Wayne A. Cornelius. 2001. "The Changing Profile of Mexican Migrants to the United States: New Evidence from California and Mexico." *Latin American Research Review* 36(3): 105–31.

Massey, Douglas S. 1987. "The Ethnosurvey in Theory and Practice." *International Migration Review* 21: 1498–1522.

————. 1990. "Social Structure, Household Strategies, and the Cumulative Causation of Migration." *Population Index* 56: 3–26.

Massey, Douglas S., Rafael Alarcón, Jorge Durand, and Humberto González. 1987. *Return to Aztlan: The Social Process of International Migration from Western Mexico*. Berkeley: University of California Press.

Massey, Douglas S., Joaquín Arango, Graeme Hugo, Ali Kouaouci, Adela Pellegrino, and J. Edward Taylor. 1998. *Worlds in Motion: Understanding International Migration at the End of the Millennium*. Oxford: Clarendon Press.

Massey, Douglas S., and Kristin E. Espinosa. 1997. "What's Driving Mexico-U.S. Migration? A Theoretical, Empirical, and Policy Analysis." *American Journal of Sociology* 102: 939–99.

Massey, Douglas S., and Felipe García España. 1987. "The Social Process of International Migration." *Science* 237: 733–38.

Massey, Douglas S., Luin P. Goldring, and Jorge Durand. 1994. "Continuities in Transnational Migration: An Analysis of Nineteen Mexican Communities." *American Journal of Sociology* 99: 1492–1533.

Mummert, Gail. 1999. " 'Juntos o Desapartados': Migración transnacional y la fundación del hogar." In *Fronteras Fragmentadas*, edited by Gail Mummert. Zamora, Mex.: El Colegio de Michoacán.

Reichert, Joshua S. 1981. "The Migrant Syndrome: Seasonal U.S. Wage Labor and Rural Development in Central Mexico." *Human Organization* 40: 56–66.

————. 1982. "A Town Divided: Economic Stratification and Social Relations in a Mexican Migrant Community." *Social Problems* 29: 411–23.

Roberts, Bryan, and Agustín Escobar Latapí. 1997. "Mexican Social and Economic Policy and Emigration." In *At the Crossroads: Mexico and U.S. Immigration Policy*, edited by Frank D. Bean, Rodolfo O. de la Garza, Bryan R. Roberts, and Sidney Weintraub. Lanham, Md.: Rowman and Littlefield.

Roberts, Bryan, Reanne Frank, and Fernando Lozano-Ascencio. 1999. "Transnational Migrant Communities and Mexican Migration to the U.S." *Ethnic and Racial Studies* 22: 238–66.

Simmel, Georg. 1971. *On Individuality and Social Forms: Selected Writings.* Chicago: University of Chicago Press.

Smith, Robert. 2001. "Comparing Local-Level Swedish and Mexican Transnational Life: An Essay in Historical Retrieval." In *New Transnational Social Spaces: International Migration and Transnational Companies in the Early Twenty-first Century,* edited by Ludger Pries. London: Routledge.

Taylor, J. Edward. 1986. "Differential Migration, Networks, Information and Risk." In *Migration Theory, Human Capital and Development,* edited by Oded Stark. Greenwich, Conn.: JAI Press.

———. 1987. "Undocumented Mexico-U.S. Migration and the Returns to Households in Rural Mexico." *American Journal of Agricultural Economics* 69: 626–38.

Vélez-Ibáñez, Carlos G. 1983a. *Bonds of Mutual Trust. The Cultural Systems of Rotating Credit Associations Among Urban Mexicans and Chicanos.* New Brunswick, N.J.: Rutgers University Press.

———. 1983b. *Rituals of Marginality: Politics, Process, and Culture Change in Urban Central Mexico, 1969–1974.* Berkeley: University of California Press.

Wirth, Louis. 1938. "Urbanism as a Way of Life." *American Journal of Sociology* 44: 3–24.

Zendejas, Sergio, and Gail Mummert. 1998. "Beyond the Agrarian Question: The Cultural Politics of Ejido Natural Resources." In *The Transformation of Rural Mexico: Reforming the Ejido Sector,* edited by Wayne A. Cornelius and David Myhre. La Jolla: University of California at San Diego, Center for U.S.-Mexican Studies.

CHAPTER 11

CUMULATIVE CAUSATION AMONG INTERNAL AND INTERNATIONAL MEXICAN MIGRANTS

Estela Rivero-Fuentes

SOCIAL NETWORKS and the cumulative causation of migration have received considerable attention in the study of the migration between Mexico and the United States (Massey 1990; Massey and Espinosa 1997; Massey and García-España 1987; Massey, Goldring, and Durand 1994; Massey and Zenteno 1999). According to recent literature, migration is perpetuated by contact between past migrants and persons who have not yet migrated as well as by changes brought to the community by prior migration. Nevertheless, studies of cumulative causation have generally ignored migration within Mexico, despite the fact that many areas of high international migration are also areas of high internal migration (Durand 1986; Escobar, Bean, and Weintraub 1999).

A handful of studies have analyzed internal and international migration simultaneously (Escobar, Bean, and Weintraub 1999; Fussell and Massey 2004; Lindstrom and Lauster 2001; Curran and Rivero Fuentes 2003; Stark and Taylor 1991; Taylor 1986). This incipient research shows that social networks are an important explanatory factor for internal as well as international migration and that the two movements are not as independent as was previously assumed. This research has also raised new questions: What does the cumulative causation of one type of migration imply for the other? Is internal migration, on which the effect of networks is less strong, also characterized by a process of cumulative causation, with networks dominating other determinants of movement? Does the expansion of international migration occur at the expense of internal migration? To answer these questions, I use Mexican Migration Project data to examine the association between rates of growth in both internal and international migration and to contrast the social and economic characteristics of communities dominated by each type of movement.

THE CUMULATIVE CAUSATION OF MIGRATION

The determinants of migration to the United States and within Mexico have been covered extensively in a huge literature (see Arias 1995; Chávez 1999; Cornelius 1990; Donato, Durand, and Massey 1992; Escobar, Bean, and Weintraub 1999; Fussell and Massey 2004; Greenwood, Ladman, and Siegel 1981; Lindstrom and Lauster 2001; Martin 1999; Massey and Espinosa 1997; Massey et al. 1987; Stark and Taylor 1991; Stark and Taylor 1989). Factors identified as important determinants thus far include economic conditions (wage differentials, labor market opportunities, and investment possibilities in places of origin), policy factors (U.S. immigration laws and border enforcement), and cultural influences (the diffusion of a "culture of migration" and the transplantation of foreign lifestyle aspirations to Mexico). Despite the multiplicity of forces found to influence migration decisions, two have received unusual attention: migrant networks and the forces of cumulative causation.

A person is said to have access to a migrant network if he or she is in contact with others who have migrated. Networks are assumed to facilitate migration by spreading knowledge about the process of moving and border crossing, diffusing information about opportunities at places of destination, providing references to jobs, housing, and services in the receiving society, and offering resources to help finance the costs of the trip (Choldin 1973; Hugo 1991; Massey and García-España 1987). A strong association between migrant networks and Mexico-U.S. migration has been firmly established in the research literature. In perhaps the most complete study to date, Douglas Massey and Kristin Espinosa (1997) find that having a relative with U.S. experience was the most important single factor in predicting the odds of taking a first or subsequent international trip, even after controlling for human capital, individual migration experience, lifecycle stage, and community-level economic conditions. Alberto Palloni and colleagues (2001) offer further proof of the importance of migrant networks by confirming the powerful effect of social ties on migration even after unobserved heterogeneity has been controlled for.

Some authors suggest that networks also operate at the collective level. For example, Massey, Luin Goldring, and Jorge Durand (1994) argue that when migration is common in a community, individuals gain access to resources that can help them migrate. With the accumulation of migratory experience among community members, migration becomes accessible to wider segments of society, and the sociodemographic profile of migrants diversifies. Each new migrant becomes, in turn, a network resource for others who previously lacked access to networks, turning migration into a self-perpetuating process.

Terming this "the cumulative causation of migration," Massey (1990) further explains that the self-perpetuation of migration occurs not only through the progressive expansion of social networks but also through transformations in the social and economic context within which migration decisions occur. For example, the arrival of migrant remittances changes the income distribution to heighten the sense of relative deprivation felt by nonmigrants, motivating them to leave in search of greater income (Stark and Taylor 1991). The investment of remittances also has second-round effects on production that heighten the need to accumulate cash to advance one's status in a changed socioeconomic hierarchy (Taylor et al. 1996).

Another aspect of cumulative causation is the development of a culture of migration. Joshua Reichert (1981) and Massey and colleagues (1987) explain that, whatever its origins and initial economic benefits, a rising rate of migration changes cultural values in the community such that migration becomes an idealized lifestyle and a rite of passage for young men entering the labor force. William Kandel and Massey (2002) show that children from families involved in U.S. migration are more likely to aspire to live and work in the United States and that these aspirations, in turn, influence their behavior, lowering motivations to continue in school while increasing the desire to leave for the United States.

The cumulative causation of international migration at the community level has been empirically tested in two ways. First, studies have shown that, controlling for individual ties to U.S. migrants, the proportion of community members who have ever migrated has a strong and positive effect on the probability of out-migration (Fussell and Massey 2004; Kanaiaupuni 2000; Massey and García-España 1987; Massey, Goldring, and Durand 1994). Massey and Espinosa (1997) find that each point increase in the share of residents with U.S. experience raised the odds of taking a first trip to the United States by a factor of five. Second, studies have demonstrated that the social, demographic, and economic characteristics of migrants diversify as the level of migration in the community increases. Massey, Goldring, and Durand (1994) find that migrants from communities with more accumulated U.S. experience were more likely than those from less experienced communities to include women, children, and younger adults and that the educational and occupational profile of migrants was more varied.

Much less attention has been devoted to studying the effects of social networks on internal migration. Most studies done to date indicate a positive link between access to networks and movements within Mexico, but the effect appears to be weaker than for international migration (see Curran and Rivero-Fuentes 2003; Fussell and Massey 2004; Lindstrom and Lauster 2001). More recently, Elizabeth Fussell and Douglas S. Massey (2004) have shown that the effects of internal and international networks are not uniform across communities and that they depend on the diffuseness of the networks as well as the labor opportunities in the community of origin.

Although these studies begin to address the role of networks in promoting internal migration, they do not test for the presence of cumulative causation. One exception is David Lindstrom and Nathanael Lauster (2001), who find that belonging to a household with at least one active internal migrant significantly raised the odds of migrating domestically while decreasing the odds of migrating to the United States. Conversely, they find that being in a household with at least one active international migrant significantly increased the odds of migrating to the United States but lowered those of moving elsewhere in Mexico. They also show that, consistent with the theory of cumulative causation, the rate of return migration from the United States had a strong positive effect on the odds of international migration and a negative effect on the likelihood of domestic migration, other things equal. They also find that the influence of community characteristics on the rate of emigration depended on relative access to U.S. migrant networks.

Together, these results suggest that as the availability of networks grows, the social and economic factors that initiated migration steadily lose their importance, increasingly leaving networks to perpetuate future outflows. Yet except for Lindstrom and Lauster (2001), most of the work has concerned international rather than internal migration. In this analysis I focus more concretely on internal migration and build on their work in several ways. First, the data used here cover a broader geographic area (Lindstrom and Lauster consider only migration from Zacatecas). Second, I explore how internal and international migration interact over time in a longitudinal study of communities. Third, I estimate individual-level models of out-migration that measure the effect of prevalence with respect to both internal and international migration on departure decisions. Finally, I consider how effects of community economic conditions vary depending on the presence or absence of internal and international network connections.

The foregoing review of theory and research leads me to formulate specific hypotheses that guide my research:

1. Internal and international migration are inversely related. At the community level, places in which international migration is more prevalent will have lower levels of domestic migration, and vice versa. At the individual level, having a tie to an internal migrant and living in a community with a high prevalence of such migrants will raise the odds of migration within Mexico and will reduce the likelihood of emigration to the United States, while the converse will be true for those with individual and community ties to international migrants.

2. Over time, international migration will tend to diminish the prevalence of internal migration, because social networks are more powerful in promoting international than internal movement.

3. International networks will generally dominate community-level socioeconomic conditions in predicting migration to the United States: individuals with access to migrant networks will be more likely to migrate, whatever the conditions in their community of origin. Internal networks will not display such dominance in predicting migration within Mexico: the effect of community socioeconomic conditions will be similar among those who possess and those who lack access to migrant networks.

DATA AND METHODS

I base my analysis on data gathered by the Mexican Migration Project from 1982 to 1998 (see chapter 16), focusing particularly on information compiled for first trips within Mexico and first and most recent trips made to the United States. From the dates of these trips I retrospectively estimate the degree to which internal and international migrants were prevalent in each community at various points in the past. I then undertake an analysis that explores the comparative evolution of U.S. and domestic migration across communities. Specifically, I classify communities into four basic types, depending on the degree to which international migration grew at the expense of internal migration and vice versa. I then determine which community-level characteristics were associated with membership in different categories.

I also use information on the date of the last trips taken within Mexico and to the United States to specify a model that predicts internal and international migration during the two years preceding the survey from theoretical variables defined at the individual, household, and community levels. To estimate the equations, I employ a matched-case binomial logit model that offers some control for selectivity and unobserved heterogeneity.

COMMUNITIES

At the community level, my hypothesis is that international migration tends to diminish the importance of internal migration: over time, the former will expand more rapidly than the latter, whatever the characteristics of the community. Following Massey, Goldring, and Durand (1994), I estimated the proportion of adults aged fifteen and over in a community who had ever made a trip to the United States. For any year t, this migration prevalence ratio is defined as the number of survey respondents aged fifteen or over in year t who took their first trip to the United States in year t or earlier divided by the total number of people aged fifteen and over who had been born in year t or earlier. I computed a comparable prevalence ratio giving the proportion of adults within each community who had ever migrated within Mexico. These data were tabulated for each of the forty years preceding the survey date.

Prevalence ratios measure the general access residents have to migrant networks within a particular community at a given point in time (see Kanaiaupuni 2000; Massey and Espinosa 1997). They do not reproduce exactly the proportion of people in a community who ever migrated to a specific destination in the past, for three reasons. First, the communities are themselves open to in-migration, meaning that some people who are in the community at the survey date may not have been there in the past. To minimize this problem, I calculated prevalence ratios only for those born in the community in question. As a result, one community was dropped from the analysis because most of its residents were born elsewhere. Second, communities also experience out-migration, so that some people who had been present in the community during earlier years were gone by the time of the survey. In the Mexican Migration Project, out-migrants can be identified and counted when at least one of their household members does not migrate. However, out-migrants cannot be counted when all the members of the household migrate. The inclusion of U.S. destination samples in the Mexican Migration Project database, though nonrandom, provides some measure of control for permanent out-migration to the United States, and the incidence of permanent domestic migration is generally low. In only 2 percent of the households that experienced a domestic migration during the prior year did all members migrate. Third, the communities are also affected by mortality, which means that some persons who had been present in the past did not survive to the survey date to report their migration histories. In response to this problem, I assume that there is no correlation between the odds of dying and migrating; if this is true, the analysis will yield unbiased estimates of prevalence ratios.

In general, I have confidence that the prevalence ratios indicate the relative importance of internal and international migration in the community at different moments in time. To explore the relationship between the expansion of internal and international migration, once these prevalence rates were calculated I divided the data into three periods of around thirteen years each: an early period, twenty-eight to forty years before the survey; a middle period, fourteen to twenty-seven years before the survey; and a late period, from thirteen years before the survey until the time of the survey. I then estimated two equations regressing the prevalence of internal or international migration on continuous time plus dummy variables indicating period. The period coefficients capture whether growth during that time was significantly above or below the average rate of growth over the forty years.

Tests of significance for differences between period coefficients in the two equations reveal that during the early period, the rate at which prevalence grew was the same in both the internal and international equations in sixty-seven of the seventy communities. However, during the middle period the rate of growth in the prevalence of international migratory was greater than that of internal migratory in seventeen communities, the same in forty-three communities, and smaller in ten communities. By the late period, the rate of growth in prevalence was greater for international migration in fifty-one communities, the same in nine communities, and smaller in ten communities. Thus it appears that over the forty years prior to the survey, international migration increasingly came to dominate internal migration in a growing number of communities.

Based on the relative rates of growth in the middle and late periods, I classified the seventy communities into one of four basic types:

Type 1: "Equal growth" communities (eight cases), in which internal and international prevalence grew at the same rate across both periods

Type 2: "International always faster" communities (seventeen cases), in which international prevalence grew more rapidly than internal prevalence across both periods

Type 3: "Internal always faster" communities (nine cases), in which internal prevalence grew more rapidly than international prevalence across both periods

Type 4: "International takes over internal" communities (thirty-six cases), in which international prevalence grew at the same rate as internal prevalence during the middle period but faster in the late period (thirty-four cases) or grew more slowly than internal prevalence in the middle period but reached parity in the late period (two communities)

To discern which factors have affected the relationship between internal and international migration in recent years, I estimated a series of bivariate multinomial models regressing the foregoing community classifications on variables mentioned in the literature as influencing the rate of emigration from Mexico. Several authors have linked the 1986 Immigration Reform and Control Act (IRCA) to an increase in the rate of U.S. migration (Cornelius 1990; Donato, Durand, and Massey 1992; Portes and Rumbaut 1996). This change coincides with Mexico's shift from an economic strategy of import substitution industrialization to a new development model of export-led growth. This shift has also been linked by some observers to changes in the patterns, rates, and directions of Mexican migration (Arias 1995; Chávez 1999; Escobar, Bean, and Weintraub 1999). Because the data included in this analysis refer to calendar periods beginning in 1957 to 1972 and ending in 1982 to 1998, some communities experienced this economic transition but others did not. This distinction is captured with a dummy variable that is set to 1 if the survey was fielded in 1994 or later (indicating a largely post-IRCA migration history) and 0 otherwise.

The level of migration at the beginning of the period is also likely to affect future trends, as higher prevalence ratios indicate larger and more diverse networks (Massey 1990; Massey, Goldring, and Durand 1994) and more-developed cultures of migration (Massey et al. 1987; Reichert 1981), both of which increase the likelihood of future movement. Some authors have noted similarities in community-level causes of internal and international migration, such as a lack of jobs, the displacement of traditional workers by new forms of production, and low wages (Arizpe 1983; Brambila 1996; Durand 1986; Escobar, Bean, and Weintraub 1999). Here I measure local job opportunities with the proportion of community workers employed in agriculture and manufacturing during the census immediately preceding the period under scrutiny. I measure recent changes in job opportunities with the percentage change in these indicators between the first and most recent censuses bounding the period under consideration. Local wage rates are indexed by the proportion of community workers earning less than two times the official minimum wage in the most recent census before the period of analysis and by the change in this percentage between the first and last census bounding the period.

Both internal and international migrants have traditionally come from small communities, though some authors have noted a change in this pattern beginning in the mid-1980s, particularly for internal migrants. Patricia Arias (1995) and Ana Maria Chávez (1999) speak of the urbanization of internal migrants' origins within Mexico, and Wayne Cornelius (1990) and Durand, Massey, and René Zenteno (2001) note the rising number of urbanites among migrants to the United States. In the present analysis, I classify communities into three categories based on population size at the last census: metropolitan centers, small urban centers, and towns or rancherías.

Table 11.1 shows the means computed for these variables. The communities are close to evenly split between those surveyed before 1994

TABLE 11.1   Means for Variables Used in Bivariate Analysis of Community-Level Analysis Type of Change in Internal Versus International Migration (Percentage)

Variable	Mean
Type of community	
Equal growth	11.4
International always faster	24.3
Internal always faster	12.9
International takes over internal	51.4
Reference period	
Before 1994	45.7
1994 or later	54.3
Initial migration prevalence	
Internal migration	4.1
International migration	3.2
Community economic conditions	
Percentage workers in agriculture	64.8
Change in percentage workers in agriculture	−43.9
Percentage workers in manufacturing	14.9
Change in percentage workers in manufacturing	150.5
Percentage workers earning less than twice minimum wage	53.2
Change in percentage workers earning less than twice minimum wage	−29.8
Metropolitan category	
Metropolitan center	20.0
Small urban center	24.3
Town or ranchería	55.7
N	70

Source: Data from Mexican Migration Project and Mexican Population Censuses.

(45.7 percent) and those surveyed in 1994 or later (54.3 percent). The initial prevalence was also similar for internal and international migrants, at 3.2 percent for the former and 4.1 percent for the latter. On average, two-thirds of workers were employed in agriculture at the time of the survey, but the share had dropped by 43.9 percent since the beginning of the period. The share of workers in manufacturing was 14.9 percent, but it had increased by 150.5 percent over the period. About half (53.2 percent) of all workers earned less than twice the minimum wage, but this share had fallen by 29.8 percent over the period. In keeping with the large share of agricultural workers, 55.7 percent of the communities were small towns or rancherías and 24.3 percent were small urban areas. Only 20.0 percent were metropolitan areas.

Table 11.2 shows the bivariate effect of each of these factors in predicting the relative growth of internal versus international migration over the two periods. The reference category is internal prevalence always greater than international prevalence. The table presents odds ratios obtained by taking the exponent of the multinomial regression coefficient associated with each variable. Values greater than 1 indicate that the factor increases the odds that a community experienced a particular growth pattern, whereas values less than 1 indicate that it decreases these odds. Owing to the limited degrees of freedom, I adopt $p < .10$ as my criterion for significance.

Coinciding with predictions derived from cumulative causation theory, the initial level of international migration is the only variable significantly associated with a pattern of international migration always dominating over internal migration. The more prevalent international migration was initially, the more likely was a community to be one in which international migration was always greater than internal migration or one in which international migration was greater than internal migration in the second period. Consistent with the findings of others (Arizpe 1983; Brambila 1996; Durand 1986; Escobar, Bean, and Weintraub 1999), the initial prevalence of internal migration has no effect in promoting the relative predominance of internal over international migration across time.

In addition to the initial prevalence of international migration, two economic variables were also significant in predicting the relative pattern of change. Specifically, the higher the percentage of workers in agriculture and the greater the share earning low wages (less than twice the minimum wage), the more likely was a community to be one in which the prevalence of international migration came from behind to surpass that of internal migration. Such a pattern of prevalence growth was also

TABLE 11.2   Odds Ratios from Bivariate Multinomial
                Regression of Type of Migratory Community on
                Selected Independent Variables

Independent Variable	Equal Growth	International Always Faster	International Takes over Internal
Reference period:			
1994 or later	1.33	1.47	0.72
Initial migration prevalence			
Internal migration	0.00	0.00[+]	0.00[+]
International migration	0.00	0.00	0.00
Community economic conditions			
Percentage workers in agriculture	0.64	3.29	5.55
Change in percentage workers in agriculture	1.00	1.01	1.03[+]
Percentage workers in manufacturing	3.56	0.28	0.40
Change in percentage workers in manufacturing	1.00	1.00	1.00
Percentage workers earning less than twice minimum wage	1.45	0.28	3.35
Change in percentage workers earning less than twice minimum wage	1.00	1.02	1.04[+]
Metropolitan category			
Small urban center	2.67	2.67	12.00[+]
Town or ranchería	1.00	4.00	5.00[+]

Source: Data from Mexican Migration Project.
Note: Reference category is internal always faster.
[+]p < .10

predicted strongly by being a small urban area and by being a small town or ranchería. In other words, a pattern of rapid increase in the relative prevalence of international migration occurred mainly outside of Mexico's large metropolitan areas. In many smaller communities where internal migration was once common, the rate of domestic migration decreased over time, and out-migration switched instead to a more exclusive pattern of international movement.

INDIVIDUALS

The limited cases available for analysis at the community level do not allow further exploration of community-level patterns. Nor are further investigations at this level necessarily desirable: by grouping people together within communities regardless of individual propensities to migrate and irrespective of personal characteristics, the foregoing analysis yields an incomplete and limited picture of the process of both internal and international migration. To provide a more detailed representation of the process of out-migration, and in particular to explore interactions between networks and community conditions, I turned to a multivariate analysis at the level of the individual, focusing on the behavior of persons who had not yet migrated and were thus "at risk" of taking a first trip.

Specifically, I selected all persons born in the sample community who were aged sixteen or older at the time of the survey and who had not yet migrated internally or internationally as of two years before the survey date. I then used specific individual, household, and community-level variables to predict whether a domestic or U.S. trip occurred during the two-year reference period. Because the Mexican Migration Project data are retrospective, however, they miss information about households that have left the study communities, making it difficult to reconstruct exactly the population at risk of migrating. If the characteristics of those missing from the community differ from those who remain, then selectivity might bias the estimated coefficients from any regression analysis.

To address this problem I used a matched case-control binomial logit approach, wherein I treat the data as if they came from matched case-control samples. Specifically, individuals who had migrated during the two years preceding the survey were considered "cases" and those who had not were considered "controls." Peter McCullagh and John A. Nelder (1989/1999) demonstrate that in a logistic regression, the sampling criterion is independent of the slope coefficients and one can therefore simulate a case-control study, reproducing a random experiment and controlling for the selectivity bias, even when data were gathered retrospectively. The only assumption necessary is that the selecting mechanism be independent of covariates in the analysis.

I therefore began by creating two independent samples. The first included as cases those persons who had migrated across state borders within Mexico at least once during the two years preceding the survey, defining as controls those who had not migrated at all during the same period. The second sample included as cases those persons who had migrated at least once to the United States during the two years preceding the survey, considering as controls those who had not migrated at all. For each sample, migrants were matched with as many nonmigrants as possible according to sex, age, and level of education. These variables were selected as the matching criteria because they are known to be related to both internal and international migration (see Curran and Rivero-Fuentes 2003; Kanaiaupuni 2000; Massey and Espinosa 1997; Taylor 1986) but are independent of the family and community variables included in my analysis.

Nonmigrants who matched the age, sex, and education of both internal and international migrants were randomly divided between the two samples to guarantee their independence. The sample for internal migration consisted of 272 individuals who migrated to another state in Mexico during the two-year window and 7,905 individuals who did not migrate at all. The sample for international migration comprised 1,105 individuals who migrated to the United States during the two-year window and 16,810 individuals who did not migrate at all. Only 17 people migrated to both destinations during the two-year period, and they were defined as international rather than internal migrants.

Table 11.3 presents descriptive statistics for independent variables in the two samples. The principal variables of interest are the levels of internal and international migration in the community, the presence of family network ties, and economic conditions in the community. During the two-year period, more people left for the United States (6.2 percent) than for a destination in Mexico (3.3 percent). The level of international migration is measured using the prevalence ratio for migrants to the United States computed exactly three years before the survey. The level of internal migration is correspondingly measured as the prevalence ratio for internal migrants three years before the survey. The overall prevalence of international migration, at 15.8 and 17.1 percent, was greater than that for domestic migration, at 7.5 percent. Since these retrospective variables are defined so close to the survey date, I expect bias to be negligible.

TABLE 11.3   Means of Variables Used in Individual Analysis of Migration to the United States and Within Mexico (Percentage)

| | Sample | |
Variable	Internal Migration	International Migration
Migrated		
Within Mexico	3.3	—
To the United States	—	6.2
Migration prevalence in community		
Internal migration	7.5	7.5
International migration	15.8	17.1
Family network		
Has internal tie	47.6	54.4
Has international tie	47.9	52.5
Reference period		
Before 1988	22.5	22.2
1988 or later	77.5	77.8
Community economic conditions		
Percentage of workers in agriculture		
Bottom quartile	15.0	26.0
Top quartile	58.2	58.3
Change in percentage workers in agriculture		
Bottom quartile	−39.5	−36.9
Top quartile	−15.9	−12.1
Percentage of workers in manufacturing		
Bottom quartile	18.9	18.4
Top quartile	32.0	32.0
Change in percentage workers in manufacturing		
Bottom quartile	4.3	8.8
Top quartile	41.8	45.9
Percentage workers earning less than twice minimum wage		
Bottom quartile	22.2	27.8
Top quartile	55.9	59.3

TABLE 11.3   Means of Variables Used in Individual Analysis
of Migration to the United States and Within Mexico
(Percentage) (*Continued*)

	Sample	
Variable	Internal Migration	International Migration
Change in percentage workers earning less than twice minimum wages		
Bottom quartile	−48.8	−48.7
Top quartile	6.2	6.2
Metropolitan category		
Metropolitan center	23.8	19.2
Small urban center	26.8	27.7
Town or ranchería	49.4	53.0
Control variables		
Family size	9.3	9.4
Education of household head		
None	23.2	27.3
One to six years	61.4	60.8
Seven or more years	15.4	11.8
Life-cycle stage		
No children	2.8	3.2
Some children under the age of eighteen	80.5	70.9
All children eighteen or older	16.7	25.9

Source: Data from Mexican Migration Project and Mexican Population Censuses.

Family network connections were measured using two dummy variables: whether any member of the household had migrated internally up to two years before the survey and whether any member of the household had migrated internationally up to this point in time. Roughly half of all people in the sample were connected to both internal and international migrants through a family tie.

Variables that measure economic conditions are similar to those used in the community-level analyses. In this case, however, change is defined as the difference in proportions (of agricultural, manufacturing, and low-wage workers) between the two censuses immediately preceding the survey date. Moreover, rather than employing continuous specifications of community-level factors, I created dummy variables indicating whether a community fell into the top or bottom quartile of the distribution (leaving the middle two quartiles to serve as the reference category). This specification was used to capture potential nonlinear effects and to facilitate interpretation of interactions with network ties. Table 11.3 shows the cutoff points corresponding to the bottom and top quartile for the percentage of workers in agriculture, manufacturing, and low-wage jobs as well as for the percentage change in these variables. The change variables show that the percentage working in agriculture was declining across communities, while the percentage in manufacturing was rising.

Period was measured using a dummy variable that equaled 1 if the survey date was 1988 or later and 0 otherwise,[1] and metropolitan category was specified as before, according to whether the respondent was from a town or ranchería, a small urban center, or a large metropolitan center. A little more than three-quarters of respondents were interviewed after 1988, and about half were from small towns or rural rancherías.

Several authors have identified life-cycle stage as an important predictor of both internal and international migration (Arizpe 1980; Massey and Espinosa 1997; Massey and García-España 1987). Here I control for life-cycle stage using a three-way categorical classification: whether, two years before the survey was taken, the household head had no children, had any children younger than eighteen, or had only children eighteen or older. Family size is measured by the number of household members. Because several investigators (Massey and Espinosa 1997; Stark and Taylor 1991; Unikel and Chiapetto 1973) have signaled socioeconomic status as an important factor in predicting both internal and international migration, I include a categorical measure of the household head's education: no formal schooling, one to six years of schooling, and seven or more years of schooling. Few household heads had education beyond the sixth grade—just 15 percent in the internal migration sample and 12 percent in the sample of international migration.

My hypotheses concerning the effect of migrant networks and community-level variables on the probability of migrating internally and internationally for the first time are tested with logistic models. Separate models are calculated for the propensity to migrate to the United States and the propensity to migrate within Mexico. Because of the matching mechanism, the observations of those individuals of the same age, sex, and education level are serially correlated. I control for this correlation, which might otherwise affect the standard errors of the coefficients, by fitting fixed-effects models within these three variables. The predicted odds of internal migration as estimated by these equations are shown in table 11.4.

The first three panels show coefficients associated with the effect of migration prevalence, family network ties, and period. The fourth panel shows the main effects of community economic conditions, and the fifth presents selected interactions between community conditions and network ties. The last two panels show the estimated effects of metropolitan category and various control variables. The columns refer to different models I specified and estimated. The first model considers the effect of prevalence and network ties on the likelihood of internal migration while controlling for period, community economic conditions, community size, and other controls. The remaining four columns show models that include various interactions between community economic conditions and network ties.

According to all models, the odds of internal migration are strongly and positively predicted by coming from a community in which internal migration is prevalent and by having an internal migrant with the family. In model 1, each point increase in the prevalence of internal migration within the community increases the odds of undertaking a first trip within Mexico by 14 percent, whereas having a family tie to someone with internal migration experience increases the odds of such a trip by 56 percent. International ties—whether measured at the individual or the community level—have no significant effect in predicting migration within Mexico.

Other coefficients in the model suggest that the likelihood of internal out-migration has fallen since 1988 and that it declines with increasing family size and rising education of the household head. Being in a community with a high proportion of agrarian workers greatly raises the odds of internal migration, whereas coming from a place with a low share in agriculture markedly reduces these odds, findings that generally support the prediction of world systems theory (see Portes 1978) that migration follows from displacement of agricultural and other traditional workers. The relative likelihood of internal migration is also increased by coming from a community in which manufacturing jobs are not increasing rapidly and one in which a large share of workers earn low wages.

The estimates of the various interaction terms in models 2 to 5 suggest that community-level economic conditions have somewhat different effects for those with and without family ties to internal migrants. Coming from a community in the top quartile of agrarian employment may increase the odds of leaving for a Mexican destination, but it has a weaker effect on those with ties than on those without them. Similarly, coming from a community in the highest quartile of change in manufacturing employment (a rapidly

TABLE 11.4   Odds Ratios from Case Matched Case-Control Logistic Regression of Migration Within Mexico on Selected Independent Variables

Independent Variable	Model 1	Model 2	Model 3	Model 4	Model 5
Migration prevalence in community					
Internal migration	1.14***	1.14***	1.15***	1.14***	1.15***
International migration	0.99	0.99	0.99	0.99	0.99
Family network					
Has internal tie	1.56***	2.23***	1.65***	2.25***	2.82***
Has international tie	0.94	0.94	0.95	0.93	0.92
Reference period: after 1988	0.42***	0.41***	0.42***	0.45***	0.45***
Community economic conditions					
Percentage workers in agriculture: bottom quartile	0.36*	0.49	0.38*	0.37*	0.39*
Percentage workers in agriculture: top quartile	4.14***	6.18***	4.17***	4.20***	4.18***
Change in percentage workers in agriculture: bottom quartile	0.59	0.60	0.56	0.60	0.59
Change in percentage workers in agriculture: top quartile	0.22***	0.23***	0.27***	0.22***	0.23***
Percentage workers in manufacturing: bottom quartile	0.94	0.93	0.93	0.93	0.93
Percentage workers in manufacturing: top quartile	1.01	1.07	1.04	1.06	1.10
Change in percentage workers in manufacturing: bottom quartile	3.44***	3.41***	3.43***	4.51***	3.34**

Change in percentage workers in manufacturing: top quartile	1.00	1.02	1.00	1.65*	0.99
Percentage earning less than twice minimum wage: bottom quartile	1.61*	1.64*	1.61*	1.56	2.43**
Percentage earning less than twice minimum wage: top quartile	0.65*	0.66	0.65*	0.64*	1.27
Change in percentage earning less than twice minimum wage: bottom quartile	0.75	0.72	0.74	0.71	0.70
Change in percentage earning less than twice minimum wage: top quartile	0.72	0.70	0.71	0.75	0.78
Interaction of internal family ties with community conditions ×					
Percentage workers in agriculture: bottom quartile	—	0.64	—	—	
Percentage workers in agriculture: top quartile	—	0.49**	—	—	
Change in percentage workers in agriculture: bottom quartile	—	—	1.10	—	—
Change in percentage workers in agriculture: top quartile	—	—	0.69	—	—
Change in percentage workers in manufacturing: bottom quartile	—	—	—	0.65	—
Change in percentage workers in manufacturing: top quartile	—	—	—	0.45***	—

(*Table continues on p. 220.*)

TABLE 11.4   Odds Ratios from Case Matched Case-Control Logistic Regression of Migration Within Mexico on Selected Independent Variables (*Continued*)

Independent Variable	Model 1	Model 2	Model 3	Model 4	Model 5
Percentage earning less than twice minimum wage: bottom quartile	—	—	—	—	0.54
Percentage earning less than twice minimum wage: top quartile	—	—	—	—	0.32***
Metropolitan category					
Small urban center	1.21	1.24	1.21	1.23	1.28
Town or rancheria	1.60	1.59	1.60	1.64	1.68
Control variables					
Family size	0.95**	0.95**	0.95**	0.95**	0.95**
Education of household head: one to six years	0.84	0.84	0.84	0.84	0.84
Education of household head: seven or more years	0.62*	0.62*	0.62*	0.63*	0.62*
Life-cycle stage: some children under the age of eighteen	0.79	0.78	0.77	0.82	0.83
Life-cycle stage: all children eighteen or older	0.75	0.74	0.74	0.78	0.76
Log likelihood	−799.35	−796.59	−798.73	−795.93	−792.64
Chi square	229.14***	234.67	230.37***	235.98	242.56***
N	7,399	7,399	7,399	7,399	7,399

Source: Data from Mexican Migration Project.

*p < 0.10   **p < 0.05   ***p < 0.01

growing industrial job sector) strongly lowers the odds of migration for those lacking ties to internal migrants. The odds of internal out-migration are particularly low in low-wage communities for those lacking social ties to internal migrants.

Table 11.5 repeats the binomial logit analysis for international as opposed to internal migration. As before, model 1 estimates only main effects, whereas models 2 to 7 add various interaction terms. No matter which specification is considered, however, there are strong and significant effects of networks at both the community and the individual level. In model 1, having a family tie to a U.S. migrant increases the odds of migrating internationally by 167 percent, and each point increase in the prevalence of U.S. migration increases the odds of such movement by 3 percent.

Apart from these network effects, family size and the life-cycle stage of the household head are also significantly associated with the odds of international migration. As family size increases, the odds of international migration increase slightly (by 2 percent). Similarly, as households proceed through the life cycle and household heads have children, the odds of U.S. migration go down, dropping by 37 percent if the household head has children eighteen or younger and by 49 percent if all the children of the household head are above this age. Once community-, family-, and individual-level variables are controlled for, there seems to be no significant difference between the odds of migration before 1988 and since 1988. The estimated coefficients for metropolitan category are consistent in showing that the odds of migrating to the United States are much greater for those respondents living in small urban centers, towns, or rancherías than those living in large metropolitan areas.

The proportion of the population employed in agriculture has a strong association with the level of international migration. Individuals living in communities in the bottom quartile of agricultural employment are 61 percent less likely to migrate than those in other quartiles. Similarly, people from communities with more job opportunities also display lower odds of leaving for the United States. Those from communities in the lowest quartile of manufacturing employment are 40 percent more likely to leave for the United States, and those in the lowest quartile of change in manufacturing employment are 143 percent more likely to do so. Finally, coming from a community in the top quartile of change in the share of low-wage workers (that is, where the number of low-wage workers is increasing) is associated with a greater likelihood of migrating abroad.

As with the models predicting internal migration, economic conditions appear to interact with network ties in the likelihood of international migration. Coming from a community in the lowest quartile of agricultural

TABLE 11.5   Odds Ratios from Case Matched Case–Control Logistic Regression of Migration to the United States on Selected Independent Variables

Independent Variable	Model 1	Model 2	Model 3	Model 4	Model 5	Model 6	Model 7
Migration prevalence in community							
Internal migration	1.00	1.00	1.00	1.00	1.00	1.00	1.00
International migration	1.03***	1.03	1.03***	1.03***	1.03***	1.03***	1.03***
Family network							
Has internal tie	0.93	0.92	0.92	0.93	0.93	0.93	0.93
Has international tie	2.67***	2.53***	2.61***	2.85**	2.84**	3.14***	3.71***
Reference period: 1988 or later	1.20	1.20	1.23	1.19	1.20	1.22	1.19
Community economic conditions							
Percentage workers in agriculture: bottom quartile	0.39***	0.28**	0.41**	0.38***	0.38****	0.37****	0.39***
Percentage workers in agriculture: top quartile	1.05	1.20	1.03	1.05	1.10	1.06	1.05
Change in percentage workers in agriculture: bottom quartile	1.15	1.14	0.84	1.16	1.15	1.19	1.15
Change in percentage workers in agriculture: top quartile	0.50*	0.49***	0.59**	0.50***	0.49**	0.50***	0.50***
Percentage workers in manufacturing: bottom quartile	1.40*	1.39***	1.42**	1.42**	1.37***	1.39***	1.39***

Percentage workers in manufacturing: top quartile	0.98	0.98	0.98	1.18	0.98	0.98	0.99
Change in percentage workers in manufacturing: bottom quartile	2.44***	2.49***	2.30***	2.42**	2.39***	2.46**	2.43**
Change in percentage workers in manufacturing: top quartile	0.62**	0.62***	0.84	0.61****	0.61***	0.62****	0.62**
Percentage earning less than twice minimum wage: bottom quartile	0.89	0.90	0.92	0.90	0.88	0.89	0.90
Percentage earning less than twice minimum wage: top quartile	1.23	1.24	1.24	1.23	1.28	1.26	1.23
Change in percentage earning less than twice minimum wage: bottom quartile	1.17*	1.27	1.15	1.18	1.18	1.16	1.17*
Change in percentage earning less than twice minimum wage: top quartile	1.30**	1.84***	1.31**	1.31**	1.31**	1.30	1.30***
Interaction of international family ties with community conditions × Percentage workers in agriculture: bottom quartile	—	—	—	—	—	1.79**	—

(Table continues on p. 224.)

TABLE 11.5   Odds Ratios from Case Matched Case–Control Logistic Regression of Migration to the United States on Selected Independent Variables (*Continued*)

Independent Variable	Model 1	Model 2	Model 3	Model 4	Model 5	Model 6	Model 7
Percentage workers in agriculture: top quartile	—	0.82	—	—	—	—	—
Change in percentage workers in agriculture: bottom quartile	—	—	1.63**	—	—	—	—
Change in percentage workers in agriculture: top quartile	—	—	0.77	—	—	—	—
Percentage workers in manufacturing: bottom quartile	—	—	—	0.98	—	—	—
Percentage workers in manufacturing: top quartile	—	—	—	0.74	—	—	—
Change in percentage workers in manufacturing: bottom quartile	—	—	—	—	1.15	—	—
Change in percentage workers in manufacturing: top quartile	—	—	—	—	0.64**	—	—
Change in percentage earning less than minimum wage: bottom quartile	—	—	—	—	—	0.90	—
Change in percentage earning less than minimum wage: top quartile	—	—	—	—	—	0.64**	—

Metropolitan category						
Small urban center	1.73**	1.66**	1.70*	1.77**	1.56***	1.70***	2.02***
Town or ranchería	1.55**	1.48*	1.52**	1.53*	1.50**	1.53**	1.92***
Interaction of metropolitan category with family network ×						
Small urban center	—	—	—	—	—	0.72	—
Town or ranchería	—	—	—	—	—	—	0.67
Control variables						
Family size	1.02*	1.02*	1.02*	1.02*	1.02*	1.02*	1.01*
Education of household head: one to six years	1.14	1.13	1.13	1.14	1.13	1.13	1.14
Education of household head: seven or more years	0.89	0.90	0.90	0.90	0.89	0.89	0.90
Life-cycle stage: some children under the age of eighteen	0.63**	0.63***	0.63***	0.62**	0.53**	0.53**	0.63**
Life-cycle stage: all children eighteen or older	0.51***	0.51***	0.51**	0.50***	0.51***	0.50***	0.51***
Log likelihood	−2,831.06	−2,826.32	−2,826.83	−2,830.06	−2,827.52	−2,828.00	−2,829.90
Chi squared	650.24***	659.72***	658.69***	652.23***	657.31***	655.94***	652.55***
N	16,617	16,617	16,617	16,617	16,617	16,617	16,617

Source: Data from Mexican Migration Project.

*p < 0.10   **p < 0.05   ***p < 0.01

employment increases rather than decreases the odds of migration for those with social ties to U.S. migrants, as does coming from a community in the quartile showing the lowest decline in the share of agrarian workers. Coming from a community in the upper quartile of manufacturing employment lowers the odds of migration generally but especially for those who have ties to U.S. migrants. Similarly, coming from a community in the top quartile of change in the share earning low wages has a weaker effect in promoting out-migration among those with ties to international migrants.

CONCLUSION

My exploration of internal and international migration in Mexico shows a complex interaction between them that does not merely imply, as I originally expected, a substitution effect. There is little evidence that growth in international migration caused internal migration to decrease in the communities studied. In approximately one-third of the communities studied, internal migration has always expanded at the same rate or even more rapidly than international migration. There are some communities where international migration gradually overrode internal migration, but these are characterized by very specific conditions. In addition, my results show that the risk factors associated with internal and international migration are different and that both movements are perpetuated through cumulative causation mechanisms. Furthermore, individual-level analysis indicates that, contrary to the findings of Lindstrom and Lauster (2001), the odds of internal and international migration are affected by neither the prevalence of migration nor the availability of networks to the alternative destination.

The difference with respect to the results of Lindstrom and Lauster (2001) may derive from two factors. First, the sample used in this study covers a broader geographical area, providing a more varied sample of communities than the state of Zacatecas, to which they restrict their study. The communities included in this sample represent, as demonstrated in the descriptive analysis, a wide variation of long-term associations between internal and international migration that might not be present in Lindstrom and Lauster's analysis. A second explanation may be that the analysis in this study includes more independent variables than that of Lindstrom and Lauster and controls not only for the prevalence of international migration but for the prevalence of internal migration, as well. The negative effects of networks and prevalence of migration to the alternative destination noted by Lindstrom and Lauster may have derived from some unobserved variables that are explicit in my analysis. Nevertheless, this is an important finding directly related to the discussion of the relationship between internal and international migration and requires further attention.

The analysis at the community level speaks to the perpetuation of internal migration because in nine of the seventy communities included in the analysis domestic migration had a larger rate of growth than international migration during the twenty-six years included in the analysis, and in eight communities internal and international migration grew at the same rate. Nevertheless, in seventeen communities international migration always grew faster than internal migration, and in thirty-six communities international migration started growing faster than internal migration only midway in the period of analysis. Furthermore, the only characteristic that distinguishes the communities in which, over the entire period, international migration expanded more than internal migration from those in which internal migration expanded at a rate higher than or equal to that of international migration is the initial level of migration to the United States from the community.

The communities in which international migration started substituting for internal migration in the middle of the period of observation are also associated with higher initial levels of international migration. Even more important, however, these communities have particular characteristics that distinguish them from behaviors in the others. Specifically, these communities are characterized by a greater prevalence of agricultural employment, an increase in the level of poverty in the community, and a greater representation by small towns and medium cities.

These results further reinforce the idea that international migration will not grow to substitute for the domestic migration from all communities but will do so only from those communities associated with some specific conditions, such as the worsening of wages or the lack of job opportunities in the industrial sector. Moreover, the results also complement the findings of other researchers (Arias 1995; Chávez 1999) that indicate a displacement of domestic migration from rural to urban origins. These results do not contradict previous findings that international migration has also expanded to the cities (Cornelius 1990; Durand, Massey, and Zenteno 2001) but rather suggest that the urbanization of international migration has not implied a decrease in the migration from rural towns, contrary to the case of domestic migration.

As other authors (Arizpe 1983; Escobar, Bean, and Weintraub 1999; Lindstrom and Lauster 2001) have suggested, some of the determinants of internal and international migration are similar. In this case, most of the similarities are found at the community level. Both types of migration are positively associated with the proportion of the labor force in agriculture, although this association is much stronger in the case of internal migration, and with changes in the occupational structure of the community such as the displacement of agriculture and the expansion of manufacturing jobs. Nonetheless, some community factors affect internal and international migration differently. Internal migration is negatively associated with the proportion of the community that earns less than twice the minimum wage but not with the change in this indicator over time. On the contrary, international migration is not associated with the proportion of the population in the community that earns less than twice the minimum wage but is positively and significantly associated with an increase in this indicator over time. Even more noticeably, international migration is more likely to come from small cities and towns than from large metropolitan areas, and internal migration has decreased with time but international migration has not.

As suggested by Lourdes Arizpe (1983), some of the largest differences between internal and international migration are in determinants at the family level. The odds of international migration are larger when family size increases and when there are no children in the household. Internal migration, on the contrary, is negatively associated with family size and is not affected by the life cycle of the family. These results suggest that internal and international migration are alternatives for different types of families (see also Lindstrom and Lauster 2001).

The results of the models of internal and international migration show evidence of a cumulative mechanism of migration in both movements. The odds of domestic and international migration are equally associated with the level of migration in the community and the presence of networks to that destination. Furthermore, in both cases the network effects dominate some of the community-level determinants, reducing the differences in the probability to migrate from communities with varying characteristics. In the case of domestic migration, individuals with family networks are less affected by the proportion of the labor force in agriculture and by the expansion of jobs in manufacturing than individuals without family networks. Similarly, the international migration of individuals with networks is less affected than that of individuals without networks by the proportion of the labor force in agriculture and by the change in the proportion of the population receiving less than twice the minimum wage.

Nevertheless, the results also indicate that the presence of networks increases (rather than decreases) the responsiveness of migration to some other characteristics in the community. In the case of internal migration, extreme levels of poverty in the community reduce the odds of migration for those individuals with networks but have no effect on the migration of individuals without internal networks. In the case of international migration, individuals with networks are more responsive to changes in the occupational structure of the community than are individuals with no networks.

These results might be an indication, as Massey, Goldring, and Durand (1994) suggest, that the action of networks varies with the migratory moment of the community. The analyses in this study control for the level of migration in the community but assume that the interaction between community-level variables and networks is the same despite the level of migration in the community. It may be the case that this interaction further varies by the level of migration in the community. When migration is not common, individuals with networks might be more responsive to the community conditions because they are better equipped than those lacking ties to embark on a costly migration. Nevertheless, as migration becomes more common, the community conditions might become less important, and migration might be dominated by networks. Further research in this aspect can help increase understanding of how migration is perpetuated within communities and whether there are any limits to this perpetuation.

NOTES

1. The periods used in this individual-level analysis differ from the periods used in the community-level analysis (before 1994, 1994, and after) because they are intended to measure the effect of IRCA on the odds of individual migration. Individuals interviewed before 1988 migrated when IRCA was not yet in effect, while individuals interviewed after 1988 migrated after IRCA.

REFERENCES

Arias, Patricia. 1995. "La migración femenina en dos modelos de desarrollo: 1940–1970 y 1980–1992." In *Relaciones de género y transformaciones agrarias: Estudios sobre el campo Mexicano*. Mexico City: González Montes.

Arizpe, Lourdes. 1980. *La migración por relevos y la reproducción social del campesinado*. Mexico City: El Colegio de México.

———. 1983. "El éxodo rural en México y su relación con la migración a Estados Unidos." *Estudios Sociológicos* 1: 9–35.

Brambila, Carlos. 1996. "A Reassessment of Migration and Urbanization in Mexico in the 20th Century." In *Migration, Urbanization, and Development: New Directions and Issues*, edited by Richard E. Bilsborrow. New York: Kluwer Academic Publishers.

Chávez, A. M. 1999. *La nueva dinámica de la migración interna en México, 1970–1990*. Cuernavaca, Mexico: Centro Regional de Investigaciones Multidisciplinarias.

Choldin, Harvey M. 1973. "Kinship Networks in the Migration Process." *International Migration Review* 7: 163–76.

Cornelius, Wayne. 1990. "Impacts of the 1986 U.S. Immigration Law on Emigration from Rural Mexican Sending Communities." In *Undocumented Migration to the United States: IRCA and the Experience of the 1980s*, edited by Frank D. Bean, Barry Edmonston, and Jeffrey S. Passel. Washington, D.C.: Urban Institute.

Curran, Sara R., and Estela Rivero-Fuentes. 2003. "Engendering Migrant Networks: The Case of Mexican Migration." *Demography* 40(2): 289–307.

Donato, Katharine M., Jorge Durand, and Douglas S. Massey. 1992. "Stemming the Tide? Assessing the Deterrent Effects of the Immigration Reform and Control Act." *Demography* 29(2): 139–57.

Durand, Jorge. 1986. "Circuitos migratorios en el Occidente de México." *Revue Européenne des Migrations Internationales* 2: 49–67.

Durand, Jorge, Douglas S. Massey, and René M. Zenteno. 2001. "Mexican Immigration to the United States: Continuities and Changes." *Latin American Research Review* 36: 107–27.

Escobar, Agustin, Frank D. Bean, and Sidney Weintraub. 1999. "The Dynamics of Mexican Emigration." In *Emigration Dynamics in Developing Countries: Mexico, Central America, and the Caribbean*, edited by Reginald Appleyard. Aldershot, U.K.: Ashgate.

Fussell, Elizabeth, and Douglas S. Massey. 2004. "Limits to the Cumulative Causation of Migration: International Migration from Urban Mexico." *Demography* 41(1): 151–71.

Greenwood, Michael J., Jerry R. Ladman, and Barry S. Siegel. 1981. "Long-term Trends in Migratory Behavior in a Developing Country: The Case of Mexico." *Demography* 18: 369–88.

Hugo, Graeme J. 1991. "Village-Community Ties, Village Norms, and Ethnic and Social Networks: A Review of the Evidence From the Third World." In *Migration Decision Making*, edited by Gordon F. DeJong and Robert W. Gardner. New York: Pergamon.

Kanaiaupuni, Shawn M. 2000. "Reframing the Migration Question: An Analysis of Men, Women and Gender in Mexico." *Social Forces* 78(4): 1311–48.

Kandel, William, and Douglas S. Massey. 2002. "The Culture of Mexican Migration: A Theoretical and Empirical Analysis." *Social Forces* 80(3): 981–1004.

Lindstrom, David P., and Nathanael Lauster. 2001. "Local Economic Opportunity and the Competing Risks of U.S. and Internal Migration in Zacatecas, Mexico." *International Migration Review* 35: 1232–54.

Martin, Philip. 1999. "Emigration Dynamics in Mexico: The Case of Agriculture." In *Emigration Dynamics in Developing Countries: Mexico, Central America, and the Caribbean*, edited by Reginald Appleyard. Aldershot, U.K.: Ashgate.

Massey, Douglas S. 1990. "Social Structure, Household Strategies, and the Cumulative Causation of Migration." *Population Index* 56: 3–26.

Massey, Douglas S., Rafael Alarcón, Jorge Durand, and Humberto González. 1987. *Return to Aztlán: The Social Process of International Migration from Western Mexico*. Berkeley: University of California Press.

Massey, Douglas S., and Kristin E. Espinosa. 1997. "What's Driving Mexico-U.S. Migration? A Theoretical, Empirical, and Policy Analysis." *American Journal of Sociology* 102: 939–99.

Massey, Douglas S., and Felipe García-España. 1987. "The Social Process of International Migration." *Science* 237: 733–38.

Massey, Douglas S., Luin P. Goldring, and Jorge Durand. 1994. "Continuities in Transnational Migration: An Analysis of Nineteen Mexican Communities." *American Journal of Sociology* 99: 1492–1533.

Massey, Douglas S., and René Zenteno. 1999. "The Dynamics of Mass Migration." *Proceedings of the National Academy of Sciences* 96(8): 5328–35.

McCullagh, Peter, and John A. Nelder. 1989/1999. *Generalized Linear Models.* 2nd ed. London: Chapman and Hall.

Palloni, Alberto, Douglas S. Massey, Miguel Ceballos, Kristin E. Espinosa, and Mike Spittel. 2001. "Social Capital and International Migration: A Test Using Information on Family Networks." *American Journal of Sociology* 106: 1262–98.

Portes, Alejandro. 1978. "Migration and Underdevelopment." *Politics and Society* 8: 1–48.

Portes, Alejandro, and Rubén Rumbaut. 1996. *Immigrant America: A Portrait.* Berkeley: University of California Press.

Reichert, Joshua S. 1981. "The Migrant Syndrome: Seasonal U.S. Wage Labor and Rural Development in Central Mexico." *Human Organization* 40: 56–66.

Stark, Oded, and J. Edward Taylor. 1989. "Relative Deprivation and International Migration." *Demography* 26: 1–14.

———. 1991. "Migration Incentives, Migration Types: The Role of Relative Deprivation." *Economic Journal* 101: 1163–78.

Taylor, J. Edward. 1986. "Differential Migration, Networks, Information and Risk." In *Migration Theory, Human Capital and Development,* edited by Oded Stark. Greenwich, Conn.: JAI.

Taylor, J. Edward, Joaquín Arango, Graeme Hugo, Ali Kouaouci, Douglas S. Massey, and Adela Pellegrino. 1996. "International Migration and National Development." *Population Index* 62(2): 181–212.

Unikel, Luis, and C. Ruiz Chiapetto. 1973. "Factores de rechazo en la migración rural en México, 1950–1960." *Demografía y Economía* 7: 24–57.

PART IV

❖

POLICY CONSIDERATIONS

CHAPTER 12

A PROFILE OF MEXICAN WORKERS IN U.S. AGRICULTURE

William A. Kandel

RECENT CHANGES in the demographic composition of the farm labor force have revealed gaps in our understanding of migration, employment, and settlement patterns among workers in U.S. agriculture. Research on agricultural labor currently relies on data from nationally based surveys that are administered either to households or to agricultural establishments. The former surveys gather individual-level demographic and labor force data, while the latter provide timely estimates of the total number employed in specific agricultural sectors. Because both types of surveys were established by government agencies in response to official mandates, however, the information they collect is oriented toward specific policy questions.

Such data carry several limitations for researchers seeking to understand farm labor more generally. First, no surveying agency collects longitudinal data, either prospective or retrospective. Second, the official sponsorship of most surveys reduces the likelihood of participation by unemployed and undocumented migrants, resulting in biased demographic profiles and an undercount of total numbers of workers (Oliveira and Cox 1989; Oliveira and Whitener 1995). Third, if all data come from surveys of farmworkers or agricultural establishments exclusively, they cannot easily be compared with samples of workers from other economic sectors. Finally, these sources do not collect information on many characteristics that influence migration and employment decisions, such as social ties to other migrants and characteristics of sending communities, that can provide insight into the changing character and dynamics of the U.S. agricultural labor force.

Given that agricultural jobs are among the most poorly paid, physically demanding, and least stable of all U.S. occupations, data that can shed light on entry into and exit from them should be particularly useful for policy analysts wishing to understand this unique labor market. One relatively untapped source of data on U.S. migrant farmworkers is the Mexican Migration Project (MMP), which captures an important but understudied segment of the U.S. farmworker population: undocumented Mexicans, particularly those who shuttle back and forth across the border with some frequency. This population has become increasingly important. Recent results from the U.S. Department of Labor's National Agricultural Workers Survey (NAWS) indicate that three-quarters of all U.S. farmworkers are Mexican born—a radical compositional shift away from the traditionally white and black workforce that shows no sign of abating (U.S. Department of Labor 2000a). Data from the survey also indicate that many farmworkers are based in Mexico rather than the United States and that a large share are undocumented. Unlike the NAWS, the MMP covers Mexican-born farmworkers exclusively and includes both those based in the United States and those who cross the border from homes in Mexico. It has also been shown to be more effective than standard surveys at sampling and interviewing undocumented migrants (Massey and Zenteno 2000).

EXTANT SOURCES OF DATA ON AGRICULTURAL LABOR

Data on the agricultural workforce originate from several sources and vary according to the target population, the definition of agricultural labor used, the age range considered, the frequency of data collection, and the reference period for employment. Table 12.1 reviews current sources of data on farm labor, classified by unit of analysis. These sources may be characterized by their relative inability to allow study of agricultural migrant workers over time as well as to compare migrant workers across occupations.

Establishment surveys interview farm operators and managers. The largest is the Census of Agriculture, conducted by the National Agricultural Statistics Service of the U.S. Department of Agriculture. Every five years it surveys all 1.9 million farms and ranches in the United States. It also conducts a quarterly Farm Labor Survey that gathers data on employment, hours worked, and hourly wages from a probability sample of farms.

Other data on farmworkers come from administrative records kept by two federal agencies: the Bureau of Labor Statistics of the U.S. Department of Labor, which compiles statistics on agricultural workers from tax reports that are filed quarterly by state employment security agencies, and

TABLE 12.1   Characteristics of Current Sources of Data on U.S. Agricultural Labor

Data Series	Agency	Target Population	Frequency
Establishment surveys			
Census of Agriculture	National Agricultural Statistics Service (U.S. Department of Agriculture)	All U.S. farms	Every five years
Farm Labor Survey	National Agricultural Statistics Service (U.S. Department of Agriculture)	Sample of U.S. farms	Every three months
Administrative records			
Unemployment insurance records	Bureau of Labor Statistics (U.S. Department of Labor)	State-mandated employers	Every three months
Employment and income records	Bureau of Economic Analysis (U.S. Department of Commerce)	Agricultural employees	Every year
Household surveys			
Census of Population	Bureau of the Census (U.S. Department of Commerce)	All households	Every ten years
Current Population Survey	Bureau of the Census (U.S. Department of Commerce)	Sample of U.S. households	Every month
National Agricultural Workers Survey	U.S. Department of Commerce	Sample of farmworker households	Every four months

Source: Adapted from Oliveira and Whitener (1995).

the Bureau of Economic Analysis at the U.S. Department of Commerce, which draws on employment and income data filed by various state and federal agencies. While both these sources provide county-level data on agricultural employment and wages, they have other shortcomings that limit their use for most micro-level and some macro-level analyses. Neither source collects much background data on the demographic or economic characteristics of farmworkers, and both cover all workers in agricultural industries, including such job categories as bookkeepers, mechanics, and workers in canning and packing plants, whose characteristics and employment profiles differ starkly from those of farm laborers. Finally, according to Bureau of Labor Statistics estimates, the Unemployment Insurance Program covers less than half of all farmworkers, sharply limiting the ability to generalize to the total population (U.S. Department of Labor 1992).

Three sources of federal statistics provide more detailed household- and individual-level data on the social, economic, and demographic characteristics of farm laborers. The Census of Population, administered by the Bureau of the Census of the U.S. Department of Commerce, collects basic demographic and employment data on members of all U.S. households every ten years, permitting detailed comparisons between occupational groups across multiple geographic levels (nation, region, state, county, and tract). The drawbacks of census data are well known, however: infrequent data collection as well as the undercounting of farmworkers, minorities, persons living in nonstandard housing, and, especially, unauthorized workers.

The Current Population Survey, which is also administered by the U.S. Bureau of the Census, solves the frequency problem but does little to remedy the various undercounting issues. The survey covers some fifty thousand civilian households containing around 160,000 individuals. It compiles demographic and employment information for all household members, including those born abroad. Like the census, however, it significantly undercounts farmworkers, undocumented migrants, and Latinos in general. In 1998, for example, the Current Population Survey estimated the size of the hired farmworker population at just 875,000 (Runyan 2000b, 11), compared with an estimate of 1.8 million from the U.S. Department of Labor (2000b, 3).

The National Agricultural Workers Survey is generally thought to provide the most representative profile of hired U.S. farmworkers, precisely because it captures foreign-born and undocumented workers (CIRS 2000; Villarejo and Baron 1999; Yuñez-Naude 2001). Since 1989, it has surveyed a random sample of crop farmworkers (that is, excluding livestock workers) three times a year using a multistage sampling design stratified by agricultural activity and size of establishment payroll. It gathers data on demographic characteristics, legal status, literacy, short-term employment histories, earnings, working conditions, and employment for all household members.

My review of data sources on farm labor reveals many sampling methodologies and primary sampling units. Different sources provide information on different classes of agricultural workers at different geographic levels. Thorough but infrequent surveys, such as the decennial census, can be supplemented with more regular data from the Current Population Survey, the NAWS, and other sources, but all extant databases miss significant shares of the population of interest, and none provides longitudinal information or data on social networks and other variables central to the process of migration. Even the NAWS, which is by far the most detailed and accurate survey of U.S. farmworkers, gathers no information on sending communities and offers no information on nonagricultural workers to provide a base of comparison.

FARMWORKERS ENUMERATED IN THE MEXICAN MIGRATION PROJECT

In contrast to sources of official statistics, the MMP contains detailed data on migrants' social networks, their sending communities, and their legal status as well as longitudinal life-history files useful in understanding the temporal dynamics of farm employment (see chapter 16). However, the MMP data have their own weaknesses: they are not a representative sample of migrant farmworkers per se but a sample of farmworkers originating in specific Mexican communities. Migrant farmworkers from these communities may or may not be representative of all Mexican farmworkers working in the United States.

To explore the representativeness of the MMP data, I selected all migrant farmworkers whose most recent trip to the United States occurred from 1993 to 1998, a period that corresponds to the years of the NAWS sample. I then compared the two surveys. The principle difference in design is that the NAWS surveys only those migrant farmworkers who are present in the United States, whereas the MMP surveys them on both sides of the border, though the sample is numerically skewed toward those surveyed in Mexico. In addition, unlike the NAWS, which misses many undocumented workers, the MMP provides excellent coverage of this clandestine population (Massey and Zenteno 2000).

The first row of table 12.2 shows the share of farmworkers identified in each data set as Mexican born. By definition, this share is 100 percent for those included in the Mexican Migration Project. In the NAWS, however,

TABLE 12.2   Characteristics of Agricultural Workers Sampled by the National Agricultural Worker Survey and the Mexican Migration Project, 1993 to 1998 (Percentage)

Population	National Agricultural Worker Survey							Mexican Migration Project
	1993	1994	1995	1996	1997	1998	Mean	Mean
Mexican-born	64	65	65	70	77	78	**70**	**100**
Shuttler migrants	29	27	35	36	42	41	**35**	**81**
Mexican-born shuttler migrants	25	23	31	33	39	39	**32**	**81**
N	2,393	2,374	2,363	2,051	2,100	2,099	**2,230**	**449**

Source: Data from Mexican Migration Project and U.S. Department of Labor (2000a).
Note: Bold added for emphasis.

this share has risen steadily in recent years, from 64 percent in 1993 to 78 percent in 1998. Moreover, of the remaining percentage of farmworkers who were not born in Mexico in 1998, nearly all are of Mexican origin. Therefore, that the MMP is designed to cover only Mexicans is becoming increasingly less relevant in distinguishing it from the NAWS.

The NAWS includes a special category, "shuttler migrants," defined as farmworkers who spent at least twenty-eight days abroad during the prior year. As can be seen in the second row of the table, the share of migrant farmworkers in the NAWS who actively shuttle back and forth between their home countries has also been increasing. The percentage of farm laborers spending at least twenty-eight days out of the country during the past year rose from 29 percent in 1993 to 41 percent in 1998. The next row indicates the share of NAWS respondents who are both Mexican-born and shuttler migrants, a percentage that has also risen rapidly in recent years from 25 percent in 1993 to 39 percent in 1998. By comparison, 81 percent of the MMP sample are Mexican-born shuttle migrants who move back and forth regularly. Though the MMP and the NAWS still cover different populations, changes over time have made the MMP increasingly representative of the U.S. agricultural workforce.

It may be most accurate to say that the MMP is weighted toward migrants at the early stages of U.S. labor force experience, whereas NAWS is weighted toward those who have become more established as U.S. farmworkers. A substantial body of research documents the self-perpetuating nature of Mexico-U.S. migration, beginning with temporary migration by a few community members and expanding over time as experienced migrants transmit migration-specific information through social networks to ultimately produce binational communities with branches on both sides of the border (Alarcón 1992; Cornelius 1992; Massey 1990; Massey et al. 1987; Mines 1981). This process is reflected in the monotonically increasing percentage of Mexico-born farmworkers in the NAWS (shown in the first row of table 12.2).

AGRICULTURAL AND OTHER WORKERS

The remaining tables in this chapter examine the demographic, migratory, social, and employment characteristics of employed migrants by their occupation while in the United States. Nonagricultural workers are divided into two categories: skilled and unskilled. Skilled workers include professionals, managers, most supervisors, pink collar workers, and technical workers. Unskilled workers include operatives, unskilled service workers such as domestics, custodians, and busboys, and manual laborers such as those working in construction. Although these broad categories necessarily mask important differences between workers, they nonetheless provide sufficient cases for reliable comparison.

Most tables cross-tabulate occupation by period. I defined three historical time periods that roughly correspond to separate immigration policy regimes and distinct economic conditions. "Before 1987" includes migrants from as far back as the early 1920s and encompasses the Bracero Program, from 1942 to 1964, as well as the epoch of significantly increased undocumented migration leading up to the passage of the landmark Immigration Reform and Control Act (IRCA) of 1986. The next period, "1987 to 1992," captures the immediate impact of IRCA. During the three years following its enactment, close to 3 million undocumented migrants with previous U.S. experience were legalized, an administrative undertaking that actually ended in 1992.

The last period, "After 1992," captures the impact of increased border enforcement and growing binational trade. In 1994 the launching of Operation Gatekeeper heralded a new era of greatly increased border enforcement, forcing Mexicans to cross the border at new points (thereby encouraging movement to nontraditional destinations) and to remain in the United States for longer periods. The Mexican economic crisis and the passage of the North American Free Trade Agreement in 1994 also created forces for increased labor migration in subsequent years (Massey, Durand, and Malone 2002). While not shown here, all cross-tabulations

were also run with five-year intervals to ensure that the three broad categories did not conceal important within-period fluctuations. Because the
aim of this descriptive analysis is to document trends, I generally do not
test for statistical significance across period or occupational categories.

All tables present individual characteristics during the most recent trip
to the United States. The MMP classifies most trips by the year in which
they began, not when they ended. For short trips, there is no disjuncture
between the two. For trips of longer duration, however, the year the trip
started and ended may differ, leaving unclear in which year a person's characteristics should be measured. I measure characteristics as of the final year
of the most recent trip. Social capital measures, on the other hand, are
structured to reflect an individual's situation at the time of the migratory
decision and are thus measured as of the first year of the most recent trip.
I measure social service participation at the midpoint of the most recent
trip because questionnaire wording asked whether services had ever been
used on the most recent trip.

Table 12.3 presents the occupational distribution of migrants identified
by the MMP. Of the 83,527 individuals surveyed in the MMP, 17,625
reported current or prior U.S. experience; of these, 11,073 were employed
on their most recent trip to the United States, 2,845 in agriculture. Among
migrant household heads, 4,758 were employed on their last trip, and 1,436
in agriculture (not shown). As table 12.3 indicates, agricultural employment
as a share of all jobs held by surveyed Mexican migrants has generally
declined over time, both for migrants based in Mexico and for those based
in the United States. Among migrants interviewed in Mexico, 51 percent of
those working in the United States before 1987 were employed in agriculture; that figure dropped to 28 percent among those who left for the United
States from 1987 to 1992 and to 15 percent among those leaving in 1993 or
later. (In these and all subsequent tabulations, the MMP data are weighted
by the inverse of the sampling fraction to adjust for differences in the sizes
of samples and communities—see Massey and Espinosa [1997] and Massey
and Parrado [1994] for a discussion of the weights.) Those migrants who
have settled in the United States are much more likely to hold nonagricultural jobs, though the general direction of the trend is still downward, shifting from 9 percent working in agriculture among migrants leaving before
1987 to 6 percent among those who left in 1993 or later.

Demographic Characteristics

Table 12.4 presents basic demographic characteristics of employed U.S.
migrants identified by the MMP. Two patterns stand out with respect to

TABLE 12.3 Occupational Distribution of Employed Mexico-U.S. Migrants Surveyed by the Mexican Migration Project, by Period of Most Recent Trip

Place of Survey	Period of U.S. Trip			All Periods
	Before 1987	1987 to 1992	After 1992	
Mexico				
Percentage skilled	12.3	20.5	28.4	19.0
Percentage unskilled	36.3	51.5	56.4	46.8
Percentage in agriculture	51.4	28.0	15.2	34.2
Total	2,934	3,281	1,526	7,741
Number in agriculture	1,508	918	232	2,658
United States				
Percentage skilled	25.5	42.1	41.9	41.5
Percentage unskilled	65.3	52.7	52.4	52.9
Percentage in agriculture	9.2	5.2	5.7	5.6
Total	98	1,193	2,041	3,332
Number in agriculture	9	62	116	187
All migrants				
Percentage skilled	12.8	26.3	36.1	25.8
Percentage unskilled	37.2	51.8	54.2	48.6
Percentage in agriculture	50.0	21.9	9.7	25.7
Total	3,032	4,474	3,566	11,072
Number in agriculture	1,517	980	348	2,845

Source: Data from Mexican Migration Project, PERSFILE.

age: migrants are getting older over time, and agricultural workers are generally older than other migrants. Among skilled workers, those migrating before 1987 had a mean age of 29.2 years, whereas those migrating after 1992 had an average age of 33.4. Among unskilled workers, the shift was from 29.0 to 34.6. During each period, however, the mean age of agricultural workers exceeded that of either skilled or unskilled workers, going from 30.8 before 1987 to 35.5 after 1992. The higher mean age of unskilled workers may reflect their more disadvantaged economic position, which requires them to spend more time in the United States to reach earnings targets.

The gender composition of U.S. migrants is also characterized both by time trends and by differences between agricultural and nonagricultural workers. In general, there are few women among migrant farmworkers and

TABLE 12.4   Selected Demographic Characteristics of Employed Mexico-U.S. Migrants, by U.S. Occupation and Period of Most Recent Trip

Characteristic and Period	Most Recent U.S. Occupation		
	Skilled	Unskilled	Agriculture
Mean age			
Before 1987	29.2	29.0	30.8
1987 to 1992	31.7	31.3	32.3
After 1992	33.4	34.6	35.5
Percentage female			
Before 1987	20	22	7
1987 to 1992	25	24	10
After 1992	33	25	8
Percentage married			
Before 1987	88	86	86
1987 to 1992	69	72	75
After 1992	71	73	77
N	2,851	5,376	2,845

Source: Data from Mexican Migration Project, PERSFILE.

no evidence of increase over time. Across the three periods under study, the percentage of females among migrant farmworkers shifted from 7 to 10 to 8 percent. Thus throughout the years studied, more than 90 percent of Mexican agricultural workers were men. The participation of migrant women in other occupational sectors is comparatively greater. Before 1987, 22 percent of migrants employed in unskilled manual occupations were women, a share that rose slightly to reach 25 percent in the post-1992 period. Among skilled migrant workers, however, the increase in female participation was sharper, from 20 percent before 1987 to 33 percent after 1992. These data suggest that female participation in U.S. labor markets is more heavily influenced by human capital attainment than for male participation, with progressively greater participation levels in skilled occupations that require more education.

The last panel of table 12.4 shows the marital status of migrants on their most recent trip. Before 1987 virtually all migrants were married, irrespective of occupation. The percentage currently married ranged from 86 percent in agricultural and unskilled manual occupations to 88 percent in skilled occupations. Thereafter the share fell somewhat, but there is no evidence of a sustained decline in marriage rates among migrants. After

1986 and across occupational categories, the share married ranged from a low of 69 percent to a high of 77 percent. Thus two-thirds to three-quarters of all Mexican migrants were married at the time of their most recent U.S. trip, and agricultural migrant workers were about as likely to be married as migrants in other occupational groups.

Human Capital and Migration Characteristics

Table 12.5 summarizes the general and migration-specific human capital held by Mexican migrants to the United States. As can be seen in the top panel, years of schooling increased for all groups across historical periods,

TABLE 12.5   Selected Human Capital and Migratory Characteristics of Employed Mexico-U.S. Migrants, by U.S. Occupation and Period of Most Recent Trip

| Characteristic and Period | Most Recent U.S. Occupation | | |
	Skilled	Unskilled	Agriculture
Mean years of schooling			
Before 1987	5.9	5.7	3.3
1987 to 1992	8.0	6.9	5.6
After 1992	10.4	7.9	6.0
Median months U.S. experience			
Before 1987	21	18	12
1987 to 1992	90	66	43
After 1992	188	114	102
Median months of trip duration			
Before 1987	12	12	6
1987 to 1992	30	18	8
After 1992	126	84	42
Total trips taken			
Before 1987	2.3	2.1	3.1
1987 to 1992	3.0	3.2	5.1
After 1992	2.1	2.1	3.5
Percentage undocumented			
Before 1987	72	78	65
1987 to 1992	69	65	43
After 1992	75	67	61
N	2,851	5,376	2,845

Source: Data from Mexican Migration Project, PERSFILE.

yet during each era, agricultural workers had significantly fewer average years than either skilled or unskilled migrant workers. Before 1987, both skilled and unskilled migrant workers had nearly six years of education, on average (5.9 for the former and 5.7 for the latter), compared with just 3.3 years among farmworkers. Although educational levels rose among migrants in all three occupational groups in subsequent years, they also increasingly diverged. Whereas the mean education of agricultural workers grew from 3.3 to 6.0 years over the period under study, that of unskilled workers rose from 5.7 to 7.9 years and that of skilled workers grew from 5.9 to 10.4 years. Results for the education levels of migrants observed during their first U.S. trip are almost identical, suggesting that self-selection into agricultural work on the basis of education occurs at the start of the migration process (results not shown).

General human capital refers to skills and abilities that, in theory, can be acquired by anyone, migrant or nonmigrant. Migration-specific human capital refers to skills and abilities acquired in the course of migration itself that render a person better able to cross the border, find housing, and obtain a U.S. job and make that person potentially more valuable to U.S. employers (Massey and Espinosa 1997; Massey et al. 1987). The acquisition of migration-specific human capital is proxied by three variables: total experience cumulated by the migrant before the most recent trip, total duration of the most recent trip, and total number of trips taken. Another migrant characteristic relevant to employment is legal status, which permits greater occupational and wage mobility.

Of the three occupation categories, agricultural workers generally display the least amount of prior U.S. experience and the shortest trips but the largest total number of trips. Historically, skilled and unskilled migrants have taken fewer trips and have remained in the United States for relatively longer periods, thereby accumulating more total migrant experience than their farmworker counterparts. Given the seasonal and unstable nature of their work, agricultural laborers make more trips of shorter duration than others, leading to the accumulation of significant skills in border crossing but less in the way of job-specific human capital that can be translated into wage gains in the United States. As of 1987, the typical migrant farmworker had accumulated 12 months of U.S. experience before the last trip, which had an average duration of six months. In contrast, unskilled workers had 18 months of prior U.S. experience and stayed for 12 months on their last trip, and skilled workers had 21 months of prior experience with the same average trip duration.

Over time, however, all occupational groups have witnessed rising amounts of cumulative migrant experience. Total prior U.S. experience for migrant farmworkers increased dramatically, going from 12 months among those leaving on their last trip before 1987 to 102 months (eight and a half years) among those leaving after 1992. The corresponding increases were from 18 months to 114 months for unskilled workers and from 21 to 188 months for those with skills.

The militarization of the Mexico-U.S. border after 1992 also produced a sharp increase in trip duration for all international migrant workers. Paradoxically, driving up the costs and risks of border crossing tends not to keep migrants from coming—it simply discourages them from going home (Massey, Durand, and Malone 2002). Whereas agricultural laborers leaving between 1987 and 1992 stayed in the United States for an average of 8 months, for example, those leaving in 1993 or later stayed an average of 42 months—a fivefold increase. Similarly, between the same two periods the average trip duration went from 18 months to 84 months for unskilled migrants and from 40 months to 120 months for skilled migrants—and these are biased downward somewhat by left-hand censoring (some of most recent trips have yet to be completed). As trip duration rose, of course, the number of trips fell, with average numbers for the two time periods after 1986 dropping from 5.1 to 3.5 for agricultural workers, from 3.2 to 2.1 for unskilled workers, and from 3.0 to 2.1 for skilled workers.

The last panel considers the percentage undocumented among workers by period and occupation. With one exception, at least 60 percent of all migrant workers in all periods were undocumented. The exception is agricultural workers between 1986 and 1993. Before this period 65 percent of agricultural workers were undocumented, and afterward 61 percent lacked papers, but from 1987 through 1992 the percentage dropped to 43 percent. This era, of course, corresponds to the massive legalization authorized by IRCA.

The IRCA legalization actually encompassed two programs, one for long-term residents of the United States that was difficult to qualify for and the other targeted specifically to migrant farmworkers, for which qualifying proved rather easy. Indeed, the latter program was so loosely administered, so nebulous in its criteria, and so plagued with opportunities for fakery that it induced many Mexicans who had never worked in U.S. agriculture, or even been in the United States, to cross the border in hopes of being legalized through fraudulent means. According to one study, the number of applicants for Special Agricultural Worker status in California alone was *three times* the size of the entire agricultural workforce during the period in question (Martin, Taylor, and Hardiman 1988). In short, IRCA for a brief period actually expanded legal migration, increasing the rate of documented out-migration from Mexico to levels not seen since the 1920s—

hence the sudden but temporary drop in the share of undocumented migrants. After 1992 the situation returned to the status quo ante.

Social Capital

The human capital characteristics examined thus far can be viewed conceptually as determinants of individual migration decision making. Migration success, however, also depends on social capital, which refers to the value attached to individuals' webs of social relationships (Coleman 1988). Social capital forms through family and community ties, strengthens from frequent contact and reciprocal exchange, and ultimately helps migrants surmount obstacles inherent in entering the United States and locating employment and housing there (Espinosa and Massey 1998; Palloni et al. 2001). Typically, it translates into direct financial assistance, housing, and information on border crossing, employment, and housing.

Table 12.6 presents four indicators of the degree to which social capital was used by migrants during their most recent U.S. trip. Unlike prior tables, data for these cross-tabulations are limited to household heads, from whom this information was collected. As can be seen, agricultural and nonagricultural migrants display distinct patterns of social capital utilization. For example, skilled and unskilled workers were quite likely to be in contact with other family members while in the United States, the proportion varying from 60 to 69 percent and displaying no time trend. In contrast, only 33 percent of agricultural laborers were in contact with family members before 1987 and 49 percent after 1992. Although the figure reached 54 percent during the period of intensive legalization under IRCA, this appears to be an aberration.

In contrast, agricultural workers were more likely than skilled or unskilled workers to be in contact with other migrants from their home community while in the United States, though this tendency has declined over time for all three groups. Whereas 74 percent of farmworkers reported contact with other community members before 1987 and 69 percent after 1992, the respective shares for skilled workers were 62 and 56 percent, and those for unskilled workers were 70 and 59 percent.

Because agricultural growers frequently provide barracks housing for their workers, farm laborers are relatively unlikely to receive housing from friends or relatives in the United States. Among those leaving before 1987, only 38 percent reported having received such assistance, and for those migrating after 1992, 45 percent. Among skilled workers arriving before 1987, however, 84 percent received housing from friends or relatives, and 80 percent did so after 1992. For unskilled migrant workers, the

TABLE 12.6   Selected Measures of Social Capital of Employed
Mexico-U.S. Migrant Household Heads, by
U.S. Occupation and Period of Most Recent Trip

Characteristic and Period	Most Recent U.S. Occupation		
	Skilled	Unskilled	Agriculture
Percentage in contact with relatives			
Before 1987	62	63	33
1987 to 1992	60	65	54
After 1992	64	69	49
Percentage in contact with community members			
Before 1987	62	70	74
1987 to 1992	57	65	61
After 1992	56	59	69
Percentage who received housing from relatives or friends			
Before 1987	84	77	38
1987 to 1992	78	86	65
After 1992	80	82	45
Percentage who received job through relatives or friends			
Before 1987	64	70	43
1987 to 1992	67	70	65
After 1992	65	73	68
N	889	1,874	1,321

Source: Data from Mexican Migration Project, MIGFILE or PERSFILE.

respective shares were 77 and 82 percent. Once again, the years of IRCA implementation proved to be an aberration for farmworkers, 65 percent of whom reported the receipt of housing from social contacts in the United States from 1987 to 1992.

Probably the most important resource that can be obtained through social networks is a U.S. job. In general, unskilled manual workers appear to be most dependent on friends and family to obtain work. In all periods, some 70 to 73 percent of migrants reported getting their job through such social contacts. Skilled migrants followed, roughly two-thirds reporting that they got their job through friends or relatives, regardless of period.

Those least dependent on networks to obtain U.S. employment have historically been agricultural workers; but this changed markedly with the passage of IRCA in 1986. This law for the first time criminalized undocumented hiring, and to protect themselves from prosecution, agricultural growers switched to indirect means of hiring (Massey, Durand, and Malone 2002). Farmworkers could no longer get work by going directly to a farm owner or manager; rather, they had to work through a subcontractor who had negotiated a arrangement with the owner or manager to provide a specific number of workers to undertake a specific set of tasks at a set rate (Taylor and Thilmany 1993). As a result, the share of farmworkers who got their job through a relative or friend (typically, subcontractors recruit friends and relatives from their home community) grew from 43 percent before 1987 to around two-thirds thereafter.

In general, differences between agricultural and other workers reflect the logistics of seasonal agricultural employment, which requires movement from one work site to the next. Under such circumstances, though agricultural migrants may move in the company of other townspeople, they are more likely to find housing on site and less likely to rely on contacts for resources such as jobs and housing, particularly during the pre-IRCA period. Although these four measures far from exhaust the potential measures of social capital available from the MMP, they suggest rather different patterns of use for rural- and urban-based migrants.

Employment Characteristics

Table 12.7 presents selected employment characteristics for household heads in each occupational group. The top panel, which considers average hours worked per week, reveals that migrants generally toil more than the normal forty-hour workweek, no matter what their sector of employment. Mean hours worked ranged from a low of 44 hours to a high of more than 49 hours. Although there were no clear trends over time, agricultural laborers tended to put in slightly more work hours than either skilled or unskilled workers. Whereas after 1992 the workweek averaged 46.7 for farmworkers, the figure was 45.1 for unskilled migrants and 44.4 for skilled migrants.

Despite the slightly greater length of their workweek, however, farm laborers tend to spend fewer months working each year compared with other migrants. Among those migrating before 1987, for example, agricultural laborers worked in the United States for an average of 5.6 months, compared with 7.5 months for unskilled manual workers and 7.8 months for skilled workers. The seasonal and unstable nature of agricultural work generally limits the work year to around three-quarters of that for skilled

TABLE 12.7   Employment Characteristics of Employed Mexico-U.S.
Migrant Household Heads, by Occupation and
Period of Most Recent Trip

Characteristic and Period	Most Recent U.S. Occupation		
	Skilled	Unskilled	Agriculture
Mean hours worked per week			
Before 1987	45	45	48
1987 to 1992	44	44	49
After 1992	44	45	47
Mean months worked per year			
Before 1987	8	8	6
1987 to 1992	10	9	6
After 1992	11	11	9
Mean hourly wage			
Before 1987	5.7	4.8	2.8
1987 to 1992	5.8	6.0	5.3
After 1992	8.2	6.3	5.5
Percentage paid by check			
Before 1987	78	75	75
1987 to 1992	79	81	85
After 1992	85	88	86
Percentage with federal taxes withheld			
Before 1987	70	69	64
1987 to 1992	79	81	82
After 1992	82	89	86
Percentage with social security taxes withheld			
Before 1987	77	72	70
1987 to 1992	80	84	84
After 1992	84	90	87
Percentage filing tax return[a]			
Before 1987	3	23	16
1987 to 1992	5	19	5
After 1992	43	57	20
N	889	1,874	1,321

Source: Data from Mexican Migration Project, MIGFILE.

[a] Data on 240 skilled workers, 308 unskilled workers, and 143 agricultural workers.

and unskilled occupations (see Gabbard, Mines, and Boccalandro 1994). Consistent with the increasing duration of trips observed earlier, however, all three groups have steadily increased the number of months worked over time. From 1993 onward, agricultural migrants worked an average of 9.2 months a year, compared with roughly 11 months for both skilled and unskilled migrant workers.

The third panel of table 12.7 shows the mean hourly wage earned by migrants in different eras and occupations. As one might expect, nominal wages have risen over time within each occupational category, but in each period there is a clear ordering by occupational status: those holding skilled occupations earn the highest wages, while those in agricultural jobs earn the lowest, the wages of unskilled manual workers falling somewhere between the two. With few exceptions, real wages of agricultural workers have not only trailed those in other occupations but also declined in real terms over the past thirty years (see also Rothenberg 1998, 16; U.S. Department of Labor 2000b, 11). As of the most recent period, the mean hourly wage of $5.50 for agricultural workers was 87 percent of that earned by unskilled laborers and 67 percent of that earned by skilled workers.

Although it is not reflected in the MMP data, agricultural work is among the most dangerous and physically grueling in the U.S. labor market, with rates of illness and injury that surpass averages for other industrial sectors (CIRS 2000; National Safety Council 2001). Harsh working conditions, remote locations, substandard living quarters, and high transportation costs, combined with unstable work schedules and low wages, provide strong incentives for agricultural migrants to switch occupations.

Numerous studies address the contentious issue of immigration's fiscal effects on the United States (see Borjas 1998; U.S. Department of Labor 1989). The next four panels of table 12.7 consider the potential fiscal contributions of Mexican migrant workers. The first of these is the percentage of migrants who were paid by check on their most recent job in the United States. Payment by check rather than cash suggests a formal job that is covered by U.S. tax laws as well as occupational safety, health, and insurance regulations. Cash payments are unlikely to have taxes withheld and forwarded to federal and state governments.

As can be seen, most migrants in all categories reported being paid by check on their last U.S. job, and there were no consistent differences by occupation, although within each occupational category the percentage who were paid by check has steadily increased over time. In the most recent period, well over 80 percent of migrant workers in each occupation were paid by check. In keeping with this apparently high rate of formal employment, rates of tax withholding are also high and have been rising over time. After 1992, 86 percent of agricultural workers, 89 percent of unskilled manual workers, and 82 percent of skilled workers reported having had federal income taxes withheld from their checks, and about the same percentages said social security taxes had also been withheld.

While the vast majority of migrants paid income and social security taxes over the years, they were much less likely to file tax returns. Thus when it comes to reclaiming overpayments, most migrants will never collect. Filing returns for federal and state taxes would undoubtedly refund migrants some portion of their withheld taxes because most Mexican migrants earn wages at or below poverty level (Runyan 2000b). The data in the bottom panel of table 12.7 need to be interpreted with caution: because of missing data, and because only those who have had taxes withheld need file, the MMP yields data on tax filing for only 240 skilled workers, 408 unskilled workers, and 143 agricultural workers.

Nonetheless, the available evidence suggests that until 1993 migrants were unlikely to file tax returns. Before 1987, the proportion filing a return ranged from 3 percent among skilled migrants to 16 percent among agricultural workers to 23 percent among unskilled migrants. During the next period, from 1987 to 1992, the respective proportions were 5, 19, and 5 percent. In other words, before 1993 migrants were likely to pay into the federal tax system but unlikely to take out. After 1992, the rate of filing increased in all categories but still only reached 43 percent among skilled migrants and 20 percent among agricultural workers, who displayed the lowest rate of tax filing. Only among unskilled workers did a majority—57 percent—report having filed a tax return.

Use of Social Services

On the other side of the fiscal equation, the use of social services by migrants, represents withdrawals from U.S. society and its economy. As noted earlier, I date program participation as of the midyear of the migrant's most recent U.S. trip because of the wording used in the MMP questionnaire. Table 12.8 shows the rate of participation of migrants in four major social service programs by period and occupation. Perhaps the most controversial program is welfare, which is displayed in the top panel of the table.

As can be seen, migrants' use of welfare programs is quite low, especially among agricultural workers. Before 1987, only 1 percent reported welfare use, whereas in the two periods following 1986 the rates were 7 and 2 percent. These low rates occurred despite the fact that 35 percent of those migrants working in the first period, 57 percent of those in the second, and 39 percent of those in the third were legal (table 12.5) and thus eligible for

TABLE 12.8   Use of Social Services by Employed Mexico-U.S.
Migrant Household Heads, by Occupation and
Period of Most Recent Trip

Characteristic and Period	Most Recent U.S. Occupation		
	Skilled	Unskilled	Agriculture
Percentage receiving welfare			
Before 1987	2	3	1
1987 to 1992	10	12	7
After 1992	16	12	2
Percentage receiving food stamps			
Before 1987	6	5	3
1987 to 1992	9	17	13
After 1992	5	6	3
Percentage receiving unemployment compensation			
Before 1987	22	17	4
1987 to 1992	29	23	28
After 1992	10	17	22
Percentage with children in public schools			
Before 1987	30	29	9
1987 to 1992	47	37	24
After 1992	19	18	20
Percentage visiting doctor or hospital			
Before 1987	58	55	27
1987 to 1992	77	71	56
After 1992	56	56	58
N	889	1,874	1,321

Source: Data from Mexican Migration Project, MIGFILE.

welfare. Although the rates were higher in other occupational groups, only small minorities of migrants in all periods reported having received welfare. In the most recent period, just 16 percent of skilled migrants and 12 percent of unskilled migrants reported themselves on welfare, compared with legalization rates of 25 and 33 percent, respectively.

Use of federally subsidized food stamp programs by migrants is equally low. Before 1987, only 6 percent of skilled migrants, 5 percent of unskilled migrants, and 3 percent of agricultural workers reported receipt of food stamps. Although the percentages rose in the IRCA years, from 1987 to 1992, after 1992 they returned to their pre-1987 rates or lower. Although relatively more migrants reported having received unemployment compensation, the same patterns can be observed over time: an increase from the first period to the second followed by a sharp decline in use rates in the latest period. As of 1993, only 10 percent of skilled migrants, 17 percent of unskilled migrants, and 22 percent of agricultural migrants received unemployment compensation, compared with figures of 29, 23, and 28 percent, respectively, in the prior period.

Not surprisingly, given the concentration of migrants in the ages of family formation, migrants tend to use schools more than other public services, though historically the percentage among agricultural workers has been quite low. Before 1987, just 9 percent of farmworkers reported having children in U.S. schools, compared with around 30 percent of skilled and unskilled migrant workers. Although from 1987 to 1992 rates of school attendance among the children of agricultural workers increased to 24 percent, after 1992 the rate subsequently fell back to 20 percent. Indeed, declining rates of school use also characterized skilled and unskilled migrants after 1982, although the migrant population itself came to include fewer shuttlers, more settlers, and larger proportions of women and children (Massey, Durand, and Malone 2002). From the period 1987 to 1992 to that beginning in 1993, the proportion of migrants with children in U.S. public schools fell from 37 percent to 18 percent among unskilled migrant workers and from 47 percent to 19 percent among skilled migrant workers.

The precipitous decline in the use of food stamps, unemployment compensation, and public schools after 1992 reflects shifts in U.S. policies toward immigrant integration, particularly the effects of 1996 welfare reform and immigration reform legislation, which sought to discourage the use of public services by legal as well as undocumented migrants. The result was what some observers have called a "chilling effect": immigrants were scared away from applying for publicly provided services, even those for which they legally qualified (see Zimmermann and Fix 1998). In addition, the 1996 legislation increased the household income necessary to qualify for the affidavit of support required of all immigrants seeking to sponsor the legal entry of a family member. To push household income above the threshold required for sponsorship, many immigrant families withdrew older children from school and put them to work.

Because portions of medical costs are often borne directly or indirectly by the public, the last panel in table 12.8 indicates the percentage of migrants who used a doctor or hospital during their most recent visit. As with other social services, the use of medical services rose from before 1987 to the period immediately afterward, going from 58 percent to 77 percent among skilled workers, 55 percent to 71 percent among unskilled workers, and 27 percent to 56 percent among farmworkers, but once again rates fell or stagnated after 1992, with the rate of medical use falling back slightly for both skilled and unskilled workers and remaining essentially constant for farmworkers, in keeping with the chilling effect mentioned in the preceding paragraph.

Of course, the cost of these doctor or hospital visits was not necessarily borne by the public. The MMP included a follow-up question asking who had paid for the most recent visit to the doctor, clinic, or hospital. The results are presented in table 12.9. A total of 2,119 employed respondents reported having used such services on their most recent trip to the United States. Although payment by Medicaid or failure to pay increased over time, the percentages remained quite low and were lowest among agricultural workers. In the most recent period, the proportion reporting such

TABLE 12.9   Source of Payment for Medical Services Used by Employed Mexico-U.S. Migrants on Most Recent Trip, by U.S. Occupation and Period of Most Recent Trip

	Most Recent U.S. Occupation		
Characteristic and Period	Skilled	Unskilled	Agriculture
Percentage paid by medicaid or no one			
Before 1987	1	4	2
1987 to 1992	4	8	3
After 1992	15	25	10
Percentage paid by employer or private insurance			
Before 1987	67	63	70
1987 to 1992	63	58	49
After 1992	65	51	57
Percentage paid by relatives or by respondent			
Before 1987	32	33	28
1987 to 1992	33	34	48
After 1992	20	25	33
N	576	1,049	494

Source: Data from Mexican Migration Project, MIGFILE.

bills stood at just 10 percent among agricultural workers and 15 percent among skilled workers, compared with 25 percent for unskilled manual workers. The majority of migrant workers rely upon employer or private insurance, often in combination with contributions from relatives and themselves. For agricultural migrants, however, there has been a clear decrease over time in the use of insurance and an increasing tendency to pay for medical expenses oneself or with the help of relatives.

PATTERNS OF OCCUPATIONAL MOBILITY

Results to this point generally indicate the marginal status of migrant agricultural workers relative to migrants in other economic sectors. Compared with skilled and unskilled workers outside of agriculture, farmworkers generally earn lower wages, work longer hours, have lower levels of education, make less use of social capital, and have less access to social services. Other things being equal, therefore, over time migrants would be expected to seek mobility out of agriculture into more-stable and better-paying occupations. The first potential opportunity for mobility occurs in moving from a

TABLE 12.10   Occupational Immobility Among Employed Mexico-U.S. Migrants, by Period of Most Recent Trip (Percentage)

Mexican Occupation and Period of Most Recent Trip	First U.S. Occupation		
	Skilled	Unskilled	Agriculture
Skilled			
Before 1987	**19**	42	39
1987 to 1992	**54**	34	12
After 1992	**80**	16	4
Unskilled			
Before 1987	9	**56**	35
1987 to 1992	9	**84**	7
After 1992	8	**88**	4
Agriculture			
Before 1987	3	21	**75**
1987 to 1992	5	22	**73**
After 1992	9	18	**73**
N	1,988	4,322	3,114

Source: Data from Mexican Migration Project, PERSFILE.
Note: Bold added for emphasis.

Mexican occupation to a first job in the United States. Table 12.10 considers patterns of mobility in making this transition by cross-tabulating the last occupation held in Mexico with the occupation held on the migrant's first trip to the United States. Within each occupational category, the data are broken down by period.

The cells along the diagonal of the table, highlighted in bold, indicate occupational immobility: that is, the migrant was employed in the same occupational class in Mexico and in the United States during his or her first trip. Given that agricultural work is relatively undesirable in both countries, one might expect considerable immobility in this occupational category. Those with farm experience in Mexico are likely to have greater stamina, more tolerance for poor working conditions, and fewer concerns about lower social standing than those from nonagricultural backgrounds and thus more amenable to working in agriculture on their first U.S. trip.

Consistent with this expectation, immobility rates were high for farmworkers in all periods, as shown in 12.10. Roughly three-quarters of migrants leaving Mexico from an agricultural occupation found employment in agriculture on their first U.S. trip. Among the quarter who did not move into agriculture, most went into unskilled manual jobs outside of agriculture. Not surprisingly, few migrants from a farm background (under 10 percent) ever went directly into a skilled U.S. occupation.

Migrants from other occupational backgrounds in Mexico experienced much less occupational immobility. Before 1987, for example, only 56 percent of unskilled migrants and 19 percent of skilled migrants remained in the same occupational category following their first move to the United States. In general, the prevailing pattern was one of downward mobility, which occurs by definition among skilled migrants, of whom, before 1987, 42 percent moved down to unskilled occupations and 39 percent ended up in agriculture. Similarly, among unskilled migrants, 35 percent shifted downward into agriculture, whereas only 9 percent moved upward into a skilled occupational category.

Over time, however, both skilled and unskilled migrants have shifted to a pattern of occupational immobility, suggesting that both groups are increasingly able to transfer their occupational skills into the U.S. labor market. From the earliest to the latest period under study, the rate of immobility shifted from 19 percent to 80 percent for skilled migrants and from 56 percent to 88 percent among those from unskilled occupational backgrounds.

Given the relative undesirability of U.S. agricultural jobs, migrants might be expected to try to move into other occupational categories as they accumulate time in the United States. Table 12.11 concludes the analysis by cross-tabulating the first and most recent occupations held by

TABLE 12.11   Occupational Immobility Among Employed
Mexico-U.S. Repeat Migrants, by Occupation and
Years of U.S. Experience (Percentage)

U.S. Experience and First U.S. Occupation	Most Recent U.S. Occupation		
	Skilled	Unskilled	Agriculture
Less than two years' experience			
Skilled	**70**	21	9
Unskilled	12	**72**	16
Agriculture	4	16	**79**
Two to five years' experience			
Skilled	**77**	20	3
Unskilled	12	**79**	9
Agriculture	9	21	**70**
Six to nine years' experience			
Skilled	**77**	21	3
Unskilled	12	**81**	8
Agriculture	13	39	**49**
Ten or more years' experience			
Skilled	**66**	33	2
Unskilled	30	**64**	6
Agriculture	16	47	**37**
N	989	2,239	1,546

Source: Data from Mexican Migration Project, PERSFILE.
Note: Bold added for emphasis.

migrants with two or more U.S. trips. Because I expect migrants with more migration-specific human capital in the United States to be better able to achieve upward mobility, the mobility matrices are stratified by total amount of U.S. experience. Once again, the diagonal cells are highlighted in bold and indicate occupational immobility.

At low levels of U.S. experience, migrant farmworkers appear to be relatively unable to move out of the agricultural sector. Among those with less than two years of cumulative U.S. experience, 79 percent of those who started out in agriculture remained in that sector on their most recent trip; even among those who have accumulated two to five years of migratory experience, the rate of immobility between first and most recent U.S. occupation is still 70 percent for those in agriculture. Only for those farmworkers with six or more years of U.S. experience do immobility rates begin to fall, reaching 49 percent among those with six to nine years of experience and 37 percent among those with ten or more years of experience. By definition, the new mobility is upward. Among those who began in agriculture and accumulated six to nine years of experience, 39 percent ended up in an unskilled manual occupation on their most recent trip, and 13 percent found work in a skilled occupation. Similarly, among those with the most experience in the United States, 47 percent moved into an unskilled and 16 percent into a skilled occupation.

Those migrants who began migrating in skilled and unskilled occupational categories generally remained in the same sort of occupation on their most recent trip. Among those whose first U.S. job was skilled, 70 percent of those with less than two years of experience remained in a skilled occupational category on their last job, as did 77 percent of those with two to five or six to nine years of experience. Paradoxically, beyond ten years of U.S. experience the degree of immobility for skilled workers drops (to 66 percent), and a larger share of those who began with a skilled occupation on their first trip (33 percent) moved into unskilled occupations on their most recent trip. Although workers who began migrating in unskilled occupations and had accumulated ten years of U.S. experience displayed a similar drop in the rate of immobility, compared with their skilled counterparts they were relatively more likely to experience upward than downward mobility in their latest U.S. job. In the absence of a multivariate analysis, which lies beyond the scope of this chapter, it is not possible to explain why people who began migrating in skilled occupational categories tended to experience downward mobility once they had accumulated high amounts of migratory experience in the United States.

CONCLUSION

Findings from this preliminary analysis of migrant agricultural workers in comparison with migrant workers in other occupational categories indicate the overall utility of the MMP database in describing the characteristics and mobility patterns of Mexican farmworkers. A comparison of recent data from the National Agricultural Workers Survey—currently the most representative source of information on farm labor—with data from the Mexican Migration Project suggests that the MMP captures roughly a third of the U.S. farmworker population that is Mexican born and regularly shuttling back and forth across the border. Because a growing proportion of farmworkers consists of such people, the MMP appears to be especially useful for conducting research into the process by which workers enter the agricultural labor market.

In addition, MMP data capture transnational migrants working in other U.S. occupations, thus facilitating comparative research across different kinds of workers. The MMP data also permit longitudinal analyses of labor market trajectories that control for the timing of critical determinants of migration, labor force participation, return migration, and settlement in the United States. Some of these determinants, including social capital characteristics and characteristics of migrants' Mexico-based households, are simply not captured by other surveys. Finally, because MMP data originate in surveys of Mexican communities, they are more likely than U.S.-based surveys to capture undocumented migrants living in nontraditional housing and engaged in unauthorized employment.

My descriptive analysis generally confirms prior quantitative and qualitative accounts of migrant farmworkers, documenting their disadvantaged economic position relative to other workers in the U.S. economy (Griffith and Kissam 1995; McWilliams 1935/2000; Rothenberg 1998). This chapter also provides a profile of the demographic characteristics, migration experiences, employment outcomes, service use, and fiscal impacts of agricultural and other migrants as a precursor to more sophisticated modeling to study entries to and exits from farm labor. This preliminary groundwork yields several notable findings.

First, given that U.S. experience is a form of human capital that determines future earnings and occupational mobility, agricultural migrants appear relatively disadvantaged. Compared to skilled and unskilled workers, farmworkers make more trips of shorter duration to the United States and accumulate less total migratory experience. They also work fewer months and longer hours, earn relatively lower wages, and experience the harshest working conditions of the three occupation categories examined. In the most recent period, examined agricultural migrants acquired roughly the same total U.S. experience as unskilled migrants by taking a larger number of shorter trips. This fact implies a relative disadvantage in the U.S. labor market, with more frequent transaction costs and sequential interruptions of work experience in the United States.

Second, the fiscal impacts of Mexican migrant farmworkers—as well as other categories of migrants—run counter to popular stereotypes about migrants' inordinate use of publicly funded social services. The vast majority of agricultural workers in this sample are paid by check, not in cash, and as a result most pay federal, state, and local taxes, along with social security and other withholdings. Agricultural migrants are far less likely than other migrants to file income tax returns, and thus they are less likely to be refunded all or part of the money they would otherwise be due owing to their low annual incomes.

Third, compared with other migrant workers, those in U.S. agriculture generally participate in fewer major social programs, a finding documented by other studies as well (U.S. Department of Labor 2000b). These findings apply particularly to that share of the farmworker population that is based primarily in Mexico, which, as noted earlier, generally represents migrants at the earliest stages of U.S. labor market incorporation. As they accumulate greater U.S. experience, migrants become more likely to use social services, although recent changes in federal legislation appear to have had a significant chilling effect on the use of most services by many Mexican migrants.

Fourth, the marginalization of agricultural workers in the U.S. economy suggests constraints on their long-term job mobility. Mobility tables indeed reveal limited prospects for movement out of agriculture among farmworkers with multiple trips but fewer than six years of total U.S. experience. Among such workers, rates of immobility between first and most recent U.S. occupations are high. Only among those farmworkers with six or more years of U.S. experience do the occupational prospects for mobility improve. Nonetheless, it remains the case that agricultural work in Mexico is a strong determinant of agricultural work on the first U.S. trip, which strongly predicts agricultural work on the latest U.S. trip.

Extensions of the work presented here would include event modeling of the likelihood of entering and leaving U.S. agricultural occupations using the methods of log-linear and event-history analysis. Such research should address how self-selection and financial, human, and social capital interact with characteristics in migrant-sending communities to determine patterns of entry into the U.S. agricultural labor market and later occupational trajectories. Modeling the supply of agricultural labor is important for policy reasons because growers have become increasingly dependent on Mexican-born and Mexican-based labor.

The U.S. Department of Labor (2000a, 5) estimates that over three-quarters of all agricultural workers are foreign born and that more than 40 percent reside abroad. If current trends continue, the demographic composition of agricultural labor is likely to be increasingly Mexican born in the coming decades. Under these circumstances, data from the Mexican Migration Project will become increasingly important as a tool for researchers to study, model, and predict the supply of U.S. agricultural labor in the coming years.

REFERENCES

Alarcón, Rafael. 1992. "Norteñización: Self-Perpetuating Migration from a Mexican Town." In *U.S.-Mexico Relations: Labor Market Interdependence*, edited by Jorge A. Bustamante, Clark Reynolds, and Raul A. Hinojosa. Stanford, Calif.: Stanford University Press.

Borjas, George. 1998. *Heaven's Door: Immigration Policy and the American Economy.* Princeton, N.J.: Princeton University Press.

California Institute for Rural Studies (CIRS). 2000. *Suffering in Silence: A Report on the Health of California's Agricultural Workers.* Woodland Hills, Calif.: California Endowment.

Coleman, James. 1988. "Social Capital in the Creation of Human Capital." *American Journal of Sociology* 94(supplement): 95–120.

Cornelius, Wayne. 1992. "From Sojourners to Settlers: The Changing Profile of Mexican Immigration to the United States." In *U.S.-Mexico Relations: Labor Market Interdependence*, edited by Jorge Bustamante, Clark Reynolds, and Raul Hinojosa. Stanford, Calif.: Stanford University Press.

Espinosa, Kristin E., and Douglas S. Massey. 1998. "Undocumented Migration and the Quantity and Quality of Social Capital." *Soziale Welt* 12(2): 141–62.

Gabbard, Susan, Richard Mines, and Beatriz Boccalandro. 1994. *Migrant Farmworkers: Pursuing Security in an Unstable Labor Market.* Washington: U.S. Department of Labor, Office of the Assistant Secretary for Policy.

Griffith, David, and Edward Kissam. 1995. *Working Poor: Farmworkers in the United States.* Philadelphia, Pa.: Temple University Press.

Martin, Philip L., J. Edward Taylor, and P. Hardiman. 1988. "California Farmworkers and the SAW Legalization Program." *California Agriculture* 42: 4–6.

Massey, Douglas S. 1990. "Social Structure, Household Strategies, and the Cumulative Causation of Migration." *Population Index* 56(1): 3–26.

Massey, Douglas S., Rafael Alarcón, Jorge Durand, and Humberto González. 1987. *Return to Aztlan: The Social Process of International Migration from Western Mexico.* Berkeley: University of California Press.

Massey, Douglas S., Jorge Durand, and Nolan J. Malone. 2002. *Beyond Smoke and Mirrors: Mexican Immigration in an Era of Economic Integration.* New York: Russell Sage Foundation.

Massey, Douglas S., and Kristin E. Espinosa. 1997. "What's Driving Mexico-U.S. Migration? A Theoretical, Empirical, and Policy Analysis." *American Journal of Sociology* 102(4): 939–99.

Massey, Douglas S., and Emilio A. Parrado. 1994. "Migradollars: The Remittances and Savings of Mexican Migrants to the United States." *Population Research and Policy Review* 13(1): 3–30.

Massey, Douglas S., and René Zenteno. 2000. "A Validation of the Ethnosurvey: The Case of Mexico-U.S. Migration." *International Migration Review* 34(3): 765–92.

McWilliams, Carey. 1935/2000. *Factories in the Fields.* Berkeley: University of California Press.

Mines, Richard. 1981. *Developing a Community Tradition of Migration: A Field Study in Rural Zacatecas, Mexico, and California Settlement Areas.* Monographs in U.S.-Mexican Studies 3. La Jolla: University of California at San Diego, Center for U.S.-Mexican Studies.

National Safety Council. 2001. *Injury Facts.* Itasca, Ill.: National Safety Council.

Oliveira, Victor J., and Jane E. Cox. 1989. "The Agricultural Workforce of 1987: A Statistical Profile." Agricultural Economics Report 609. Washington: U.S. Department of Agriculture, Economic Research Service.

Oliveira, Victor J., and Leslie A. Whitener. 1995. "Agricultural Labor: A Review of the Data." In *Immigration Reform and U.S. Agriculture*, edited by Philip L. Martin, Wallace Huffman, Robert Emerson, J. Edward Taylor, and Refugio I. Rochin. Davis: University of California, Division of Agriculture and Natural Resources.

Palloni, Alberto, Douglas S. Massey, Miguel Ceballos, Kristin Espinosa, and Mike Spittel. 2001. "Social Capital and International Migration: A Test Using Information on Family Networks." *American Journal of Sociology* 106(5): 1262–98.

Rothenberg, Daniel. 1998. *With These Hands: The Hidden World of Migrant Farm Workers.* Berkeley: University of California Press.

Runyan, Jack L. 2000a. "Almost Half of Hired Farmworkers 25 Years and Older Earn Poverty-Level Wages." *Rural Conditions and Trends* 11(2): 47–50. Washington: U.S. Department of Agriculture, Economic Research Service.

———. 2000b. "Profile of Hired Farmworkers, 1998 Annual Averages." Agricultural Economic Report 790. Washington: U.S. Department of Agriculture, Economic Research Service.

Taylor, J. Edward, and Dawn Thilmany. 1993. "Worker Turnover, Farm Labor Contractors, and IRCA's Impact on the California Farm Labor Market." *American Journal of Agricultural Economics* 75(2): 350–60.

U.S. Department of Labor. 1989. *The Impact of Immigration on the U.S. Labor Market.* Washington: U.S. Department of Labor, Office of the Assistant Secretary for Policy.

———. 1992. *BLS Handbook of Methods.* Bulletin 2414. Washington: U.S. Department of Labor, Bureau of Labor Statistics.

———. 2000a. "Findings from the National Agricultural Workers Survey (NAWS), 1997–1998: A Demographic and Employment Profile of United States Farmworkers." Washington: U.S. Department of Labor, Office of the Assistant Secretary for Policy.

———. 2000b. *Report to Congress: The Agricultural Labor Market—Status and Recommendations.* Washington: U.S. Department of Labor, Office of the Assistant Secretary for Policy.

Villarejo, Don, and Sherry Baron. 1999. "The Occupational Health Status of Hired Farm Workers." *Occupational Medicine* 14(3): 613–35.

Yuñez-Naude, Antonio. 2001. "How Changes in Mexican Agriculture Affect Mexico-U.S. Migration." Paper presented at the Immigration and the Changing Face of Rural California Workshop, Focus on the Imperial Valley and the U.S.-Mexican Border. Holtville, California (January 16–18, 2001).

Zimmermann, Wendy, and Michael Fix. 1998. *Declining Immigrant Applications for Medi-Cal and Welfare Benefits in Los Angeles County.* Washington, D.C.: Urban Institute.

CHAPTER 13

RETURN VERSUS SETTLEMENT AMONG UNDOCUMENTED MEXICAN MIGRANTS, 1980 TO 1996

Fernando Riosmena

DOUGLAS MASSEY, Jorge Durand, and Nolan Malone (2002) have depicted the social and economic process of Mexican-U.S. migration as a machine that was working properly until U.S. governmental actions upset its internal mechanisms. The massive legalization of undocumented migrants and the criminalization of unauthorized hiring by the 1986 Immigration Reform and Control Act (IRCA), together with intensification of border enforcement in 1993 and the enactment of new penalties for immigration violations in 1996, were intended to reduce the stock of undocumented migrants in the United States while limiting their inflow. Rather than achieving these aims, however, U.S. policies appear to have upset the smooth workings of the North American migratory system.

Aside from the apparent contradiction of trying to stop flows of labor within a free trade zone in which the movement of goods and capital are encouraged, Massey, Durand, and Malone (2002) argue, U.S. immigration policies have failed in their own right. Not only have they failed to curb unauthorized migration, they have actually encouraged more rapid growth of the undocumented population, for two reasons. First, IRCA's amnesty and other policy initiatives fortified migrant networks by augmenting the number of U.S. citizens and legal residents among Mexicans living in the United States, thereby increasing the amount of migration-specific social capital accessible to friends and relatives still living in Mexico (Massey and Phillips 1999). Second, by raising the psychic and economic costs of border crossing, U.S. policies paradoxically lowered the likelihood of return migration to Mexico. Because of the increased costs of undocumented border crossing, migrants have to work longer to pay off the debts incurred while moving, crossing the border, and looking for work; and because of the higher risks, migrants are less willing to undertake multiple border crossings for fear of injury or death (Massey, Durand, and Malone 2002).

In this way, U.S. immigration policies contributed to the escalation of the flow-stock dynamics of Mexican immigration. Borrowing Massey, Durand, and Malone's (2002) machine metaphor, U.S. policies greased the gears of migrant settlement. This chapter departs from earlier studies by using life-table methods to measure and track changes in the propensity of undocumented Mexicans to settle or return from 1980 to 1996. Specifically, I employ multiple-decrement period life tables to study annual variations in the likelihood that an undocumented migrant remained in the United States, returned to Mexico, or became a legal U.S. resident. When used to study fertility or mortality, life tables normally employ age to bracket events such as birth and death, which are highly contingent on years of life. Here I construct life tables using cumulative U.S. experience to bracket migratory events, thus creating synthetic cohorts defined by amount of migratory experience. Although migration also varies by age, prior work has identified cumulative time spent in the country of destination as the most important factor determining the likelihood of return migration (Massey and Espinosa 1997; Massey et al. 1987).

This methodological approach differs from that employed by Massey, Durand, and Malone (2002) in three ways. First, their analysis computed raw probabilities, while I adopt a life-table approach. Second, whereas they focus on the biennial likelihood of return migration, I consider annual probabilities of return. Finally, I define legalization to be a competing risk—not because I view legalization as a proxy for settlement but because return decisions are likely to be very different for documented and undocumented migrants.

If the conclusions of Massey, Durand, and Malone (2002) hold under this more refined analysis, I expect to observe a decrease in the probability of return migration after IRCA's implementation in 1986, followed by an acceleration of the decline after the implementation of Operation Blockade in 1993 and Operation Gatekeeper in 1994. I also anticipate a significant increase in the probability of legalization from 1987 to 1990, the period corresponding to the IRCA legalization programs (U.S. Immigration and Naturalization Service 1997).

I do not expect to find that controlling for legalization will eliminate the secular decline in return probabilities, however. For one thing, legalization occurs in annual fixed amounts regardless of the number of applications made in a given year, and we know that undocumented flows remained fairly stable after IRCA (Bean, Edmonston, and Passel 1990; Massey, Durand, and Malone 2002). In addition, regularization is not the only policy-related issue at stake: as already mentioned, the costs of undocumented crossing accelerated markedly in the 1990s, which I expect to countervail any effect of legalization.

MODELING RETURN MIGRATION

One other set of analyses apply life-table methods to studying undocumented migration. Massey (1985) bases his analysis on event-history data gathered in four Mexican communities in 1982 and 1983, and Massey and colleagues (1987) draw on that analysis to define three basic migration strategies: temporary, recurrent, and settled. These studies show that as one moved from the former to the latter category, migratory experience and the number of social ties in the United States increased. Based on this insight, they propose a five-part typology of migrants: new, temporary, recurrent, retired, and settled, with the latter defined as those who spent at least three continuous years in the United States. They find that settled migrants were more likely to possess legal documents, to work outside of agriculture, and to have more formal and informal social ties in the United States.

In this analysis I employ retrospective life histories of household heads gathered by the Mexican Migration Project in seventy-one sending communities and their U.S. branches (see chapter 16). From these event histories I selected person-years spent by undocumented males in the United States as the unit of analysis. I focus on males because they are typically the initiators of migration in Mexico, whereas women who migrate generally follow other family members (Cerrutti and Massey 2001; Donato 1993). Since the Mexican communities and their U.S. branches vary widely by size, I employ weighted data, where weights are defined to equal the inverse of the sampling fraction (for detailed description of the weights, see Massey and Parrado 1997).

Using these data, I construct multiple-decrement life tables to compute duration-specific probabilities of leaving the undocumented population. The likelihood of exiting the undocumented state in a given year is determined by counting the number of unauthorized migrants who either legalized or returned to Mexico in that year and dividing that by the number of who were present in the United States for at least one month during that year. The resulting probabilities are then tabulated by years of cumulative migratory experience.

After deriving this two-decrement table, I estimate the two associated single-decrement life tables for return migration and legalization. Such a life table is a hypothetical exercise in which competing causes of decrement are eliminated to observe how a probability process would function in their absence (Preston, Heuveline, and Guillot 2001). In this case, the associated single-decrement probability of return migration captures the likelihood of exiting the undocumented population if leaving for Mexico were the only decrement. All probabilities were computed using the method of Chin Long Chiang (1968), which assumes a proportional distribution of decrements across intervals. The general formula for the survival function is as follows:

$$*_n\rho_z^i[0,T] = {}_n\rho_x[0,T]^{(nDz^i/nDz)},$$ (1)

where $*_n\rho_z^i$ is the associated single-decrement probability of remaining in the undocumented population if only cause i (that is, return or legalization were prevalent) during the period from 0 to T; $_n\rho_x$ is the probability that a migrant remains in the United States in undocumented status during the period; and $_nD_z^i/_nD_z$ is the proportion of exits from the undocumented population owing to cause i.

Because of practical considerations, several simplifying assumptions must be made. First, I assume that patterns of return migration and legalization for migrants who died before the interview were the same as those who survived and responded to the survey. In other words, I assume that return and legalization are the only sources of decrement from a population that in reality experienced decrements from mortality as well. Second, return migration or legalization at time T is assumed to occur if a person is observed to have returned or legalized by time T + 1. In other words, the change observed at T + 1 is assumed to have occurred at the beginning of the period. Third, I assume that a person migrating in undocumented status during year T has made no more than one U.S. trip during that year. Finally, although the communities are not homogeneous with respect to hazards of return, I perform an aggregate analysis of data across all survey sites to yield the broadest possible perspective on the issue of return migration.

The seventy-one communities include many in western Mexico, the traditional heartland for U.S. migration (see Durand 1986), as well as newer sending communities in the northern and southern regions of the country. Although households within this sample of communities were randomly selected, the communities themselves were not, raising the possibility that the changes in probabilities of return and legalization modeled here are an artifact of community selection, especially in later years, for which the data have not been systematically validated (see Massey and Zenteno 2000; Zenteno and Massey 1999). In addition, right-hand censorship might also bias the estimates because respondents' migrant experiences are truncated at the survey date. I plan to address the issue of censorship in future research using hazard-rate models (Allison 1995).

TRENDS IN LEGALIZATION AND RETURN MIGRATION

For simplicity, in the rest of this chapter when I use the term "probabilities" with reference to the likelihood of either legalization or return, I mean associated single-decrement probabilities. This statement does not apply to the overall probability of survival in the undocumented population, however, as this hazard is determined by dividing the number of undocumented migrants who did not return or legalize in a given period by the number of all those present during the period. It will also be implicit in my discussion that the term "migrant" refers to those without documents.

Table 13.1 presents the associated single-decrement life-table probabilities for legalization and return migration during the period 1980 to 1996. Figure 13.1 graphs these data along with the associated survival curve for remaining in the United States without documents. Although the data in table 13.1 reveal a few significant (p < .05) year-to-year shifts in the probability of return migration (from 1980 to 1981, from 1988 to 1989, from 1991 to 1992, and from 1993 to 1994), the data in figure 13.1 suggest a fairly clear picture of the long-term trends. Throughout most of the 1980s, the probability of return migration remained stable at around 0.30 per year, falling slightly below this level during the early 1980s and rising slightly above it by mid-decade. After 1988, however, there was a sustained decline in the probability of return migration, one that seemed to accelerate in 1993 before bottoming out at less than 0.10 in 1996, a shift that is highly significant statistically (p < .001).

Probabilities of legalization were generally quite low in most years—under 5 percent. The notable exception is the period 1986 to 1989, corresponding to the implementation of IRCA's legalization programs. According to the data in table 13.1, the likelihood of legalizing before 1986 hovered around zero, but with IRCA's passage in that year the probability climbed to 0.35 and then peaked at 0.41 in 1987 before dropping to 0.25 in 1988, 0.10 in 1989, 0.04 in 1990. Thereafter, the likelihood of legalization fluctuated around zero. This rise and fall in the probability of legalization is highly significant (p < .001), and the shape of the curve is virtually the same as that derived from U.S. Immigration and Naturalization Service (1997) data on legal admissions, except that it is displaced to the left by around two years, reflecting the fact that Mexican Migration Project respondents reported the year they applied for amnesty or legalization whereas the immigration office tabulates data by the year they

TABLE 13.1   Associated Single-Decrement Probabilities of Return
Migration and Legalization Among Undocumented
Mexican Males Observed in the United States,
1980 to 1996

Year	Migrants in Interval	Return Migration		Legalization	
		Exits	Probability	Exits	Probability
1980	843	217	0.3391	9	0.0361
1981	780	154	0.2617	5	0.0080
1982	771	169	0.2540	3	—[a]
1983	751	155	0.2734	7	0.0170
1984	829	183	0.2747	6	0.0032
1985	894	210	0.2945	19	0.0433
1986	929	205	0.3225	118	0.3547
1987	632	129	0.3220	102	0.4120
1988	462	112	0.3568	56	0.2506
1989	414	106	0.2655	15	0.1020
1990	399	111	0.2479	7	0.0409
1991	313	79	0.2470	5	0.0181
1992	271	54	0.1491	3	—[a]
1993	267	61	0.1853	2	—[a]
1994	206	26	0.1096	3	—[a]
1995	178	30	0.1030	2	—[a]
1996	154	17	0.0913	2	—[a]

Source: Data from Mexican Migration Project.
[a] Insufficient cases for reliable estimation.

adjusted status to become permanent residents. The low probabilities of legalization before 1986 and after 1990 are explained by the mandated limits on documentation and the increasing number of restrictions placed on immigrants from Mexico (see Massey, Durand, and Malone 2002). After 1991, the number of legalizations was so small that reliable estimation becomes a problem (see Runyon et al. 1996).

Figure 13.1 also plots year-to-year probabilities of remaining in the United States as an undocumented migrant. In general, the graph line has an inverted U-shape, mirroring the trajectory of probabilities of legalization and return, since it is a (nonadditive) function of both numbers (see equation 1). Consequently, the yearly probability of remaining in the United States without documentation was high (at 0.70 or greater) over the entire period except for the brief period corresponding to IRCA imple-

FIGURE 13.1   Probabilities of Return Migration, Legalization, and Remaining in the United States Without Documentation, 1980 to 1996

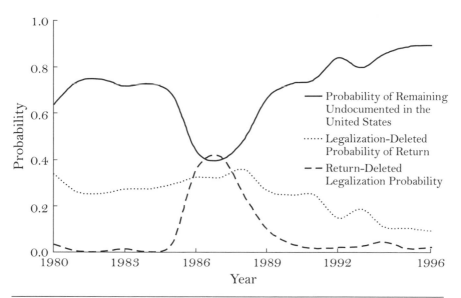

Source: All data come from the Mexican Migration Project database.
Note: Time series are smoothed using three- to four-year moving averages.

mentation (which was associated with a slight increase in the likelihood of return). After 1987, as probabilities of both legalization and return migration fell, the likelihood of remaining in the United States in undocumented status rose sharply, reaching almost 0.90 in 1996.

Table 13.2 shows associated single-decrement probabilities of return migration computed separately for agricultural and nonagricultural workers, and figure 13.2 plots these data along with the proportion of migrants working in agriculture. The latter has generally declined over time: whereas in 1981 around 30 percent of migrants were farmworkers, over the next fifteen years the share steadily fell, reaching less than 5 percent by 1996. As one might expect, throughout the entire period the likelihood of return migration was greater for agricultural than for nonagricultural workers. Whereas the former generally experienced return probabilities in the range of 0.40 to 0.60, the latter never experienced a return probability in beyond 0.30.

Among agricultural workers the likelihood of return migration remained fairly flat through 1986, then increased to 0.65 by 1990 before dropping

TABLE 13.2   Associated Single-Decrement Probabilities of Return
Migration Among Undocumented Mexican Males
Observed in the United States, by Occupation,
1980 to 1996

	Nonagricultural Workers			Agricultural Workers		
Year	Migrants	Exits	Probability	Migrants	Exits	Probability
1980	508	168	0.2351	335	194	0.5265
1981	469	121	0.2037	311	173	0.3948
1982	491	155	0.2020	280	153	0.3836
1983	480	140	0.2185	271	156	0.4162
1984	529	161	0.2093	300	182	0.4302
1985	568	181	0.2537	326	197	0.4008
1986	602	184	0.2899	327	160	0.4295
1987	442	137	0.2850	190	82	0.4549
1988	343	116	0.3048	119	58	0.5739
1989	322	115	0.2292	92	53	0.4624
1990	319	112	0.2005	80	58	0.6475
1991	258	81	0.1831	55	39	0.6547
1992	224	62	0.1252	47	28	0.3155
1993	214	66	0.1487	53	37	0.4130
1994	183	47	0.0957	23	11	0.3909
1995	158	39	0.0915	20	8	0.3655
1996	137	27	0.0737	17	11	—[a]

Source: Data from Mexican Migration Project.
[a] Insufficient cases for reliable estimation.

sharply and significantly (p < .001) through 1993, whereupon it rose once
again to wipe out most of the aforementioned decline (an increase that was
also highly significant, p < .001). Although farmworkers generally experienced a rising propensity to return, fewer and fewer migrants worked in
agriculture; thus the overall trends for undocumented migrants were dominated by the behavior of nonagricultural workers. Among migrants working in nonfarm occupations, the prevailing trend was one of decline. From
1981 through 1988, the likelihood of return migration rose from around
0.20 to around 0.30, but thereafter the probabilities steadily fell, dropping
from a peak of 0.30 in 1988 to just 0.07 in 1996, a highly significant (p <
.001) decline of 23 percent in just six years.

Table 13.3 presents associated single-decrement life-table probabilities
of return migration broken down by trip number, and figure 13.3 plots the
smoothed series for migrants on their first, second, and third or later trips.

FIGURE 13.2   Probability of Return Migration by Occupation and Percentage of Migrants in Agricultural Occupations, 1980 to 1996

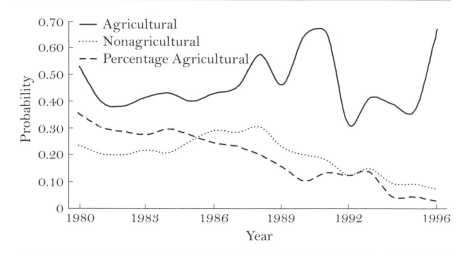

Source: All data come from the Mexican Migration Project database.
Note: Time-series are smoothed using three- to four-year moving averages.

In general, the likelihood of returning to Mexico from an undocumented trip is much greater for those who have made three or more trips than for those on their first or second trip, who display similar levels and patterns of return. Whereas the probability of return ranged from 0.06 to 0.33 for migrants with one or two trips, among those with three or more trips behind them it ranged from 0.46 to 0.80.

In terms of trends, migrants on their first or second trip generally experienced a slight increase in the likelihood of return through around 1988, followed by a steady decline thereafter. In contrast, recurrent migrants with three or more trips experienced a high and stable probability of return from 1980 through 1986, followed by sharp up and down fluctuations during the years IRCA was enacted. Following the buildup in border enforcement in 1993, therefore, all migrants, regardless of the number of trips they had made, displayed a decline in the propensity to return to Mexico.

EXPLAINING THE TRENDS

Consistent with the arguments of Massey, Durand, and Malone (2002), the foregoing analyses consistently show a decline in the odds of return migration probably partly in response to the militarization of the Mexico-U.S.

TABLE 13.3   Associated Single-Decrement Probabilities of Return Migration Among Undocumented Mexican Males Observed in the United States, by Trip Number, 1980 to 1996

Year	Number of Migrants			Number of Departures			Probabilities		
	First Trip	Second Trip	Third or Later Trip	First Trip	Second Trip	Third or Later Trip	First Trip	Second Trip	Third or Later Trip
1980	594	123	126	217	51	94	0.324	0.218	0.693
1981	535	110	135	154	43	97	0.214	0.200	0.691
1982	532	96	143	169	31	108	0.217	0.144	0.692
1983	501	98	152	155	29	112	0.231	0.169	0.701
1984	558	112	159	183	42	118	0.222	0.204	0.707
1985	599	121	174	210	38	130	0.249	0.201	0.707
1986	598	157	174	205	61	78	0.298	0.264	0.606
1987	405	92	135	129	26	64	0.313	0.189	0.581
1988	335	54	73	112	17	45	0.329	0.316	0.696
1989	301	57	56	106	25	37	0.253	0.224	0.455
1990	289	63	47	111	23	36	0.233	0.217	0.485
1991	231	50	32	79	16	25	0.247	0.125	0.804
1992	194	40	37	54	9	27	0.131	0.091	0.709
1993	183	44	40	61	13	29	0.161	0.113	0.739
1994	134	46	26	26	13	19	0.078	0.105	0.672
1995	125	37	16	30	8	9	0.083	0.111	—a
1996	95	36	23	17	9	12	0.058	0.074	0.496

Source: Data from Mexican Migration Project.
a Insufficient cases for reliable estimation.

FIGURE 13.3   Probability of Return Migration, by Trip Number, 1980 to 1996

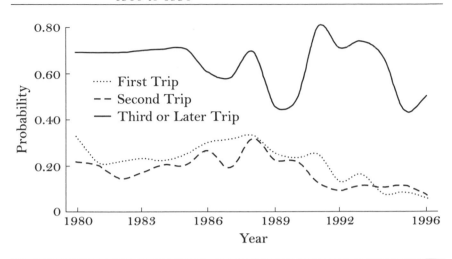

First Trip
Second Trip
Third or Later Trip

Source: All data come from the Mexican Migration Project database.
Note: Time-series are smoothed using three- to four-year moving averages.

border. However, it has also been shown that the likelihood of return is contingent on occupation in the United States, cumulative U.S. experience, and the total number of U.S. trips. As the data in table 13.4 indicate, all three variables vary over time. The average total experience of undocumented migrants rose from 5.3 years in 1981 to 7.5 years in 1985 and 1986, then dropped to around 5.8 years from 1988 to 1990 (following IRCA's amnesty, which targeted experienced migrants). Thereupon it increased to fluctuate between 6.0 and 7.0 years from 1991 through 1996. Similarly, the number of trips rose from 1.8 in 1980 to 2.0 in the mid-1980s before falling to 1.4 in 1990, where it basically remained throughout the 1990s. Finally, as has already been noted, the proportion of migrants in agriculture dropped from 0.35 in 1980 to 0.03 in 1996.

Given these trends, it is possible that some or all of the changing likelihood of return migration observed among undocumented migrants stemmed from the changing composition of the migrant population, not from any shift in the probabilities themselves. To address this issue, I divided the data into periods and then undertook a statistical decomposition analysis of differences between periods, using the approach of Evelyn Kitagawa (1955). Kitagawa's method was originally developed to compare differences in mortality rates but has been subsequently adapted to study differences in other rates, including interperiod differences in probabilities

TABLE 13.4   Annual Means and Standard Deviations for Variables Used in the Decomposition Analysis of Legalization and Return Migration Probabilities

Year	N	Cumulative Experience		Number of Trips		Percentage in Agriculture	
		Mean	Standard Deviation	Mean	Standard Deviation	Mean	Standard Deviation
1980	843	5.26	15.75	1.82	9.66	0.35	0.48
1981	780	6.02	16.15	1.93	10.40	0.30	0.46
1982	804	6.20	17.13	1.89	10.74	0.29	0.45
1983	756	6.86	18.16	1.99	11.60	0.28	0.45
1984	829	7.15	18.18	2.00	11.00	0.30	0.46
1985	894	7.49	20.20	1.97	10.96	0.27	0.45
1986	929	7.49	21.08	1.99	11.04	0.25	0.43
1987	646	7.07	18.26	1.92	8.67	0.23	0.42
1988	535	5.81	18.99	1.51	4.93	0.20	0.40
1989	446	5.79	18.43	1.55	5.22	0.16	0.36
1990	438	5.87	18.67	1.38	4.64	0.10	0.31
1991	376	6.43	18.69	1.42	5.20	0.13	0.34
1992	310	5.99	15.26	1.42	4.35	0.12	0.33
1993	280	6.47	16.15	1.43	4.63	0.14	0.34
1994	252	7.00	16.22	1.46	5.06	0.05	0.21
1995	224	6.93	16.20	1.43	5.23	0.04	0.21
1996	181	7.17	17.01	1.43	2.91	0.03	0.17
Total	9,523	6.58	18.21	1.80	9.17	0.25	0.43

Source: Data from Mexican Migration Project.

(see, for instance, Smith, Morgan, and Koropeckyj-Cox [1996], who follow a subsequent adaptation of the Kitagawa methodology developed by Das Gupta [1993]).

Table 13.5 presents three separate standardization exercises, considering the effect of compositional changes with respect to cumulative experience, U.S. occupation, and trip number. Three interperiod comparisons are considered: the late 1980s versus the early 1980s, the early 1990s versus the late 1980s, and the mid-1990s versus the early 1990s. The three left-hand columns consider interperiod differences with respect to probabilities of return migration; those on the right repeat the analysis for probabilities of legalization. All interperiod differences are statistically significant ($p < .05$).

Whereas the comparison of the late 1980s to the early 1980s yields a positive difference, both comparisons involving the 1990s are negative,

TABLE 13.5   Decomposition of Interperiod Differences in Probabilities of Return Migration and Legalization, 1980 to 1996

Compositional Factor	Difference in Probabilities of Return Migration			Difference in Probabilities of Legalization		
	1985 to 1989 Versus 1980 to 1984	1990 to 1994 Versus 1985 to 1989	1995 to 1996 Versus 1990 to 1994	1985 to 1989 Versus 1980 to 1984	1990 to 1994, Versus 1985 to 1989	1995 to 1996 Versus 1990 to 1994
Cumulative experience						
Percentage owing to change in composition	31.8	21.9	26.4	1.0	11.3	10.1
Percentage owing to change in rates	68.2	78.1	73.6	99.0	88.7	89.9
Number of trips						
Percentage owing to change in composition	10.7	20.8	0.3	1.2	2.0	3.7
Percentage owing to change in rates	89.3	79.2	99.7	98.8	98.0	96.3
Percentage in agriculture						
Percentage owing to change in composition	23.3	27.5	28.7	0.4	0.3	15.5
Percentage owing to change in rates	76.7	72.5	71.3	99.6	99.7	84.5
Interperiod difference	0.0294**	−0.1159****	−0.0973****	0.2221****	−0.2044***	−0.0126+

Source: Data from Mexican Migration Project.
+p < .1   *p < .05   **p < .01   ***p < .001

reflecting the decline in probabilities of return that accompanied the buildup of border enforcement. Compositional changes with respect to cumulative migrant experience account for only 22 to 32 percent of inter-period differences in the probability of return migration, the greatest contribution occurring for the comparison between the early and late 1980s, when the odds of return were rising. The declines observed during the 1990s mostly follow from actual shifts in probabilities of return migration (78 and 74 percent) rather than from changes in composition.

Compositional changes with respect to trip number generally account for a low share of the interperiod differences, ranging from just 0.3 percent in the comparison of the middle and early 1990s to 21 percent in the early 1990s to late 1980s comparison. Given the steady downward trend in the relative number of migrant farmworkers, compositional shifts with respect to agricultural employment have a relatively constant effect across all periods, accounting for 23 percent of the small increase during the 1980s, 28 percent of the decline to the early 1990s, and 29 percent of that observed during the mid-1990s. In short, the decline in the propensity to return appears mostly to represent a real change in behavior rather than a mere change in the distribution of variables related to the odds of return.

As the right-hand columns show, compositional factors explain relatively few of the changes in the probability of legalization. The huge increase from the early to the late 1980s was almost entirely (99 percent) a reflection of changing rates rather than changing composition, as was the huge drop from the late 1980s to the early 1990s (89 percent) and then to the mid-1990s (90 percent). The rise and fall in legalization probabilities reflects the exogenous effect of the IRCA legalization programs rather than any underlying change in the composition of the migrant population.

CONCLUSION

My analysis of the competing risks of legalization and return migration as exits from undocumented Mexican population of the United States confirms the dramatic effect of the 1986 Immigration Reform and Control Act on legalization probabilities during the late 1980s. Following the enactment of IRCA, the annual likelihood of acquiring documents abruptly rose from levels below 0.05 to peak at 0.41 before falling back again to levels near zero. The wide swing in this competing risk had little effect on the probability of return migration, however. From 1980 through 1988 the annual probability of return migration fluctuated from 0.25 to 0.36, where it peaked in 1988. Thereafter, however, it steadily fell, replicating earlier findings by Massey, Durand, and Malone (2002) using a more rigorous measurement model.

When I disaggregated the data by occupation and number of trips, I found that farmworkers and recurrent migrants (those with three or more trips) generally displayed higher probabilities of return migration and that the steady decline in return probabilities was characteristic primarily of nonagricultural workers and those with one or two trips. Agricultural migrants and those with multiple trips experienced more variable trends with respect to return migration.

This observation led me to undertake a statistical decomposition analysis to determine whether the decline in the likelihood of return migration observed during the 1990s and attributed by Massey, Durand, and Malone (2002) to underlying policy changes might actually have reflected underlying shifts in the composition of the migrant population with respect to occupation, trips, or cumulative experience. In the case of return migration, compositional changes were indeed sizable but accounted for a minority of the decline in return propensities for the early and mid-1990s. At least three-quarters of the shift was unrelated to changes in composition. With respect to legalization, virtually all of the increase during the late 1980s was attributable to an underlying change in rates of documentation rather than to shifts in population composition.

Together, these analyses reaffirm the preponderant role of immigration and border policies in shaping patterns of Mexican migration. The Immigration Reform and Control Act's amnesty drove up the probability of legalization to unprecedented heights for a brief period in the late 1980s, and the escalation of border enforcement operations after 1993 dramatically reduced the probability of return migration. The end result has been a remarkable growth in the number of Mexicans in the United States—both documented and undocumented. If U.S. policy makers intended to reduce the number of Mexican immigrants to the United States, they failed utterly.

REFERENCES

Allison, Paul D. 1995. *Survival Analysis Using the SAS System: A Practical Guide.* Cary, N.C.: SAS Institute.

Bean, Frank D., Barry Edmonston, and Jeffrey Passel. 1990. *Undocumented Migration to the United States: IRCA and the Experience of the 1980s.* Washington, D.C.: Urban Institute.

Cerrutti, Marcela, and Douglas S. Massey. 2001. "On the Auspices of Female Migration from Mexico to the United States." *Demography* 38(2): 187–200.

Chiang, Chin Long. 1968. *An Introduction to Stochastic Processes in Biostatistics.* New York: Wiley.

Das Gupta, Prithwis. 1993. *Standardization and Decomposition of Rates: A User's Manual.* Washington: U.S. Government Printing Office.

Donato, Katharine M. 1993. "Current Trends and Patterns of Female Migration: Evidence from Mexico." *International Migration Review* 27(4): 748–72.

Durand, Jorge. 1986. "Circuitos Migratorios en el Occidente de México." *Revue Européenne des Migrations Internationales* 2: 49–65.

Kitagawa, Evelyn M. 1955. "Components of a Difference Between Two Rates." *Journal of the American Statistical Association* 50(272): 1168–94.

Massey, Douglas S. 1985. "The Settlement Process among Mexican Migrants to the United States: New Methods and Findings." In *Immigration Statistics: A Story of Neglect,* edited by Daniel B. Levine, Kenneth Hill, and Robert Warren. Washington, D.C.: National Academy Press.

Massey, Douglas S., Rafael Alarcón, Jorge Durand, and Humberto González. 1987. *Return to Aztlán: The Social Process of International Migration from Western Mexico.* Berkeley: University of California Press.

Massey, Douglas S., Jorge Durand, and Nolan J. Malone. 2002. *Beyond Smoke and Mirrors: Mexican Immigration in an Era of Free Trade.* New York: Russell Sage Foundation.

Massey, Douglas S., and Kristin E. Espinosa. 1997. "What's Driving Mexico-U.S. Migration? A Theoretical, Empirical, and Policy Analysis." *American Journal of Sociology* 102(4): 939–99.

Massey, Douglas S., and Emilio Parrado. 1997. "International Migration and Business Formation in Mexico." *Social Science Quarterly* 79(1): 1–20.

Massey, Douglas S., and Julie A. Phillips. 1999. "The New Labor Market: Immigrants and Wages After IRCA." *Demography* 36(2): 233–46.

Massey, Douglas S., and René Zenteno. 2000. "A Validation of the Ethnosurvey: The Case of Mexico-U.S. Migration." *International Migration Review* 34(3): 766–93.

Preston, Samuel H., Patrick Heuveline, and Michel Guillot. 2001. *Demography: Measuring and Modeling Population Processes.* Oxford: Blackwell Publishers.

Runyon, Richard P., Audrey Haber, David J. Pittenger, and Kay A. Coleman. 1996. *Fundamentals of Behavioral Statistics.* Boston: McGraw-Hill.

Smith, Herbert L., S. Philip Morgan, and Tanya Koropeckyj-Cox. 1996. "A Decomposition of Trends in the Nonmarital Fertility Ratios of Blacks and Whites in the United States, 1960–1992." *Demography* 33(2): 141–51.

U.S. Department of Justice. Immigration and Naturalization Service. 1997. *1996 Statistical Yearbook of the Immigration and Naturalization Service.* Washington: U.S. Government Printing Office.

Zenteno, René M., and Douglas S. Massey. 1999. "Especificidad versus representatividad: Enfoques metodológicos para el estudio de la migración internacional." *Estudios Demográficos y Urbanos* 40: 75–116.

CHAPTER 14

THE EFFECT OF U.S. BORDER ENFORCEMENT ON THE CROSSING BEHAVIOR OF MEXICAN MIGRANTS

Pia M. Orrenius

HUNDREDS OF thousands of undocumented immigrants cross the Mexico-U.S. border each year. Over the past decade, to stem the inflow of migrants, the U.S. Border Patrol launched a series of site-specific crackdowns starting with Operation Hold-the-Line in El Paso, Texas, in 1993. Operation Gatekeeper followed in San Diego in 1994, and then Operation Rio Grande in South Texas in 1997 and Safeguard in Tucson in 1999.[1] A stated objective of these Border Patrol offensives was to force migrants into rural terrain where they are more readily apprehended. As part of this effort, the number of Border Patrol officers nearly doubled between 1994 and 1999, and officer "linewatch" hours—the number of person-hours spent patrolling the Mexico-U.S. border—increased almost 300 percent. At the same time, the geographic concentration of migrant apprehensions began to change, gravitating away from heavily trafficked areas such as San Diego–Tijuana and El Paso–Juárez to more remote sectors along the western portion of the border in California and the eastern section in Arizona and southern Texas (Orrenius 2001).

The changing pattern of migrant border crossings is well documented in the literature. Douglas Massey, Jorge Durand, and Nolan Malone (2002), using data from the Mexican Migration Project, illustrate the shift in border-crossing locations away from Tijuana following the launch of Operation Gatekeeper in 1994 and away from California in general following the expansion of Gatekeeper eastward in 1995 and 1996. Wayne Cornelius (2001, 667) observes that "an indisputable consequence of concentrated border enforcement operations has been the spatial redistribution of illegal entry attempts."

These changing crossing patterns have had potentially severe consequences for undocumented migrants. Cornelius (2001) shows that as a result of border crackdowns like Gatekeeper, the number of migrant deaths along the border with the U.S. Southwest has risen steeply, increasing faster than the estimated rate of illegal immigration, with the bulk of the increase in fatalities attributable to deaths by exposure and dehydration. Using Mexican government data, Cornelius graphically demonstrates the spatial shift eastward in migrant deaths coincident with the eastward expansion of Operation Gatekeeper.

Karl Eschbach and his colleagues (1999) also indicate that additional deaths are a result of the deflection of migrant flows from traditional populous crossing points to more remote and hazardous locations. Using death records collected in the U.S. border counties, the authors present evidence on border deaths similar to the findings of Cornelius. Although they do not document a significant increase in total deaths between 1993 and 1997, they find sharp increases in deaths owing to environmental causes and to drowning in the All-American Canal in Imperial County, California.[2]

The studies mentioned here point to a convincing link between enforcement and migrant crossing patterns. However, with Mexico-U.S. migration in a constant state of evolution, a complete analysis also has to take into account socioeconomic and demographic variables that drive migrant crossing choices. It is necessary to model crossing-site choice in a multivariate framework. There are many reasons crossing locations might have changed that are not related to border enforcement. For example, crossing patterns might be expected to move away from California as, in the 1990s, migrant destinations became more dispersed geographically than they had been in the past. Migrant-sending states have also become more heterogeneous than in the past, as have the characteristics of migrants. Mexican migrants now hail not only from western Mexico but also from the southern and eastern parts of the country. Migrant traits have changed, as well: flows of primarily young men engaging in seasonal labor have evolved into flows composed of both male and female migrants with year-round employment prospects in the services and manufacturing industries.

This chapter also evaluates the impact of current immigration policy. If border crackdowns such as Gatekeeper and Hold-the-Line are found to be directly related to more remote crossings and hence an increased likelihood of migrant injury and death, this finding could bolster the arguments for setting up a large-scale temporary legal migration plan like a Mexico-U.S. guest worker program. The perceived link between enforcement and deaths has already led to other positive changes such as public service announcements to warn potential migrants, the placement of water stations in the desert, and a Border Patrol safety initiative in which rescues of stranded migrants play a central role.[3]

I investigate the impact of an increase in border enforcement on an undocumented migrant's choice of crossing site. The results indicate that migrants are, in fact, discouraged from crossing into more heavily enforced states. As a result, Border Patrol enforcement strategy has reinforced general trends in crossings away from California and toward Texas and Arizona over the past twenty years. Looking at city-level data over a longer period, I also find that enforcement has had a role in redistributing crossings not only across states but also within states, with increasing trends toward crossings in less-populated areas.

GEOGRAPHIC TRENDS IN ENFORCEMENT AND CROSSING SITES

Border enforcement began to intensify in the mid-1980s, in response to rising illegal immigration and to President Ronald Reagan's declaration of a "war on drugs" as well as the 1986 Immigration Reform and Control Act (IRCA). The law marked a turning point for U.S. enforcement policy. It gave amnesty to 2.7 million undocumented immigrants, increased funding for the Border Patrol, criminalized the hiring of unauthorized workers; and strengthened penalties against migrant smugglers (Rosenblum 2000). The late 1980s were marked by an intensification of interdiction efforts and a decline in the relative importance of internal enforcement actions, such as raids on homes and businesses. Although IRCA mandated sanctions against employers who knowingly hired undocumented workers, this enforcement mechanism has always been unpopular, and over the past decade few employers have been prosecuted.

The Immigration Reform and Control Act represented a structural shift not only in enforcement policy but also in Mexico-U.S. immigration more generally. Durand, Massey, and Parrado (1999, 535) argue that IRCA and the amnesty that followed transformed what had been a "temporary and regionally concentrated flow of undocumented, predominantly male, and disproportionately rural workers into a settled, urbanized population of immigrant families dispersed throughout the nation." Although their analysis indicates that some of these changes began long before IRCA, it stands to reason that the massive legalization

FIGURE 14.1   Border Patrol Apprehensions and Rate of Illegal
                   Immigration, 1960 to 1999

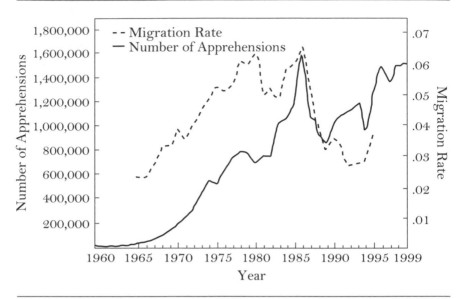

Source: Data from Mexican Migration Project; U.S. Department of Justice (n.d.).

of immigrants and tightened border controls after 1986 intensified these trends.

Figure 14.1, for example, shows the number of migrant apprehensions (from INS data) and the rate of undocumented migration (from Mexican Migration Project data) for the years 1960 to 1999. For several years following IRCA's passage in 1986, both the number of apprehensions and the rate of undocumented migration fell quite sharply. The most likely explanation for this decline is that IRCA legalized more than 2 million previously undocumented Mexican migrants, who then ceased crossing the border illegally. Eventually, however, apprehensions along the Mexico–U.S. border began to increase again as new migrants attempted the journey.

The increase in the number of crossings into Texas, especially, provided the impetus for Operation Hold-the-Line, launched in El Paso in 1993. Specifically, it was intended to make clandestine migration into El Paso costly, thereby diverting the flow of undocumented migrants away from residential neighborhoods, roads, and urban infrastructure into more sparsely populated areas (U.S. General Accounting Office 1999b). Agents took up fixed positions along the most commonly used crossing paths in the city and installed new fencing and surveillance equipment to dissuade migrants from crossing there.

Within a few months, undocumented traffic through El Paso had slowed to a trickle (Bean et al. 1994). The success of Operation Hold-the-Line quickly led to the launching of Operation Gatekeeper in San Diego in 1994, followed by Operation Rio Grande and Operation Safeguard in McAllen and Nogales, respectively (Andreas 2000). As a result, the budget for enforcement along the Mexico-U.S. border more than doubled between 1993 and 1997, and the number of Border Patrol officers rose from forty-two hundred in 1994 to seventy-seven hundred in 1999 (U.S. General Accounting Office 1999a).

All these operations followed the same site-specific application of enforcement resources. The concentration of Border Patrol in specific locations had strong effects on the geography of undocumented border crossing. Figure 14.2 shows Mexican Migration Project data on the location of border crossings by state from 1965 through 1994. Between 1965 and 1990, one-half to three-fourths of all border crossings occurred in California. Following the implementation of IRCA, however, there was a decline in the fraction of crossings into California and a corresponding

FIGURE 14.2   Preferred Border Crossings Sites, by State, 1965 to 1994 (Percentage)

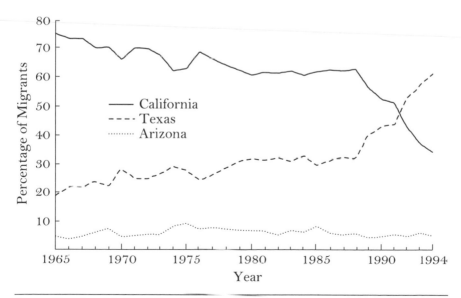

Source: Data from Mexican Migration Project.

increase in the proportion crossing into Texas. The trend in crossings away from California intensified following the implementation of Operation Gatekeeper in 1994, and more recent INS data on apprehensions indicate a growing share of crossings into Arizona during the late 1990s. Thus empirical data are consistent with the interpretation that the enactment of IRCA and Operation Gatekeeper made border enforcement in California more effective relative to elsewhere along the border, causing migrants to shift their preferred crossing locations eastward into Arizona and Texas.

Changes in crossing patterns not only shifted between states: changes within states are equally striking. Figure 14.3 tabulates INS data on apprehensions in Texas sectors from 1960 through 1999. The increase in Texas crossings after 1990 was almost entirely concentrated in the El Paso sector, prompting the launching of Operation Hold-the-Line. The result was a 75 percent decrease in apprehensions in El Paso during the following year. The subsequent rise in apprehensions in the other Texas sectors suggests that migrants simply responded by crossing farther to the south and east. The change in preferred border crossing sites is particularly noticeable following the devaluation of the Mexican peso in December 1994 as apprehensions in the McAllen-Laredo sector rose to unprecedented levels over the following two years.

FIGURE 14.3   Border Patrol Apprehensions, by Texas Sector, 1960 to 1999

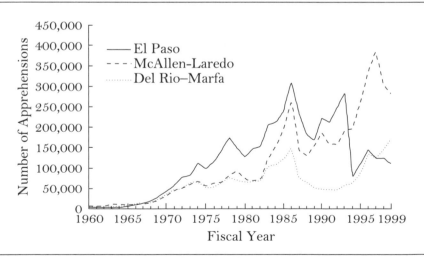

Source: Data from U.S. Department of Justice (n.d.).

DETERMINANTS OF CROSSING SITE CHOICE

The intensity of enforcement is not the only variable affecting a migrant's decision about where to cross the Mexico-U.S. border. The choice of a crossing site depends principally on a migrant's ultimate destination and then, conditional on destination, on factors that minimize the costs of the trip. Migrants' choice of destination is determined by their migration experience and the geographic structure of their network connections as well as by economic conditions at alternative destinations(Massey and Espinosa 1997; Massey et al. 1987).

Transportation and nonpecuniary costs generally increase as distance to destination rises, and fall as the accessibility of the crossing site to origin and destination communities grows. Fees to coyotes (border-crossing guides or smugglers) are likely to be a function of both enforcement intensity (the probability of apprehension) and the risk of injury or hardship during crossing. Finally, a migrant's willingness to bear risk is an important consideration in border-crossing decisions. Risk taking is most likely related to factors such as a migrant's age, education, and family size as well to the amount of prior migratory experience and the number of prior apprehensions. In general, younger, less educated migrants are more willing to bear risks, whereas educated, older individuals are less willing—either because they have access to better information or because they have "more to lose." Being married and having children also lowers the tolerance for risk, as an unfortunate accident or death could leave families destitute.

Obviously, the determinants of crossing-site choice include many of the same variables that explain the decision to migrate. As migration patterns and migrant characteristics change, so too do the determinants of crossing-site choice. Some of the changes may amplify what are perceived to be the effects of selective border enforcement, and herein lies the importance of studying this question in a multivariate framework. Other things being equal, a growing dispersion of migrants to destinations throughout the United States would increase the likelihood of crossings through states other than California, whatever U.S. policies might be at the time. Similarly, the declining share of Mexican migrants working in agriculture would have a similar effect. In contrast, the feminization of migration would mitigate against more remote crossings, as families are wary of subjecting wives and daughters to risks of injury or death (Eschbach et al. 1999; Massey, Durand, and Malone 2002). Sorting out all these potential effects requires a multivariate econometric model.

DATA

To test the effect of border enforcement on the crossing behavior of undocumented Mexican migrants, I rely on several data sources. The border crossing and demographic data at the individual level come from fifty-two communities in western Mexico sampled by the Mexican Migration Project from 1987 to 1997 (excluding the four original communities sampled in 1982 and 1983). The survey asks randomly sampled heads of households to provide family, job, and migration histories. The latter include information on the timing, place, and mode of border crossing (where mode is either alone, with family, or with a coyote), as well as the migrant's legal status and, if applicable, the amount of money paid to coyotes and the number of times apprehended by the Border Patrol.

Using these migration histories, I constructed a panel of all Mexico-U.S. border crossings undertaken by undocumented male household heads aged fifteen to sixty-five from 1985 to 1996. Over this period, 5,752 crossings were made, the majority of which were through California (70 percent), followed by Texas (25 percent) and Arizona (5 percent). There were no reported crossings into New Mexico. I link yearly data on crossings to longitudinal data from the INS on "linewatch" hours, tabulated separately for each of the Border Patrol's nine sectors: San Diego, El Centro, Yuma, Tucson, El Paso, Marfa, Del Rio, Laredo, and McAllen (going from west to east).

Average sector linewatch hours by state are reported in the top line of table 14.1; not surprisingly, the number of Border Patrol person-hours in California (San Diego and El Centro) exceeds that in Arizona (Yuma and Tucson) and Texas (El Paso, Marfa, Del Rio, Laredo, and McAllen) by 120 and 82 percent, respectively. The table also reports means and standard deviations for economic variables in U.S. border states and Mexico. Data on earnings and employment by state, shown in the second panel of the table, were obtained from the Bureau of Economic Analysis. California is by far the largest state, with an average workforce of 15.6 million workers over the time period covered. Average annual earnings were also highest in California at $35,373, and the state's unemployment rate (estimated from the Current Population Survey data), at 6.6 percent, was the lowest of the three states. Interestingly, Arizona had the highest level of farm earnings, despite limited farm employment compared with Texas and California, which both averaged about 260,000 farmworkers over the period.

I measure economic conditions in Mexico using an index of Mexican manufacturing wages obtained from the Banco de México. Individual

TABLE 14.1   Means of Variables Used in Analysis of Border-Crossing Sites, by State, 1985 to 1996

| | | | State of Border Crossing | | | | | |
| | California | | Arizona | | Texas | | |
Variable	Mean	Standard Deviation	Mean	Standard Deviation	Mean	Standard Deviation
U.S. enforcement effort: sector linewatch hours (thousands)	419.68	78.74	190.50	28.35	230.42	40.59
U.S. economic conditions						
Unemployment rate (%)	6.60	1.12	6.70	0.61	7.50	0.97
Average earnings (thousands of 1996 dollars)	35.37	0.50	28.55	0.42	30.46	0.52
Total employment (millions)	15.60	0.98	1.81	0.16	9.02	0.51
Average farm earnings (thousands of 1996 dollars)	32.60	3.42	41.48	6.00	9.93	2.27
Farm employment (thousands)	258.3	12.1	20.2	0.873	260.7	7.67
Mexican economic conditions: real wages in manufacturing (index)	18.89	1.30	18.89	1.30	18.89	1.30
Individual and social characteristics						
Age (years)	33.40	9.84	33.06	10.38	33.50	10.53
Education (years)	4.95	3.41	4.83	3.22	4.91	3.19
Number of migrant siblings	1.78	1.74	2.10	1.76	1.43	1.65
Number of prior U.S. trips	6.82	6.46	10.33	6.32	7.95	7.00
Median coyote price (1996 dollars)	377.16	74.98	398.76	77.81	358.11	84.02

Source: Data from Mexican Migration Project, U.S. Department of Justice (n.d.); U.S. Department of Labor (various years); U.S. Department of Commerce (various years); Banco de México (various years).

demographic and social data are taken from the Mexican Migration Project. These data reveal several important patterns. California migrants, for example, have more sibling migrants, make fewer U.S. trips, and pay more for coyotes than do migrants crossing into Texas. The average cost of a coyote was greatest in Arizona, at around $400, compared with $377 in California and $358 in Texas. Migrants into Arizona appear to be the most experienced, having made an average of 10.3 U.S. trips compared with 6.8 for migrants to California and 8.0 for migrants to Texas.

ECONOMETRIC MODEL

The multivariate analysis employs a standard approach for estimating a choice model with attributes that vary both by individual and choice. Following David Jaeger (2000), I assume that migrants choose among J states and that for individual i, crossing through state j gives a utility level U_{ij}. Individuals choose the crossing site that gives them the most utility. I assume that individual i's utility at a particular crossing site is a linear function of the site's characteristics, S_j (for example, enforcement hours, earnings), the interaction between the site and the individual's characteristics X_{ij} (for example, age, education), and an error term, ϵ_{ij}. Thus

$$U_{ij} = S_j \Phi + X_{ij} \prod + \epsilon_{ij}. \tag{1}$$

If $\epsilon_{ij} \sim$ i.i.d. Weibull, the parameters of the model can be estimated using a conditional logit framework (McFadden 1984). The probability of individual i choosing site s is

$$P\left(y_i = s\right) = \exp(Z_{is}\beta) / \sum_{j=1}^{J} \exp(Z_{ij}\beta), \tag{2}$$

where y_i is individual i's site choice, $Z_{ij} = (S_j X_{ij})$, and $\beta = (\Phi\Pi)'$ is the parameter vector. The parameters can then be estimated by maximum likelihood.

This analysis requires estimation using $N \times J$ observations (where N is the number of individuals and J is the number of states), and the resulting coefficients are not marginal effects.[4] In the model, one choice has to serve as the baseline, and in this case it is Arizona. Hence there are no coefficient estimates for Arizona, which serves as the reference category.

The set of regressors S and X include most of the determinants of crossing choice outlined earlier in this chapter. For the state-level analysis, S includes state linewatch hours (average per Border Patrol sector in given state), state fixed effects, and state time trends. State fixed effects pick up fixed attributes of crossing points like distance, topography, average climate, and vegetation. State time trends absorb other factors in crossing-site choice that may intensify or diminish over time, including propensity to migrate to certain areas and trends in occupational composition of migrants.

To capture the labor market conditions in each border state, I include real average earnings, real average farm earnings, and the unemployment rate. In the second specification, to control for job growth, I also include total employment and farm employment. To control for economic conditions in Mexico, I include the Mexican manufacturing wage. Although a region-specific variable would be preferable (since variations across local labor markets are not captured in a single aggregate measure), such an indicator is not available going back to 1985. Nonetheless, much work has shown that the Mexican manufacturing wage has considerable explanatory power with regard to Mexico-U.S. migration (see Hanson and Spilimbergo 1999). Individual-level regressors, represented in equation (1) by X, consist of age, education, number of sibling migrants, number of prior U.S. trips, and the median coyote price paid by migrants from the individual's state of origin. Because the number of parameters proliferate with the number of choices, continuous variables are entered linearly. Entering age, education, and network variables nonlinearly as categorical variables do not affect the main results but make exposition cumbersome.

CHOICE OF STATE FOR BORDER CROSSING

Table 14.2 presents the results of estimating equation (2) for all undocumented crossings reported by household heads from 1985 to 1996. The estimated coefficients support the hypothesis that increased linewatch hours along a state's border significantly decrease the probability that undocumented migrants will cross into that particular state. This finding partly explains the shift away from California toward Arizona and Texas that is so apparent in the raw data on apprehensions and crossings. However, other factors also contribute to fewer crossings into California. For example, the time trend is negative and significant, which suggests that the probability of crossing into California has been diminishing over time in any case, apart from changes in border enforcement.

The economic variables suggest that high U.S. earnings, especially farm earnings, constitute a pull factor and low Mexican wages represent a significant push factor—at least for migrants going to California.

TABLE 14.2   Logistic Regression Analysis of Choice of State for
             Border Crossing: Undocumented Mexican Migrants,
             1985 to 1996

Independent Variable	Baseline Model Coefficient	Standard Error	With Employment Coefficient	Standard Error
U.S. enforcement effort				
Linewatch hours	−1.073*	0.648	−2.167**	1.099
California fixed effect	0.317	0.518	0.518	0.545
Texas fixed effect	−0.463	0.738	0.791	1.331
California time trend	−0.312**	0.124	−0.558**	0.244
Texas time trend	−0.030	0.115	−0.199	0.213
U.S. economic conditions				
Real earnings per worker	5.686	12.214	24.059	20.651
Real farm earnings per worker	2.012**	0.822	1.178	1.065
Total employment	—	—	−13.896	11.854
Farm employment	—	—	0.259	2.209
Unemployment rate	3.447**	1.537	3.395**	1.566
Mexican economic conditions				
Manufacturing				
wage × California	−9.341**	2.862	−9.782**	3.079
Manufacturing wage × Texas	−3.132	2.673	1.340	4.486
Individual and social characteristics				
Age × California	0.015	0.015	0.015	0.015
Age × Texas	0.007	0.016	0.006	0.016
Education × California	−0.020	0.042	−0.021	0.042
Education × Texas	−0.015	0.044	−0.016	0.044
Number of sibling migrants × California	−0.061	0.063	−0.060	0.063
Number of sibling migrants × Texas	−0.205**	0.068	−0.204**	0.068
Number of U.S. trips × California	−0.064**	0.017	−0.064**	0.017
Number of U.S. trips × Texas	−0.028	0.018	−0.026	0.018
Real coyote price × California	−0.002	0.001	−0.002	0.001
Real coyote price × Texas	−0.006**	0.002	−0.006**	0.002
Pseudo R squared	0.352		0.353	
Log likelihood	−1175.195		−1174.407	
Number of observations	4,955		4,955	

Source: See table 14.1.
Note: Arizona is the omitted category. Linewatch hours, earnings, emp, and unemployment are in logs.
*p < .1   **p < .05

However, the U.S. earnings result is sensitive to specification, most likely because the time series is so short. Other work has shown the importance of U.S. wages in attracting migrants (Hanson and Spilimbergo 1999; Orrenius and Zavodny 2000). The coefficient for the unemployment rate has the opposite sign from what economic theory might suggest. Tighter labor markets—lower unemployment rates—should attract migrants, while looser markets should deter them. This anomalous result may again reflect the short time series and the annual frequency of the data.

Age and education are not significant in predicting crossing choice. I originally postulated that age and education would be correlated with risk taking and access to information about border crossing, but at the state level these variables appear to have little explanatory power. Network variables, however, are interesting in that they show that migrants going into Texas have significantly fewer sibling migrants than do migrants into other border states. Migrants into California, meanwhile, have significantly lower cumulations of U.S. experience (as measured by number of U.S. trips), suggesting that they are less likely to circulate and perhaps more likely to settle north of the border.

Finally, migrants going into Texas also pay significantly less for a coyote to guide them in crossing. Coyote price is most likely an outcome of both of supply and demand, as well as the relative risk of crossing along the Texas border versus the borders with Arizona and California. Abundant ground cover in Texas, particularly around Laredo and in the Rio Grande Valley, might make it easier to escape detection by Border Patrol agents (lowering the probability of apprehension), although in recent years the long walk to circumvent the Border Patrol checkpoints has proved fatal for some migrants (Eschbach et al. 1999).

CHOICE OF CITY FOR BORDER CROSSING

The results show that migrants respond to border enforcement by crossing in areas that are less patrolled, but state-level results are too broad to address whether this has led to more crossings in remote areas. In recent years, border crackdowns have focused on big metropolitan border areas like Tijuana–San Diego and Juárez–El Paso and not coincidentally, these have traditionally been the preferred crossing sites of most migrants. By also conducting a city-level analysis, I see whether enforcement in general has led to fewer crossings through large cities. On the border, cities with smaller populations are generally located in more remote locations. The significance of this analysis is to link enforcement with crossings in more remote areas as a way in which to explain the increased border crossing deaths.

Given the paucity of data on border deaths, there is not a long enough time series available to run an econometric model exploring whether linewatch hours directly explain the increased incidence of border-crossing deaths. Several studies have highlighted the link nonetheless, as discussed above. Cornelius (2001) finds a 509 percent increase in deaths along the Mexico border with California from 1994 to 2000. For the Southwest border as a whole, reported deaths among undocumented border-crossers rose 474 percent from 1996 to 2000.

In order to estimate equation (2) at the city level, I have to reduce the number of site and individual-specific attributes included and extend the time series. The need for parsimony stems from the dimensionality considerations of the conditional logit model as the number of choices increases (in this case from three to twelve). Moreover, sector-specific linewatch hours are not available prior to 1985, so in this specification I interact aggregate linewatch hours with city fixed effects. I also include city fixed effects, a time trend, an IRCA time trend, and migrant's age, education and number of U.S. trips. Table 14.3 shows the estimation results for all undocumented crossings reported during the period from 1965 to 1996. The city pairs are listed in order of size from largest to smallest. Among the six largest city pairs, five show a significant deterrent effect of enforcement on the likelihood of crossing there (Tijuana–San Diego is not listed in the table because it is the baseline choice).

These estimates suggest that enforcement has had a role in pushing border-crossers out of larger, more populated areas. The results also suggest that the trend away from urban crossings may have started before IRCA and Gatekeeper. The time series does not extend far enough into the 1990s to capture the full effect of the new border patrol operations, so it is important to note that this estimated impact is likely an underestimate of the current effect of enforcement on migrant crossing choice. The same is true for the results in table 14.2.

CONCLUSION

Undocumented Mexico-U.S. migrants today avoid formerly popular crossing points in California in favor of Texas and Arizona. Within states, the change is also noticeable. In California, migrants choose to cross the deserts of El Centro rather than risk a crossing south of San Diego. In Texas, migrants are less likely to attempt an El Paso

TABLE 14.3   Logistic Regression Analysis of Choice of City for
Border Crossing: Undocumented Mexican Migrants,
1965 to 1996

Independent Variable	β Coefficient	Standard Error
Log of linewatch hours × city		
Tijuana– San Diego	—	—
Juárez–El Paso	−1.464*	0.803
Reynosa-McAllen	−0.371	0.870
Matamoros-Brownsville	−1.133*	0.560
Mexicali-Calexico	−1.561*	0.709
Nuevo Laredo–Laredo	−0.806*	0.445
Acuña–Del Río and Piedras		
Negras–Eagle Pass	−0.995*	0.584
San Luís–Yuma	−0.631	0.713
Nogales-Nogales	−0.402	0.889
Agua Prieta–Douglas	−0.569	1.936
Tecate-Tecate	−1.317	1.368
Ojinaga-Presidio	5.519	6.514
City fixed effects		
Tijuana–San Diego	—	—
Juárez–El Paso	17.023	10.998
Reynosa-McAllen	2.656	11.906
Matamoros-Brownsville	12.884	8.239
Mexicali-Calexico	17.904*	9.701
Nuevo Laredo–Laredo	8.922	6.111
Acuña–Del Rio and Piedras		
Negras–Eagle Pass	12.656	8.003
San Luis–Yuma	−10.334	9.818
Nogales-Nogales	2.161	12.177
Agua Prieta–Douglas	2.481	26.645
Tecate-Tecate	15.623	18.742
Ojinaga-Presidio	−78.331	89.354
Pseudo R squared	0.42	
Log likelihood		−11,951
Number of observations		68,520

Source: See table 14.1.
Note: The following variables are controlled for but not shown in table: age, education, number of prior U.S. trips, time trend, and interaction between IRCA and time trend. Some Mexican border cities were combined due to a lack of data in certain years. Tijuana–San Diego is the omitted category.
*p < .10   **p < .05

crossing, preferring to cross in south Texas through Laredo, McAllen, or Brownsville. The literature suggests that increased border enforcement is the driving force behind these changes and behind the rising death rates that seem to have come with them.

This chapter's contribution is to address the question of enforcement and crossing patterns within the context of multivariate analysis that controls for both site and migrant characteristics. Using a combination of data sources on economic and enforcement conditions and the Mexican Migration Project for individual-level crossing and demographic data, the results from a conditional logit model suggest that enforcement has played a significant role in deterring migrant crossings in California. The results from a longer time series on city-level crossings also suggests that enforcement has deterred crossings in larger border cities more generally. The latter is important in order to establish a definitive link between border enforcement and the increasing remoteness of crossing sites.

These are the author's opinions and do not necessarily reflect the views of the Federal Reserve Bank of Dallas or the Federal Reserve System.

NOTES

1. Operation Safeguard was officially launched in 1994 but did not receive sufficient funding and resources until 1999.
2. Cornelius (2001) and Eschbach and colleagues (1999) use different data sources on migrant deaths. Cornelius relies on data from the Mexican Ministry of Foreign Relations and Mexican consulates, while Eschbach and colleagues use data gathered from vital statistics registries in U.S. border counties. U.S. Immigration and Naturalization Service data on migrant deaths start in 1998 and show no clear trends in cause of death from 1998 to 2000 but do show a marked increase in the number of deaths (42 percent).
3. According to the Immigration and Naturalization Service, the Border Patrol rescued 1,041, 2,454, and 1,233 migrants, respectively, in 1998, 1999, and 2000 as part of the border safety initiative.
4. The parameters can be presented either as coefficients or odds ratios. I choose to report coefficients. The sign, significance, and relative magnitudes of the coefficients are straightforward, although they do not indicate the magnitude of the change in the probability of choosing a particular location resulting from a unit change in a regressor.

REFERENCES

Andreas, Peter. 2000. *Border Games: Policing the U.S.-Mexico Divide*. Ithaca, N.Y.: Cornell University Press.

Banco de México. Various years. "Indicadores Economicos." *Informe Annual*. Mexico, D.F.: Banco de México.

Bean, Frank D., Roland Chanove, Robert G. Cushing, Rodolfo de la Garza, Gary P. Freeman, Charles W. Haynes, and David Spener. 1994. *Illegal Mexican Migration and the United States/Mexico Border: The Effects of Operation Hold-the-Line on El Paso/Juárez*. Washington: U.S. Commission on Immigration Reform.

Cornelius, Wayne A. 2001. "Death at the Border: Efficacy and Unintended Consequences of U.S. Immigration Control Policy." *Population and Development Review* 27: 661–85.

Durand, Jorge, Douglas S. Massey, and Emilio A. Parrado. 1999. "The New Era of Mexican Migration to the United States." *Journal of American History* 86: 518–36.

Eschbach, Karl, Jacqueline Hagan, Nestor Rodriguez, Rubén Hernández-León, and Stanley Bailey. 1999. "Death at the Border." *International Migration Review* 20: 430–54.

Hanson, Gordon H., and Antonio Spilimbergo. 1999. "Illegal Immigration, Border Enforcement, and Relative Wages: Evidence from Apprehensions at the U.S.-Mexico Border." *American Economic Review* 89: 1337–57.

Jaeger, David A. 2000. "Local Labor Markets, Admission Categories, and Immigrant Location Choice." Working paper. Hunter College and Graduate School, CUNY, June.

Massey, Douglas S., Rafael Alarcón, Jorge Durand, and Humberto González. 1987. *Return to Aztlan: The Social Process of International Migration from Western Mexico*. Berkeley: University of California Press.

Massey, Douglas S., Jorge Durand, and Nolan J. Malone. 2002. *Beyond Smoke and Mirrors: Mexican Immigration in an Era of Free Trade*. New York: Russell Sage Foundation.

Massey, Douglas S., and Kristin E. Espinosa. 1997. "What's Driving Mexico-U.S. Migration? A Theoretical, Empirical, and Policy Analysis." *American Journal of Sociology* 102: 939–99.

McFadden, Daniel. 1984. "Econometric Analysis of Qualitative Choice Models." In *Handbook of Econometrics*, edited by Zvi Griliches and M. D. Intriligator, vol. 2. Amsterdam, Netherlands: North-Holland.

Orrenius, Pia M. 2001. "Illegal Immigration and Enforcement Along the U.S.-Mexico Border: An Overview." Federal Reserve Bank of Dallas *Economic and Financial Review* (1st quarter): 2–11.

Orrenius, Pia M., and Madeline Zavodny. 2000. "Self-Selection Among Undocumented Immigrants from Mexico." Working paper 00-05. Dallas, Tex.: Federal Reserve Bank of Dallas (November).

Rosenblum, Marc R. 2000. "U.S. Immigration Policy: Unilateral and Cooperative Responses to Undocumented Immigration." Policy paper 55. La Jolla, Calif.: Institute on Global Conflict and Cooperation (May).

U.S. Department of Commerce. Bureau of Economic Analysis. Various years. "Regional Economic Accounts." Washington: U.S. Department of Commerce. Available at http://www.bea.gov/bea/regional/statelocal.htm (accessed on May 10, 2004).

U.S. Department of Justice. Immigration and Naturalization Service (INS). n.d. Unpublished data on sector linewatch hours and sector apprehensions. Washington: INS.

U.S. Department of Labor. Bureau of Labor Statistics. Various years. "Local Area Unemployment Statistics." Washington: U.S. Department of Labor. Available at http://www.bls.gov/lau/ (accessed on May 10, 2004).

U.S. General Accounting Office. 1999a. *Border Patrol Hiring: Despite Recent Initiatives, Fiscal Year 1999 Hiring Goal Was Not Met.* GAO/GGD-00-39. Washington: U.S. General Accounting Office.

———. 1999b. *U.S.-Mexico Border: Issues and Challenges Confronting the United States and Mexico.* GAO/NSIAD-99-190. Washington: U.S. General Accounting Office.

CHAPTER 15

U.S. IMMIGRATION POLICY AND THE DURATION OF UNDOCUMENTED TRIPS

Belinda I. Reyes

MEXICAN MIGRATION has long been characterized by its cyclical nature (Massey et al. 1987). Historically, most Mexican immigrants enter the United States to work temporarily and then return to Mexico within a few years or months (Calavita 1992). However, it is well known that the probability of return migration declines as migratory experience accumulates across trips (Massey et al. 1987), and in recent years trip duration may have changed as more and more immigrants built up significant amounts of experience and social ties north of the border (Massey 1990).

Also at play is U.S. immigration policy. The legalization of over two million previously unauthorized immigrants under the Immigration Reform and Control Act (IRCA) could also have led more immigrants to settle permanently in the United States (Alarcón 1995a, 1995b). Some authors have identified the recent buildup of enforcement resources at the Mexico-U.S. border as another important factor leading immigrants to stay longer in the United States (Cornelius 1998; Marcelli and Cornelius 2001). This chapter seeks to understand which factors are most important in determining trip duration among undocumented Mexican migrants to the United States.

DATA AND METHODS

To model the probability of return migration by unauthorized Mexican migrants, I use retrospective data on U.S. trips provided by respondents to the Mexican Migration Project (MMP) (see chapter 16). I restricted the sample to the persons located in communities surveyed after 1990, so that a large fraction of the migrants would have had migratory experience following implementation of IRCA. I also restricted the sample to adults aged sixteen to thirty-five and considered males and females separately.

To study return migration by men and women, I estimated a discrete-time hazard model for two different samples: the first is made up of all respondents, the second of only those located in communities surveyed after 1994. After this date, the MMP made special efforts to broaden the sample, moving away from an exclusive focus on western Mexico, the historical heartland for immigration to the United States, to incorporate communities in newer sending regions—namely, the states of Guerrero, Oaxaca, Puebla, and Baja California Norte. These models allow me to determine changes in the probability of return as well as trends in the duration of trips.

My model assumes that the probability of return migration varies depending on how long migrants have been in the United States. Specifically, I assume that there is an underlying response variable, Z_{it}, defined by the relationship

$$Z_{it} = \beta_0 + \beta_1 X_{it} + \beta_2 N_{it} + \beta_3 C_{it} + \beta_4 M_{it} + \beta_5 T_{it} + \delta_1 Y_i + \xi_{it},$$

where X_{it} represents the characteristics of individual i in year t, N_{it} stands for family resources and experiences, C_{it} indicates the characteristics of the community of origin, M_{it} is the person's own migratory experience, Y_i comprises a set of dummy variables for years 1970 through 1997, and T_i is a set of dummy variables indicating duration of stay. The various βs are coefficients to be estimated, and ξ_{it} is the error term, which I assume follows a logistic distribution so that the formal probability is given by the equation

$$\text{Prob}\left(Z_{it} = 1\right) = \frac{\exp\left(\beta_0 + \beta_1 X_{it} + \beta_2 N_{it} + \beta_3 C_{it} + \beta_4 M_{it} + \beta_5 T_{it} + \delta_1 Y_i\right) *}{*1 + \exp\left(\beta_0 + \beta_1 X_{it} + \beta_2 N_{it} + \beta_3 C_{it} + \beta_4 M_{it} + \beta_5 T_{it} + \delta_1 Y_i\right)}, \quad (1)$$

specified for each person-year. The dependent variable is whether person i returns home after t years in the United States. This equation allows me to model the probability of return over time better than would a simple logistic equation while maintaining the simplicity of discrete-time analysis. It also allows me to observe and measure the time-varying effects of independent variables by interacting the independent variables with duration.

The MMP database contains variables defined at the individual, household, and community levels, some fixed and some time varying. To correct for the hierarchical nature of the data, I estimated a two-stage model. The first stage used person-level data to estimate the discrete-time hazard model defined in equation (1). This stage explored whether temporal changes in the characteristics of people or communities led to changes in the probability of return migration. Next, using time-varying data, a second-stage OLS regression took the estimated coefficients for δ_1 generated in the first stage as a dependent variable and regressed them on indicators of macroeconomic conditions and measures of border enforcement to assess their role in accounting for the time trend. I address the issue of heteroskedasticity by weighting the second-stage equation by $1/N^2$, where N is the number of observations available for each year. Because, owing to smaller sample sizes, data for later years are more imprecise, this weighting scheme corrects for rising standard errors of estimate.

BASIC TRENDS IN RETURN MIGRATION

Figure 15.1 shows the proportion of unauthorized Mexican immigrants in the MMP sample who returned to Mexico within one year of migration. Most of the yearly differences from 1979 to 1986 are not statistically significant, except for the years 1980 and 1982. But starting in the mid-1980s, all years are statistically significant, except 1990.

Although many of the year-to-year changes may not be statistically significant, the overall trend is clear. For men, the probability of return

FIGURE 15.1   Proportion of Unauthorized Immigrants Returning to Mexico Within One Year After Migrating, 1979 to 1997

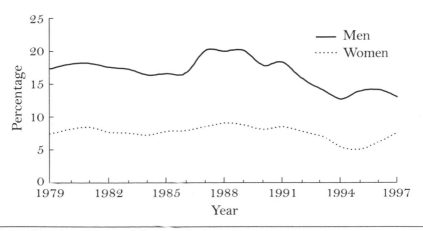

Source: Data from Mexican Migration Project.
Note: Three-year moving average.

migration increased dramatically after the 1986 passage of IRCA, a finding echoing that of Jorge Durand, Douglas Massey, and René Zenteno (2001). Although several researchers (Johnson 1996; Martin 1994; Warren 2000) have found an increase in unauthorized immigration after the passage of IRCA, it appears that, in general, these migrants made only short trips (Durand, Massey, and Zenteno 2001). For men, the probability of returning to Mexico within one year was close to 17 percent before 1986 but increased to more than 20 percent for three years following IRCA's passage. It declined again throughout the 1990s, reaching its lowest historical level at mid-decade (see also Cornelius 1998; Marcelli and Cornelius 2001).

For women, the probability of return within one year of entry was lower, around 7 percent during most of the years under study. There were, however, significant increases during the late 1980s and early 1990s and a decline in the mid-1990s. Until 1987, most of the year-to year differences are not statistically different from one another; but following IRCA implementation, the pattern is, for the most part, statistically significant (p < .05).

Figure 15.2 considers the effect of declining probabilities of return by plotting the cumulative likelihood of return migration among men who entered the United States in the 1985, 1988, 1991, and 1994 migrant cohorts. Whereas two-thirds of the men who arrived in 1988 had returned to Mexico within three years of entry, only 54 percent of those arriving in 1994 had done so. If 500,000 undocumented Mexican males enter the

FIGURE 15.2   Cumulative Distribution of the Probability of Returning to Mexico, Men, Various Years

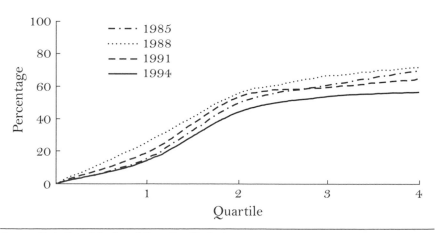

Source: Data from Mexican Migration Project.

United States every year, this difference implies that, relative to 1988 figures, an additional 63,333 would have been in the United States for at least three years in 1994, yielding a sharp increase in the size of the undocumented population present in the United States at any point in time.

To examine the reasons for these changing probabilities of return migration, I compute the likelihood of going home while controlling for cumulative experience in the United States as well as selected individual, household, and community characteristics. Variables employed in this analysis are defined in table 15.1. The model includes measures of age, education, headship, family migratory experience, legalization experience, ownership of home and land in Mexico, and size of home community in Mexico. I measure individual migratory experience using the number of U.S. trips, occupation while in the United States, and destination. Dummy variables represent the various Mexican states included in the MMP database. Estimates of the full model are included in table 15.2.

This exercise allows me to determine whether shifts in return probabilities and trip duration stem from fluctuations in independent variables or from other exogenous factors. Figure 15.3, for example, shows a simulation of return migration based on the estimated model. Predicted probabilities of return are generated by inserting mean values for control variables into the regression equation and then letting year vary. Even after accounting for the temporal changes in underlying variables, a transformation clearly took place in the duration of stay following the passage of the Immigration Reform and Control Act. Part of the difference between figures 15.2 and 15.3 is attributable to changes in the MMP sample, which in the later years surveyed communities in nontraditional sending regions. Migrants from these communities generally have a lower probability of return than those from the traditional sending regions. Because in the late 1990s the sample is disproportionately from those regions, more of the sample stays longer in the United States, as can be seen in figure 15.2. Once the differences in duration by community of origin are accounted for, however, part of the decline from 1988 to 1994 shown in figure 15.2 disappears.

For men in general, the probability of return migration before the passage of IRCA was around 11 percent; but soon thereafter it increased dramatically, an increase that is statistically significant ($p < .05$). In the 1990s the probability of return declined, although it remained above the pre-IRCA levels. For women, the probability of return within one year of migration was about 7 percent for most of the 1980s. It increased above 10 percent in the late 1980s and early 1990s, but declined again in the mid-1990s.

It is also clear from this figure that most of IRCA's effect was concentrated in the major sending regions. When the sample is restricted to the

TABLE 15.1   Definition of Variables Used in Analysis of Return Migration

Variable	Definition
Return	Equals 1 if returned during person-year, 0 otherwise
Year	Dummy variables for years 1970 to 1998 (reference category is 1989)
Age	Age during person-year
Education	Years of school completed during person year
Head	Equals 1 if household head, 0 otherwise
Own land	Equals 1 if family owns land, 0 otherwise
Own home	Equals 1 if family owns home, 0 otherwise
In U.S. before	Equals 1 if family in United States, 0 otherwise
Legal	Equals 1 if someone in family legalized during person-year or before, 0 otherwise
Change status	Equals 1 if person became legalized during person-year or before, 0 otherwise
Male agriculture	Proportion of males in community who work in agriculture during person-year
Medium	Equals 1 if community population between five thousand and fifty thousand in person-year, 0 otherwise
Large	Equals 1 if community population fifty thousand or more in person-year, 0 otherwise
Guanajuato	Equals 1 if community in Guanajuato, 0 otherwise
Jalisco	Equals 1 if community in Jalisco, 0 otherwise
Michoacán	Equals 1 if community in Michoacán, 0 otherwise
Nayarit	Equals 1 if community in Nayarit, 0 otherwise
Zacatecas	Equals 1 if community in Zacatecas, 0 otherwise
Guerrero	Equals 1 if community in Guerrero, 0 otherwise
San Luis Potosí	Equals 1 if community in San Luis Potosí, 0 otherwise
Colima	Equals 1 if community in Colima, 0 otherwise
Oaxaca	Equals 1 if community in Oaxaca, 0 otherwise
Sinaloa	Equals 1 if community in Sinaloa, 0 otherwise
Puebla	Equals 1 if community in Puebla, 0 otherwise
Baja California	Equals 1 if community in Baja California, 0 otherwise (reference category)
Aguascalientes	Equals 1 if community in Aguascalientes, 0 otherwise
Skilled	Equals 1 if skilled worker on first U.S. trip, 0 otherwise
Unskilled	Equals 1 if unskilled worker on first U.S. trip, 0 otherwise
Unemployed	Equals 1 if unemployed on first U.S. trip, 0 otherwise
Trips	Number of prior U.S. trips

TABLE 15.1   Definition of Variables Used in Analysis of Return
Migration (*Continued*)

Variable	Definition
Rest of California	1 if went to California other than Los Angeles on first U.S. trip, 0 otherwise
Texas	1 if went to Texas on first U.S. trip, 0 otherwise
Illinois	1 if went to Illinois on first U.S. trip, 0 otherwise
Other state	1 if went to other state on first trip, 0 otherwise
GDP per capita	GDP per capita in Mexico during person-year
Unemployment rate	Rate of unemployment in United States during person-year
Exchange rate	Number of pesos per dollar during person-year (official rate)
Legal admissions	Number of legal admissions to United States during person-year
Linewatch hours	Number of person hours spent by INS guarding Mexico-U.S. border

Source: Data from the Mexican Migration Project.

communities surveyed after 1994, which were primarily new sending regions, return probabilities are more-or-less flat throughout the period of this study. (Sample-size limitations prevent me from looking at return rates for female migrants in the restricted sample.) This could be because most of the people legalized through IRCA were from the western part of Mexico; hence the policy affected the return rates of people in those regions only.

Figure 15.4 considers the cumulative effect of the return rates observed in figure 15.3 for cohorts of undocumented men who entered the United States in 1985, 1988, 1991, and 1994. Even after controlling for changes in household, community, and personal characteristics, there is still a difference in trip duration over time. Of the men who entered the United States in 1991, 66.5 percent returned to Mexico within the first three years after migrating, compared with 64.7 percent of those who moved in 1994. Assuming that 500,000 Mexican men enter illegally every year, almost 10,000 more undocumented men would still be in the United States after three years if they entered in 1991 as opposed to 1994. The figures for both of these groups are substantially higher than for those who migrated in 1985. Of the men who migrated in 1985, 225,000 (55 percent) would still be in the United States after three years, compared with 167,500 in the 1994 cohort.

TABLE 15.2   Parameter Estimates and Standard Errors from Discrete Time Hazard Model of Return Migration

| | Men | | | | Women | | | |
| | Whole MMP | | Restricted Sample | | Whole MMP | | Restricted Sample | |
Variable	Ratio	Error	Ratio	Error	Ratio	Error	Ratio	Error
Yr1970	0.59***	0.20	0.53	0.49	0.85	0.67	1.95	1.16
Yr1971	0.65**	0.18	1.18	0.36	1.30	0.45	33.0*	1.17
Yr1972	0.59***	0.17	0.92	0.36	0.42*	0.52	2.01	1.41
Yr1973	0.61***	0.15	0.77	0.34	0.30***	0.46	0.00	314.4
Yr1974	0.54***	0.15	0.77	0.34	0.51**	0.33	0.36	1.11
Yr1975	0.58***	0.14	0.74	0.31	0.28***	0.35	0.58	0.66
Yr1976	0.70***	0.13	0.66	0.29	0.46***	0.29	0.41	0.62
Yr1977	0.62***	0.13	1.04	0.27	0.52**	0.27	0.89	0.52
Yr1978	0.57***	0.13	0.85	0.27	0.50***	0.25	1.14	0.50
Yr1979	0.68***	0.12	1.12	0.24	0.53***	0.24	0.25**	0.78
Yr1980	0.69***	0.11	0.86	0.24	0.57**	0.22	0.63	0.50
Yr1981	0.63***	0.12	0.88	0.24	0.70*	0.21	1.35	0.40
Yr1982	0.70***	0.12	0.75	0.24	0.69*	0.22	0.99	0.45
Yr1983	0.69***	0.12	1.23	0.22	0.47***	0.25	0.81	0.48
Yr1984	0.67***	0.12	0.98	0.23	0.65*	0.22	1.30	0.41
Yr1985	0.61***	0.11	0.76	0.22	0.63**	0.21	1.09	0.41
Yr1986	0.82*	0.11	1.12	0.20	0.77	0.20	1.15	0.39
Yr1987	0.89	0.11	1.13	0.20	0.85	0.19	1.28	0.38
Yr1988	1.57***	0.10	0.96	0.20	0.91	0.18	0.72	0.43
Yr1990	1.07	0.10	0.77	0.19	0.80	0.18	0.97	0.35
Yr1991	1.35***	0.10	1.01	0.18	1.01	0.18	0.83	0.35

Yr1992	1.39***	0.11	1.09	0.19	1.38*	0.18	1.22	0.33
Yr1993	0.68****	0.14	0.89	0.19	0.69**	0.22	1.12	0.33
Yr1994	1.22*	0.12	1.13	0.18	0.78	0.21	1.06	0.32
Yr1995	1.19	0.13	1.34*	0.17	0.90	0.21	1.16	0.32
Yr1996	1.06	0.14	0.95	0.19	0.61*	0.28	0.48*	0.41
Yr1997	1.19	0.15	1.48*	0.19	1.05	0.28	1.41	0.36
Yr1998	0.79	0.21	1.07	0.24	1.43	0.31	1.83	0.39
Year1	2.05***	0.06	1.25**	0.11	1.59***	0.12	0.56**	0.23
Year2	7.65****	0.06	5.92****	0.09	5.18****	0.10	3.19****	0.17
Year3	3.63****	0.07	2.70****	0.11	3.45**	0.11	2.07****	0.19
Year4	2.33****	0.08	2.00****	0.13	2.28****	0.13	2.09****	0.20
Age	1.24****	0.03	1.26****	0.06	1.15**	0.07	1.09	0.12
Age squared	1.00****	0.001	0.99****	0.001	1.00**	0.001	0.99	0.002
Edyrs	0.97	0.020	0.99	0.030	0.99	0.035	1.04	0.070
Edyrs squared	1.00****	0.001	1.00	0.002	1.00	0.002	0.99	0.004
Head	1.91****	0.05	2.14****	0.09	1.70***	0.19	1.53	0.33
Land	1.20***	0.05	1.37****	0.08	1.12	0.09	1.06	0.14
Ownhome	1.20***	0.04	1.30****	0.08	0.94	0.07	0.85	0.13
Inusbft	0.60****	0.05	0.58****	0.08	0.72****	0.10	0.77	0.16
Legal	0.92	0.05	0.72****	0.10	0.98	0.08	0.68**	0.14
Change status	0.93	0.09	0.73**	0.15	1.98**	0.17	0.82	0.27
MeninAg	2.90***	0.15	1.42	0.35	4.52***	0.31	3.17	0.88
Medium	1.00	0.05	0.94	0.01	1.10	0.09	0.64**	0.20
Large	1.61***	0.10	1.06	0.32	1.79***	0.20	3.65*	0.68
Guanajuato	2.05****	0.10	1.02	0.16	1.38	0.17	0.37***	0.36
Jalisco	2.50***	0.10	0.56****	0.18	1.62**	0.17	0.25***	0.50

(*Table continues on p. 308.*)

TABLE 15.2 Parameter Estimates and Standard Errors from Discrete Time Hazard Model of Return Migration
(Continued)

| | Men | | | | Women | | | |
| | Whole MMP | | Restricted Sample | | Whole MMP | | Restricted Sample | |
Variable	Ratio	Error	Ratio	Error	Ratio	Error	Ratio	Error
Michoacán	3.39***	0.11	0	—	1.97***	0.17	0	—
Nayarit	2.58***	0.13	0	—	1.51**	0.21	0	—
Zacatecas	2.16***	0.10	1.69***	0.16	1.25	0.15	1.75**	0.25
Guerrero	0.84	0.14	0.47***	0.21	0.67*	0.22	0.25**	0.43
San Luis Potosí	1.16	0.11	1.34	0.18	0.70**	0.18	0.67	0.38
Colima	0.91	0.16	0.81	0.21	0.25***	0.33	0.17**	0.50
Oaxaca	0.86	0.15	0.65**	0.20	0.68	0.25	0.62	0.35
Sinaloa	0.99	0.17	0.63**	0.20	0.66	0.34	0.48*	0.40
Puebla	0.97	0.20	0.65	0.32	0.84	0.30	0.22***	0.51
Aguascalientes	1.80***	0.12	1.29	0.16	0.78	0.26	0.71	0.31
Skilled	0.46***	0.06	0.59***	0.11	0.43***	0.16	0.54**	0.29
Unskilled	0.54***	0.05	0.65***	0.09	0.55***	0.13	0.76	0.25
Unemployed	1.47***	0.12	1.82***	0.21	0.43**	0.13	0.55**	0.24
Trip	1.00	0.0001	1.00	0.0001	1.00	0.0002	0.89	0.11
Other California	1.03	0.05	1.19**	0.09	1.02	0.09	1.50***	0.15
Texas	1.70***	0.07	1.46**	0.13	1.26	0.15	1.22	0.29
Illinois	1.07	0.09	1.14	0.18	0.99	0.17	1.05	0.45
Other state	0.99	0.06	1.13	0.11	1.19	0.12	1.58**	0.20

Source: Data from Mexican Migration Project.

*p < .1   **p < .05   ***p < .001

FIGURE 15.3   Simulation of the Probability of Returning to Mexico
                Within One Year After Migrating, 1979 to 1997

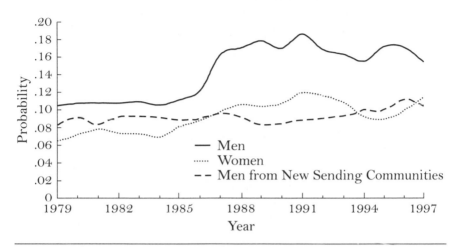

Source: Data from Mexican Migration Project.
Note: Three-year moving average.

FIGURE 15.4   Simulation of the Cumulative Probability of Returning
                to Mexico, Men, Various Years

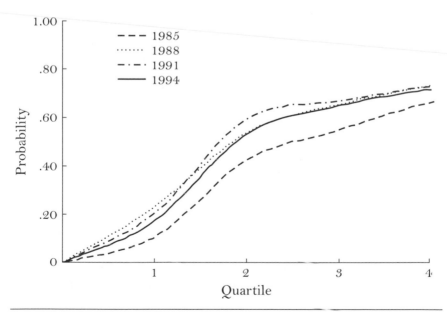

Source: Data from Mexican Migration Project.

EXPLAINING THE TRENDS

I estimated a second set of equations to explore the effects of economic conditions in Mexico and the United States and of changes in U.S. immigration policy on the probability of return. Unstandardized coefficients for these models are presented in table 15.3. This second-stage model has its limitations: I have only twenty-eight years of data, and the sample may not be large enough to capture effects of complex variables with squared terms. Although a particular variable may have an effect on the probability of return migration, unless that effect is large the effect will not be significant, owing to small sample size. Hence this model captures only the effects of variables that have a large effect on the probability of return.

The first model examines the effect of conditions in Mexico and the United States without controlling for changes in the sample. The second examines the effect of conditions in the United States and Mexico on the probability of return after controlling for changes in household, community, and personal characteristics. The last model shows the effect of economic conditions and immigration policy on the restricted sample of communities surveyed after 1994. Of all macro-level factors, IRCA appears to have had the strongest effect on the probability of return migration.

In 1989, the number of immigrants who either were admitted as legal permanent residents or changed their status was 1,090,900. According to my model, this massive legalization would lead to an increase in the probability of return migration from 7 percent in 1988 to 11 percent in 1989. This increase may occur because some people went to the United States only temporarily, to join newly legalized family members, or because many more people than those legalized crossed the border in a short period to legalize their status, especially under the Special Agricultural Workers provision of IRCA. This might explain the unexpectedly high number of immigrants legalized under IRCA hypothesized by other authors (Martin 1994).

In most of the models, the enforcement buildup at the Mexican-U.S. border has a negative effect on the probability of return, indicating that increases in the number of person-hours spent patrolling the border increases the duration of stay in the United States. But it is statistically significant only in the model without controls. I estimated another model with interactions for duration and year of migration (not shown) and found that indeed there was a decline in the probability of return during the period of enforcement and that the effect of linewatch hours approaches statistical significance ($p < .11$ with a two-tailed test but $p < .05$ with a one-tailed test).

Table 15.4, which presents odds ratios for regressions on selected independent variables, indicates which are the most important predictors of

TABLE 15.3 Parameter Estimates and Standard Errors for Second-Stage OLS Equation Modeling the Probability of Return Migration for Male Undocumented Migrants

	No Controls		With Controls		Restricted Sample	
Variable	Betas	Standard Error	Betas	Standard Error	Betas	Standard Error
Men						
Mexican economic conditions						
Mexican GDP per capita	0.0003	0.0003	0.0003	0.0003	−0.0001	0.0004
Mexican GDP per capita squared	−0.0007	0.0005	−0.0005	0.0005	−0.0001	0.0005
Exchange rate	0.030	0.060	0.080	0.060	−0.050	0.060
U.S. economic conditions:						
U.S. unemployment rate	−0.060	0.050	−0.060	0.060	−0.050	0.060
U.S. immigration policy						
Legal admissions	0.225*	0.127	0.300*	0.130	0.170	0.140
Legal admissions squared	−0.009	0.005	−0.010*	0.006	−0.007	0.006
Linewatch hours	−0.770**	0.360	−0.160	0.380	0.420	0.390
Linewatch hours squared	0.070	0.040	−0.003	0.040	−0.040	0.040
Intercept	−0.530	0.480	−1.100**	0.500	−0.920	0.560
Adjusted R-squared	0.340		0.540		0.110	

(*Table continues on p. 312.*)

TABLE 15.3   Parameter Estimates and Standard Errors for Second-Stage OLS Equation Modeling the Probability of Return Migration for Male Undocumented Migrants (*Continued*)

Variable	No Controls		With Controls		Restricted Sample	
	Betas	Standard Error	Betas	Standard Error	Betas	Standard Error
Women						
Mexican economic conditions						
Mexican GDP per Capita	0.0005	0.0004	0.0001	0.0004	−0.0005	0.0020
Mexican GDP per capita squared	−0.0009	0.0006	−0.0003	0.0007	0.0006	0.0030
Exchange rate	−0.080	0.070	−0.040	0.080	−0.210	0.330
U.S. economic conditions:						
U.S. unemployment rate	−0.100	0.070	−0.070	0.070	0.180	0.320
U.S. immigration policy						
Legal admissions	0.440***	0.150	−0.480***	0.170	0.540	0.690
Legal admissions squared	−0.018*	0.006	−0.019***	0.007	−0.020	0.030
Linewatch hours	−1.060***	0.440	−0.490	0.490	0.800	2.100
Linewatch hours squared	0.140*	0.050	0.070	0.060	−0.020	0.220
Intercept	−0.320	0.630	−1.460*	0.730	−4.500	3.300
Adjusted R-squared	0.260		0.370		0.000	

Source: Data from Mexican Migration Project.

*p < .1   **p < .05   ***p < .01

TABLE 15.4   Odds Ratios and Standard Errors for Regression of the
Probability of Return Migration on Selected
Independent Variables

	Men		Females	
Variable	Odds Ratio	Standard Error	Odds Ratio	Standard Error
Household characteristics				
Head	1.90***	0.045	1.70***	0.190
Owns land	1.20***	0.050	1.10	0.090
Owns home	1.20***	0.040	0.94	0.070
Family in United States before	0.60***	0.050	0.72***	0.100
Documented	0.90	0.050	0.98	0.080
Change status	0.90	0.090	1.98***	0.170
Community characteristics				
Proportion males in agriculture	2.90***	0.150	4.52***	0.300
Large size	1.60***	0.100	1.79***	0.200
State of origin				
Colima	—	—	—	—
Guanajuato	2.10***	0.100	1.38*	0.170
Jalisco	2.50**	0.100	1.63***	0.170
Michoacán	3.40***	0.110	1.97***	0.170
Nayarit	2.60**	0.130	1.50**	0.210
Zacatecas	2.20***	0.100	1.25	0.150
Guerrero	0.80	0.100	0.67*	0.200
San Luis Potosí	1.16	0.110	0.70**	0.180
Oaxaca	0.91	0.160	0.25***	0.330
Sinaloa	0.86	0.150	0.68	0.250
Puebla	0.99	0.170	0.66	0.340
Baja California Norte	0.97	0.200	0.84	0.300
Aguascalientes	1.80***	0.120	0.78	0.260
U.S. work experience				
Agriculture	—	—	—	—
Skilled	0.46***	0.060	0.43***	0.160
Unskilled	0.54***	0.050	0.55***	0.130
Unemployed	1.47***	0.120	0.43***	0.130
Texas	1.70***	0.070	1.26	0.150

Source: Data from Mexican Migration Project.
*p < .1   **p < .05   ***p < .01

return migration in the hazard model. Being a household head in Mexico, originating from the western region, and being from an agricultural community or a town with more than fifty thousand people all increase the probability of return for both men and women. Migratory experience in the United States has a strong effect on the probability of return. Among women, those who worked in U.S. agriculture were most likely to return to Mexico; but for men the odds of return migration are greatest for those who were unemployed. Skilled women and women out of the labor force or unemployed were the least likely to return. For men, skilled workers were the least likely to return.

Household social networks are also important in predicting return migration. Originating in a family with significant migration experience reduced the probability of going home, even if other household members were present illegally in the United States. Legalization increased the probability of return migration for women, but it had no effect among men. In general, there has been a decrease over time in the probability of return among those residing in households with large migrant networks.

Figure 15.5 illustrates the trend in the probability of return within a year of migration depending on the migration experience of household members and their legal status. The probability of return is substantially

FIGURE 15.5   Probability of Returning to Mexico Within One Year of Migrating, Men, by Experience and Legal Status of Household Members, 1979 to 1997

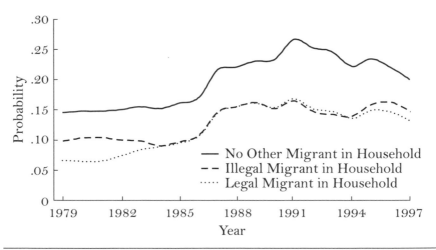

Source: Data from Mexican Migration Project.
Note: Three-year moving average.

higher for men who originate from households without other migrants. But the decline in the probability of return during the period of rising linewatch hours (1995 to 1997) is steeper for these migrants than for individuals with other migrants in the household. For men from households with one or more legalized migrants, the model indicates a greater decline in the probability of return migration during the period of heightened enforcement. Such people may be staying on in the United States in hopes of legalizing their own status through the newly legalized household member.

Similar patterns are observed for women (not shown in figure); but there is a convergence between the return probability for women without networks and those in households containing illegal household members. A woman who had a household member with legal status was substantially less likely to return during the period of the buildup of border enforcement. The buildup may have made it more important to remain in the United States and attempt to legalize, increasing the duration of stay for those with possibilities for legalizing their status through kinship with a legal resident alien.

QUALITATIVE PERSPECTIVES ON RETURN MIGRATION

As part of an ongoing study of Mexican migration and border enforcement, the Public Policy Institute of California conducted focus groups with undocumented migrants in California as well as a household survey of some households in a migrant-sending community in the state of Michoacán. These samples provide qualitative interview data that can be used to supplement the quantitative analysis already presented, allowing migrants to speak for themselves about the issue of return migration. Naturally, these data are not representative and cannot readily be used to generalize about the experience of all unauthorized immigrants from Mexico. Nonetheless, they offer honest reports of people's experiences crossing the Mexico-U.S. border.

Five focus groups were conducted in California—one in Fresno, one in Madera, and three in Los Angeles. A total of fifty-two respondents (twenty-one women and thirty-one men) participated in the sessions. The focus groups lasted close to an hour and were conducted on May 25, June 29, and June 30, 2000. Respondents were selected to include a mix of people in terms of year of migration, migration experience, occupation, gender, and region of origin.

In addition, Public Policy Institute researchers visited the town of Chavinda, Michoacán, to gather information about migrants and prospective migrants at a point of origin. For two weeks in January 2001, the researchers attempted to interview 184 households included on a list of households compiled for a previous survey, seeking to visit the same families to learn about changes that had occurred since the original interviews. By the beginning of 2001, 20 percent of the 184 housing units surveyed in 1982 were vacant because the entire family had moved to the United States; an additional 10 percent were vacant and the whereabouts of the inhabitants unknown. In the end, researchers were unable to determine the location of all but eighteen of the households originally surveyed (for more details on the sample, see Reyes, Johnson, Sweringer 2002).

In the 2001 interviews, people talked about having to stay longer in the United States because of the buildup in enforcement efforts at the border. People were staying longer for three reasons: the greater difficulty of crossing the border, which makes it risky to go back and forth between Mexico and the United States; the higher cost of migration, which makes it necessary to stay longer to pay for the cost incurred; and a desire to stay in hopes of legalizing one's status, so as to make it easier to move back and forth between Mexico and the United States without fear of apprehension.

Many were reluctant to return to Mexico for fear of not being able to reenter the United States: "It has been already four years since my children left because my mom became ill. They went only to save money to pay the doctor bills, but they did not come back . . . because then how would they be able to return to the [United States] afterwards?" (respondent in Chavinda). Others, noting the increased cost of border crossing relative to costs in the past, said a longer stay was required for them to pay back those who financed their trip and then save money to bring home.

> There are hundreds of people, and thousands of people, who work for the minimum, in restaurants, in factories . . . and the minimum is $5.75. . . . With much work and much effort, they put together [enough to repay] . . . the money they got from their brothers, their cousins. They pay in installments. And that's how they do it. . . . To pay five thousand something. . . . Well, it will take them about two years. . . . But we all, the majority of us, have family in Mexico . . . and we send money home. . . . We also have to pay apartment and food here. . . . Then you have, what, three years; you need three years to pay the money. (Respondent in West Los Angeles)

The same sentiment was echoed by another respondent:

> To be able to pay $1,500 to $2,000 [to a coyote], it takes people at least a year. . . . But what happens is that the $1,500 you got cannot be

paid as soon as you start working. . . . With the money you're earning, you also have to eat and pay [for] many things. . . . You cannot pay back as soon as you arrive, . . . you also have to live. . . . And it seems that now when you borrow money, you also have to pay interest; every month they charge 10 percent interest, 10 percent on the $1,500 you borrowed. . . . It takes longer because of the interest . . . because most people come to do seasonal work, for a short time, . . . and in such amount of time, they don't get to even save for the coyote. . . . [They have] to wait until next season . . . [and get] into more debt. They have to stay because otherwise they can't make the money. So, even if they didn't like it, they have to save to pay back anyway; and then go back. (Respondent from Fresno)

The increasing intensity of enforcement has also made it more important for people to legalize their status in the United States. Many hope for and some expect a future legalization program, and in our limited sample many people said they were staying longer in the hope of eventually adjusting their status, so as to be able to move back and forth freely and to overcome legal barriers to employment. As one respondent in Mexico reported, "My daughter Maria says that once she has papers it will be easy for her to come every year to visit, but that now it is too difficult. She says her husband needs two more years to legalize her situation" (respondent in Chavinda). The sister of several young men who had just left for the United States explained her situation as follows:

Just now three of my brothers left: Jesus, Jose, and, Fernando, who is only sixteen and is on his first trip. They hired a coyote and will pay twelve hundred [U.S.] dollars each. They will go through the hills, and we are very worried. We have been crying all day, but I tell my mom that rather than crying we should be praying. Jesus had not been back in three years precisely because he feared the crossing. He says that they have to walk and run a lot and pay the coyote so much sometimes just to be deported later. They begin working and paying for the coyote, but there is not always work in the fields. They say that if they had papers, they would come see my mom every year and would live without worries. Jose has not been back in four years for the same reasons as Jesus. (Respondent in Chavinda; names have been changed to protect privacy)

Finally, after having spent many years in the United States, people change their expectations about return (Massey et al. 1987). They become accustomed to life in the United States and readjust their plans. Some begin to bring their family members north as part of a plan to resettle completely in the United States.

> To tell you the truth, it's not that I want to stay, but once you are here, you get used to it. The comfort you have here, you can't get there. Even with things being more expensive here, you make money a little easier than in Mexico. It's hard to make money in Mexico. . . . It's easier to have a car or air conditioner here. All the comforts are better here than there. I want to go back, but I wouldn't get used to it again. (Respondent in Fresno)
>
> Well, I went back in '95, . . . and I wanted to work during the four months I was going to be there. But I realized that what they pay there, it wasn't enough. . . . And I didn't feel comfortable, . . . I couldn't get used to being there. And it's true, in this country you have more comfort, so it seems you learn something: to live in a different way. So it's hard for you to adapt back to what you came from. And that's why you don't force yourself to live there again. (Respondent in Fresno)

CONCLUSION

My findings indicate a dramatic increase in the probability of return migration after the implementation of IRCA (reflecting its massive legalization) but a sharp decline in the probability of return in the 1990s (may be due to the militarization of the Mexico-U.S. border). Statistical analysis reveals a rather sharp decline in the probability of return in the last two years of the period studied, corresponding to the massive increase in linewatch hours. Such a migratory response to increasing enforcement is also suggested by qualitative interviews conducted in both Mexico and the United States.

This study suggests important unintended consequences of U.S. immigration policy. Through its legalization of more than 2 million Mexican migrants, IRCA led to an increase in the volume of authorized immigration. But paradoxically, the receipt of documents facilitated back-and-forth movement across the border, yielding a pattern of short trip duration in the immediate aftermath of the legislation. According to my analysis, in the immediate post-IRCA period, only about a third of male migrants stayed in the United States for longer than three years.

This pattern changed in the 1990s, and the buildup of enforcement efforts at the border appears to have been played an important part in the change. As undocumented migration revived after 1986, the size of migrant cohorts once again rose in the 1990s, and those who migrated increasingly had incentives to stay longer in the United States to avoid the rising costs and risks of border crossing that accompanied the militarization of the border after 1993. The change in migrant behavior could be part of the explanation for the unexpectedly large number of unauthorized immigrants reported in the 2000 U.S. census.

Finally, this study underscores the importance of social networks for migration. Only communities in the western part of Mexico experienced a change in migration patterns following passage of IRCA, probably because the existence of networks in this region yielded significant social capital that migrants could draw upon to shape their behavior as they responded to changes in U.S. immigration policy. Migrants from families with migration experience were less likely to return to Mexico, either because they had better knowledge and resources, allowing them to advance in the United States, or because they were more reliant on networks as a source of income. In any event, with the increase in border enforcement, those with family members who have been legalized are choosing to stay longer in the United States so as to legalize their own status.

REFERENCES

Alarcón, Rafael. 1995a. *Immigrants or Transitional Workers? The Settlement Process Among Mexicans in Rural California.* Davis: University of California, California Institute for Rural Studies.

————. 1995b. "Transnational Communities, Regional Development, and the Future of Mexican Immigration." *Berkeley Planning Journal* 10: 36–54.

Calavita, Kitty. 1992. *Inside the State: The Bracero Program, Immigration and the INS.* New York: Routledge.

Cornelius, Wayne. 1998. "The Structural Embeddedness of Demand for Mexican Immigrant Labor: New Evidence from California." In *Crossings: Mexican Immigration in Interdisciplinary Perspective*, edited by Marcelo Suarez-Orozco. Cambridge, Mass.: Harvard University Press.

Durand, Jorge, Douglas S. Massey, and René M. Zenteno. 2001. "Mexican Immigration to the United States: Continuities and Changes." *Latin American Research Review* 36: 107–27.

Johnson, Hans P. 1996. *Undocumented Immigration to California: 1980–1993.* San Francisco: Public Policy Institute of California.

Marcelli, Enrico, and Wayne Cornelius. 2001. "The Changing Profile of Mexican Migrants to the United States: New Evidence from California and Mexico." *Latin American Research Review* 36: 105–31.

Martin, Philip L. 1994. "Good Intentions Gone Awry: IRCA and U.S. Agriculture." *Annals of the American Academy of Political and Social Sciences* 534: 44–57.

Massey, Douglas S. 1990. "Social Structure, Household Strategy, and the Cumulative Causation of Migration." *Population Index* 56: 3–26.

Massey, Douglas S., Rafael Alarcón, Jorge Durand, and Humberto González. 1987. *Return to Aztlán: The Social Process of International Migration from Western Mexico.* Berkeley: University of California Press.

Reyes, Belinda I., Hans P. Johnson, and Richard Van Sweringer. 2002. *Holding the Line? The Effect of the Recent Border Build-up on Unauthorized Immigration.* San Francisco: Public Policy Institute of California.

Warren, Robert. 2000. "Annual Estimates of the Unauthorized Population Residing in the United States and Components of Changes: 1987 to 1997." Unpublished paper. U.S. Department of Justice, Immigration and Naturalization Service.

CHAPTER 16

APPENDIX:
THE MEXICAN MIGRATION PROJECT

Jorge Durand and Douglas S. Massey

AS UNDOCUMENTED migration has come to account for a larger share of total immigration to developed countries, an increasing fraction of demographic growth lies outside the usual modes of statistical measurement, creating major problems for demographers seeking to forecast the size and composition of national populations and serious headaches for social scientists seeking to study the determinants and processes of immigration. As Douglas Massey and Chiara Capoferro (forthcoming) point out, the data sources normally used to study immigration have serious inadequacies with respect to measuring undocumented migration. We therefore developed an alternative methodology, known as the ethnosurvey, to study patterns and processes of undocumented migration from Mexico.

Unlike other sources of information on Mexican immigration, ethnosurveys yield data that allow investigators to

- compare the characteristics and behavior of documented and undocumented migrants

- measure trends in the characteristics of both groups over time

- undertake longitudinal studies of the migration process

- discern the background and characteristics of migrants before and after they enter the United States

- undertake detailed cross-tabulations of Mexican migration based on large samples

- study transitions between different legal statuses and model selective movements back and forth across the border

- provide an ongoing source of longitudinal data that allows researchers to monitor the effect of shifting U.S. and Mexican policies

METHODOLOGY OF AN ETHNOSURVEY

The basic idea underlying an ethnosurvey is that qualitative and quantitative procedures complement one another and that, when properly combined, the weaknesses of one become the strengths of the other, yielding a body of data with greater reliability and more internal validity than would be possible using either method alone (Massey 1987). The ethnosurvey shifts back and forth between quantitative and qualitative modes during all phases of design, data collection, and analysis. Consequently, ethnographic and survey methods inform one another throughout the study. Once a site is selected for study, the ethnosurvey begins with a phase of conventional ethnographic fieldwork, including participant observation, unstructured in-depth interviewing, and archival work. Early materials from this fieldwork are then made available for use in designing the survey instrument.

After the instrument has been designed, it is applied to a probability sample of respondents selected according to a carefully designed sampling plan. Qualitative fieldwork continues during the implementation of the survey or resumes after the survey's completion. The flow of analysis is organized to make preliminary quantitative data from the survey available to ethnographic investigators before they leave the field, allowing patterns emerging from quantitative analysis to shape qualitative fieldwork, just as insights from early ethnographies guide later statistical studies.

Quantitative data are gathered using a *semi-structured interview schedule* that lies midway between the highly structured instrument of the survey researcher and the guided conversation of the ethnographer. The schedule is laid out in a series of tables with variables arranged in columns across the top and rows referring variously to persons, events, years, or other meaningful categories. The interviewer holds a natural conversation with the subject and fills in the cells of the table by soliciting required information in ways that the situation seems to demand, using his or her judgment as to the timing and wording of specific questions or probes. Each table is organized around a particular topic, giving coherence and order to the "conversation," and certain specialized probes may be included to elaborate particular themes of interest.

A second fundamental feature of an ethnosurvey is the *collection of life histories*. Within the quantitative survey, the semistructured questionnaire is readily adapted to compile event histories on various aspects of social and economic life, such as employment, migration, marriage, childbearing, and property ownership. Various facets of a respondent's life are recorded in separate tables in the event-history questionnaire. Rows refer to specific years or periods in the respondent's life, and columns correspond to variables relating to the facet of life under investigation. These tables provide structure to the gathering of life histories by guiding the flow of conversation between interviewer and respondent.

When properly compiled and coded, the various event histories (employment, marriage, fertility, migration, property ownership, border crossing) can be combined, with the aid of a computer, to construct a comprehensive life history for each respondent, summarizing key events for each person-year of life from birth (or some other relevant starting point) to the survey date. The construction of such retrospective life histories takes the ethnosurvey design considerably beyond the cross-sectional approach usually applied to census or survey data and permits the estimation of dynamic developmental models using sophisticated methods of longitudinal data analysis.

Although individuals may be the ultimate units of analysis, their decisions are typically made within larger social and economic contexts. These contexts structure and constrain individual decisions so that analyses conducted only at the micro level are perforce incomplete. Although individuals ultimately decide whether to migrate or stay, the decision is typically reached within some larger family or household unit; these households exist within larger communities that influence family decision making; and communities, in turn, exist within regions and nations.

A third feature of the ethnosurvey is that it is designed for the *collection of multilevel data.* Information is solicited from all household members, not only yielding individual information relevant to the migration decision but also enabling the estimation of household contextual variables like dependency, family income, life-cycle stage, and kinship connections to other migrants. At the same time, other modules gather information on variables that pertain directly to the household itself, such as property ownership, dwelling construction, home furnishings, length of residence, and tenure in the home.

If communities themselves are sampling units, and quantitative information is gathered on multiple communities as part of a cluster sampling design, then fieldworkers also complete community inventories that later enable researchers to construct aggregate-level data files. Data at the individual, household, and community level may be organized into separate data sets or combined into a single multilevel file. Either way, variables defined at various levels are available for analysis.

A fourth distinguishing feature of the ethnosurvey is its reliance on *representative multisite sampling*—the purposive selection of sites and the use of random sampling methods within them. Communities may be chosen according to specific criteria designed to enable comparative analysis between settings, or they may be chosen randomly from a universe of possible sites to represent a population of interest. The latter procedure yields a representative cluster sample that generates unbiased statistical estimates. Whether chosen randomly or according to a priori specifications, however, both internal and external validity are greatly enhanced by the inclusion of multiple field sites. A variety of sites also enhances the strength of inference in qualitative as well as quantitative analyses.

Because migration is a social process that transcends distinct geographic and cultural areas, a fifth characteristic of the ethnosurvey is *parallel sampling*, which involves gathering contemporaneous samples in the different geographic locations that serve as loci for the social or economic process under study. In the case of migration, representative samples of respondents are surveyed in both sending and receiving areas.

This strategy is necessary because migration, like most social and economic processes, is selective. The population of people with U.S. migratory experience contains two classes of migrants: those who have returned home and those who have remained abroad. Since the decision to stay or return is highly selective of different characteristics and experiences, neither class is representative of all those with migrant experience. The use of origin or destination samples alone produces biased statistical analyses and misleading statements about migratory processes (Lindstrom and Massey 1994).

Parallel sampling raises certain troubling technical issues, however. Whereas designing a representative sample of returned migrants who live in a particular sending community is a straightforward process, it is more difficult to generate a representative sample of settled emigrants from that community who reside elsewhere. The main difficulty lies in constructing a sampling frame that includes all out-migrants from a community, since they are typically scattered across a variety of towns and cities, both domestic and foreign. To solve this problem, the final characteristic of an ethnosurvey is the use of *multiplicity sampling* (Kalton and Anderson 1986).

In a multiplicity sample of out-migrants, respondents in sending communities provide information not only about themselves and others in the household but also about some well-defined class of relatives—usually siblings—who live outside the community. When the survey of households in the sending community is complete, a sampling frame for settled out-migrant siblings will have been compiled, and a random sample of emigrants may be chosen from it. Researchers return to households containing relatives of the sampled siblings to obtain information necessary to locate them in destination areas. They then go to these destination areas to administer the interview; the result is a representative sample of the out-migrant community.

THE MEXICAN MIGRATION PROJECT DATABASE

The ethnosurvey was first developed for implementation in four Mexican communities and their U.S. branch settlements during 1982 and 1983. Designed to serve as a demonstration project, these ethnosurveys yielded detailed information about patterns and processes of documented and undocumented migration to the United States as well as transitions between these legal statuses. The data were analyzed and the results summarized in Massey and colleagues (1987) and a series of related articles (reviewed and included in the bibliography of Massey et al. 1998). The methodology for an ethnosurvey was first laid out by Massey (1987).

Having demonstrated the potential of ethnosurveys to gather data on subjects resistant to study using the normal sources, in 1987 we proposed a five-year project that would annually survey selected communities throughout Mexico to build up, over time, a large and reliable base of data about the characteristics and behavior of documented and undocumented migrants to the United States. This proposal was funded by the National Institute of Child Health and Human Development and ultimately became known as the Mexican Migration Project (MMP).

Soon after its initial funding, the MMP was granted a Merit Award by National Institute of Child Health and Human Development that allowed for automatic renewal (subject to administrative approval) for a second five-year period. It was renewed competitively again in 1997 and in 2002 and as of this writing is completing its sixteenth year of continuous support. Including the four communities originally surveyed in 1982 and 1983, the MMP to date has surveyed eighty-one Mexican communities and U.S. branch settlements to build a binational database that contains information on 17,625 current or former migrants to the United States, 59.8 percent of whom (10,549 persons) were undocumented on their most recent U.S. trip. Among household heads, 5,512 had been to the United States, yielding 258,910 person-years of information. Data and documentation are publicly available through the project website, which may be found simply by typing the project name into a search engine such as Google (see also http://mmp.opr.princeton.edu/).

Basic data about the communities surveyed by the MMP and the resulting samples are shown in table 16.1. As can be seen, the MMP covers a variety of Mexican states, focusing on those that constitute the traditional heartland for U.S. migration: the western states of Aguascalientes,

(Text continues on p. 330.)

TABLE 16.1 Information on Community Samples Included in the Mexican Migration Project

Community Number	State	1990 Population	2000 Population	Survey Year	Mexican Sample	U.S. Sample	Refusal Rate
1	Guanajuato	52,000	65,000	1987	200	21	0.034
2	Guanajuato	868,000	1,135,000	1987	200	0	0.119
3	Jalisco	4,000	5,000	1988	200	22	0.140
4	Guanajuato	17,000	18,000	1988	200	22	0.057
5	Guanajuato	2,000	2,000	1988	150	10	0.085
6	Jalisco	5,000	6,000	1988	200	20	0.115
7	Jalisco	3,000	4,000	1988	200	15	0.010
8	Michoacán	6,000	8,000	1989	200	20	0.050
9	Michoacán	32,000	36,000	1989	200	20	0.037
10	Michoacán	2,000	1,000	1990	150	20	0.152
11	Nayarit	20,000	25,000	1990	200	20	0.029
12	Nayarit	12,000	13,000	1990	200	20	0.010
13	Guanajuato	21,000	25,000	1990	200	20	0.047
14	Michoacán	7,000	8,000	1990	200	20	0.057
15	Guanajuato	265,000	319,000	1991	200	20	0.057
16	Guanajuato	1,000	1,000	1991	100	10	0.029
17	Jalisco	31,000	35,000	1991	200	20	0.044
18	Zacatecas	8,000	7,000	1991	365	20	0.127
19	Michoacán	428,000	550,000	1991	200	20	0.083
20	Jalisco	3,000	3,000	1982	106	0	0.038

21	Jalisco	2,000	2,000	1982	94	0	0.037
22	Michoacán	7,000	7,000	1982	200	0	0.015
23	Jalisco	12,000	18,000	1982	200	0	0.038
24	Jalisco	1,650,000	1,646,000	1982	200	16	0.048
25	Jalisco	1,000	1,000	1992	100	7	0.029
26	Guanajuato	34,000	34,000	1992	200	15	0.095
27	Guanajuato	24,000	22,000	1992	200	15	0.127
28	Jalisco	73,000	85,000	1992	200	20	0.074
29	Michoacán	138,000	226,000	1992	200	13	0.083
30	Zacatecas	1,000	1,000	1991	187	0	0.025
31	Guerrero	83,000	105,000	1993	100	12	0.089
32	San Luis Potosí	489,000	629,000	1993	200	25	0.048
33	Colima	7,000	8,000	1994	200	20	0.087
34	Zacatecas	2,000	2,000	1994	149	0	0.063
35	Zacatecas	100,000	114,000	1994	239	10	0.142
36	San Luis Potosí	13,000	13,000	1994	201	5	0.024
37	San Luis Potosí	1,000	1,000	1994	102	5	0.000
38	San Luis Potosí	42,000	47,000	1994	200	15	0.052
39	San Luis Potosí	1,000	1,000	1994	100	0	0.000
40	Zacatecas	34,000	38,000	1995	201	30	0.107
41	Guerrero	7,000	6,000	1995	153	11	0.186
42	Guerrero	1,000	1,000	1995	100	0	0.107
43	Guerrero	515,000	621,000	1995	200	0	0.074
44	San Luis Potosí	1,000	1,000	1995	99	17	0.000
45	San Luis Potosí	1,000	1,000	1996	142	11	0.000

(*Table continues on p. 328.*)

TABLE 16.1   Information on Community Samples Included in the Mexican Migration Project (*Continued*)

Community Number	State	1990 Population	2000 Population	Survey Year	Mexican Sample	U.S. Sample	Refusal Rate
46	Zacatecas	1,000	1,000	1995	111	0	0.142
47	San Luis Potosí	3,000	4,000	1996	197	11	0.032
48	San Luis Potosí	3,000	4,000	1996	94	0	0.021
49	Oaxaca	1,000	1,000	1996	100	0	0.000
50	Oaxaca	1,000	1,000	1996	100	10	0.000
51	Oaxaca	9,000	9,000	1997	199	0	0.083
52	Oaxaca	213,000	252,000	1996	200	9	0.087
53	Sinaloa	2,000	1,000	1998	100	6	0.020
54	Puebla	1,007,000	1,272,000	1997	201	1	0.016
55	Guanajuato	1,000	1,000	1997	80	8	0.000
56	Guanajuato	1,000	1,000	1998	87	9	0.033
57	Jalisco	4,000	6,000	1998	201	20	0.057
58	Jalisco	1,000	1,000	1998	100	10	0.029
59	Puebla	2,000	2,000	1997	100	0	0.010
60	Puebla	2,000	3,000	1997	100	0	0.010
61	Puebla	9999	9999	1998	199	0	0.050
62	Sinaloa	3,000	4,000	1998	150	11	0.020

63	Baja California Norte	699,000	1,149,000	1998	150	8	0.068
64	Baja California Norte	699,000	1,149,000	1998	150	7	0.011
65	Baja California Norte	699,000	1,149,000	1998	150	8	0.085
66	Baja California Norte	699,000	1,149,000	1998	152	7	0.080
67	Colima	3,000	4,000	1998	72	10	0.029
68	Colima	1,000	1,000	1998	100	10	0.000
69	Aguascalientes	18,000	4,000	1998	150	1	0.013
70	Sinaloa	5,000	6,000	1998	202	0	0.010
71	Aguascalientes	2,000	2,000	1997	100	6	0.010
72	Guanajuato	41,000	41,000	2000	155	16	Pending
73	Durango	16,000	23,000	1999	203	24	Pending
74	Durango	9,000	9,000	1999	151	11	Pending
75	Durango	1,000	1,000	1999	101	6	Pending
76	Durango	348,000	427,000	1999	200	20	Pending
77	Nuevo León	198,000	226,000	2000	200	0	Pending
78	Chihuahua	4,000	5,000	2000	200	0	Pending
79	Chihuahua	3,000	4,000	2000	150	0	Pending
80	Chihuahua	516,000	516,000	2000	201	0	Pending
81	Chihuahua	1,000	1,000	2000	100	0	Pending

Source: Data from Mexican Migration Project.

Colima, Guanajuato, Jalisco, Michoacán, Nayarit, San Luis Potosí, and Zacatecas. As far back as data exist, these states have accounted for at least half of all Mexican migration to the United States (Durand, Massey, and Zenteno 2001). More recently, the project has broadened its coverage to incorporate newer sending states in Mexico's south-central region (Guerrero, Oaxaca, and Puebla) as well as the north (Baja California, Chihuahua, Durango, and Sinaloa).

Following standard procedures, within each state we selected a range of different-sized communities for study, from small rural villages of one thousand or less to major metropolitan centers with populations in the millions, with all sizes in between. In choosing communities for study, the goal was not to find international migrants but to incorporate a wide range of different kinds of communities with contrasting patterns of social and economic organization and then to enumerate whatever migrants turned up at each site. The success of the ethnosurvey in securing respondent cooperation is indicated by the low refusal rates encountered by MMP interviewers, ranging from zero in several communities to 18.6 percent in one community in the state of Guerrero (which happened to be near a zone of guerrilla activity). The average refusal rate was just 4.7 percent.

Because communities themselves were not randomly selected, the MMP does not yield a probability sample of Mexico, even for the states in which the samples are located. Technically, the eighty-one community samples are representative only of the combined population of those communities. Thus it is relevant to ask how accurate a portrait the MMP sample paints of U.S. migrants and their characteristics. Massey and René Zenteno (2000) use Mexico's 1992 National Survey of Population Dynamics to validate the accuracy of the MMP. This survey includes a question to identify those members or former members of selected households aged twelve and over who have been to the United States, either to work or to look for work, during the preceding five years, thus yielding a nationally representative population of persons with U.S. migratory experience with which similarly defined migrants captured by the MMP could be compared. Massey and Zenteno's (2000) analysis demonstrates that apart from geographic background, the MMP accurately captures the characteristics and behavior of U.S. migrants.

Here we update that earlier study by comparing the current MMP database of eighty-one communities with the most recently available round of Mexico's National Survey of Population Dynamics (known by its Spanish acronym, ENADID), which was fielded in 1997. Table 16.2 presents the regional distribution of U.S. labor migrants aged twelve and over identified from both sources using the regional coding scheme devel-

TABLE 16.2   Regional Distribution of U.S. Migrants Identified by
the Mexican Migration Project (MMP) and Mexico's
1997 National Survey of Population Dynamics
(ENADID) (Percentage)

Region and State	ENADID	MMP
Historical region	47.5	85.5
Aguascalientes	1.6	2.3
Colima	1.0	2.4
Durango	3.8	4.3
Guanajuato	9.3	16.1
Jalisco	14.0	16.7
Michoacán	8.6	14.3
Nayarit	1.9	3.1
San Luis Potosí	3.6	11.0
Zacatecas	3.9	15.3
Border region	28.2	7.9
Baja California Norte	5.8	3.2
Baja California Sur	0.2	0.0
Chihuahua	6.0	2.7
Coahuila	2.8	0.0
Nuevo León	3.8	0.4
Sinaloa	2.5	1.6
Sonora	3.0	0.0
Tamaulipas	4.1	0.0
Central region	22.0	6.5
Distrito Federal	3.9	0.0
Guerrero	3.5	2.6
Hidalgo	1.7	0.0
México	4.6	0.0
Morelos	2.0	0.0
Oaxaca	2.1	2.3
Puebla	2.5	1.6
Querétaro	1.3	0.0
Tlaxcala	0.4	0.0
Southern region	2.3	0.0
Campeche	0.1	0.0
Chiapas	0.3	0.0
Quintana Roo	0.2	0.0
Tabasco	0.1	0.0
Veracruz	1.2	0.0
Yucatán	0.4	0.0

Source: Data from Mexican Migration Project and ENADID (1997).

oped by Durand (1998). Given the purposive selection of communities for the MMP, it is hardly surprising that its migrants are not geographically representative of all U.S. migrants in Mexico. Because the MMP started in Mexico's historical region of migration and only later branched out to embrace other locations, the western states are clearly overrepresented in the MMP data. Whereas 86 percent of all migrants in the latest version of the MMP were from the historical sending region, only 48 percent of those captured by the ENADID were from this zone.

Although the border and central regions are underrepresented with respect to their actual contribution of migrants to the national population, their experience is nonetheless included in the MMP. Whereas 28 percent of all Mexican migrants to the United States originated in the border region, and 22 percent were from the central region, the respective figures among migrants identified by the MMP were 8 and 7 percent. Only the relatively unimportant southern region, which contributes very few (2 percent) migrants to the national pool, is still unrepresented in the MMP.

More relevant than geography are the social characteristics of Mexican migrants. Table 16.3 assesses how accurately the MMP sample represents the traits and behaviors of the population of migrants to the United States. As can be seen, the only MMP distribution to depart markedly from that found in the ENADID is that for community size. Compared with the national population of U.S. migrants, the MMP underrepresents those in rural communities with fewer than twenty-five hundred inhabitants (only 10 percent, compared with 36 percent in the ENADID) as well as metropolitan centers of 1 million or more (14 percent, compared with the ENADID's 30 percent). Migrants from the two middle categories (2,500 to 19,999 and 20,000 to 99,999) are correspondingly overrepresented.

Aside from this distinctive feature of the MMP, which follows from its nonrandom sample selection method, the distributions of other variables are quite close. According to the MMP, 86 percent of Mexican migrants to the United States are male, whereas the ENADID figure is 84 percent. The median age of migrants was forty in the MMP and thirty-eight in the ENADID, and mean ages were even closer, with respective figures of forty-three and forty-two. With respect to marital status, the ENADID finds 79 percent of all U.S. migrants to be married, compared with 78 percent so identified by the MMP. The educational distributions are also quite similar. In the MMP sample, 50 percent of migrants have less than six years of schooling, 27 percent have six to eight years, 13 percent nine to eleven years, and 10 percent have twelve or more years of schooling, compared with respective figures of 46, 29, 16, and 8 percent in the ENADID sample. These two distributions yield mean education levels of

TABLE 16.3   Social Characteristics of U.S. Migrants Identified by the Mexican Migration Project (MMP) and Mexico's 1997 National Survey of Population Dynamics (ENADID) (Percentage Except as Indicated)

Characteristic	ENADID	MMP
Size of community		
Under 2,500	36.1	9.7
2,500 to 19,999	20.6	35.4
20,000 to 99,999	13.5	40.9
Over 100,000	29.9	14.0
Gender		
Male	84.4	86.0
Female	15.6	14.0
Age (years)		
Median age	38.0	40.0
Mean age	42.2	43.1
Standard deviation	16.2	16.8
Relation to household head		
Household head	73.4	71.6
Spouse	8.8	7.5
Son or daughter	13.1	19.0
Other	4.7	1.9
Marital status		
Currently married	78.8	77.8
Never married	12.3	16.7
Formerly married	8.9	5.5
Years of schooling		
Less than six years	46.4	50.1
Six to eight years	28.6	26.7
Nine to eleven years	16.4	13.4
Twelve or more years	8.0	9.8
Median	6.0	5.0
Mean	5.6	5.1
Duration of last trip (months)		
Median	7.0	8.0
Mean	17.6	18.7
Number of unweighted cases	8,297	6,766

Source: Data from Mexican Migration Project and ENADID (1997).

5.1 years for migrants identified by the MMP and 5.6 years for those identified by the ENADID.

The only other significant difference in distribution between the two
sources is that for household position. In general, the MMP contains a
larger number of sons and daughters than the ENADID: whereas the
MMP identifies 19 percent of migrants in the MMP as children of household heads, in the ENADID sample that figure is only 13 percent; but
Massey and Zenteno (2000) have determined that this difference occurs
because the MMP, owing to its careful procedures for determining household membership, was more successful in enumerating absent sons and
daughters (mostly the former) who had been away for some time but were
expected to rejoin the household upon their return.

In a study of international migration, perhaps the most important variables are those associated with migratory behavior itself. The only indicator of migratory behavior available from the ENADID is the duration
of the most recent trip to the United States. In the MMP data, the average trip duration is nineteen months and the median eight months, indicating a long-tailed distribution skewed to the left. Trip durations as
reported by migrants identified by the ENADID display a mean of eighteen months and a median of seven months, suggesting essentially the
same distribution. Figure 16.1 presents the cumulative distribution of U.S.
trips by duration for both MMP and ENADID respondents to demonstrate how closely the two sets of data correspond.

The foregoing systematic comparison suggests that, despite the non-
representativeness of the its selection of sample communities, the MMP
nonetheless captures the social and economic characteristics of U.S.
migrants quite accurately, including the timing of their departures and
returns. The great advantage of the MMP, however, is that it allows
investigators to identify those migrating with and without documents,
thus permitting detailed analyses of the characteristics and behavior of
unauthorized migrants (see Massey and Espinosa 1997). In addition, the
MMP elicits a detailed series of migration-specific data (about social ties
to other migrants, for example) that are simply unavailable from standard
demographic surveys such as the ENADID.

Each year since 1987, we have supervised the gathering of data from
representative samples of households in four to six Mexican communities. Following the principles of the ethnosurvey design, each Mexican
sample is supplemented with a survey of settled out-migrants from the
same community who are located in the United States, using snowball
sampling methods. Using a procedure developed by Massey and Emilio
Parrado (1994), the Mexican and U.S. surveys may be weighted to

FIGURE 16.1   Months Spent by Return Migrants on Most Recent
Trip to the United States, Cumulative Percentage

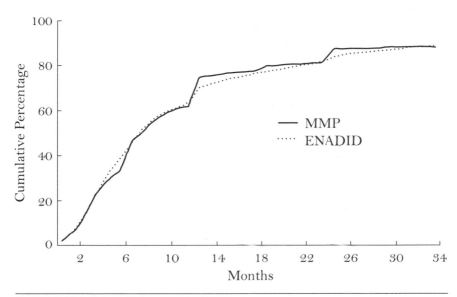

Source: Authors' compilation.

reflect their relative contributions to the total transnational population of each community.

The resulting information is organized into five basic data files: PERSFILE contains data on individuals enumerated in sample households; HOUSFILE contains data on the households themselves; MIGFILE contains information about the household head's most recent trip to the United States; LIFEFILE contains detailed life histories for all household heads; and SPOUSFILE contains labor histories for all spouses.

After administering the ethnosurvey to sample households, MMP fieldworkers complete an inventory of information on the community from a variety of sources: phone directories, interviews with local officials, archives, and Mexican statistical sources. These community inventories yield a community-level data file, COMMUN, which provides information on community characteristics from 1950 to the time of the survey. Included is information on population, labor force, industrial distribution, natural resources, agriculture, standard of living, community development, infrastructure, institutions, and migration prevalence.

Three additional quantitative files are also available from the database. MSACROSS is a cross-sectional file that gives cost-of-living indicators for U.S. metropolitan areas contained in the Mexican Migration Project database, allowing researchers to adjust for differences in price levels across urban destination areas. MSAYEAR is a longitudinal file containing information on employment, unemployment, legalization, and population for all metropolitan destination areas from 1972 to the present; and NATLYEAR contains national-level indicators of macroeconomic performance in the United States and Mexico from 1950 to the present.

REFERENCES

Durand, Jorge. 1998. "¿Nuevas regiones migratorias?" In *Población, desarrollo y globalización*, edited by René M. Zenteno, vol. 2, *V reunión de investigación sociodemográfica en México*. Mexico City: Sociedad Mexicana de Demografía and El Colegio de la Frontera Norte.

Durand, Jorge, Douglas S. Massey, and René M. Zenteno. 2001. "Mexican Immigration to the United States: Continuities and Changes." *Latin American Research Review* 36: 107–27.

ENADID. 1997. *Encuesta Nacional de la Dinámica Demografica: Metodología y Tabulados* (National Survey of Population Dynamics). Aguascalientes, Mex.: Instituto Nacional de Estadística Geografiae la firmática.

Kalton, Graham, and D. W. Anderson. 1986. "Sampling Rare Populations." *Journal of the Royal Statistical Society A* 149: 65–82.

Lindstrom, David P., and Douglas S. Massey. 1994. "Selective Emigration, Cohort Quality, and Models of Immigrant Assimilation." *Social Science Research* 23: 315–49.

Massey, Douglas S. 1987. "The Ethnosurvey in Theory and Practice." *International Migration Review* 21: 1498–1522.

Massey, Douglas S., Rafael Alarcón, Jorge Durand, and Humberto González. 1987. *Return to Aztlan: The Social Process of International Migration from Western Mexico*. Berkeley: University of California Press.

Massey, Douglas S., Joaquín Arango, Graeme Hugo, Ali Kouaouci, Adela Pellegrino, and J. Edward Taylor. 1998. *Worlds in Motion: Understanding International Migration at the End of the Millennium*. Oxford: Clarendon.

Massey, Douglas S., and Chiara Capoferro. Forthcoming. "Measuring Undocumented Migration." *International Migration Review*.

Massey, Douglas S., and Kristin Espinosa. 1997. "What's Driving Mexico-U.S. Migration? A Theoretical, Empirical, and Policy Analysis." *American Journal of Sociology* 102: 939–99.

Massey, Douglas S., and Emilio A. Parrado. 1994. "Migradollars: The Remittances and Savings of Mexican Migrants to the United States." *Population Research and Policy Review* 13: 3–30.

Massey, Douglas S., and René Zenteno. 2000. "A Validation of the Ethnosurvey: The Case of Mexico-U.S. Migration." *International Migration Review* 34: 766–93.

INDEX